# Precision
## Handloading

# Precision
# Handloading

John Withers

Stoeger Publishing Company

Published by Stoeger Publishing Company
55 Ruta Court
South Hackensack, New Jersey 07606

ISBN 0-88317-132-5

Library of Congress Catalog Card No.: 85-051162

Manufactured in the United States of America

Distributed to the book trade and to the sporting goods
trade by Stoeger Industries, 55 Ruta Court, South Hackensack, New Jersey 07606

In Canada, distributed to the book trade and to the sporting
goods trade by Stoeger Canada Ltd., 169 Idema Road,
Markham, Ontario L3R 1A9

# CONTENTS

# Dedication

This book is dedicated to my wife, Carol.
Without her work, it would not be finished.
Without her support, it would have never
begun.

# Acknowledgments

I extend my gratitude to the following people, and with respect in memory of those now deceased, for their kind assistance over many years in the gathering of information for this book: Tag Anderson—sportsman, outdoor expert, guide, and sporting products distributor, Richardson, Texas; David F. Andrews—Marketing Services Manager, Omark Industries, Lewiston, Idaho; Bob Barry—tool technician and mechanical designer, Arlington, Texas; Ralph Bone—gunsmith, Lubbock, Texas; Leo H. Bradshaw, Jr.—sportsman, firearms expert, and president of Cogdell's Westview Sporting Goods, Waco, Texas; Luther A. Brock, Ph.D., "The Letter Doctor"—professional writer, Denton, Texas; G. B. Chambers—gunsmith, Dallas and Lone Oak, Texas (deceased); Larry Chance—fellow sportsman, Fate, Texas; R. M. Downing—Plant Technical, Potomac River Works, E.I. Du Pont De Nemours & Co., Martinsburg, West Virginia; Dean Grennell—Managing Editor, *Gun World* magazine, Capistrano Beach, California; Gene Henderson—President, Gene Henderson and Associates, Inc., Fine Printing, Carrollton, Texas; Roy Koonce—sportsman and photographer, Dallas, Texas; David R. Miller—electrical engineer and fellow photographer, Los Altos, California; Robert E. Miller—consulting engineer, Dallas, Texas; Bill Mowry—fellow writer, St. Petersburg, Florida; Frank O'Brien—firearms expert, Dallas, Texas; Doug Painter—Director of Communications, National Shooting Sports Foundation, Riverside, Connecticut; Arthur Rawlings—sportsman and president of American Guns, Dallas, Texas; Charlie Reed—Manager, Elm Fork Shooting Park, Dallas, Texas; James B. Withers—fellow sportsman, Dallas, Texas; John T. Withers, III—sportsman, outdoorsman, and mentor, Dallas, Texas (deceased); the directors and members of The Dallas Pistol Club, Carrollton, Texas; and the gun writers of America, whose experience and information keep our pastime alive, safe, and well.

# About the Author

John Withers was born in Dallas, Texas, but just barely. According to his mother, she was rushed back home in 1940 by his father, from out-of-state, so John could be born in Texas.

Still a resident of the Lone Star State, Withers has enjoyed, studied, and promoted the outdoor sports of the Southwest for years. It all began with his father, John T. Withers III, who founded Withers and Co., the store "where sportsmen serve sportsmen." The store was one of the largest sporting goods retailers in the Southwest in the 1940s, 50s, and 60s, attracting hunting, fishing, and outdoor authorities of the region. In addition, the store's gunsmiths helped introduce young Withers to the world of firearms, an interest that has never been exhausted.

After schooling at Texas Tech University in Lubbock, Withers served with the U.S. Army and the Texas Army National Guard as an officer in the Airborne Corps. During this time, he taught soldiers the fundamentals of small arms marksmanship and mortar gunnery.

Withers' involvement with handloading began around 1956. He considers handloading to be a fascinating part of the shooting and hunting sports, offering a positive way for shooters to improve their equipment and shooting.

John lives in Dallas with his wife, Carol, and their two daughters, Jennifer and Catherine. The Withers' family time is often spent camping and fishing, but John still reserves a portion for hunting, shooting, and handloading.

# Preface

When I first loaded ammunition, only a few of the methods mentioned in this book were available. That was long ago, but I remember the experience well.

After hearing about the things that handloading could do, I decided to try it myself to improve the accuracy of my own rifle, which was a Christmas present from my father on my eagerly awaited seventeenth birthday.

After collecting a box of empty brass cases and some instructions from the local experts, I began to load, using the loading tables supplied by both the bullet maker and the powder maker. But foolishly, I only used the tables to locate the maximum charge and loaded all twenty cartridges just that way—maximum charge!

The next weekend, I put the handloads and rifle in the family auto and drove to the range. After posting a target, I returned to the bench and began firing. My rifle kicked a bit more and opened a little harder than usual. My shooting was worse than usual, too. But all twenty cartridges fired perfectly and I was proud of my accomplishment.

If you think this story sounds dangerous, you are correct. I was flirting with danger and didn't know it. Others have done the same. Some of us have been lucky; others have not. I was lucky and so was my rifle. Neither of us was injured. I was lucky because my rifle was built so strongly, and fortunate because the powder and bullet makers had incorporated some safety limits into their loading tables. I owe them a debt of gratitude. Their wisdom compensated for my lack of it.

It wasn't until later that I realized the danger in my handloading. It took even longer for me to admit the hardest confession of all—that my hand loads were inferior to factory ammunition. That is a bitter truth indeed.

It has been many years since my first experience with handloading. Since then, I've heard others tell stories like mine. We started handloading without a proper method to ensure safety and success. I don't mean that good methods weren't available. We had them, but we didn't use them. We didn't use good, safe methods for handloading because they didn't offer enough incentive for us. If a method doesn't provide incentive for success, it won't be used.

The method for handloading presented in this book provides positive incentives for rewarding and safe handloading. The incentives are promises. The method in this book *promises positive, measurable results, clearly identifying the best ammunition for the shooter.* By providing such results, this method also *promises greater confidence in one's shooting.* But in order for the method to work—for the handloader to reap the promises of *results* and *confidence*—the method must be used as it is taught. And its teaching is built on safe handloading procedures.

*Precision Handloading* offers a new, positive approach to handloading. It uses new concepts borrowed from respected professions. It provides expected results through measurable goals, and takes the handloader to new levels of achievement. It allows the handloader to accomplish what he wants to do with complete confidence in the result, while using good, safe procedures.

*Precision Handloading* will work for you.

# Chapter 1

# A Better Method

There are two groups of shooters who load ammunition—reloaders and handloaders. Reloaders, both amateur and commercial, load ammunition to lower the cost of shooting. Their purpose is to make usable ammunition in generous quantities at low cost. Quality is a consideration for most reloaders, but less important than quantity and cost. If reloaded ammunition works and can be made cheaply in quantity, the reloader is satisfied. Reloaders can achieve success in several of the shooting sports while concentrating their efforts on overall cost and quantity.

Handloaders are a different variety of shooter. They are a curious bunch of people. They read everything that is written about loading techniques and the shooting experiences of others. They continually try to gain new insights and greater knowledge of their pastime. Handloaders read to prepare themselves for the things that happen at the bench, on the range and in the field. They read of others'

experiences to reinforce their own findings. They search for the highest quality ammunition to improve their own shooting.

Handloaders participate heavily in the shooting sports and they continually try to make their shooting better, even when established procedures are accepted by others. They like to find out for themselves which ones work, which ones do not work, and, most importantly, which ones work best. Handloaders are willing to sacrifice time, effort, and money to find which methods are best, and then to improve them. These people appreciate precision, efficiency, and positive results. They also like facts and they realize that facts can often be found only by actual experiment. These shooters know that handloading is an excellent way to find which methods are best for their individual needs. The fact that they can, and often do, develop better ammunition is very satisfying to handloaders. Some claim that they load ammunition to save money, but

These are the 13 most often loaded cartridges in America. In order of increasing popularity, from left to right they are: .22-250 Remington, 9mm Luger, 7mm Remington Magnum, .270 Winchester, .308 Winchester, .243 Winchester, .30-30 Winchester, .45 ACP, .223 Remington, .44 Magnum, .38 Special, .30-06 Springfield, and .357 Magnum. Actual ranking changes some each year.

most are really trying to create the best possible ammunition for specific purposes.

Those purposes may be to break shooting records, kill game more surely, humanely and at greater distances, and provide greater security for home and family. Along the way they will gain confidence in their efforts, and confidence is crucial to shooting success.

My own interests in shooting and loading match those of the handloader group. I suspect that yours do, too. If so, this book will be of interest, as it is written for you, the handloader. Its purpose is to help you find the best ammunition for your shoot-

ing needs. But finding that ammunition can be a very difficult task, due to the many considerations and the lack of specific information for our own particular needs.

The many choices of loading components available for any popular caliber of firearm can be a real problem. If you consider all the choices of bullets made for a cartridge such as the .30–06 Springfield, times all the usable powders, primers and cases, the number of cartridge combinations becomes enormous. The choices are staggering if you also consider the proliferation of different powder charges, bullet seating depths, case sizing techniques, and so forth. If these things were not already enough, don't forget all the factory-loaded cartridges. They add more to the problem. All these choices require decisions and can create confusion. The handloader, faced with so much, can become confounded and indecisive. Worse yet, he can lose confidence in his ammunition, his gun, and even himself.

Some handloaders load all the combinations of components for a cartridge that they consider useful. Sometimes they have success with this method. But when such attempts to find the perfect cartridge are questioned, the handloader often devel-ops dissatisfaction with his results. He loses confidence in his results. Confidence often suffers when questions like the following are asked: Am I entirely satisfied with my results? Do my handloads give equal or better accuracy than factory ammunition? Better velocity? Better pressure? Do I really know what I want in the way of results with my handloading? Have my time, effort, and money been justified by my results? These questions have caused a loss of confidence for many handloaders for many years.

Another method used by some handloaders is the "pet load" or "recommended load" theory. This

Another shooting sport where handloading is a way of life. These shooters are participating in a match called "The Iron Man." It consists of six shooting disciplines with one gun and lots of shooting. (Dallas Pistol Club, Carrollton, Texas)

A Better Method

All the choices of handloading components can create problems of confusion and disturb shooting confidence. Clear objectives and proper use of loading manuals will narrow the choices.

is loading based on the belief that "what works for one should work equally well for someone else." The supposed advantage to this method is the lack of any need for further testing by the shooter. But a handload which may work well for one shooter seldom performs identically for another. The varying factors of guns, equipment, technique and materials never offer identical situations. Even if the load works satisfactorily in someone else's gun, the handloader never knows if "pet" or "recommended load" ammunition is the best he can make. Confidence suffers again when a "pet load" is questioned.

Neither of the above methods is really satisfac-

tory but they are all we handloaders have had until now. Until now, we haven't had the right kind of information to handload with maximum confidence in our results. We haven't had a proper method for handloading ammunition.

The above statement may sound ridiculous with all the information available for handloaders, but it is true. Let me explain.

Almost all manuals, magazines, books and pamphlets for handloading are similar in content. They are basic guides for handloaders to make ammunition. They are similar to, but more thorough than, the guides of 25, 50, and even 100 years ago.

Precision Handloading

Their *purpose* is to provide good, safe data for handloaders to use as guides, basic mechanical instruction, information about components, and even ballistic tables. Their reason is often to sell products and to provide some liability protection for the manufacturer underwriting the publication.

Most of the information available for handloaders is excellent for *its* purpose. The different writers and manufacturers accomplish this well. They provide us handloaders with valuable data that we really need. But as well written and thorough as most of the above information sources are, they cannot answer all of our questions about handloading. They were not intended to do that and we can't expect them to. Such questions, however, affect our results and must be answered before full confidence can be gained.

In a sense, the various guides to handloading are all written *to* the handloader. They tell us what we should achieve if we do as *they* say, regardless of what we may want to do. There should be a method for handloading that is written *for* us. It should teach us how to use our tools, materials, and data to achieve what *we* want. It should also teach us how to decide what we want and how to recognize success.

For a long time, I have read and experimented

Modern handloading guides provide good, safe data for handloaders. They also give mechanical instruction, component information, and ballistic tables.

Any hunter can be justifiably proud of a trophy whitetail, especially if it has been "rattled up" in the South Texas brush country. Keen shooting and hunting skills are needed for success in this demanding type of hunting. Confidence in the ammunition is needed, too.

with the information provided by new writings about handloading, believing that each new book or magazine article would throw some light on all my unanswered questions. Sometimes the material was helpful, but usually I found little that was new.

A few years ago, I began to realize that my own purpose and reason for handloading did not coincide with most of the handloading literature, which, it seemed, lacked objectivity. The manuals, books, and pamphlets accomplish their purpose as guides for safe component use and mechanical procedures, but they don't tell us how to use that information fully to achieve our own purpose. Questions

are left unanswered. We need to know more. The old and familiar procedures and principles are limiting, to some extent.

Fortunately, a better method for handloading now exists. The method allows *us* to obtain *our* expected results in handloading through the achievement of *our* objectives. This method is used for finding direction, solving problems, and reaching goals. It is used by leaders in industry, education, theology, science, government, and the armed forces. This method, although identified by several names, is often called Management by Objective, or MBO.

Precision Handloading

# Chapter 2

# Management of Handloading

In the early 1960s, American businessmen began using a new method for management. Known by various names such as Management by Objective, and Management by Result, that method is now used by business leaders, scientists, the military, the medical profession, and many other groups in our society and the world. Management by Objective, or MBO, is a management tool for getting things done. Many of the groups that practice MBO have become the best at what they do.

This chapter will acquaint you with Management by Objective and will explain the adaptation of its principles to handloading. It will give you a method for attaining positive results with your own handloading efforts.

It also gives you a set of objectives to use as steps in reaching each goal, methods to measure those objectives, and a method for determining when and how well the final result has been achieved. MBO gives you methods to answer your own questions as they occur while working up handloads. MBO is a method for management and decision-making by which overall objective achievements and final re-

sults can be planned. No other method for handloading can do what MBO can do for you.

Management by Objective consists of four steps. Those steps answer the *what, how, where,* and *when* questions of managing work projects. They are:

I. Decide *what* the desired result or outcome is to be.

II. Develop detailed operating plans to determine *how* each of the necessary, intermediate objectives will be met. The plans must include methods for measuring the objectives.

III. Control all activities to ensure conformance with the operating plans that determine *how* and *where* each objective will be accomplished. Eliminate all activities that are nonproductive in achieving the objectives and the desired result.

IV. Establish a time frame to determine *when* each intermediate objective and the final result are to be completed and stick to it.

Notice that MBO does not answer any *why* questions. Such answers are the justifications for any result. They are often assumed, but should be clearly understood. As handloaders, the answer to *why* questions is our purpose and reason for handloading. Our purpose, from Chapter 1, is to develop the best ammunition for our shooting needs. The reason we do this is to develop maximum confidence in our shooting for better results.

The most important step in using MBO is the first one. Decide what you want to accomplish. This chapter will deal with that step in MBO, and partly with step II, which concerns planning. The detailed methods and measurements for objective achievement will be covered in subsequent chapters. Step III, the controls for ensuring compliance with the operating plans, will also be explained and used throughout. The methods used in steps II and III answer the *how* and *where* questions of individual handload development.

MBO also uses time as a factor in reaching objectives and results. Although important in business for fiscal reasons, time use in MBO is not always needed for handloading, unless for commercial reasons or the need for completion by a certain date. As a hunter, I have, at times, needed to complete a handloading project before a scheduled hunt. Time was important in such circumstances, but not in the same way as managing a business. Therefore, time will not be discussed in great detail with the other handloading objectives in this book. If you feel that time planning will be needed, simply allow for it. Give yourself a few weekends for load development before that big hunt or important target match. The best handloads are not brewed overnight. Some need to "simmer" a while.

As stated, MBO requires that a specific desired result be decided upon before any other activities are begun. Certain objectives must also be planned to develop a successful, orderly path to the final result. Not knowing where you want to go is like the man who "got on his horse and rode off in all directions." You can't go anywhere unless you pick a path. The horseman probably wore out several horses and never got anywhere. He may have gotten himself lost, as many handloaders have done. If you've ever felt like that, don't think you're alone. Others, like myself, have taken several paths and wound up with uncertain, confusing results in our handloading. Those results were usually poor,

which does not lead to confident shooting. Perhaps the following will help you decide where you want to go in handloading before you start using MBO.

Many gun writers have compiled and published lists of reasons or purposes for handloading one's own ammunition, such as:

### Reasons for Handloading

1. To develop greater accuracy
2. To develop greater velocity
3. To develop better bullet performance
4. To correct cartridge and gun malfunctions
5. To lower the cost of ammunition and permit more shooting
6. To be able to duplicate a cartridge at some future time
7. To develop better ammunition per se
8. To shoot with increased confidence

Six of these statements could be considered good ideas for objectives, but are not really the ultimate motivations for handloading. Numbers 7 and 8 come close, however.

Number 7, with some elaboration, should be the result we want and also our main purpose for handloading; to develop the best ammunition possible for our shooting needs. Consequently, number 7 satisfies the *what* question and is the answer to step I in the MBO method.

Reason number 8 on the list is the final reward. We would all like to shoot better and handloaded, superior ammunition builds confidence. Thus, the *why* question is answered.

But what about reasons 1 through 6? Aren't they also important to handloaders? Of course they are, but not to the same degree. These are the intermediate objectives which must be met on the way to the final product—the best ammunition for our shooting needs.

All the preceding may seem complicated. Actually, it's not. To reiterate, handloading, using the methods of Management by Objective, requires four steps:

I. Decide what you want.
II. Develop a plan of operation.
III. Control the procedure, eliminating non-productive activities.
IV. Establish a time schedule (optional).

There are many books about management. Most are written for business and industry but the principles apply to other disciplines as well; handloading is one. Good handloading management is needed for positive, successful shooting results.

With the possible exception of step IV, each progression follows logically. When all are completed successfully, the end result should be achieved.

Next to deciding what you want to accomplish, the most important decisions will be in setting the intermediate objectives. They answer the *how* and *where* questions of MBO. Without measurable objectives in handload development, the outcome would have no meaning. You would not know if your objective had really been attained.

The process of setting intermediate handloading objectives is the chief planning phase using MBO methods in this book. Objective-setting and the equally important step of objective-measurement are the backbone of good MBO practice. Most books about MBO state that the objective-setting process should include the following questions:

**Objective-Setting Questions**

    A. Is the objective worth setting?
    B. Is the objective practical?
    C. Is the objective attainable?
    D. Is the objective clearly stated in terms of:
        1. the task?
        2. the method of measurement?

3. the time period required?
E. Is the objective compatible with the overall expected result?

Again, with the possible exception of a structured time period, each of the above questions must be asked of each possible objective before it is put into the plan for handloading.

To set objectives in handloading, as in any other management job, it is good practice first to list all of the possible objective considerations. This doesn't mean all considerations will be included in the final planning; however, it does help to ensure that no important, practical, compatible, and necessary objective will be left out. This is vital. A neglected objective can prevent the successful completion of a project. Confidence in the "product" is threatened. Further testing may be required. Leaving out an objective can send you back to square one with a lot of time and effort having been wasted. This will become apparent as you progress.

Theoretically, there's no limit to the number of objectives relative to any handloading project. It's common to develop more objectives than are practical, manageable, or needed. One of your jobs is deciding which objectives can be established pertaining to the five questions above. It's not easy to do this the first time around, but we have a good starting point. Consider those first six *reasons* for handloading mentioned earlier. They will be used to start the objective-setting process.

The best way to learn the process is simply to observe it. I will describe a handloading situation where MBO is used. The shooter will try to decide what objectives are needed. He will test them with the five objective-setting questions. The practical, remaining objectives will be used in developing a plan for handloading.

Let's take a typical fellow sportsman named Jim, who has a problem and chooses the MBO approach to solving it. Jim believes that there must be something worthwhile in all this handloading business because so many top-notch shooters take it so seriously. In fact, several of his hunting and shooting friends load their own ammo.

In the past, Jim has loaded and fired a few rounds, but he soon realized that there is more to handloading than simply reloading spent cases. He now appreciates the need for better planning to get better results from handloading, but he isn't exactly sure what he wants. Different people say different things about what handloading is and what it does for them. That's because there can be many objectives in loading. Each individual must determine which objectives are necessary, practical, and compatible with *his* needs. Jim decides to list his needs as potential objectives for planning, using the prior list of *reasons* for handloading as a starting point. After a good deal of thought, he decides that he wants to cover the first six objectives or reasons: better accuracy; velocity; bullet performance; consistent results; lower cost ammo; and being able to duplicate a round precisely.

Each of the objectives is tested against the questions from the objective-setting process, for example, "Is the objective worth setting?" Jim answers "yes" to this question for each of his objectives. The second and third questions ask if the objectives are practical and attainable. Again, the answer is "yes," but with some reservations. He's not sure if all his objectives are actually attainable or even practical. Question D of the process asks, "Is the objective clearly stated in terms of the task, the method of measurement, and the measuring period?" Our subject is beginning to feel uncomfortable now. He doesn't know how to answer. The last question, asking if the objective is compatible with the overall result expected, is very confounding. Jim realizes that he is not prepared to answer all the questions and must look for assistance elsewhere.

Before you too begin to feel uncomfortable, let's explain one of his troubles in listing his objectives. The reason for Jim's inability to answer is due to the fact that he has listed "wants and needs" without knowing if they are genuine objectives. *A good objective is a statement that can provide a "yes" answer to each of the objective-setting questions.* The handloader must try to state his objectives so they will relate to these questions positively.

The objectives must also be stated in terms that compare quality and quantity. Jim wants his handloaded ammunition to be "better," but better than what? He needs a standard for comparison. For starting handloads, the accepted standard of comparison is factory-loaded ammunition. More precisely, the standard for handload comparison should be the factory ammunition that most nearly achieves the purpose of the shooter.

Knowing the above, Jim can better state his objectives and he tries again, as follows:

1. To achieve better accuracy than from factory ammunition
2. To achieve higher velocity than from factory ammunition
3. To achieve better bullet performance than from factory ammunition
4. To achieve more uniform results than from factory ammunition
5. To achieve lower cost than that of factory ammunition
6. To be able to duplicate ammunition at any time

These new objectives sound more explicit than Jim's first statements, but they must be tested with the five objective-setting questions. Again, these objectives will fail the test because they lack definitiveness. More details are needed. Jim is not stating his objectives in the ways necessary to satisfy all the objective-setting process questions—a process that must be completed in order to achieve his overall results successfully. It is imperative that each objective is practical and attainable. The chief concern comes with questions D and E. Question D asks, "Is the objective clearly stated in terms of the task, the method of measurement, and the time period required?" Question E asks, "Is the objective compatible with the overall result expected?" Jim is now quite frustrated, and rightfully so. Developing a complete and satisfactory list of handloading objectives requires a lot of thought and more experience than he has at present. The better part of this text will be used to explain the things that are needed to state, satisfy, and meet these handloading objectives. Although such objectives are difficult to set, they are the best way to develop positive results.

Because Jim does not yet have all the knowledge to state his handloading objectives, let's rephrase his objectives *so they will satisfy* the objective-setting questions and eliminate any more confusion. Note that two additional objectives, which should not be overlooked, are now included:

1. To achieve equal or better target precision (accuracy potential) with handloaded ammunition than that of factory ammunition.

Precision of fired shot groups is to be measured and compared using:
   (a) uniform methods of target measurement
   (b) accepted methods of statistical comparison
2. To achieve equal or higher bullet velocity with handloaded ammunition than that of factory-loaded ammunition. Velocity is to be measured using a chronographic instrument and compared to factory ammunition velocity using the same firearm under conditions that are as nearly equal in temperature, barometric pressure, and relative humidity as possible.
3. To achieve equal or better bullet consistency and performance as to controlled expansion, penetration, and downrange ballistic potential than with factory-loaded ammunition. This comparison is to be made using available manufacturing information and ballistic data, individual testing, and observed effect.
4. To achieve equal or greater consistency in handloaded ammunition as to precision, velocity, pressure, and bullet performance than that available from various lots of factory ammunition. This is to be done with:
   a. target precision data
   b. velocity data
   c. positive component identification
   d. cartridge component weights and measurements
   e. probability assumptions based on graphic, statistical data
5. To be able to duplicate the chosen cartridge at any time. This is to be done by:
   a. recording all necessary loading data
   b. recording all necessary precision, velocity, and pressure data for the handloaded ammunition
   c. retention and use of the same size die, neck expander, and case holder as used to develop the handload
6. To achieve correct firearm functioning with handloaded ammunition or better functioning with handloaded ammunition than with factory ammunition as to:
   a. magazine loading

b. chambering

c. locking

d. firing

e. unlocking

f. extraction

g. ejection

h. cocking and chambering (semiautomatic). This is to be accomplished by adhering to cartridge dimensions, component usage, and firing and function testing with the handload and factory ammunition in the firearm.

7. To achieve proper, consistent, and safe pressure in the handloaded ammunition. This is to be accomplished by comparing:

a. the heard, felt, and seen results of handloaded and factory ammunition during and after firing

b. the case head expansion of handloaded ammunition and factory ammunition after firing

8. To determine that ammunition which best achieves the above objectives with the least expense of time, labor, materials, and money for testing.

Now, that's better! The above eight handloading objectives are worth setting. They are practical and attainable. Furthermore, each is clearly stated in terms of the task and the methods of measurement (which will be covered in greater detail further on). Lastly, the objectives are compatible with the expected result. Their achievement will determine the best ammunition for his shooting needs. Only the question of a time period has been left unanswered, as this is optional.

These particular objectives are important to all deer hunters. But the same list is not for all shooters. A target shooter may not be interested in developing high velocity or correct bullet performance with regard to the killing effect on game. A benchrest shooter would not be very concerned with firearm function if his rifle is the single-shot-type. The target shooter and the varmint hunter may think other objectives such as reducing recoil, muzzle flash, muzzle blast, and barrel fouling are important also. The wind-bucking characteristics of bullets are very important to long-range shooters.

All of this is to say that you must determine the handloading objectives that best suit your own spe-

cific needs. Other objectives will be discussed in Chapter 12.

For simplicity, I will use the objectives that have been developed here for two reasons: First, they suit a great many hunting handloaders. Secondly, these are the most difficult objectives for most handloaders to achieve, regardless of their shooting needs and experience. Considerations needed for other shooting sports will be covered later.

The concepts of Management by Objective and objective-setting have been presented and adapted to handloading. Real-life handloading objectives have been established and are suitable for most hunting-type cartridges. Furthermore, the objectives have been set and further defined with regard to the task involved, and the methods of measurement. Also, the objectives are compatible with the overall result expected. These objectives will be used in practical ways to expand your understanding and use of handloading for better results in your shooting. Now it is time to move on to other aspects of MBO.

The second step of MBO is to develop detailed operating plans and determine how each of the intermediate objectives will be achieved. Those plans must include the methods for measuring the objectives. Each of these handloading objectives will be accomplished, but that can't be done by dealing with each objective independently of the others. The actions needed to accomplish some objectives are closely allied with those of others. An overall handload operating plan, composed of several stages, will be used to mesh each objective into a smooth-flowing set of procedures. Basically, this plan will consist of the following parts, which are listed in sequence.

- Decisions and selections before loading
- Loading the ammunition and preparing control standards
- Firing
- Target measurement
- Velocity measurement
- Case measurement
- Graphing
- Study of the data
- Making the final decision

This plan corresponds to the chapters in this book. As each objective is developed and achieved, it will be noted. This use of handload planning is

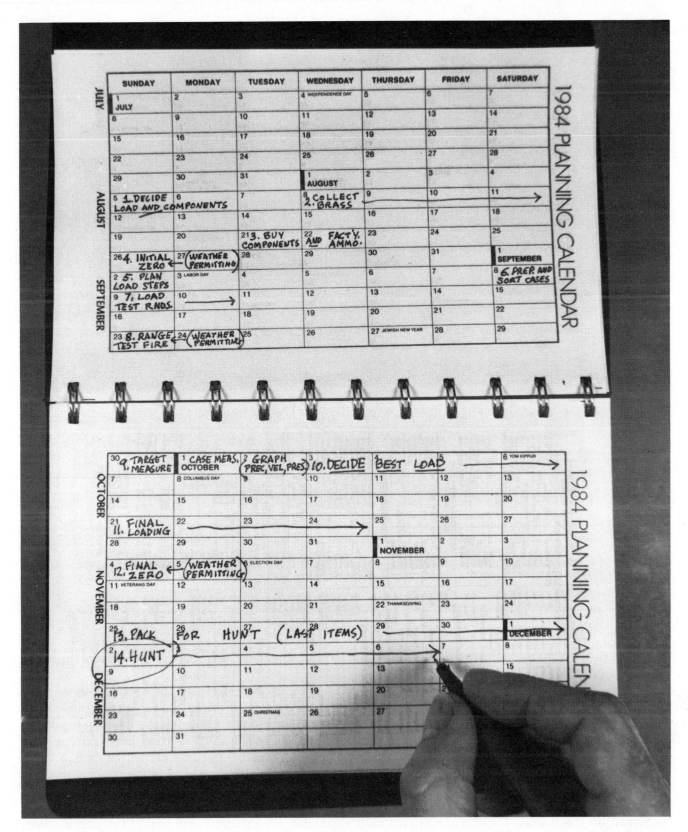

Give yourself time to develop a handload for an important event. Each necessary step should be included in your planning.

**COVERAGE OF OBJECTIVES BY CHAPTER**

| Chap. No. | Chapter Title | Objectives | 1. Precision | 2. Velocity | 3. Bullet Performance | 4. Consistency | 5. Duplication | 6. Functioning | 7. Pressure | 8. Expense |
|---|---|---|---|---|---|---|---|---|---|---|
| 1 | A Better Method | | | | | | | | | |
| 2 | Management of Handloading | | X | X | X | X | X | X | X | X |
| 3 | Decisions before Handloading | | X | X | X | X | X | X | X | X |
| 4 | At the Loading Bench | | X | | | X | X | X | X | X |
| 5 | At the Range | | X | X | | X | | | X | X |
| 6 | Precision | | X | | | | X | | | X |
| 7 | Velocity | | | X | X | | | | X | X |
| 8 | Pressure | | X | X | | X | | X | X | |
| 9 | Using Handload Data | | X | X | X | X | X | X | X | X |
| 10 | Completing the Project | | X | X | | X | | | | |
| 11 | Handgun Cartridges: Loading and Testing | | X | X | | X | | X | | |
| 12 | Other Handloading Points | | X | X | X | X | | X | X | |
| 13 | Other Handloading Examples | | X | X | | X | | | X | |
| 14 | Review of Objective Handloading | | X | X | X | X | X | X | X | X |

not a departure from good MBO practice. It is a practical way of placing the objectives into a plan with more meaning for you. Complete, satisfactory accomplishment of all the individual objectives will still occur.

The third step of MBO is to control all activities to ensure conformance with the operating plans. This determines how and where each objective will be accomplished. All activities that are nonproductive in achieving the objectives and the desired result must be eliminated. These requirements and procedures will be covered as each part of the handloading plan is revealed.

Finally, the fourth step of MBO planning is the establishment of a time frame to determine when each intermediate objective and the final result is to be completed. It will be discussed in detail later on. The establishment of a time schedule for handloading can only be suggested here. Some shooters couldn't care less; to others, it's an important factor. If the final result must be accomplished by a specific date, make sure that each part of the plan is sched-

The best ammunition is that which best meets your needs and gives you the most confidence.

uled and accomplished on time. Otherwise, the expected result will not occur when needed. A simple calendar will help you do this.

The statements made in this chapter are the most important to the methods presented in this book. Their complete understanding is vital to your purpose as a handloader and getting your expected result. These statements about MBO will be made again, in more detail, as you progress to a better understanding of handloading using the principles of MBO.

In coming chapters, I will take the objectives, again using Jim as a guinea pig, and explain the ways for meeting them using factory ammunition as a basis of comparison. Those objectives will develop the final result. The chart here shows where the eight objectives will be discussed and used.

With this understanding of Management by Objective, you are ready to begin handload development with a genuine purpose—to find the best ammunition for your shooting needs.

Management of Handloading

Hunters achieve successful results with handloaded ammunition. They have confidence in their own handcrafted work.

# Chapter 3

# Decisions before Handloading

This chapter will help you start a successful handloading project. The decision and selection methods given here will permit a smooth flow from objective- setting into actual loading. The eight intermediate objectives from Chapter 2 are directly influenced by the points in this chapter. Your success depends on the decisions and selections made at this time. In addition, the essential points of safety, facility, equipment, supplies, storage, and record-keeping are presented. Some of these points will be expanded further after handloading and firing. Others are not dealt with so completely, but their need will be seen as you progress.

The first point prior to loading should be safety. This means safety for you while working, and safety for others when you are absent. Handloading does not jibe with smoking, drinking, conversation, television, children, or even uncomfortable conditions. All of these things can add to the chance of an accident. In your absence, the loading bench must be secure from curious adults and children. You need a good light, but no open flames or sparks should be near the bench or near any explosives.

The bench can be almost any height as long as your seat is the right height for easy use of the press, scales, and other equipment. The bench doesn't have to be large or rock solid. Most commercially made benches are adequate to support your loading press and the other required tools. The compound linkage presses require even less bench strength.

The size of the loading bench is another matter, however. If your bench is used only for actual loading, you may be able to operate in a small space. If shotshell loading is also performed, you will want to expand. If other activities, such as planning, gunsmithing, cleaning, record-keeping, reading, bullet casting, and other shop activities are done at the same bench, you will need more room. Personally, I like to separate loading from paperwork and

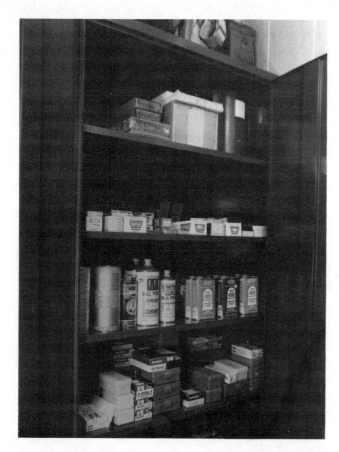

Keep the flammable and explosive supplies locked and away from the living area. A steel cabinet is excellent but several types of containers may be used. All should be lockable.

the least damage in case of fire, yet still be secure from curious adults and children. Your situation may be different from mine, but it's a good idea to store all ammunition, powder, and primers in one location, away from firearms. A storage location apart from the living quarters of your house is also an added safety factor. All of these potentially dangerous items should be located so as to minimize their effects in case of fire. I don't subscribe to the advice from some authorities who suggest distributing flammable components about your home in small quantities to lessen their concentration at any one point. If your handloading requires storage of several pounds of powder, primers, and ammunition, you are safer if those components are stored in a single, secure place, located away from the living area and fire escape routes. I use an old steel office cabinet with ventilated front and sides and a good lock. This cabinet is in the hallway between my house and garage. Temperatures are fairly cool there in summer. The cooler air in my house passes into the hall. A smoke detector is installed near the steel cabinet. It can be heard throughout the rest of my house. A fire extinguisher is a few feet away from the cabinet. This may seem a bit overdone for such a relatively low fire hazard, but an ounce of prevention is worth at least a pound of cure.

reading. This allows me to use a small, efficient loading bench in the corner of my garage. Reading and planning are done indoors in a separate study room. The choices are yours, and not too important, except for the safety and security aspects.

### Storage

Personal choice is also a factor in deciding where to store components and ammunition. The layout of your home or workshop may dictate whether you store components near or away from the loading bench. Loaded ammunition, propellants, primers, and guns are your chief concerns when considering safety. There are many thoughts as to the best storage location for these flammable, explosive items. Probably the best choice for component storage location is where each component concerned will do

### Safety

Another safety consideration is that of mechanical dangers around the loading bench. Priming devices, powder measures, sharpened cutting tools, hand tools, and loading presses present some dangers, especially to small children; keep these items out of their reach. Bench-mounted loading presses have great leverage and shearing action. They can pinch and cut near the working area at the press and ram and also around the press linkage at the bottom. On most presses, this part is below the bench top. Mount your press so that you won't pinch your hand or leg when working. Be certain to provide some form of restraint on the press when it is unused, especially if the loading bench can be reached by small children. A simple restraint for most loading presses can be made out of a piece of coat hanger wire. The linkage on most presses can do harm. Children like to pull and push things that move. Let your own imagination determine the possible results. Take steps to prevent an accident before it happens.

While loading, be sure to follow the "no smoking" and "no drinking" rules. Neither has a place at the loading bench while work is underway. Have others observe the "no smoking" rule at the bench also. Keep a small fire extinguisher nearby. Sweep up all spilled powder granules after loading and pick up all dropped primers immediately. Primers may present the greatest single danger during and after loading. A primer underfoot, scraping against a concrete floor, can explode. If loading over a carpet, place newspapers underneath your bench to catch any dropped primers. A child might locate a primer lost in carpeting pile and suffer the consequences of your carelessness. For these reasons, it is a good idea to count primers before and after loading. Jot down the amounts. If the difference doesn't

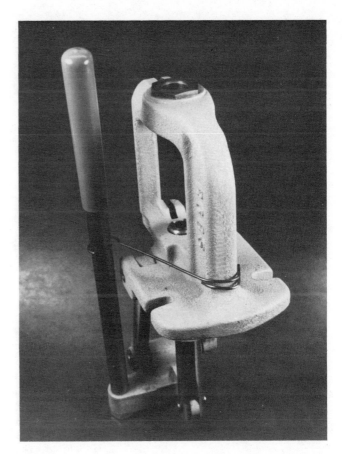

This simple restraint, made from a coat hanger, provides a measure of safety for small children.

Mounting some sort of fire alarm near the components' storage space is a good idea. A smoke alarm or heat sensor will give warning if mounted correctly. Just make sure you can hear the alarm in the other rooms of your home.

equal the number of primed cartridges, you'd better start looking for the lost ones. Don't give up until you find them all. Your wife may not appreciate the lost primer being sucked into her vacuum cleaner, either.

Be sure to follow the handloader's rule and never put more than one can of powder on your bench at one time. This is not only a basic safety rule, but an excellent way to prevent confusion and waste, due to improperly loaded cartridges and mixed propellants. And, keep the lid on the can.

Disposing of unusable powder and primers is another matter. Burning old powder may not be possible in your neighborhood and dousing primers with oil does not necessarily destroy them. Believe me! Probably the best thing to do when getting rid of unusable powder and primers is simply to bury them. Place them in moist soil, about two feet deep. Nature will perform the destruction job quickly and safely.

Don't ever try to resize a loaded cartridge. Imagine the results if the primer exploded while the cartridge is squeezed into the sizing die!

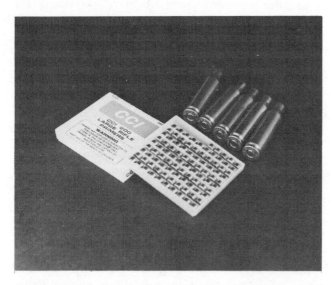

Count primers before and after priming. The difference should match the number of primed cases. If you're still missing a primer, start looking and don't quit until you find it.

Keep a pair of approved safety glasses near your bench and don't ever begin loading until you put them on. Don't take them off until you leave the bench. If a primer pops, you could be hurt without eye protection. I have violated most of the previous suggestions at one time or another, but I do wear safety glasses religiously. Aside from just plain common sense, good glasses are the cheapest safety investment you can make. Buy a pair and wear them for your eyes' sake.

While we're on the subject of safety, one of the most dangerous acts an unthinking handloader may try is to resize a *loaded* cartridge. Don't do it! Remember this: the loaded cartridge will be contained within the sizing die. If the primer were to ignite, there's no way to release the explosion of the cartridge. The effect would be like that of a bomb. Another very dangerous act is to try and seat a primer in a loaded cartridge. Both of the above actions are extremely dangerous. Again, the consequences will be left to your own imagination.

## Organizing the Work Area

Now let's consider some other aspects of the loading bench. Keep in mind that some of these suggestions reflect my own preferences. They are offered only as ideas. Your needs may be different.

If your bench is used for other work, you may not like the idea of permanently fastening your different loading tools, such as the powder measure, case trimmer, priming tool, and so forth, to the bench top. This is unnecessary and takes up room that's needed for other activities. I recommend mounting only two pieces of equipment on the bench—the loading press and a bench vise. Obviously, if you are right-handed the press should be set up for convenience on the right side of the table, and over the bench leg for stability. Over on the left, near the other front bench leg, is where the vise should be mounted. Powder measures, case trimmers, and priming tools can all be mounted on hardwood T-blocks, which can be clamped in the vise when they are needed. At all other times, this equipment can be stored off the bench top.

Experience has proven that the vise and wooden mounting blocks are better than C-clamps for holding loading equipment to the bench. Each block is

Various loading tools mounted on wooden T-blocks. A vise will hold any of these tools rigidly when needed. The bench top remains uncluttered and usable for other jobs.

constructed of two pieces of hardwood. Screw a standard-width "vise" block to the base of each mounting block. The standard-size block allows the vise to be used more conveniently and quickly, since the vise opening remains essentially unchanged. (Consult the accompanying photo and drawing.) Any hard, dense wood will do. A standard-width "vise" block should be about 2½" wide and ¾" thick, and the same length as the "tool" block, also ¾" thick; its width and length will vary according to the specific piece of equipment.

Do not fasten your powder scale to the bench. Precision equipment like this can be damaged if subjected to shock. The powder scale should be mounted above the bench on a separate shelf that is not attached to the bench and not likely to receive a blow. Mount the scale shelf so that the indicator needle on the scale will be at your eye level while you work. The shelf can be used to store other items of equipment and supplies such as books, loading dies, and measuring equipment. All of your hand-loading tools should be placed so that you can operate them comfortably, and with good material flow. You don't want to have to look around for something when you need it. Everything ought to be in a familiar place.

Two other pieces of equipment necessary for the handloading methods described in this book are

Decisions before Handloading

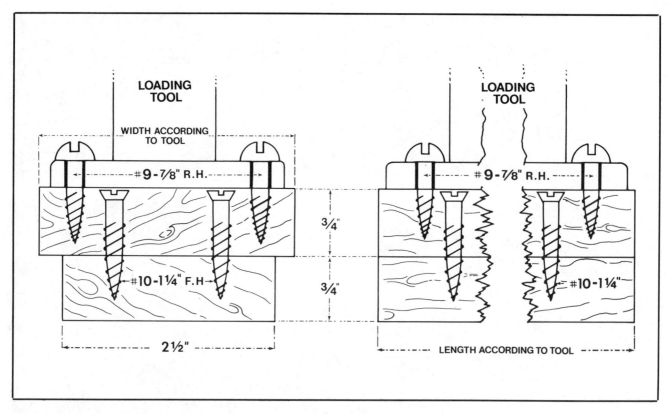

This shows typical T-block construction for mounting loading tools.

precision measuring devices: a caliper, and a micrometer. Both are essential.

Measuring calipers are devices for measuring inside and outside distances, heights, and depths. They are made in two types: vernier and dial. Calipers are accurate to one-one thousandth of an inch ($\pm 0.001''$). It doesn't matter whether you use the vernier lines or dial gauge. Both are equally accurate. The dial-type caliper costs more, but is faster, easier to use, and eliminates reading errors that happen with the vernier. A six-inch caliper is the best size for handloading needs. The caliper is used for finding cartridge case dimensions and measuring targets.

A micrometer is the other precision device you'll need for handloading. The zero-to-one-inch size is all that's needed. Be sure that the micrometer has a vernier scale on the barrel for four place measurements. That means that the micrometer must be able to measure to $\pm 0.0001$ inch. It is ten times as precise as the caliper, but can only measure up to one inch. The micrometer is used to measure cartridge case heads for pressure expansion. A mi-

crometer is needed because cartridge case head measurements must be ten times as precise as those obtainable with calipers.

Some micrometers come with direct, digital read-out features but the digits only read to thousandths of an inch ($\pm .001''$). For ten thousandths measurements ($\pm .0001''$) you must still read the vernier scale on the barrel and add that figure to the digital figure just like on the standard types. The digital feature on some micrometers is nice, but not as much of an advantage as the dial indicator is on calipers. You're after quick, accurate readings.

If you're wondering how to spend your money, purchase a good six-inch dial-type caliper but buy a standard, one-inch micrometer with the vernier scale on the barrel. This will measure to $\pm .0001$ inch. Since your micrometer readings will be to four places for all case head measurements, it is best to buy a micrometer with a friction-type thimble. The friction thimble, rather than the ratchet-type thimble, is better for making measurements to the fourth place ($\pm .0001''$).

The measurements you need to make with the

calipers and micrometer are only needed when working up a handload. Unless you plan to handload other cartridges, you may wish to rent or borrow these devices. That's good for objective number 8—meeting your objectives with the least expense.

The last item of equipment is not absolutely necessary, but very nice to have. It is a small, portable air compressor with a few feet of hose and a blow gun. This is a great timesaver when cleaning and drying cartridge cases if you do much reloading. It can also be used for many other shooting, fishing, automotive, and household chores. A $^{1}/_{4}$ to $^{3}/_{4}$ HP compressor is fine. But use caution whenever using the blow gun, even the OSHA approved type. Do not blow air directly against your skin. Air pressure can force dirt, rust, metal chips, and chemicals into your skin and bloodstream. When using the blow gun, always hold a rag between your hand and whatever you are cleaning or drying.

## Materials and Supplies

The categories of materials and supplies include factory ammunition, cartridge reloading components, and lubricants. These will be discussed individually. Materials, supplies, and the standards for good cartridge making will be discussed so that nothing important for successful handloading is overlooked before work at the loading bench actually begins.

At first glance one might think it strange that handloading materials include factory ammunition. However, this is important. Factory ammo will be the standard by which many of your results and decisions will be made. The better the standard, the better the result. The cartridge standard often referred to in this text is factory ammunition that most nearly meets your *objectives* for handloading; in other words, the factory ammunition that would be best for your shooting needs if you were not a handloader. Be certain that the factory ammunition that you choose is loaded with the correct bullet for your use. This means a bullet that is of the correct weight and of the correct construction for your needs. For instance, if you are a deer hunter and you shoot a .30-06, choose ammunition loaded with a 150–165-grain expanding-type bullet. Reputable, factory-loaded .30-06 ammunition with 150-grain

expanding bullets is designed for proper penetration and expansion on deer-sized game. Lighter bullets tend to self-destruct too easily and only wound game. Heavier bullets do not expand well in deer and do not kill as positively. Each suitable rifle caliber has a best bullet weight range for deer-sized animals, for example: the 100-grain bullet with the 6mm or .243; the 120-grain with the .257 or .264; the 130-grain with the .270; the 140- to 150-grain with the 7mm Mag or .284; and the 150- to 165-grain bullets with the .308.

These bullet weights are best for deer because they have good sectional density, ballistic coefficient, and are still light enough to be driven at speeds that result in good expansion and enough shock for quick kills.

Greater bullet penetration is needed on larger animals such as elk, moose, brown bears, and several African species. Accordingly, heavier bullets

Place your powder scale at eye level and on a shelf that is not attached to the bench. This scale is at eye level when the loader is sitting on the bench stool.

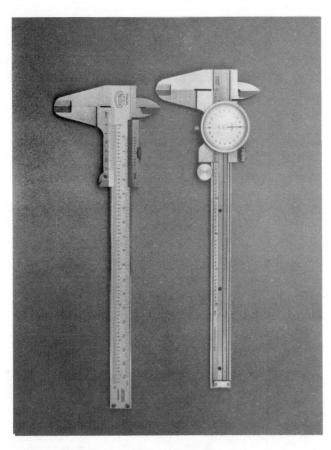

Calipers are available in dial-type (right), and vernier-type (left). Either kind works well.

standard. You'll want to be able to compare velocities of your handloads with the factory standard (objective 2). It is also important to be sure of correct bullet expansion and penetration with your handloads (objective 3). If identical weight bullets are not available or are impractical, try and stay within 4 percent of the factory-loaded bullet. For example, if you handload the 7mm Magnum, using one of the 150-grain factory cartridge loadings as your standard, your component bullet should be no less than 144 grains and no more than 156 grains in weight for a fair comparison. Buy about 200 bullets and try to obtain identical lot numbers on each box. You should also purchase two boxes of factory-loaded ammunition with the same factory lot number. This is important.

The handloading component with which you will spend the most time is the cartridge case. You can collect cases that have been fired in your own gun or once-fired cases from other sources. Remember that you must use cases made by the same manufacturer, having the same head stamp on the cartridge case head. It doesn't really matter which brand of case you select for your handloads as long as those cases are all the same. This is because cartridge cases must be as nearly equal in weight, in-

are made with thicker, tougher jackets. This controls bullet expansion and penetration on heavy-bodied, muscular animals. Heavier bullets will kill deer, but they don't do the job as quickly and positively as the lighter-weight, thinner-jacketed ones. Bullet choice is important.

Don't stay up nights worrying about best bullet weights or overall quality. American ammunition manufacturers all make excellent products to meet the needs of the hunter and the range shooter. You can't go wrong with any major ammo supplier. They all publish much useful ballistic information and you can trust their recommendations. By choosing the correct factory ammunition for your needs, you set the correct standard of comparison for your handloads.

The same reasoning holds true for choosing your component bullets. These must be the same weight, or very close, to that of the bullets used in the factory-loaded ammunition chosen as your

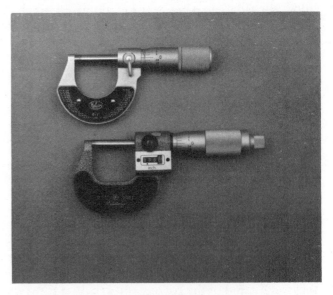

A micrometer is needed for finding relative chamber pressure. Make sure it measures to four places (0.0001″). Whether standard (top), or digital (bottom), the micrometer must have a vernier scale on the thimble barrel. The vernier scale provides the fine measurements you will need.

ternal shape, and brass alloy as possible for the precise loading and performance comparisons you will make later. This is necessary to achieve handloading objectives: (1) precision; (4) consistency; (5) duplication; and (7) pressure. For handload development projects, you should collect about 150 to 200 once-fired, selected cases of the same caliber, manufacturer, and head stamp. Much more discussion about cartridge case selection, grading, and preparation will be presented in Chapter 4.

The next cartridge component is the propellant or powder. The choice of powder is important in at least six ways for achieving the handload objectives. First, it must be able to achieve equal or better target precision with your handloaded ammunition than the factory standard (objective 1). Second, the powder must give comparable or higher velocity with your handloaded ammunition than the factory ammunition (objective 2). Third, it can help to achieve higher consistency than that from factory ammunition (objective 4). Fourth, the powder in the handload must enable the firearm to function as well as or better than the way it functions with factory ammunition (objective 6). Fifth, the powder must produce proper, consistent, and safe pressure in the handloaded ammunition (objective 7). Sixth, being able to specify and identify the propellant gives you the ability to duplicate a cartridge at any time (objective 5). The contribution that the pow-

You have four component decisions to make after deciding to develop any handload: which bullet, which powder, which primer, and which case.

der makes in reaching each of these objectives underlines its importance in gaining your final handloading result.

In addition to the preceding facts, the powder should be chosen with some thought to its availability in the future. If the manufacturer should decide to eliminate the powder you select from future production, you will have to choose another powder and duplicate all of your prior efforts. This

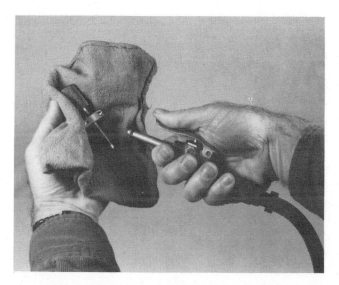

When using compressed air to operate a blowgun, always keep some protection between the air jet and your skin. Wear safety glasses, too.

Some of the many propellants for centerfire cartridges. The propellant you choose should have a history of good sales and continued availability. All of these do.

would create expenses you don't need (objective 8). Choose an established powder with a history of good sales. Let someone else experiment with new products for now. You have more basic needs to satisfy at present.

As you can see, the powder will have a tremendous influence on the effectiveness of your finished product. But choosing the correct powder, like choosing bullets, is not difficult if a few things are understood before you make your choice.

Always remember that you should follow a decision process for powder choice. The decision should be based on your need. If you don't lose sight of your needs, your decision will be easier.

## Modern Propellants

Shortly before the turn of this century, smokeless propellants began to replace black powder for use in firearms. Smokeless powders were safer, more stable, and did not produce as much fouling as black powder, which was also called gunpowder. The new powder did not hide the target behind a screen of smoke, and it did not mark the location of the rifleman for enemy observers. In addition, smokeless powders had many other highly desira-

There is more variety in bullets than any other component. These are just a few. Most major bullet makers publish elaborate catalogs and manuals that describe their products including their use, how to load them, and their external ballistics.

Bullets have lot numbers because it is impossible to make such highly precise products exactly the same every time. American bullet makers come very close, however. They are the world's best.

ble qualities which allowed newer and more powerful ammunition and arms to be developed.

There are two basic types of smokeless propellants for use in small arms. They are known simply as single-base and double-base powders. Both types use the compound, nitrocellulose. Nitrocellulose, also called gun cotton or pyrocellulose, is the basic ingredient in smokeless powders. Single-base powder is composed mainly of nitrocellulose. Double-base powder is generally made of about 90 percent nitrocellulose and 10 percent nitroglycerine to burn faster and develop pressure faster. Both types, single- and double-base, can be used in rifle, pistol, and shotshell cartridges. Double-base powders are used mostly in handgun and shotshell cartridges. Single-base powders are used mostly in high-powdered rifle cartridges.

Smokeless powders are made to burn efficiently at different pressures and at different speeds: shotshell powders burn best at 7,000 to 12,000 pounds per square inch of pressure; handgun powders at 10,000 to 40,000 psi; and rifle powders at 35,000 to 60,000 psi. Various powders differ from one another by the speed and the characteristics with which they burn. These characteristics are used to great advantage with the different types of firearms, as we will see.

High-powered rifles fire bullets at much higher

velocities than do handguns or shotguns. This is accomplished by making rifle bores long in relation to their diameters, and by utilizing the unique characteristics of some powders. Slow-burning powders are used to advantage in the longer-bored rifles. The long barrel length gives slow propellants time to build high pressure. The relatively small chamber size of the rifle can be strengthened to withstand high pressures developed with slow-burning powders. Furthermore, this pressure is sustained better through the long, but small diameter rifle bore. Rifle bullets achieve higher velocities than possible in handguns and shotguns. These mechanical facts were understood for a long time, but it wasn't until the invention and perfection of smokeless powder that they were effectively used. Almost all modern rifle ammunition was developed during and after the 1890s, when smokeless powders replaced black powder.

In the 1920s, smokeless powder was further improved with an additional characteristic or feature, known as progressive rate of burning. Progressive, smokeless propellants allow even higher bullet velocities at lower pressure. Progressive rate of burning, in contrast to neutral and degressive burning rates, is achieved by changing the shape, size, and density of the powder granules. Surface coatings, known as deterrents, are used to slow the burning rate further and sustain pressure for even longer periods. Modern powders also contain additives for reducing muzzle flash, preservatives and stabilizers to lengthen storage life, and lubricants to improve measure and flow characteristics for loading, while decreasing the nuisance and danger of static electricity. Most of these modern, single-base powders evolved into the present flake and tubular or "stick"-shaped powders. Ball or spherical powders, developed later, have been controlled sufficiently for some high-powered cartridges and offer some unique advantages. All ball-type powders, at present, are double-base propellants. They are best used in shotshells, handgun cartridges, and small case rifle cartridges.

Despite the differences among powders, their chief ingredient, nitrocellulose, is still the same. It is common to all. The different features merely allow us to match the powder precisely to the specific loading requirement. But powders are all still made of the same basic stuff.

In addition to knowing something about the

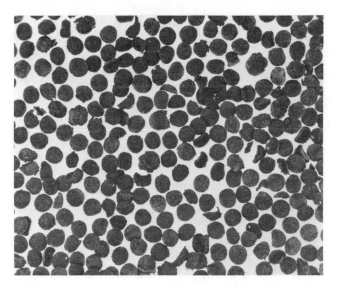

Flake propellant. Hercules Unique.

physical properties of modern powders, you also should be familiar with two terms—canister powders, and powder lots.

When powder intended for factory-loaded ammunition is manufactured, its characteristics are not controlled unequivocally, or with finite precision. To attempt to do so is considered impractical from a production standpoint. Even with controlled blending procedures, some differences still exist. The resulting lots of any given propellant, while similar in character to one another, are still slightly different in energy level and burning

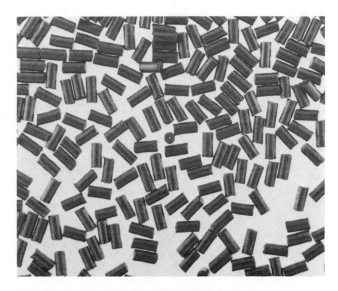

Tubular propellant, DuPont IMR 4350.

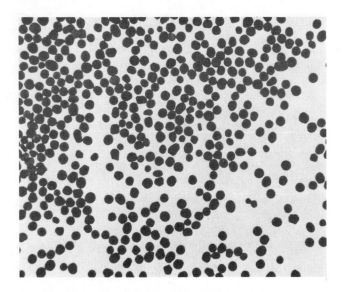

Ball propellant (flattened ball). Winchester-Western 760.

speed. To a large commercial ammunition maker, these differences in lots are acceptable. Appropriate loading adjustments are made along the production line to keep velocity and pressure to the company's acceptance standards. But if this same type powder is sold to the public for reloading, the differences in production batches and lots must be further lessened. This is because of the safety, liability, and convenience considerations accorded the small users and handloaders. The powder must be carefully blended to ensure that correct energy levels are achieved on the same weight and volume ba-

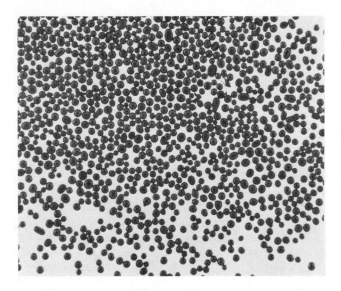

Spherical propellant. Hodgdon H380.

sis, because handloaders use both weighed and metered (volume) methods for loading.

Metering requires the use of a fixed or adjustable device to dispense the same volume of powder each time the device is operated. Handloaders know such loading devices as powder measures, although they do not measure, they only meter.

The other method of loading cartridges is to measure the amount of propellant by weight. This is done using balances or scales to determine the exact weight of the powder placed into each cartridge. Such measuring devices are normally capable of measuring within $\pm 0.1$ grain of weight on the avoirdupois scale.

Because both of the above methods, weighed measurement and volumetric metering, are used by handloaders, and because handloaders rely on loading data supplied to the public by the powder makers, special blending and matching is required for these selected propellants. These specially prepared lots of propellant are poured into small containers or canisters. Such lots of powder are termed canister lots and are reserved for sale to the public.

Canister powders are the most closely controlled and blended powders available from the powder suppliers—they are also the most costly. Yet with all these precise, careful, and costly attentions to detail, it is still not possible to duplicate batches of canister powder exactly. There are still some differences from lot to lot. That is one reason why batch or lot numbers are placed on each canister. The lot number is the only way of determining if one can of powder is exactly the same as another. For some, these differences in powder lots are of no concern. But for the handloader, who wants to duplicate and load at some future time and who has the ability to measure the resulting performance differences (objectives 4 and 5), a powder's lot number becomes almost as important as the powder itself.

For these reasons, once you have chosen a powder for handloading, purchase enough to complete your basic loading determinations and also to make the extra cartridges for your future needs. For a once-a-year deer hunter shooting a high-powered rifle, at least two pounds of the same stock number and lot number powder is needed. The exact quantity depends on the caliber, the amount of handload testing required, the chosen powder, and the amount of shooting you intend to do in the future. It is less expensive, and certainly easier, to purchase an extra pound or two of powder initially than to have to retest all over again in the future due to a change in lot numbers.

When developing any new handload, start loading at least 10 percent below the maximum recommended charge weight for the bullet weight, caliber, and powder you are using. This is for safety's sake, but it also lets you see results more clearly as you test. As double security, use the recommendations of both the powder manufacturer *and* the bullet manufacturer for that caliber and bullet weight. This requires two documents: the guide furnished by the powder maker, and the guide or manual from the bullet maker. You need both.

By cross-referencing information available from the powder maker and the bullet maker, you should be able not only to find the correct powder, but also the correct range of powder charge weights for proper, safe, and complete testing. With this knowledge, it is possible to determine accurately how much propellant and other components will be necessary for testing.

### Comparing Powders

Now that the important propellant facts have been stated, let's decide how to go about choosing a powder for your shooting requirements.

In addition to satisfying the intermediate objectives and the basic reason of confidence, the list of powders you may choose from must be narrowed using available information. The term "list" of powders is used because there is often more than one powder that will do the job. Several powders may be able to meet your objectives equally well. Seldom will it be necessary to rely on a single powder to accomplish the objectives we've been talking about.

Your initial list of correct powders should be made up using the information supplied by the propellant makers. They know more about what their products will do than anyone else. Next, use substantiating information supplied by the bullet makers. The best powder selections are usually obvious once the caliber and the bullet weight have been chosen.

When using loading information from the powder supplier, pay attention to the details of data collection such as the barrel length and rate of rifling twist used, and the velocity and pressure obtained.

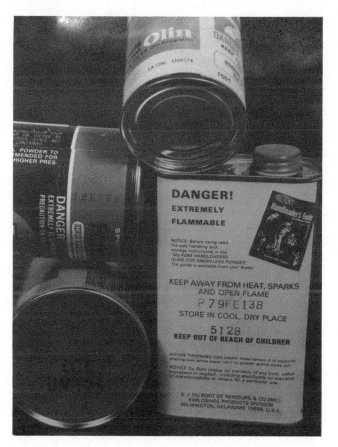

Propellant lot numbers are important to the handloader. They are the only way to ensure identical results. All powder makers and distributors supply lot numbers on the cans.

Cartridge cases must be sorted according to manufacturer and head stamp. These are just a few commonly seen head stamps for one caliber.

Any big differences between those constants and your own firearm (e.g., barrel length) can affect your results. If so, consult another information source whose standards are closer to your own particular situation.

There are many common views expressed about the relative performance and correct use of different powders. The statement, "slow-burning powders are better for heavy bullets, and fast powders are needed for light bullets," is often heard and read. This advice can be accepted as a rough guide to powder selection, but only if the handloader understands its relative meaning. Granted, the statement does contain some truth, overall, but the subject is much more involved than this simplistic opinion would suggest.

Likewise, another statement, "big cases require slow-burning powders, and small cases require fast-burning powders," is also too inconclusive for reliable use. You should treat this generality with the same regard as the previous one. The sensible approach is to research data thoroughly from the powder maker and also the bullet maker to determine a proper powder for any handloading project. Their loading tables make it possible for you to compare extensive factory results and make your choice accordingly. Then use that powder in working up your loads.

If you want to experiment further at a later time, choose a second powder, determine a best loading for it, and then compare the results of the two powders against your objectives. Then make your decision. All other methods eventually lead to this same process. By using the bullet and powder makers' data, you are doing this.

The handloading techniques in this text simplify and help determine which handloading combination is best with the components you choose for testing. Near identical results can often be achieved with similar propellants and similar bullet weights.

As noted earlier, the most important prerequisite to powder selection is to study the powder maker's loading data first, then use the chosen bullet maker's data to substantiate pertinent facts. First, obtain loading tables from several leading powder makers. Locate the data appropriate to the bullet weight and caliber of interest. Then determine which powder gives the highest bullet velocity, and which most nearly fills the cartridge case.

Second, consult the bullet maker's loading tables

in regard to the caliber and the bullet you intend to use. From these tables, find the powders that give the highest bullet velocity. At this point, the selection of propellants normally will have narrowed considerably. Sometimes this method turns up only one best powder, but usually two or three powders will show equal or nearly equal potential. Unless velocity differences are greater than 100 feet per second in the tables, any of these recommended propellants should allow you to achieve your objectives. And, they should be readily available.

Another thought; the most precise, usable loadings usually involve charge weights that are less than maximum. This means slightly less than maximum use of case volume; therefore, if a powder selection indicates slightly compressed charges for maximum velocity, your best load may not require compression at all. Such an occurrence, from a loading standpoint, is ideal. The utilization of space in the cartridge case will be near maximum. No air space will be left to allow powder shifting and changes in ignition, pressure, velocity, and precision. It doesn't always work out this way, but it is nice when it happens. If a powder is chosen correctly, you can often come close to this situation. Some examples are presented to better illustrate this comparison process.

**Example 1. Cartridge—.270 Winchester, Bullet—130-grain Sierra.** The *Du Pont Handloader's Guide* (see photo) shows the highest velocity for the 130-grain bullet in the .270 Winchester should occur with IMR 4831 powder. To quote from the Du Pont guide, "The powder charge weights specified represent loads that developed *maximum allowable chamber pressures* with the test components specified—with the exception of loads that are specified as "compressed charges" (C), which may represent case capacity rather than maximum chamber pressure." Using the selection procedure as described, the choice appears to be IMR 4831. Not only are the highest velocities achieved with IMR 4831 among the Du Pont powders, but the best loading densities may also be achieved and at a lower pressure than with some of the other powders. IMR 4350 would be the next best choice according to Du Pont data. Now let's look at the bullet maker's data before making our decision.

The *Sierra Reloading Manual* shows five powders capable of near equal velocity in the .270 Winches-

DU PONT CHARGE VELOCITY CHAMBER
POWDER (grains) (ft/sec) PRESS. (cup)

DU PONT CHARGE VELOCITY CHAMBER
POWDER (grains) (ft/sec) PRESS. (cup)

DU PONT CHARGE
POWDER (grains)

## .270 WINCHESTER

REM. N.F.P. CASE;
REM. 100 GR. PSP
.277" DIA.; 23" BBL.; 3.075" C.O.L.

| DU PONT POWDER | CHARGE (grains) | VELOCITY (ft/sec) | CHAMBER PRESS. (cup) |
|---|---|---|---|
| SR 4759 | 33.0 | 2755 | 54000 |
| IMR 4227 | 30.0 | 2710 | 53300 |
| IMR 4198 | 37.5 | 3025 | 53500 |
| IMR 3031 | 49.0 | 3300 | 53400 |
| IMR 4064 | 51.5 | 3340 | 53900 |
| IMR 4895 | 49.5 | 3260 | 54000 |
| IMR 4320 | 50.5 | 3230 | 54000 |
| IMR 4350 | 60.0C | 3365 | 53900 |
| IMR 4831 | 60.0C | 3245 | 49800 |

## 7 x 57 MM MAUSER

REM. N.F., REM. 9 1/2 P. CASE;
SPEER 160 GR. SPITZER
.284" DIA.; 24" BBL.; 3.065" C.O.L.

| DU PONT POWDER | CHARGE (grains) | VELOCITY (ft/sec) | CHAMBER PRESS. (cup) |
|---|---|---|---|
| SR 4759 | 22.5 | 1855 | 45700 |
| IMR 4227 | 22.5 | 1890 | 46000 |
| IMR 4198 | 28.5 | 2135 | 44900 |
| IMR 3031 | 38.0 | 2430 | 45800 |
| IMR 4064 | 40.0 | 2480 | 46000 |
| IMR 4895 | 35.0 | 2325 | 45800 |
| IMR 4320 | 36.0 | 2295 | 45200 |
| IMR 4350 | 45.0 | 2510 | 45800 |
| IMR 4831 | 47.5C | 2540 | 45600 |

## .284 WI[N]

WIN. N.
SPEER 16(
.284" DIA.; 24"

| DU PONT POWDER | CHARGE (grains) |
|---|---|
| SR 4759 | 27.5 |
| IMR 4227 | 28.0 |
| IMR 4198 | 34.5 |
| IMR 3031 | 45.0 |
| IMR 4064 | 47.0 |
| IMR 4895 | 41.0 |
| IMR 4320 | 43.5 |
| IMR 4350 | 52.0 |
| IMR 4831 | 52.0 |

## .270 WINCHESTER

REM. N.F.P. CASE;
REM. 130 GR. P SPCL
.277" DIA.; 23" BBL.; 3.250" C.O.L.

| DU PONT POWDER | CHARGE (grains) | VELOCITY (ft/sec) | CHAMBER PRESS. (cup) |
|---|---|---|---|
| SR 4759 | 30.5 | 2390 | 53400 |
| IMR 4227 | 28.5 | 2305 | 53500 |
| IMR 4198 | 36.0 | 2630 | 54000 |
| IMR 3031 | 46.0 | 2915 | 53000 |
| IMR 4064 | 49.0 | 2995 | 53400 |
| IMR 4895 | 44.0 | 2825 | 53600 |
| IMR 4320 | 46.0 | 2860 | 54000 |
| IMR 4350 | 55.0 | 3035 | 53100 |
| IMR 4831 | 59.0C | 3110 | 53600 |

## .280 REMINGTON

REM. N.F.P. CASE;
REM. 125 GR. PTD. SPCL
.283" DIA.; 24" BBL.; 3.250" C.O.L.

| DU PONT POWDER | CHARGE (grains) | VELOCITY (ft/sec) | CHAMBER PRESS. (cup) |
|---|---|---|---|
| SR 4759 | 30.0 | 2445 | 49700 |
| IMR 4227 | 28.5 | 2375 | 48400 |
| IMR 4198 | 36.0 | 2680 | 50000 |
| IMR 3031 | 47.0 | 2975 | 48900 |
| IMR 4064 | 50.0 | 3055 | 49700 |
| IMR 4895 | 44.0 | 2845 | 49100 |
| IMR 4320 | 46.5 | 2880 | 49900 |
| IMR 4350 | 56.5 | 3055 | 48600 |
| IMR 4831 | 60.0C | 3115 | 50000 |

## 7 MM REM[INGTON]

REM. N.
HORNADY 12[?]
.284" DIA.; 24"

| DU PONT POWDER | CHARGE (grains) |
|---|---|
| SR 4759 | 36.[?] |
| IMR 4227 | 37.[?] |
| IMR 4198 | 44.[?] |
| IMR 3031 | 52.[?] |
| IMR 4064 | 55.[?] |
| IMR 4895 | 54.[?] |
| IMR 4320 | 55.[?] |
| IMR 4350 | 65.[?] |
| IMR 4831 | 68.[?] |

## .270 WINCHESTER

REM. N.F.P. CASE;
REM. 150 GR. SPCL
.277" DIA.; 23" BBL.; 3.220" C.O.L.

| DU PONT POWDER | CHARGE (grains) | VELOCITY (ft/sec) | CHAMBER PRESS. (cup) |
|---|---|---|---|
| SR 4759 | 30.0 | 2225 | 53900 |
| IMR 4227 | 27.5 | 2115 | 53400 |
| IMR 4198 | 35.0 | 2450 | 53700 |
| IMR 3031 | 43.0 | 2690 | 54000 |
| IMR 4064 | 47.5 | 2830 | 52600 |
| IMR 4895 | 42.5 | 2675 | 53600 |
| IMR 4320 | 44.0 | 2680 | 53000 |
| IMR 4350 | 54.0 | 2930 | 53400 |
| IMR 4831 | 57.0C | 2980 | 53900 |

## .280 REMINGTON

REM. N.F.P. CASE;
REM. 150 GR. PTD. SPCL
.284" DIA.; 24" BBL.; 3.325" C.O.L.

| DU PONT POWDER | CHARGE (grains) | VELOCITY (ft/sec) | CHAMBER PRESS. (cup) |
|---|---|---|---|
| SR 4759 | 29.5 | 2200 | 50000 |
| IMR 4227 | 27.5 | 2115 | 49500 |
| IMR 4198 | 34.5 | 2375 | 49200 |
| IMR 3031 | 45.5 | 2745 | 48800 |
| IMR 4064 | 48.0 | 2810 | 50000 |
| IMR 4895 | 42.5 | 2635 | 49300 |
| IMR 4320 | 44.5 | 2655 | 50000 |
| IMR 4350 | 55.0 | 2895 | 50000 |
| IMR 4831 | 57.0 | 2930 | 50000 |

## 7 MM REMI[NGTON]

REM. N.
REM. 150 [GR.]
.284" DIA.; 24"

| DU PONT POWDER | CHARGE (grains) |
|---|---|
| SR 4759 | 35.0 |
| IMR 4227 | 36.0 |
| IMR 4198 | 43.0 |
| IMR 3031 | 51.0 |
| IMR 4064 | 54.0 |
| IMR 4895 | 52.0 |
| IMR 4320 | 54.0 |
| IMR 4350 | 63.0 |
| IMR 4831 | 66.5 |

Example 1—.270 Winchester, 130-grain bullet. A page from Du Pont's *Handloader's Guide* shows the powders that give the greatest velocities. All these loads are maximum. The letter "C" indicates a compressed charge. When working up a load, always begin at least 10 percent below maximum and go up gradually.

ter cartridge and 130-grain bullet. Each is capable of about 3,100 feet per second. They are Du Pont IMR 4350 and IMR 4831, Hodgdon H450 and H4831, and Winchester 785. Three of these powders (IMR 4350, IMR 4831, and H4831) are single-base, tubular-grained powders. The other two powders (H450 and W-W785) are ball-type, double-base powders. Four would work well with this loading. Only one of the five, Winchester 785, is not entirely suitable for our loading methods as outlined in this book. A check of their loading data shows that Winchester specifically cautions against the use of any charge weight other than that shown for W-W785. This restriction does not allow the freedom to start below the maximum charge weight and work up to find the best loading. The other four powders are all acceptable for our needs. Incidentally, the 4831 powders (Du Pont or Hodgdon) have been considered best choices for the 130-grain .270

Winchester cartridge for many years by knowledgeable writers, shooters, and experienced handloaders. That advice could be time-saving.

Let's look at another powder choice problem to gain more experience.

**Example 2. Cartridge—.308 Winchester, Bullet—150-grain Speer.** For this excellent deer hunting cartridge, the *Du Pont Handloader's Guide* shows IMR 3031 and IMR 4064, as the two "fastest" propellants in this 150- grain grouping. Comparing the data, we note that IMR 3031 holds a very slight edge in velocity over IMR 4064.

The *Speer Reloading Manual No. 10* shows the "fastest" choice for this cartridge combination to be Du Pont IMR 4064, followed very closely by Hodgdon H335. Different testing procedures, equipment, and components are the reason for these slight differences.

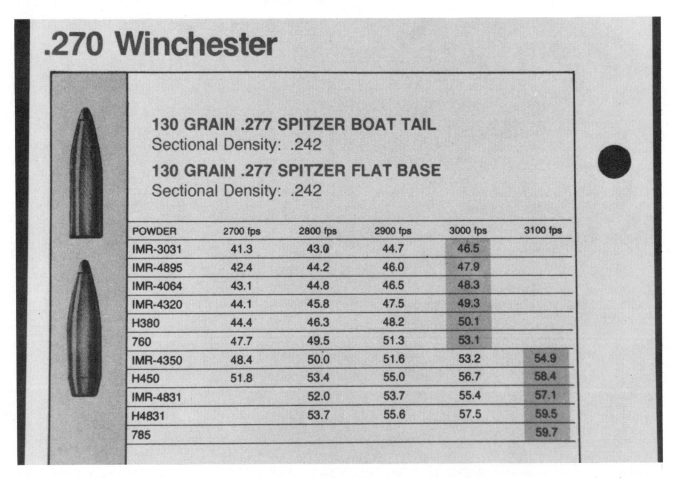

# .270 Winchester

**130 GRAIN .277 SPITZER BOAT TAIL**
Sectional Density: .242

**130 GRAIN .277 SPITZER FLAT BASE**
Sectional Density: .242

| POWDER | 2700 fps | 2800 fps | 2900 fps | 3000 fps | 3100 fps |
|--------|----------|----------|----------|----------|----------|
| IMR-3031 | 41.3 | 43.0 | 44.7 | 46.5 | |
| IMR-4895 | 42.4 | 44.2 | 46.0 | 47.9 | |
| IMR-4064 | 43.1 | 44.8 | 46.5 | 48.3 | |
| IMR-4320 | 44.1 | 45.8 | 47.5 | 49.3 | |
| H380 | 44.4 | 46.3 | 48.2 | 50.1 | |
| 760 | 47.7 | 49.5 | 51.3 | 53.1 | |
| IMR-4350 | 48.4 | 50.0 | 51.6 | 53.2 | 54.9 |
| H450 | 51.8 | 53.4 | 55.0 | 56.7 | 58.4 |
| IMR-4831 | | 52.0 | 53.7 | 55.4 | 57.1 |
| H4831 | | 53.7 | 55.6 | 57.5 | 59.5 |
| 785 | | | | | 59.7 |

Example 1—.270 Winchester, 130-grain bullet. The *Sierra Bullets Reloading Manual (Second Ed.)* showing the powders that give highest velocities.

## .308 WINCHESTER
### REM. N.F.P. CASE;
### HORNADY 110 GR. SPIRE PT.
### .308" DIA.; 23" BBL.; 2.600" C.O.L.

| | | | |
|---|---|---|---|
| SR 4759 | 31.0 | 2710 | 51600 |
| IMR 4227 | 32.0 | 2835 | 51900 |
| IMR 4198 | 38.5 | 3015 | 51100 |
| IMR 3031 | 45.0C | 2990 | 42200 |
| IMR 4064 | 47.0C | 2955 | 43300 |
| IMR 4895 | 49.0C | 3130 | 49200 |
| IMR 4320 | 49.0C | 3010 | 47600 |
| IMR 4350 | 47.0C | 2500 | 32000 |
| IMR 4831 | 47.0C | 2330 | 29200 |

## .308 WINCHESTER
### REM. N.F.P. CASE;
### REM. 150 GR. PTD. SPCL
### .308" DIA.; 23" BBL.; 2.700" C.O.L.

| | | | |
|---|---|---|---|
| SR 4759 | 27.5 | 2325 | 51500 |
| IMR 4227 | 26.0 | 2260 | 51100 |
| IMR 4198 | 35.5 | 2595 | 51300 |
| IMR 3031 | 45.0C | 2830 | 52000 |
| IMR 4064 | 46.0C | 2800 | 51500 |
| IMR 4895 | 44.5 | 2780 | 52000 |
| IMR 4320 | 45.0 | 2710 | 52000 |
| IMR 4350 | 46.0C | 2415 | 36600 |
| IMR 4831 | 46.0C | 2265 | 32600 |

## .308 WINCHESTER
### REM. N.F.P. CASE;
### REM. 180 GR. PTD. SPCL
### .308" DIA.; 23" BBL.; 2.725" C.O.L.

| | | | |
|---|---|---|---|
| SR 4759 | 26.5 | 2085 | 51200 |
| IMR 4227 | 27.0 | 2110 | 52000 |
| IMR 4198 | 33.5 | 2350 | 51600 |
| IMR 3031 | 41.5C | 2550 | 51700 |
| IMR 4064 | 43.5C | 2580 | 51700 |
| IMR 4895 | 42.5C | 2540 | 50900 |
| IMR 4320 | 44.5C | 2550 | 52000 |
| IMR 4350 | 46.0C | 2365 | 38900 |
| IMR 4831 | 46.0C | 2225 | 36900 |

Example 2—.308 Winchester, 150-grain bullet. *DuPont Handloader's Guide* loading tables show which powders give the highest velocities.

Any of the above medium-speed rifle powders would be an excellent choice and would easily fit the requirements for handloading by objective and result. Both Du Pont products are tubular, single-base; the Hodgdon product is a double-base, spherical propellant.

The above example shows that slow-burning powders are not always the best choice for some cartridge combinations. There are several factors that determine the best choice for powders in each cartridge and bullet combination, but the data supplied by the powder and bullet makers are still the best guides for your needs. You will see later that the final, exact charge weight will be the factor that only you, the handloader, can supply.

The last three examples of powder selection are used to show the effects of different bullet weights and sectional density (ratio of bullet weight to the square of its diameter) on powder selection. Each of these examples will use the same caliber, the .30-06 Springfield, but with light, medium, and heavy bullets to illustrate the points.

**Example 3. Cartridge—.30-06 Springfield, Bullet—110-grain Hornady.** For this example, the *Du Pont Handloader's Guide* shows the first choice in propellants should be IMR 3031, followed closely by IMR 4064. IMR 3031 is the fastest of the Du Pont medium-speed propellants suitable for large rifle cases. The .30-06 is considered a large case. The *Hornady Handbook* also indicates that IMR 3031 and IMR 4064 are the best choices of the Du Pont products. The Hornady data indicates that Norma 202 and Winchester 748 may yield even higher velocities than the Du Pont products. All of these powders are considered fast- to medium-burning-rate rifle propellants. All will do the job.

**Example 4. Cartridge—.30-06 Springfield, Bullet—150-grain Nosler.** For this popular high-powered deer cartridge, Du Pont shows five of their products to give almost equal velocities in the .30-06 case with a 150-grain bullet. IMR 4064 gives the highest velocity, followed closely by IMR 3031, 4895, 4320, and 4350. This is not surprising. Many of these propellants were originally designed for the .30-06 Springfield cartridge and similar bullet weights during the last World War.

Nosler data does not list Du Pont IMR 3031 for this loading. Du Pont IMR 4895 and IMR 4350 are

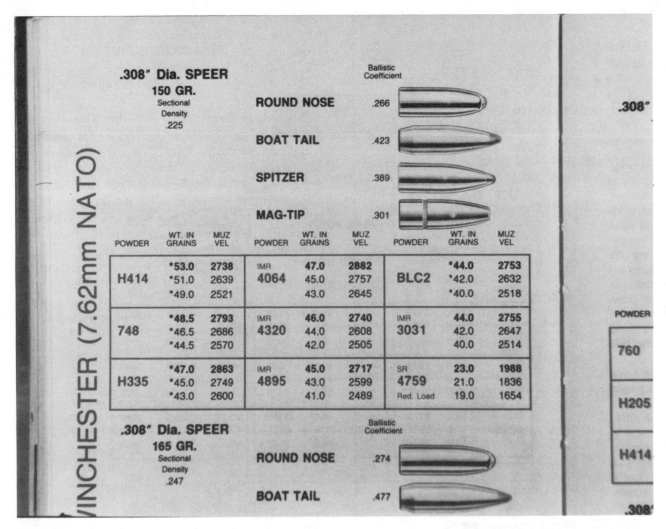

**.308" Dia. SPEER**
**150 GR.**
Sectional Density .225

| | Ballistic Coefficient |
|---|---|
| ROUND NOSE | .266 |
| BOAT TAIL | .423 |
| SPITZER | .389 |
| MAG-TIP | .301 |

| POWDER | WT. IN GRAINS | MUZ VEL | POWDER | WT. IN GRAINS | MUZ VEL | POWDER | WT. IN GRAINS | MUZ VEL |
|---|---|---|---|---|---|---|---|---|
| H414 | *53.0 | 2738 | IMR 4064 | 47.0 | 2882 | BLC2 | *44.0 | 2753 |
| | *51.0 | 2639 | | 45.0 | 2757 | | *42.0 | 2632 |
| | *49.0 | 2521 | | 43.0 | 2645 | | *40.0 | 2518 |
| 748 | *48.5 | 2793 | IMR 4320 | 46.0 | 2740 | IMR 3031 | 44.0 | 2755 |
| | *46.5 | 2686 | | 44.0 | 2608 | | 42.0 | 2647 |
| | *44.5 | 2570 | | 42.0 | 2505 | | 40.0 | 2514 |
| H335 | *47.0 | 2863 | IMR 4895 | 45.0 | 2717 | SR 4759 | 23.0 | 1988 |
| | *45.0 | 2749 | | 43.0 | 2599 | | 21.0 | 1836 |
| | *43.0 | 2600 | | 41.0 | 2489 | Red. Load | 19.0 | 1654 |

**.308" Dia. SPEER**
**165 GR.**
Sectional Density .247

| | Ballistic Coefficient |
|---|---|
| ROUND NOSE | .274 |
| BOAT TAIL | .477 |

**WINCHESTER (7.62mm NATO)**     **.308"**

| POWDER |
|---|
| 760 |
| H205 |
| H414 |

.308"

Example 2—.308 Winchester, 150-grain bullet. The *Speer Reloading Manual* loading tables show which powders give the highest velocities.

shown, but Nosler indicates that IMR 4350 and Hodgdon H205 are the best choices of propellants in this instance. Using data for the 150-grain-weight bullets from other bullet makers shows that all of the above-mentioned propellants give nearly equal results in this cartridge. When loaded according to the methods of objective and result, they should be quite similar ballistically, and usually at slightly less than the maximum charge weights.

If you really want to be picky about the propellant choice in such a circumstance, you may wish to consider chamber and cartridge case volumes as a factor. By this I mean that if the cartridge cases you're using are light and you know the gun chamber is larger than average, the slower, bulkier propellant may be the best choice. If the reverse is true, a small chamber and heavy cases, you should favor the use of the faster, less dense propellant. Keep in mind that your best precision and accuracy will probably occur at slightly less than the maximum charge weights and velocities in the loading tables regardless of which powder you choose.

**Example 5. Cartridge—.30-06 Springfield, Bullet—180-grain Sierra.** Example 5 also involves the .30-06 cartridge, but this time with a relatively heavy bullet. Here the Du Pont guide shows that the slow powders have a definite superiority. IMR 4350

| DU PONT POWDER | CHARGE (grains) | VELOCITY (ft/sec) | CHAMBER PRESS. (cup) |
|---|---|---|---|

### .30-06
#### REM. N.F.P. CASE;
#### HORNADY 110 GR. SPIRE PT.
#### .308" DIA.; 23" BBL.; 3.130" C.O.L.

| Powder | Charge | Velocity | Pressure |
|---|---|---|---|
| SR 4759 | 35.0 | 2820 | 49700 |
| IMR 4227 | 32.0 | 2730 | 49400 |
| IMR 4198 | 39.5 | 2980 | 49400 |
| IMR 3031 | 56.0 | 3365 | 49300 |
| IMR 4064 | 58.0C | 3320 | 49400 |
| IMR 4895 | 54.5 | 3265 | 49600 |
| IMR 4320 | 57.5 | 3255 | 49100 |
| IMR 4350 | 59.0C | 2960 | 36900 |
| IMR 4831 | 59.0C | 2780 | 32500 |

### .30-06
#### REM. N.F.P. CASE;
#### REM. 150 GR. PTD. SPCL
#### .308" DIA.; 23" BBL.; 3.200" C.O.L.

| Powder | Charge | Velocity | Pressure |
|---|---|---|---|
| SR 4759 | 31.0 | 2365 | 49700 |
| IMR 4227 | 30.0 | 2310 | 50000 |
| IMR 4198 | 38.0 | 2600 | 50000 |
| IMR 3031 | 49.5 | 2850 | 49800 |
| IMR 4064 | 52.0 | 2885 | 50000 |
| IMR 4895 | 49.5 | 2845 | 50000 |
| IMR 4320 | 51.0 | 2825 | 50000 |
| IMR 4350 | 59.0C | 2825 | 47800 |
| IMR 4831 | 59.0C | 2715 | 42900 |

Example 3—.30-06 Springfield, 110-grain bullet. The *DuPont Handloader's Guide* shows powders that give the highest velocities for a relatively light bullet.

tionship of relatively fast, medium, and slow powder-burning rates with light, medium, and heavy bullets in the same cartridge.

Light bullets provide less inertial resistance to gas pressure. Faster powders can be used safely with light bullets and they yield high velocities with those bullets. A heavy bullet, in the same barrel, gives higher inertial and frictional resistance to pressure from the burning powder. The slower powders can be used to push the heavy bullets at a more gradual rate of acceleration within the barrel and achieve high velocity while still keeping pressure at a safe level. This explanation is more detailed but it is still only a generality. Other factors, such as chamber and cylinder dimensions, throat and forcing cone dimensions, and shape, barrel length, type of rifling and twist, and the land and groove dimensions, which vary with individual firearms, have an effect on internal ballistics, even when the same cartridge case is used. If the cartridge case is altered by substituting a different primer, a different brand of bullet, or even changing the bullet seating depth, without altering the powder or charge weight, more variables begin to act inside. All of these factors have effects on your result. The choice of best propellant, and to some extent primer choice, depends on case capacity relative to both bullet weight and sectional density.

If the above explanation is confusing, don't be too concerned. Remember, the powder and bullet suppliers have already determined the best choices for each bullet weight with actual test firings. They present their findings in their guides, pamphlets, and books. Using their information, any slight variations caused by your gun and your handloaded cartridges will be minor. Techniques, presented later in this book, will compensate for even those small differences. You will be able to accomplish each of your objectives, achieve desirable results, and satisfy your purpose and reason for handloading. However, it will take some serious effort.

Incidentally, Du Pont loading data for the above five examples was used for two reasons. First, Du Pont products are used by many handloaders and the guides the company furnishes are reliable. Second, any attempt to include the loading data of other powder makers would tend to overcomplicate the example unnecessarily. The intent of this book is to help, not to confuse. Certainly, other produc-

appears to be the first choice, with IMR 4831 a close second. Note that compressed charges will be necessary for maximum charge weights with both.

The Sierra manual shows the 180-grain bullet performs best in the .30-06 when pushed by Du Pont IMR 4350, IMR 4831, Hodgdon H205, H4831, and Norma MRP. Again, each of these powders should be a suitable choice for use in precision handloading.

These last three examples help explain the rela-

## 30 CALIBER (.308" Dia.)
## 110 GRAIN SPIRE POINT #3010

CARTRIDGE OVERALL LENGTH 3.170"

| POWDER | VELOCITY | | | | |
| --- | --- | --- | --- | --- | --- |
| | 3100 fps | 3200 fps | 3300 fps | 3400 fps | 3500 fps |
| IMR 3031 | 50.2 gr. | 51.8 gr. | 53.4 gr. | 55.0 gr. | |
| H4895 | 50.2 gr. | 52.0 gr. | 53.7 gr. | 55.5 gr. | |
| N201 | 52.1 gr. | 53.6 gr. | 55.1 gr. | | |
| IMR 4320 | 51.2 gr. | 53.7 gr. | 56.2 gr. | | |
| IMR 4064 | 53.0 gr. | 54.6 gr. | 56.2 gr. | 57.8 gr. | |
| N202 | 53.9 gr. | 55.7 gr. | 57.4 gr. | 59.1 gr. | 60.8 gr. |
| WIN 748 | 55.0 gr. | 56.7 gr. | 58.5 gr. | 60.2 gr. | 62.0 gr. |
| H205 | 61.4 gr. | 62.9 gr. | 64.5 gr. | | |
| WIN 760 | 60.3 gr. | 62.5 gr. | 64.6 gr. | | |

Example 3—.30-06 Springfield, 110-grain bullet. *Hornady Handbook of Cartridge Reloading (Third Ed.)* shows which powders give highest velocities for a relatively light bullet.

ers and suppliers such as Winchester-Western, Hodgdon, Hercules, and Norma all offer excellent, quality products for handloading needs and the methods presented in this text. The final choices are often those of personal taste or notion. No favoritism is intended.

## Primer Selection

The last cartridge component selection that must be discussed is the primer. It is a much simpler selection than that of powder.

All primers currently made in the United States for use in commercial and handloaded metallic ammunition are of the Boxer style. The Boxer-type primer requires a flash hole through the center of the cartridge case head for powder ignition. It is easily removed with simple tools after being fired. The other type of primer, the Berdan, used in Europe, is more difficult to remove from the case after firing, and should be ignored by domestic shooters. American primers are made in two sizes and they are simply called small primers and large primers. Small primers have a diameter of 0.175"; large primers measure 0.210". Both sizes are used in different rifle and handgun ammunition.

Since World War II, even some very small differences in shape and primer dimension have been standardized. This was due largely to the demands of the military. In the 1960s, one of the last changes was made—the adoption of the flat primer cup as standard by all U.S. makers.

Since the early 1930s, all American primers for use in commercial ammunition have been made with materials that do not produce chemical compounds harmful to steel barrels or brass cartridge cases. The terms "nonmercuric" and "noncorrosive" are applied to all such primers. The military adopted these changes a little later in the early 1950s.

All of the above statements also apply to pistol primers, but primers intended for use in handgun ammunition differ slightly. The first difference is in the thickness of the metal used for the primer cup. This is because most pistols don't have as much firing pin strike force as rifles. Secondly, pistol primers contain less explosive mixture compared to rifle primers.

Metallic primers are available in four categories

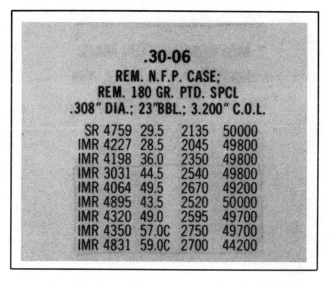

| .30-06 REM. N.F.P. CASE; REM. 150 GR. PTD. SPCL .308" DIA.; 23" BBL.; 3.200" C.O.L. | | | |
|---|---|---|---|
| SR 4759 | 31.0 | 2365 | 49700 |
| IMR 4227 | 30.0 | 2310 | 50000 |
| IMR 4198 | 38.0 | 2600 | 50000 |
| IMR 3031 | 49.5 | 2850 | 49800 |
| IMR 4064 | 52.0 | 2885 | 50000 |
| IMR 4895 | 49.5 | 2845 | 50000 |
| IMR 4320 | 51.0 | 2825 | 50000 |
| IMR 4350 | 59.0C | 2825 | 47800 |
| IMR 4831 | 59.0C | 2715 | 42900 |

Example 4—.30-06 Springfield, 150-grain bullet. *DuPont Handloader's Guide* loading tables show which powders give the highest velocities.

| .30-06 REM. N.F.P. CASE; REM. 180 GR. PTD. SPCL .308" DIA.; 23"BBL.; 3.200" C.O.L. | | | |
|---|---|---|---|
| SR 4759 | 29.5 | 2135 | 50000 |
| IMR 4227 | 28.5 | 2045 | 49800 |
| IMR 4198 | 36.0 | 2350 | 49800 |
| IMR 3031 | 44.5 | 2540 | 49800 |
| IMR 4064 | 49.5 | 2670 | 49200 |
| IMR 4895 | 43.5 | 2520 | 50000 |
| IMR 4320 | 49.0 | 2595 | 49700 |
| IMR 4350 | 57.0C | 2750 | 49700 |
| IMR 4831 | 59.0C | 2700 | 44200 |

Example 5—.30-06 Springfield, 180-grain bullet. *DuPont Handloader's Guide* loading tables show which powders give the highest velocities.

based on size, cup strength, and the amount of explosive mixture. These categories are: small rifle; large rifle; small pistol; large pistol.

The large rifle primer is used in all calibers of modern U.S. and many foreign cartridges intended for larger game, with the single exception of the .256 Winchester. Small rifle primers are used chiefly in small-case, .22-caliber centerfire cartridges. Therefore, almost all cartridges suitable for deer and larger game require large rifle primers.

Primers also come in standard and magnum form. Magnum primers are the same size as standard primers, but they contain a greater amount and different type of explosive mixture. They explode with a hotter flame of longer duration than a standard primer. Magnum primers are generally recommended by their manufacturers for use in one or more of the following three situations: (1) heavy charges of slow-burning powder in large cases; (2) hard-to-ignite ball propellants; and (3) extreme cold weather conditions.

The only indecision in choosing primers for handloading could arise in this area of standard versus magnum. Primers differ in terms of their energy level and their ability to ignite the powder charge. The various primers are not standardized with regard to strength of ignition. This appears to be true when comparing both standard primers and magnum primers. Some publications have attempted to clarify these differences, for they do exist. The most popular and generally best use of standard and magnum primers are specified in most of the manufacturers' loading tables. These tables generally show the use of standard rifle primers in cases up through .30-06 size. Larger rifle cases are often loaded with magnum primers. Magnum-type primers are used in both rifle and handgun cartridges. The choice is not as simple for handgun cartridges. Magnum primers are even available in small rifle and small pistol sizes, too.

Some tests have shown excessive primer power to have a bad effect on pressure level, velocity, precision, and resulting accuracy. Such studies indicate that the use of a standard or normal intensity primer tends to give the best overall result with normal-sized cartridge cases. But cases larger than the standard .30-06 sometimes give less pressure and velocity variations when their powder charge is ignited by a magnum-type primer. Magnum primers can be a better choice when hard-to-ignite, slow-burning powders are used, regardless of case size. Most American primer manufacturers offer both standard and magnum primers under various stock numbers. One manufacturer, Winchester-Western, has opted to manufacture only one large rifle primer. The intensity of this large rifle primer is comparable to the magnum large rifle primers of the other manufacturers.

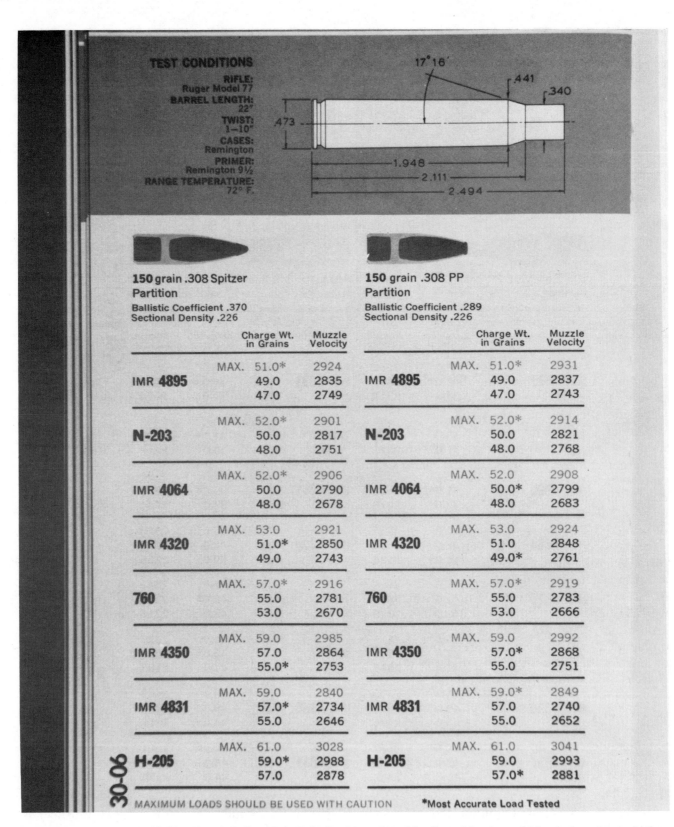

**TEST CONDITIONS**
RIFLE: Ruger Model 77
BARREL LENGTH: 22"
TWIST: 1—10"
CASES: Remington
PRIMER: Remington 9½
RANGE TEMPERATURE: 72° F.

17°16'  .441  .340  .473  1.948  2.111  2.494

**150** grain .308 Spitzer Partition
Ballistic Coefficient .370
Sectional Density .226

**150** grain .308 PP Partition
Ballistic Coefficient .289
Sectional Density .226

| | | Charge Wt. in Grains | Muzzle Velocity | | | Charge Wt. in Grains | Muzzle Velocity |
|---|---|---|---|---|---|---|---|
| IMR **4895** | MAX. | 51.0* | 2924 | IMR **4895** | MAX. | 51.0* | 2931 |
| | | 49.0 | 2835 | | | 49.0 | 2837 |
| | | 47.0 | 2749 | | | 47.0 | 2743 |
| **N-203** | MAX. | 52.0* | 2901 | **N-203** | MAX. | 52.0* | 2914 |
| | | 50.0 | 2817 | | | 50.0 | 2821 |
| | | 48.0 | 2751 | | | 48.0 | 2768 |
| IMR **4064** | MAX. | 52.0* | 2906 | IMR **4064** | MAX. | 52.0 | 2908 |
| | | 50.0 | 2790 | | | 50.0* | 2799 |
| | | 48.0 | 2678 | | | 48.0 | 2683 |
| IMR **4320** | MAX. | 53.0 | 2921 | IMR **4320** | MAX. | 53.0 | 2924 |
| | | 51.0* | 2850 | | | 51.0 | 2848 |
| | | 49.0 | 2743 | | | 49.0* | 2761 |
| **760** | MAX. | 57.0* | 2916 | **760** | MAX. | 57.0* | 2919 |
| | | 55.0 | 2781 | | | 55.0 | 2783 |
| | | 53.0 | 2670 | | | 53.0 | 2666 |
| IMR **4350** | MAX. | 59.0 | 2985 | IMR **4350** | MAX. | 59.0 | 2992 |
| | | 57.0 | 2864 | | | 57.0* | 2868 |
| | | 55.0* | 2753 | | | 55.0 | 2751 |
| IMR **4831** | MAX. | 59.0 | 2840 | IMR **4831** | MAX. | 59.0* | 2849 |
| | | 57.0* | 2734 | | | 57.0 | 2740 |
| | | 55.0 | 2646 | | | 55.0 | 2652 |
| **H-205** | MAX. | 61.0 | 3028 | **H-205** | MAX. | 61.0 | 3041 |
| | | 59.0* | 2988 | | | 59.0 | 2993 |
| | | 57.0 | 2878 | | | 57.0* | 2881 |

**30-06**

MAXIMUM LOADS SHOULD BE USED WITH CAUTION     *Most Accurate Load Tested

Example 4—.30-06 Springfield, 150-grain bullet. *Nosler Reloading Manual No. 1* loading tables show which powders give the highest velocities.

# .30-'06

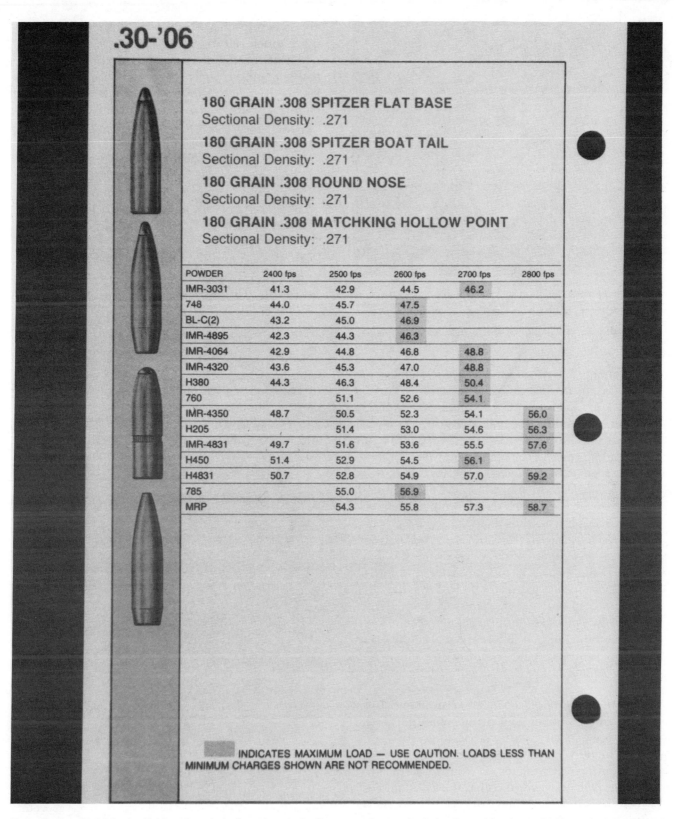

### 180 GRAIN .308 SPITZER FLAT BASE
Sectional Density: .271

### 180 GRAIN .308 SPITZER BOAT TAIL
Sectional Density: .271

### 180 GRAIN .308 ROUND NOSE
Sectional Density: .271

### 180 GRAIN .308 MATCHKING HOLLOW POINT
Sectional Density: .271

| POWDER | 2400 fps | 2500 fps | 2600 fps | 2700 fps | 2800 fps |
|---|---|---|---|---|---|
| IMR-3031 | 41.3 | 42.9 | 44.5 | 46.2 | |
| 748 | 44.0 | 45.7 | 47.5 | | |
| BL-C(2) | 43.2 | 45.0 | 46.9 | | |
| IMR-4895 | 42.3 | 44.3 | 46.3 | | |
| IMR-4064 | 42.9 | 44.8 | 46.8 | 48.8 | |
| IMR-4320 | 43.6 | 45.3 | 47.0 | 48.8 | |
| H380 | 44.3 | 46.3 | 48.4 | 50.4 | |
| 760 | | 51.1 | 52.6 | 54.1 | |
| IMR-4350 | 48.7 | 50.5 | 52.3 | 54.1 | 56.0 |
| H205 | | 51.4 | 53.0 | 54.6 | 56.3 |
| IMR-4831 | 49.7 | 51.6 | 53.6 | 55.5 | 57.6 |
| H450 | 51.4 | 52.9 | 54.5 | 56.1 | |
| H4831 | 50.7 | 52.8 | 54.9 | 57.0 | 59.2 |
| 785 | | 55.0 | 56.9 | | |
| MRP | | 54.3 | 55.8 | 57.3 | 58.7 |

░░░░ INDICATES MAXIMUM LOAD — USE CAUTION. LOADS LESS THAN MINIMUM CHARGES SHOWN ARE NOT RECOMMENDED.

Example 5—.30-06 Springfield, 180-grain bullet. *Sierra Reloading Manual (Second Ed.)* loading tables show which powders give the highest velocities.

The parts of a Boxer-type primer. A complete primer is shown at the top. Below, from left to right: cup and explosive pellet, paper cover, and anvil.

Personally, I have never had a primer ignition failure occur in any rifle cartridge when using standard or magnum primers, and only twice in handgun ammunition. For this reason, I don't believe that standard rifle primers are responsible for any faulty ignition. However, some velocity variations do seem to occur, which indicates that powder ignition may be happening at a more erratic rate in the large cases when primed with standard primers. I have fired many rounds from the shooting bench and while hunting on days that were below freezing. But I have not honestly tested primers in magnum cartridges when the thermometer read zero or 20 below. It doesn't get that cold in Texas.

It would help to see some controlled, independent testing of powders at different temperatures, in small, medium, and large cases using standard and magnum primers. A lot of marketing claims and personal opinions have clouded this whole question for years.

In choosing primers, go by the recommendations of the powder, bullet, and primer manufacturers. If they don't specify, start your testing with a standard primer. You can always test further by using the magnum primer later. If you do switch to a magnum primer, lower the charge weight about 5 percent for safety and then work back up to the velocity you want. Five percent in a .30-06 case is only

about two grains of powder. This should not require much retesting.

All of the discussion in this chapter about cartridge components is concerned with internal ballistics. Internal ballistics do affect the exterior ballistics of bullet velocity, precision, and accuracy. Chapters 5 through 8 go into more detail concerning external ballistics.

The last items of supply you need for handloading are not cartridge components. The bullet, case, powder, and primer decisions have now been covered. You still need a supply of lubricants, however.

Many brands and types of lubricants are available. You will need two types to begin your handloading: case and die lubricant; and a good spray lubricant and rust preventive. If you decide to use the common grease-type case lubricant, you should also use a lubricant pad. The pad allows uniform, light application of lubricant to the case body and it speeds the job. For all types of case lubricants, follow the manufacturer's instructions, as discussed in Chapter 4.

The spray lubricants stop rust on your loading dies and hand tools. They are excellent on some gun parts also. Brands such as WD-40 and LPS-1 and LPS-2 are popular examples of this type.

Different brands of primers may vary somewhat. They should always be stored in their original containers for safety. They are the most hazardous components in loading ammunition. Don't ever store them loose in any container. If one goes off, they all do.

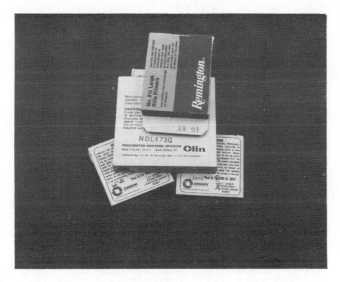

Primers, like powder, vary slightly from lot to lot. Use the same lot number if exact duplication is a must. It's part of confidence in your ammunition.

## Record-Keeping

The last portion of this chapter is devoted to record-keeping for handloading requirements. Four record-keeping forms, plus targets, are necessary:

1. Handload data list
2. Handload precision graph
3. Handload velocity graph
4. Handload pressure graph
5. Targets

Each form will be discussed only briefly here, but detailed explanations are given in subsequent chapters where they apply.

The first form is the handload data list, which is composed of all the information needed for successful handloading by objective. It contains all the data needed for achieving handloading objectives 1, precision, 2, velocity, 4, consistency, 5, duplication, and 7, pressure. You may wish to use this same format (see illustrations), or make your own list. In any case, the data will be used and discussed and it is all needed to accomplish your purpose and result. The data will be compiled before, during, and after test firing. This information is used to develop handloads under the techniques presented here. You can also refer to it later to duplicate any of your handloads without guesswork or the need for more testing.

The handload data list is made of three basic parts; two parts are on the front of the form and the third part is on the back. There's a line in the top left corner to record the cartridge and bullet weight data.

Below that are information blocks with spaces to record the firearm used, the type of target, and the shooting distance in yards. The next blocks cover the important details of the factory cartridge used as a standard of comparison, along with the case, bullet, powder, and primer used for the handloads. Each of the data blocks contains enough information about each item to specify and identify the components properly and meet objective 4, uniformity, and objective 5, duplication.

The major portion of the handload data list contains observations from test firing. This part includes the categories of loads, internal and external factors, precision, velocity, and pressure. A load number is assigned to each group of handloads which differ in charge weight. The internal and external factors column shows charge weight, date loaded, date fired, number of rounds fired, and the weather conditions relative to wind velocity and direction, temperature, and barometric pressure, plus any other factors that might affect a particular load number.

Precision data columns show the measurements taken from targets fired with the test handloads. Velocity data is gathered from chronographic measurements of the various load numbers. Pressure data are relative chamber pressure findings made by measurement of cartridge case head expansions. The last area of note on this side of the form is at the bottom. This is precision, velocity, and pressure data taken from the factory cartridge used as your standard for comparison. Seven data items appearing on this form are used in the construction of precision, velocity, and pressure graphs. These items are numbered accordingly and the numbers are cross-referenced with the same numbered items on the appropriate graphs.

The remainder of the handload data list appears on the reverse side. As on the front side, the caliber, bullet, and powder used are indicated at the top of the form. Space is provided below for notes taken before and during loading, and also during and

# HANDLOAD DATA

Cal._____ Bullet_____

CALIBER_____ BULLET WGT._____gr.

FIREARM:mfgr._____
model_____
barrel length_____in
twist rate 1:_____in
TARGET:mfg/no._____
RANGE:dist._____yd

FACTY STD CARTRGE
mfgr_____
mfgr no._____
lot no._____
bullet wgt_____gr

CASE:mfgr_____
avg wgt. ± . _____gr
trim length . _____in
c.o.a.length . _____in
sized head . _____in

BULLET:wgt_____gr
mfgr_____
mfgr no._____
lot no._____
type_____
clearance_____in

POWDER:mfgr_____
mfgr no._____
lot no._____
PRIMER:mfgr_____
mfgr no._____
lot no._____

| LOAD no. | charg wgt. gr. | date load | date fire | no. rds | INTERNAL AND EXTERNAL FACTORS — wind velocity, direction, temperature, bar. pres., precip., visibility, ch. pressure observations, other. | PRECISION | | | VELOCITY | | | | PRESSURE |
|---|---|---|---|---|---|---|---|---|---|---|---|---|---|
| | | | | | | Dat1 Std Vert Dev. in. | Dat2 Extm Vert Sprd in. | Dat3 HtAb Aim Pt. in. | Dat4 Std Vel. Dev. fps. | Dat5 Extm Vel. Sprd. fps. | Dat6 Avg Vel. fps. | no. rds rcrd | Dat7 Case Head Exp. in. |
| 1 | | | | | | | | | | | | | |
| 2 | | | | | | | | | | | | | |
| 3 | | | | | | | | | | | | | |
| 4 | | | | | | | | | | | | | |
| 5 | | | | | | | | | | | | | |
| 6 | | | | | | | | | | | | | |
| 7 | | | | | | | | | | | | | |
| 8 | | | | | | | | | | | | | |
| 9 | | | | | | | | | | | | | |
| 10 | | | | | | | | | | | | | |
| 11 | | | | | | | | | | | | | |
| 12 | | | | | | | | | | | | | |
| 13 | | | | | | | | | | | | | |
| 14 | | | | | | | | | | | | | |
| 15 | | | | | | | | | | | | | |
| 16 | | | | | | | | | | | | | |
| 17 | | | | | | | | | | | | | |
| 18 | | | | | | | | | | | | | |
| 19 | | | | | | | | | | | | | |
| 20 | | | | | | | | | | | | | |
| 1 | facty ld. | | | | | | | | | | | | |
| 2 | " | | | | | | | | | | | | |
| 3 | " | | | | | | | | | | | | |
| 4 | " | | | | | | | | | | | | |
| 5 | " | | | | | | | | | | | | |

facty avgs =

Data 1,2,3,4,5,6 and 7 above, refer to data used in construction of the PREC.,VEL. and PRESS. graphs

Sample handload data list blank form (front side).

Caliber _____ Bullet _____ Powder _____

NOTES

Planning:

Loading:

Firing:

Conclusions:

Sample handload data list blank form (reverse side).

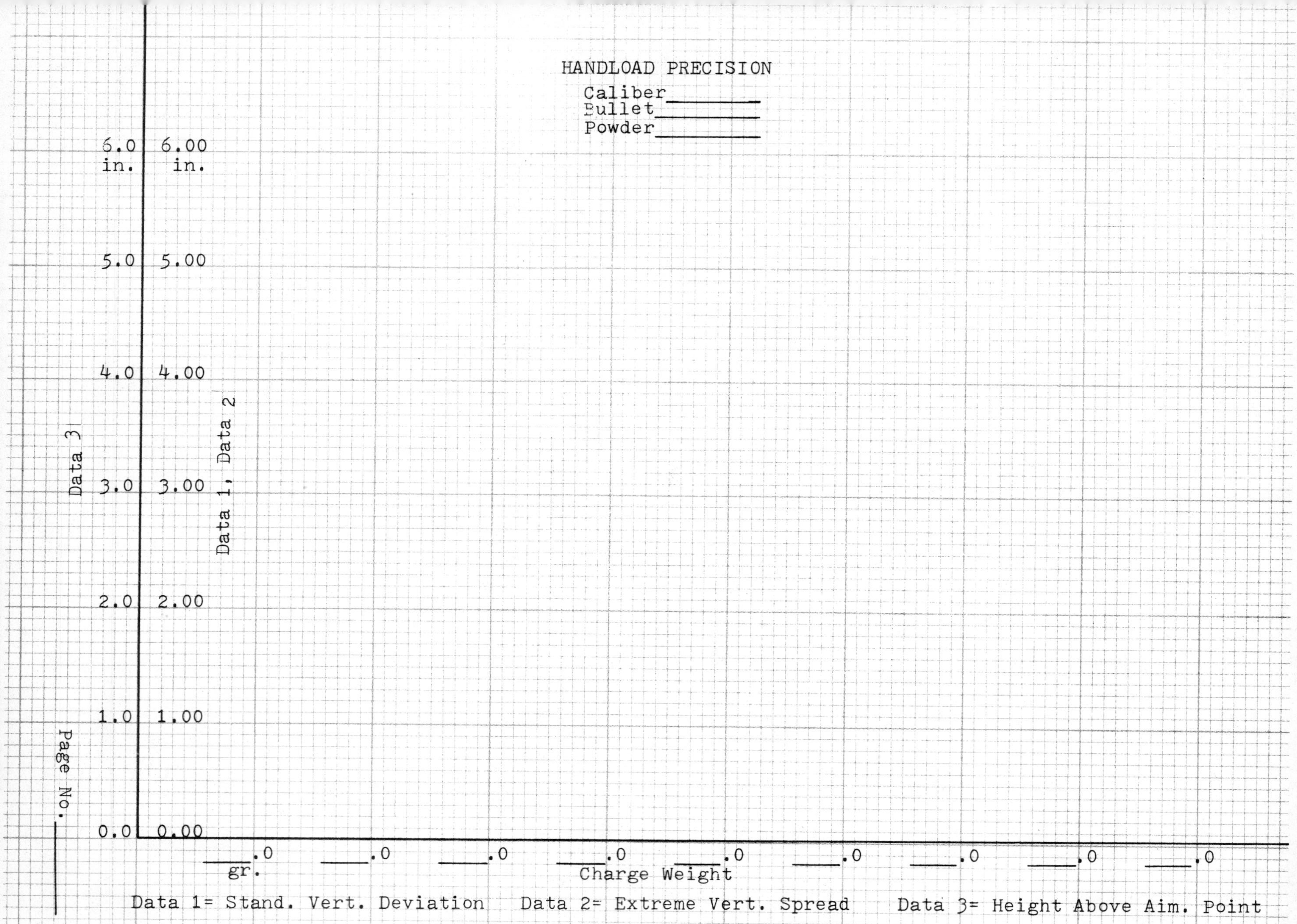

HANDLOAD PRECISION

Caliber _____
Bullet _____
Powder _____

6.00
in.

5.00

4.00

3.00

2.00

1.00

0.00

Data 1, Data 2

6.0
in.

5.0

4.0

3.0

2.0

1.0

0.0

Data 3

Page No. _____

.0
gr.

.0

.0

.0

.0

.0

.0

.0

.0

Charge Weight

Data 1= Stand. Vert. Deviation    Data 2= Extreme Vert. Spread    Data 3= Height Above Aim. Point

Sample handload precision graph form,

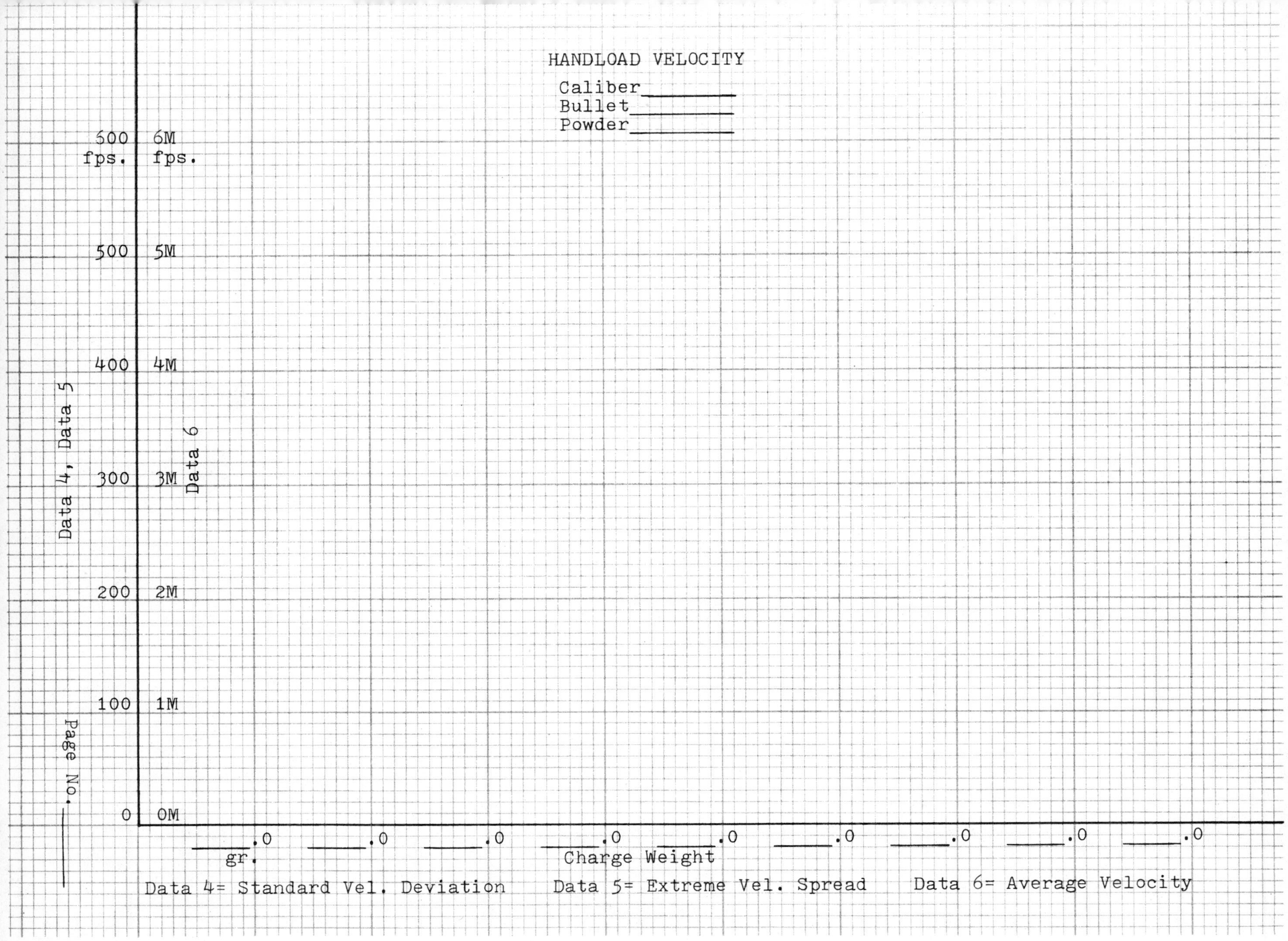

HANDLOAD VELOCITY

Caliber _____
Bullet _____
Powder _____

| | | | | | | | |
|---|---|---|---|---|---|---|---|
| 500 6M | | | | | | | |
| fps. fps. | | | | | | | |
| 500 5M | | | | | | | |
| 400 4M | | | | | | | |
| 300 3M | | | | Data 6 | | | |
| 200 2M | | | | | | | |
| 100 1M | | | | | | | |
| 0 0M | | | | | | | |

Data 4, Data 5

Page No. _____

gr.          Charge Weight

Data 4= Standard Vel. Deviation   Data 5= Extreme Vel. Spread   Data 6= Average Velocity

Sample handload velocity graph form.

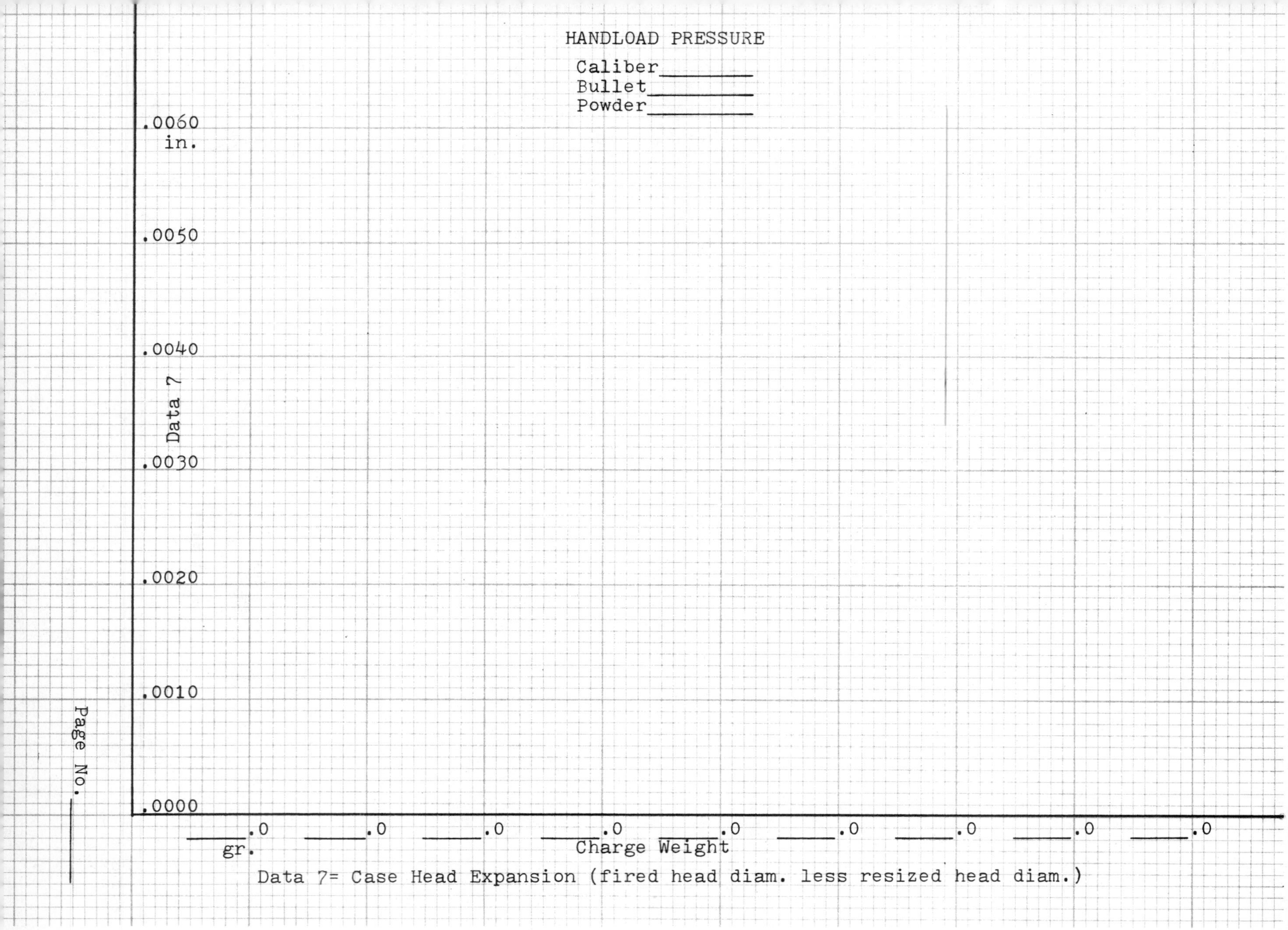

HANDLOAD PRESSURE

Caliber _____
Bullet _____
Powder _____

.0060
in.

.0050

.0040

Data 7

.0030

.0020

.0010

.0000

gr.

.0    .0    .0    .0    .0    .0    .0    .0

Charge Weight

Data 7= Case Head Expansion (fired head diam. less resized head diam.)

Page No. _____

Sample handload pressure graph form.

after firing. Such notes are often required as they are too specific for the data columns on the front side. These notes would include such things as special reloading procedures, die adjustments, scope adjustments and power settings, procedure changes, unusual happenings while firing, observations, and the reasons for final choice of any one of the handloads.

Each part of the handload data list contains some data that is entered at the loading bench. In addition, there is provision for data developed during range firing and during the collection, measurement, and comparison of results from firing.

The handload data list is the single most important document for your handloading needs. This back-to-back form is a record of the notes and comments needed for your final decision, and will be used and discussed extensively throughout the following chapters, for it contains the results of your handloading project.

The handload precision graph is developed with measurements taken from the targets after firing with your handloads. This graph balances the charge weights of the handloads against target group measurements. It helps to locate the charge weights that produce the most precise shot groups. These are compared against factory ammunition precision. This graph will be used in meeting handload objective 1, precision.

The handload velocity graph is developed with data from chronographic measurements of the numbered handloads. The handload velocity graph balances charge weight against measured velocities. It is used to find the most uniform velocities and the actual velocities, and enables the shooter to make a comparison against factory ammunition velocity. This graph will be used for achieving handload objective 2, velocity, objective 4, uniformity, and objective 5, duplication.

The handload pressure graph consists of relative chamber pressures determined by measuring cartridge case expansion. This graph, like the precision and velocity graphs, uses factory-loaded ammunition as a standard of comparison. The graph's use will be discussed in detail in another chapter. It will be used to achieve handloading objective 7, proper, consistent, and safe pressure.

The last necessary element is the target itself. The kind of target is mostly a matter of personal choice but certain considerations must be included for success at the range and the accomplishment of your objectives. The first concern is target size. A vertical dimension of 14 inches is about the minimum for developing a new handload, even with a firearm that has been previously zeroed or sighted in. The width of the target depends on several factors. It should be at least 8 to 9 inches wide. The aiming point should be outlined for easy sighting with a four-power scope, and for good visibility if using metallic sights. The aiming point can be centered or placed about two inches above the center point on a 14-inch target. This helps ensure against lost shots due to bullet drop, which can happen with initial, low-pressure rounds. Additionally, the target may include a grid system composed of one-inch squares and enough space for entering essential information. The data developed from test firing and target measurement will be used to accomplish handloading objective 1, precision.

If you've become apprehensive over any of the points presented in this chapter, don't be too concerned. Each point will be expanded, explained, and used in the actual handload development example in coming chapters. In reality, the explaining takes longer than the doing. It is entirely possible to develop a handload, using the techniques in this book and meeting all of your objectives, in as little as two or three evenings of work and one afternoon at the shooting range. And it is possible to do all of these things while using as few as 80 rounds of factory and handloaded ammunition. In the next chapter, handload development will begin.

If you separate loading chores from paperwork, a small bench and a little space is all that's needed.
Note safety glasses and gloves for priming

# Chapter 4

# At the Loading Bench

This chapter is about the mechanics of reloading, and more. The basic mechanical procedure for good loading will be discussed, plus some of the finer points of handloading. More importantly, the mechanical steps will be presented with the equipment and record-keeping that must be done to achieve the intermediate handloading objectives. Successful completion of all eight objectives stated in Chapter 2 greatly depends on actions you take at the loading bench. This fact is one important reason why so much has been written about the loading process itself.

It is not practical, in one chapter, to repeat all of the things that have been said about metallic cartridge reloading in other books. The intent of *Precision Handloading* is to present a better, more advanced handloading method. It must be assumed that you are already familiar with the basic mechanics of reloading. If not, any of the following excellent reference materials are recommended:

*ABC's of Reloading* by Dean Grennel
*The Complete Book of Practical Handloading* by John Wooters
*Complete Guide to Handloading* by Philip B. Sharpe
*Handbook of Metallic Cartridge Reloading* by Edward Matunas
*Handloader's Guide* by Stanley W. Trzoniec
*Metallic Cartridge Reloading* by Robert S. L. Anderson
*Modern Handloading* by Maj. George C. Nonte
*NRA Handloader's Guide*
*Reloader's Guide* by Bob Steindler
*Why Not Load Your Own?* by Col. Townsend Whelen

*Hodgdon's Data Manual*
*Hornady Handbook*
*Lyman Reloading Handbook*
*Nosler Reloading Manual*

*Sierra Reloader Manual*
*Speer Reloading Manual*
Instructions and guides furnished with hand-loading tools and equipment.

This chapter is divided into two main parts: part 1 is an introduction to the planning, record-keeping, and loading procedures needed to satisfy your objectives; part 2 will follow our new handloading friend, Jim, through an actual handloading project.

The process of metallic cartridge reloading is usually explained using several basic steps. Generally, these steps are called case preparation, de-priming and sizing, priming, powder charging, and bullet seating. These basic procedures are fine, but they have to be expanded for our needs. For our handloading project, the steps of planning and record-keeping must be considered in more depth to achieve our objectives and help answer those questions that arise when objective decisions must be made. For these reasons, this chapter will discuss the mechanics of reloading in a slightly altered manner from that usually presented in books of this kind.

The mechanics of loading will not be broken into numbered steps, but the entire process of loading

At first glance, these head stamps may all look alike. Closer inspection reveals the differences. The three cases are from three different eras, and they are not the same.

will be discussed in three stages: planning, record-keeping, and loading.

## Planning

Handloading is often the beginning of a never-ending project for some shooters. That's fine if one likes continuous experimentation, but most people would rather do things that have some immediate purpose and a successful conclusion. That is why this book stresses the objective requirements. Your purpose in any handloading project should be to develop the best possible ammunition that will fulfill your shooting needs. This is the answer to what you are doing. Your reason for developing any handload should be to gain the greatest possible confidence in your shooting. This, after all, is why we handload.

To refresh your memory, the steps involved in the method for handloading using Management by Objective, as described in Chapter 2, are briefly:

    I.  Determine the desired handloading result.
    II.  Develop operating plans for achieving the intermediate objectives.
    III.  Control all activities for meeting the objectives, eliminating all nonproductive activities.
    IV.  Make a time schedule for completion of each intermediate objective and the final result.

The result you want is the best possible ammunition that will fill your shooting need. Since this result and your purpose for handloading are the same thing, you have already achieved step I of managing your handloading project; to make the best ammunition possible for your shooting. Steps II and III of MBO are where the real work begins. You must develop the plans to achieve the intermediate handloading objectives. You must control the activities for meeting those objectives to arrive at your desired result. You cannot be sidetracked by nonproductive activities. This brings us to the planning stage of handloading.

Since planning a handloading project with MBO methods requires the setting of intermediate objectives, it is good to review the objective-setting process and restate the intermediate objectives developed back in Chapter 2 before beginning the actual planning.

As you'll recall, the objective-setting process asks five questions:

A. Is the objective worth setting?
B. Is the objective practical?
C. Is the objective attainable?
D. Is the objective clearly stated in terms of:
   a. the task?
   b. the method of measurement to be used?
   c. the measuring period?
E. Is the objective compatible with the expected result?

Each of the above questions must be asked of each objective and the answer must be "yes" for that objective to be included in planning. In Chapter 2, a list of eight worthy, practical, attainable, clearly stated, compatible objectives was developed. They should be reviewed again before proceeding with further handload planning. They will become increasingly important as we continue.

### Intermediate Objectives

1. To achieve equal or better target precision (accuracy potential) with handloaded ammunition than that of factory ammunition.
2. To achieve equal or higher bullet velocity with handloaded ammunition than that of factory-loaded ammunition.
3. To achieve equal or better bullet consistency and performance as to controlled expansion, penetration, and downrange ballistic potential than with factory-loaded ammunition.
4. To achieve equal or greater consistency in handloaded ammunition as to precision, velocity, pressure, and bullet performance than that available from factory ammunition.
5. To be able to duplicate the chosen cartridge at any time.
6. To achieve correct firearm functioning with handloaded ammunition or better functioning with handloaded ammunition than with factory ammunition.
7. To achieve proper, consistent, and safe

pressure in the handloaded ammunition.
8. To determine which ammunition best achieves the above objectives with the least expense of time, labor, materials, and money for testing.

Each of these objectives can be challenged by the five objective-setting questions. In each case, a positive response can be given. The exact details for achieving each of them will require more explanation. With that brief review, let's see what is needed to plan for handloading.

The first item of planning is deciding on the cartridge and firearm. The choice should be based on your shooting needs. You may be content to use your present gun. If not, ask for and listen to the advice of experienced shooters and sportsmen. Reading is another way of collecting information leading to a logical decision. But don't rely solely on one writer or one expert. Shooting authorities, as individuals, sometimes spout opinions as if they were gospel. One fact is usually clear: most any shooting requirement can usually be met by more than one cartridge and more than one gun, with equal results. You usually have a choice. Do some research. Listen to opinions of those you trust. See what the manufacturers recommend. However, you must make the final selection, which is as it should be. You will be more satisfied with your result because it is based on your own decisions.

After choosing the cartridge and the gun, determine the best factory cartridge for your shooting. This is an important decision also. The factory-loaded cartridge you choose will become the standard by which your own handloading efforts will be judged. Again, follow respected advice and pay particular attention to bullet choice; type and weight being the most important aspects.

Next is the matter of cartridge components, beginning with the bullet. There's a bullet for every need: wadcutter for target pistol, hollow point for varmints, spitzer-type for hunting, and so forth. The bullet should be the same type and weight as the factory load standard, or at least within 4 percent of the factory bullet weight for valid comparison. Purchase at least 100 bullets; 200 is probably better.

The brass cartridge case you use should be the same brand and carry the same head stamp as the factory-loaded standard. Use once-fired brass.

You'll need about 200 or more cases.

Powder is next on the list. First, decide which manufacturer and type of powder you wish to use: for instance, Winchester-Western for double-base, Ball rifle and pistol powder; Du Pont for single-base, tubular rifle powder; Hodgdon for both of these types of powder; or Hercules for double-base, flake powder for pistols and revolvers.

Remember, the choice of powder should be based both on the powder manufacturer's data and on the bullet manufacturer's data. As mentioned earlier, generally, for a hunting cartridge, the best powder is that which the manufacturer shows to yield the highest velocity for the given bullet.

You will need about two pounds of powder for most high-powered rifle cartridges. This sounds excessive but it will give you enough of the same lot for load testing and future stock. The quantity should be based on planned powder consumption for testing and your anticipated future needs. You will see how to plan for this later. When purchasing powder, make certain that the lot numbers of the canisters are the same to ensure that each can is from the same process and blending batch.

When buying primers be sure to get the correct size; that is, large rifle or small rifle, large pistol or small pistol. It may be a standard or magnum primer. Normally, magnum primers are recommended by the manufacturers for large cases, when heavy charges of slow-burning powder are used, or when shooting in extremely cold weather. The bullet and powder makers often indicate the types of primers used in their loading tables. Here, too, lot numbers have importance. It is best to buy primers in enough quantity to balance against the amount of powder you purchase. Some simple calculations should quickly tell you how many rounds of ammunition your powder supply will accommodate. Purchase primers accordingly, rounded off to the next highest 100, and be sure that the lot numbers match.

A handloader who wishes to achieve loading objectives must make his component selections carefully. His objectives and result will depend on his choice of factory ammunition and handload components. After testing begins, he can't change cartridges, firearms, or components. Testing must be accomplished using the original ingredients for the results to be measured and compared against fixed references. A handload can consist of only one set of components at a given time. By changing a single component, he would be creating a new handload and confound the efforts to narrow the selection process.

## Record-Keeping

With these decisions of firearm, ammunition, and reloading components out of the way, it is time to start documenting the project. This job can be aided with the use of a printed form. The handload data list, as explained in the preceding chapter, is the chief record-keeping document for handloading and the single most important record for developing handloads utilizing the techniques offered in these pages. The handload data list is a record of all essential data. There is only one variable factor— the powder charge weight. Everything on the list applies to one specific set of components for one handload determination.

The handload data list, as described briefly in Chapter 3, contains three basic parts. Parts 1 and 2 are on the front; part 3 is on the back.

The first part of the form concerns the particulars about components of the handload, the factory-loaded cartridge used for comparison, the firearm for which the handload is being developed, the type of target, and the range distance.

The second part includes the load numbers, internal and external factors of charge weight, dates of loading and firing, number of rounds fired, and the wind, weather, and other influences encountered during firing. Of great importance in Part 2 are the precision, velocity, and pressure data which are entered in their respective columns. Lastly, Part 2 of the handload data list also provides space for this type of data obtained from the factory standard cartridge. These figures are written in at the bottom of the form.

Part 3 of the handload data list, on the reverse side, is largely space for notes. These notes contain specific items of planning and observations during loading and firing, but not on the same basis as that in parts 1 and 2 of the list. The notes collected during any handload development are very important and contain information that is often vital in the final selection of a single best handload. The back of the form is a good place to list the reasons why a final selection was made (i.e., conclusions).

CALIBER _____ BULLET WGT. _____ gr.          HANDLOAD DATA                                          Cal. _____ Bullet ____

| FIREARM:mfgr. _____ | FACTY STD CARTRGE | CASE:mfgr _____ | BULLET:wgt _____ gr | POWDER:mfgr _____ |
| model _____ | mfgr _____ | avg wgt . ± . gr | mfgr _____ | mfgr no. _____ |
| barrel length . in | mfgr no. _____ | trim length . . in | mfgr no. _____ | lot no. _____ |
| twist rate 1: . in | lot no. _____ | c.o.a.length . . in | lot no. _____ | PRIMER:mfgr _____ |
| TARGET:mfg/no. _____ | bullet wgt _____ gr | sized head . in | type _____ | mfgr no. _____ |
| RANGE:dist. _____ yd | | | clearance _____ in | lot no. _____ |

| LOAD | INTERNAL AND EXTERNAL FACTORS | | | | | PRECISION | | | VELOCITY | | | | PRES-SURE |
|---|---|---|---|---|---|---|---|---|---|---|---|---|---|
| no. | charg load wgt. gr. | date load | date fire | no. rds | wind velocity, direction, temperature, bar. pres., precip., visibility, ch. pressure observations, other. | Dat1 Std Vert Dev. in. | Dat2 Extm Vert Sprd in. | Dat3 HtAb Aim. Pt. in. | Dat4 Std Vel. Dev. fps. | Dat5 Extm Vel. Sprd fps. | Dat6 Avg Vel. fps. | no. rds rcrd | Dat7 Case Head Exp. in. |
| 1 | . | | | | | . | . | . | . | . | . | | . |
| 2 | . | | | | | . . | . | . | . | . | . | | . |
| 3 | . | | | | | . | . | . | . | . | . | | . |
| 4 | . | | | | | . | . | . | . | . | . | | . |
| 5 | . | | | | | . | . | . | . | . | . | | . |
| 6 | . | | | | | . | . | . | . | . | . | | . |
| 7 | . | | | | | . | . | . | . | . | . | | . |
| 8 | . | | | | | . | . | . | . | . | . | | . |
| 9 | . | | | | | . | . | . | . | . | . | | . |
| 10 | . | | | | | . | . | . | . | . | . | | . |
| 11 | . | | | | | . | . | . | . | . | . | | . |
| 12 | . | | | | | . | . | . | . | . | . | | . |
| 13 | . | | | | | . | . | . | . | . | . | | . |
| 14 | . | | | | | . | . | . | . | . | . | | . |
| 15 | . | | | | | . | . | . | . | . | . | | . |
| 16 | . | | | | | . | . | . | . | . | . | | . |
| 17 | . | | | | | . | . | . | . | . | . | | . |
| 18 | . | | | | | . | . | . | . | . | . | | . |
| 19 | . | | | | | . | . | . | . | . | . | | . |
| 20 | . | | | | | . | . | . | . | . | . | | . |
| 1 | facty ld. | | | | | | | | | | | | |
| 2 | " | | | | | | | | | | | | |
| 3 | " | | | | | | | | | | | | |
| 4 | " | | | | | | | | | | | | |
| 5 | " | | | | | | | | | | | | |

facty avgs =

Data 1,2,3,4,5,6 and 7 above, refer to data used in construction of the PREC., VEL. and PRESS. graphs

The front page of the handload data list format.

Caliber _____ Bullet _____ Powder _____

<u>NOTES</u>

Planning:

Includes specific details of planning stage such as objectives, special requirements, component selections and reasons for selection, factory standards, recommended range of charge weights from propellant <u>and</u> bullet maker.

Loading:

Includes specific details of factory standard components, special loading procedures, die adjustments, case sorting, powder meter settings, load densities, location of warm-up rounds, pressure test rounds, factory rounds and handloads in storage containers.

Firing:

Includes other specific details of range conditions, atmosphere, wind, times, sight settings, procedure changes, pressure observances, other observations and impressions.

Conclusions:

Compares results of precision, velocity and pressure of factory and handloaded ammunition. States which handloads met objectives. States which handload best met all objectives and why. Final selection is stated here.

The reverse side of the handload data list, with explanations of the sort of information noted there.

Keep in mind that the handload data list is for one set of handload components with only one variable factor. All loads listed are for the same bullet, powder, primer, and case. The one variable factor on the list is the powder charge weight shown opposite the load number. If you decide to change any of the other cartridge components, you must make up a new handload data list. By changing the bullet or case or powder or primer, a new and different handload is created. With this understanding, let's begin discussion of work at the loading bench.

Using the handload data list format, the record-keeping steps for handloading will be explained first. The data list parallels a logical loading sequence that's easy to follow.

At the top of the data form the caliber and bullet weight are recorded. This helps locate a specific sheet if several are kept in the same notebook. The caliber and bullet are also listed at the bottom right of the form for easier reading if the sheet is kept in a ringed notebook and holes are punched in the top of the page. The page number is on the bottom left of the form.

Data for the firearm used is entered next. Indicate the manufacturer, the model name and number, barrel length, and the rate of twist of the rifling. Twist rates are usually specified by the manufacturer. If the twist rate is not available, it can be determined with a cleaning rod and tight patch. Mark the rod and measure how far the rod must be pushed through the bore before the mark makes one complete revolution. This is the twist rate and is usually stated in such terms as one turn in 10 inches or 1:10. The patch-and-cleaning-rod method is a practical way of finding the twist rate of any rifle barrel.

Write in the target information. State the maker of the target and the stock number. This information can be useful when identifying precision data later on. In the space labeled "Range" enter the distance at which firing will occur from muzzle to target in yards.

Next, examine the factory ammunition to be used as the standard. First enter what you know from its container. This includes the manufacturer, the manufacturer's stock number, the lot number, and the bullet weight and type. You should disassemble five to ten of the factory cartridges to find the average charge weight of the powder and the average weights of the bullets and cases. This re-

quires a quality bullet puller and a handpunch for removing the live primers from the cases. Be sure to wear a pair of safety glasses and thick gloves for this operation. **Don't tap the primer! Press it out with a press or a weight on the punch.** It is safe if you use a punch and block as shown in the illustration. Don't throw these factory components away. They will be used now for setting some of the standards, and later for pressure-testing.

The factory components must be weighed on your powder scale. Write the individual component weights of ten factory cartridges on a piece of paper. Find the average weight of each component by adding the sums and dividing by ten. List these average weights in the notes on the back of the handload data list.

In addition to finding the average weights of factory components, observe how much the heaviest and lightest individual components weigh. The difference in these weights and the average weight are called variances. The greatest of these variances, whether low or high, determines a standard. Include these in the notes also. Let me explain this, using bullet weight as an example.

Let's say the average bullet weight from ten factory cartridges is 130.0 grains. The lightest bullet is 129.9 grains and the heaviest is 130.2 grains, so the greatest variance is 0.2 grains. This is written as $130.0 \pm 0.2$ grains. The same bullet weight variance can be expected throughout this lot of factory ammunition. That figure is your quality standard for comparison against the bullets you'll be handloading. Factory case weights and factory charge weights are determined using the same method. Having these factory component weight standards in your notes will enable you to satisfy part of objective 4, consistency.

The component that demands the most toil and time from the handloader is the cartridge case. But it's worth the effort. The case is the single most expensive part of any cartridge, but it is reusable. In the long run, a reused case is a cost-saving factor when reloading ammunition. It is a consideration as a loading objective for some types of shooting. The cartridge case is also one of the two components that gives the handloader a real opportunity to improve ammunition and shooting significantly; powder is the other.

There is space on the handload data list for all the data needed to describe treatment and selection of the case. The line labeled "Case: mfgr" should also include the head stamp. This is the printing on the base of the case head. It usually identifies the manufacturer and the caliber. Different head stamps, even from the same maker, help to identify changes in manufacturing that affect the case. These can be things such as internal case shape, volume, weight, and hardness. Next is the average case weight and the amount of weight variance permitted. Case weight is measured in grains, as are bullets and powder charge weights. How to determine this tolerance or standard was described above. Grading and selecting brass cases leads to better ammunition for your needs.

The cartridge case trim length is usually .010 inch less than the specified maximum case length. The trimming is done to ensure safety when cases have been used several times and stretched beyond their normal length. The handload data list is a con-

venient place to keep this measurement for future loading. It saves time; objective 8.

The cartridge overall length (COAL) includes the seated bullet. It is a total length of a completed round. This length is found after the bullet-seating die has been adjusted to provide correct bullet clearance in the chamber of the gun. This space on the handload data list is left blank until the bullet clearance is determined and the first handload rounds are complete. The last entry under the "Case" block is the diameter of the resized cartridge case head. The method of measuring the cartridge case head will be described later in this chapter and also during the discussion of pressure-testing in Chapter 8.

The bullet chosen for this handload project is entered by its weight, the bullet manufacturer, the manufacturer's stock number, lot number, type of bullet tip (such as round nose, spitzer, hollow point,

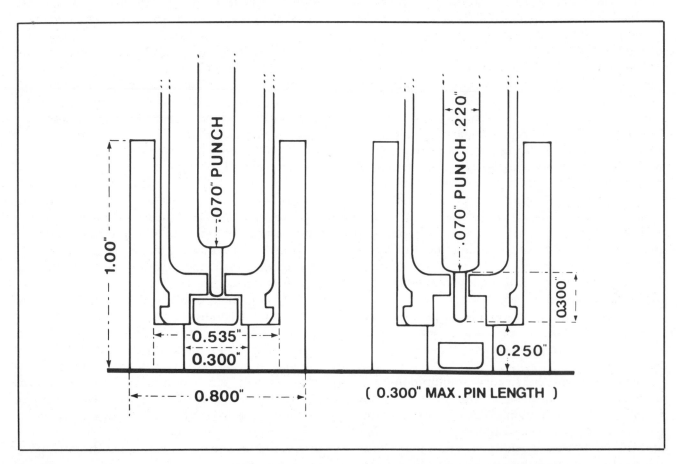

It is necessary to disassemble factory rounds for comparison. This is a relatively safe way to do it. Follow the directions and don't stand over the case mouth when you press out the primer. Don't strike the punch or primer with a hammer! Use gentle, controlled force to remove the primer.

and so forth), and the type of bullet base (such as flat-base or boat-tailed).

Bullet clearance is the distance from the barrel lands to the bullet when the cartridge is chambered. This distance must also remain the same throughout testing. For target rifles, zero clearance is sometimes best for maximum accuracy. For hunting rifles, some bullet clearance must exist for reliable and safe operation.

Zero clearance might be best for maximum precision if nothing else were involved. But zero bullet clearance is not always possible or desirable. This is true for hunting ammunition. With zero clearance, there is some risk of extracting the case while leaving the bullet stuck in the barrel and spilling powder into the action. This effectively puts a gun out of commission. In most hunting guns, the chamber is cut to provide some bullet clearance for the rea-

son just stated. This is called freebore or leade, which is the distance in a rifle's chamber from the case mouth to the rifling lands. Some rifles have so much freebore that it is impossible to obtain zero clearance, regardless of how the bullet is seated in the case. When this happens, it is usually best to seat the bullet so that its base is even with the bottom of the case neck. Just be sure that the cartridge overall length does not exceed the maximum. This method ensures a positive grip between bullet and case neck with maximum space available for the powder.

Remember that you must have some bullet clearance in all hunting guns. For hunting rifles with normal or short leades, adjust the bullet clearance as follows: use $1/8''$ bullet clearance for new rifles with less than 100 firings. If the rifle has had 100 or more firings, you may tighten the bullet clearance to $1/32''$. A clearance of $1/16''$ is a happy medium and

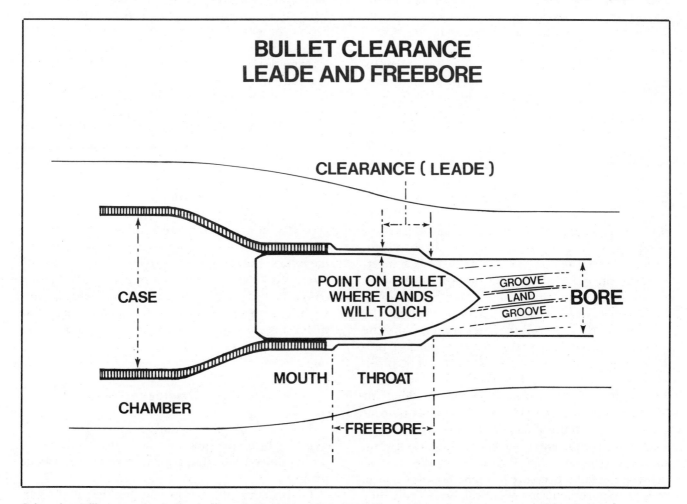

It is easier to illustrate what bullet clearance (or leade) is rather than define it (dimensions are exaggerated for clarity).

will function well in most modern hunting rifles.

Any discussion of bullet clearance tends to give the impression that great differences of precision, velocity, and pressure will result from different clearance settings. In most rifles, especially hunting rifles, bullet clearance, as long as it remains the same, is simply not an important factor affecting precision or accuracy. Many experiments in bullet clearance and precision don't take into account the effects that pressure changes have on precision. Different clearances do cause changes in pressure. For hunting rifles, just be sure you have some bullet clearance for reliable and safe functioning. Few hunting rifles show much performance variation with any reasonable clearance settings. Once the clearance has been set and some rounds have been completed, measure a few with your six-inch calipers. Double-check the cartridge overall length dimension of your completed handloads against the factory data to verify you have not exceeded the maximum. Enter this measurement in the "Case" data block.

After you measure the cartridge overall length, measure the case head diameter of the handloads. Use the one-inch micrometer for this measurement. The best procedure for doing this will be explained later. Take an average using at least five randomly selected cases. Determine this average dimension to four places ($\pm$.0001 inch). Each time you resize cases, so long as you use the same resizing die and the same adjustment, the case should return to this dimension. The average resized head dimension is entered in the "Case" data block.

The powder, or propellant if you want to be technically correct, is identified by the manufacturer, stock number, and also by lot number. Any powder manufacturer's product will vary a little from lot to lot. One powder lot seldom performs precisely the same as another, even if the stock numbers are the same. No propellant maker achieves perfect uniformity from one lot to the next; it might be possible, but the cost and selling price would be prohibitive. This fact challenges the "pet load" or "favorite load" theory. Different lots of any powder seldom yield identical ballistic results. You can expect charge requirements to vary as much as a grain or more from one lot of powder to the next to achieve the same pressure level. Sometimes charge weight requirements are identical, but usually they

are not. Needless to say, the powder lot number on your handload data list is important for results now and later.

A good procedure to follow when purchasing powder for a new handload is always to buy matching lot numbers if more than one canister is required. With large rifle cases, two pounds is about minimum. This will allow thorough testing with plenty of powder remaining for more of your best load.

The last component to be entered on the handload data list is the primer for your cartridge. The primer stock number identifies if the primer is small or large, for rifle or pistol, and if it is a standard or magnum-type. Primers, like powder, vary somewhat during manufacturing and their lot numbers should be listed on the data form. The relative merits of standard and magnum primers have already been discussed in Chapter 3.

Coverage of the first part of the handload data list is now complete. Keep in mind that the cartridge overall length and the bullet clearance information can't be calculated until the first bullets are seated.

Part 2 of the handload data list has several items that can be entered now, although most data for this section is entered during and after firing. The selected charge weights for each load number, date loaded, and the number of test rounds can be entered. Except for the caliber and bullet entries at the lower right-hand corner, and any notes you may wish to record on the reverse side, all the needed record-keeping is complete at this point.

Now that basic planning and record-keeping have been covered, loading can begin. As already stated, there are any number of excellent books on basic handloading. Your needs will differ only slightly from ordinary, basic instructions, but those differences are important to MBO techniques. This chapter covers those differences.

### Loading

Before we get into actual loading at the bench, here's a brief preview of what's involved. All of these points will be discussed in greater detail as we progress.

Of primary concern in handloading is the cartridge case. The case and charge weight are the handloader's most controllable elements in load development. Once-fired cartridge cases, from your own gun or someone else's, chosen by make and head stamp, must first be cleaned of dirt, grease, and corrosion. They should be given a detergent bath if needed, and inspected for obvious flaws. Cases with flaws such as head separation, enlarged primer pockets, off-center flash holes, split necks, split shoulders, heavy corrosion pits, or dense and deep scratches should be tossed into a scrap brass container. Use a hammer or pair of pliers and squash each defective case to ensure that it doesn't work its way back into your handloading project. Fortunately, with once-fired cases, most such defects are rare.

After the initial cleaning and inspection, the outside of the case bodies and necks will be lubricated very lightly. Light lubrication cannot be seen, only felt. The inside of the case necks are lubricated more liberally with a case neck brush. Your sizing die will need to be adjusted so that bottle-neck-type cases chamber properly but head space on the case shoulder, with zero clearance. This same sizing procedure should be used for belted cases as well. Straight-walled cases must be fully sized.

After the sizing die has been adjusted and the decapping pin set for correct stroke, all of the lubricated cases will be run through the sizing die. After sizing, all cases will be trimmed to length if required. The inside and outside edge of each case neck mouth will be deburred, including chamfering the inside slightly. All sizing lubricant is then removed with a solvent bath followed by a good washing in household detergent. The cases are then rinsed in warm water until the water stays clear, then blown dry with compressed air. They are allowed to dry overnight on a towel or newspaper if needed. If any more cases show defects that might present a danger, imprecision, or loss of confidence, they are discarded also.

Next, the cases will be separated and sorted by weight. After this, the cases will be primed and inspected for full primer seating. They are then placed in a loading tray in groups of five.

Carefully weighed individual powder charges will then be loaded into the five primed cases, each group of five cases representing one load number.

The bullet-seating die will be adjusted for clear-ance, and the bullets seated. The process of charging and bullet-seating of each group of five cases will be repeated. Completed loads will be checked off on the handload data list opposite the load reference number.

Each round will need to be inspected for straight bullet-seating and then placed in an ammunition box. The box will be labeled as to its contents and load numbers by row number.

And that's about it for bench work. Now we'll get into loading in detail. The following text is written as if the reader were looking over someone's shoulder, in this case our friend from Chapter 2, Jim, the deer hunter.

The remaining part of this chapter will be used to explain, in operating plan steps, the requirements for planning, record-keeping, and loading by objective and result. These are the planned steps that are best completed at the loading bench. Let's observe the first handloading step—the planning.

Jim has become an avid deer hunter in recent years and believes that this kind of hunting will account for most of his big game efforts. He wanted a rifle that would also be suitable for pronghorn antelope and perhaps even elk, if the opportunity ever presents itself. After some reading, and listening to advice from hunting friends and the experts at the local sporting goods store, he decided to purchase a bolt action rifle in the .270 Winchester caliber, topped with a good, four-power telescopic sight. Although there are other suitable calibers and scopes that would meet his needs, he has decided on the .270 Winchester and four-power scope as they will perform well under each of his hunting considerations. This first decision is a good one.

This brings up another fact of which we should be aware; that is, handloads best enhance the abilities of a gun and ammunition if that gun and ammunition are correctly chosen for their intended use. These first, important choices help achieve the best handloading and shooting results.

The available factory ammunition will perform well, but Jim wants to develop maximum shooting confidence. Making the very best ammunition possible for the recognized shooting needs is one way to do this. He wants results that will satisfy his purpose and he has adopted the previously stated list of intermediate objectives. He believes that they are worthy, practical, reasonably attainable, clearly stated objectives that are compatible with the desired result.

Jim has also followed the good advice of knowledgeable hunters as to the choice of factory ammunition—130-grain, expanding point ammunition will be used as the standard for comparison. This cartridge will perform well for each of the three hunting requirements—deer, antelope, and elk. He has purchased two boxes of factory ammo with the same lot number: Remington brand, stock number R270W2, lot L25UD2452. This is a .270 Winchester loading with a 130-grain, spitzer-type, expanding bullet.

Because Jim wishes to sight in the rifle and work up the handloads on the same day at the rifle range, all the components needed for this project have been collected. He has gathered some once-fired cases, most of which have the same head stamp as the new, factory ammunition.

Two boxes of bullets have been purchased for the handloaded cartridges. The bullets are 130-grain, spitzer-type, flat-base bullets made by Sierra. Their stock number is 1830 and the lot number on both boxes is 40520.

The chosen powder is Du Pont IMR 4831. This selection has been based on the *Du Pont Handloader's*

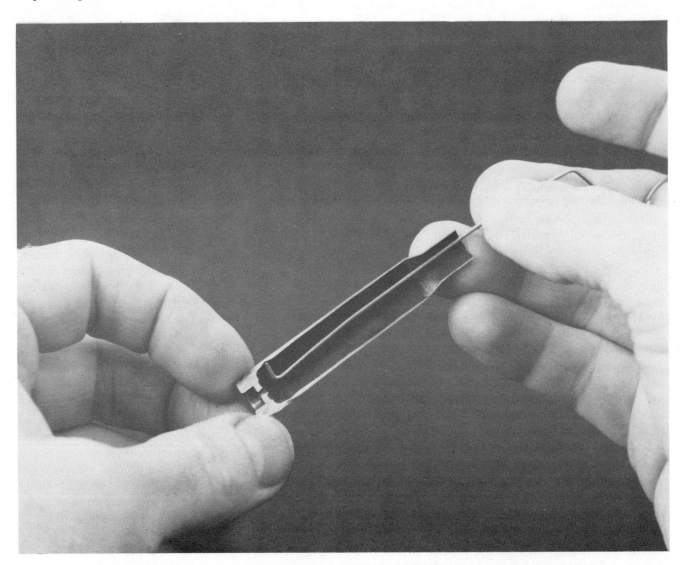

A case cross-sectioned to show how a wire "feeler" can be used to detect head stretch. Cases that are stretched like this should not be reloaded.

Precision Handloading

*Guide* and the *Sierra Bullets Reloading Manual.* The powder lot number is P81JY29A-74.

Jim knows that the final handloads may take as much as 60 grains of powder per round. To estimate the powder requirements, he multiplies 60 grains times the 200 component bullets, which shows that up to 12,000 grains of powder may be needed. Since a one-pound can hold 7,000 grains, two cans, or 14,000 grains, of the chosen powder have been purchased.

Jim decides to use the CCI brand of primer. The standard large rifle primer is selected based on available information. This primer is cataloged as CCI #200. The lot number is L25L. He decides to buy three boxes, or 300 primers. This is done for two reasons. First, the two cans of powder will provide an excess of 2,000 grains, even if a maximum charge is used in all handloads. Secondly, the best charge weight will probably be less than 60 grains of powder, which means that the two pounds of powder may yield considerably more than 200 rounds of handloaded ammunition. The extra box of primers is a small cost, but good insurance for future results.

In addition, a package of Leupold and Stevens-type 100-yard targets is purchased.

All of this information is carefully recorded on the handload data list.

The component that will require the most effort to prepare for loading is the cartridge case. A total of 167 cases, which are believed to be identical, have been collected. After all the cases have been cleaned to remove dirt and grease, the first inspection is begun, starting with the case heads. Only the same brand and same head stamp cases will be used, as described earlier. The first inspection shows that 12 of the cases are Winchester brass. These cases are put away for other uses. It is also discovered that three Remington cases have a different style of head stamp. Instead of "R-P" stamps, they are the older "Rem-UMC" head stamp. These three cases, like the Winchester cases, are segregated and isolated from the bulk lot. This leaves 152 cases.

Next, the remaining cases are carefully inspected for case head separation. This includes cases that show early signs of separation such as a bright band or slight crack around the base. All are checked for irregularities in the body such as dents, abrasions, splits, deep scratches, and heavy corrosion. Lastly,

all cases are inspected for shoulder and neck flaws such as splits, dents, and malformations that could affect safety or precision. No other flawed cases are found during this inspection, and the remaining 152 cases are ready to be resized.

Before resizing begins, Jim decides to learn about the chamber of the new rifle. With no ammunition, powder, or primers on the bench, he lights a candle and places one of the cases in the flame. The burning candle deposits a layer of carbon on the case shoulder. He is careful not to let the brass get too hot. This would anneal the metal and soften the case. This is prevented by passing the case shoulder back and forth through the middle and coolest part of the flame. This prevents overheating while depositing a good layer of carbon on the case. Three cases (for purposes of instruction) are "smoked" in this manner. Next, the chamber of the rifle is wiped clean with a large, fresh patch.

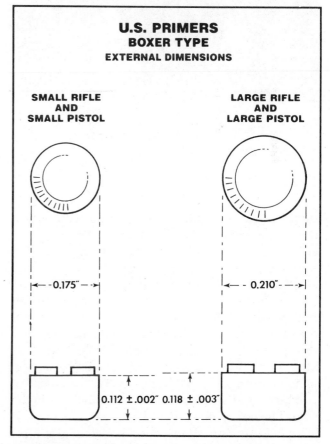

U.S. primers come in only two sizes, but cup strength, intensity, and duration of ignition change with different brands and models. Choose carefully.

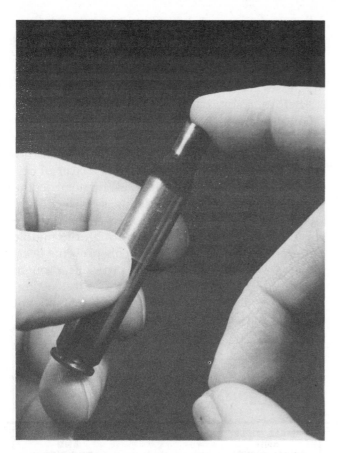

Before smoking the case, clean any lubricant from the shoulder. Carbon will deposit better on clean brass, as seen here.

With the muzzle held up, the first of the smoked cartridge cases is chambered in order to find how the once-fired case fits this rifle. As the case easily enters the chamber and the bolt closes the action smoothly, it is obvious that the case was fired in a chamber no larger than this one. As the case is removed, the smoked case shoulder shows light but well-defined contact all around. This indicates that the case was fired in a chamber similar in length and shoulder angle to that of the test rifle. Case 1 is identified and set aside for another use to be explained later.

The second case does not chamber as easily in the rifle. The bolt is more difficult to close. The smoked area on the case shoulder shows strong contact everywhere. Case 2 came from a rifle with a slightly longer chamber. This case is also identified for further use.

The third case chambers very easily. The shoul-

der area shows little or no contact. Case 3 was fired in a smaller chamber than this one.

In order to ensure good chambering, with proper fit and minimal case stretching, the first case is used for precise adjustment of the full-length sizing die. (Note: if the test rifle had been fired with new factory ammunition, any of those cases could have been used for the adjustment procedure explained here.) Each of the three cases is "resmoked" and then lightly lubricated on the outside case wall using the lubricant pad. The necks are carefully lubricated outside and inside, but not so much as to remove the carbon on the shoulder.

Now attention focuses on the loading press. The lever restraint is removed, and the proper shell holder is cleaned and installed on the ram of the press. Next, the correct sizing die is taken from its box and the decapping rod removed. The decap-

Smoking a case prior to adjusting the sizing die. Pass the case neck back and forth through the flame while rolling the case in your fingers. Don't let it get too hot. Use the middle of the flame—more carbon, less heat.

Precision Handloading

ping pin is inspected for straightness and tightness. The expander ball is measured at its widest point with the six-inch calipers. It measures .275″, which is .002″ less than the diameter of the component bullets (.277″). This measurement tells us that the correct expander ball is installed in the sizing die. The undersized ball ensures that the expanded case mouth will be slightly undersized to grip the seated bullet securely in the completed cartridge.

Next, a paper clip or similar-sized soft wire is used to push any material out of the small "bleed hole" in the wall of the die body. A solvent-soaked patch is used to clean all the inside surface of the die carefully. A dry patch completes the job. Without reinstalling the decapping rod and pin, Jim screws the sizing die body into the press. With the ram and shell holder in the fully extended or "up" position, the sizing die is screwed down into the press until contact is made between the base of the die and the top of the shell holder. At this point, we must pause to perform a small calculation needed for precision die adjustment.

We do not want to push the case shoulders back any farther than the first case chambered in the previous exercise. That was case 1, which fit the rifle chamber closely. This case will be used for adjusting the sizing die.

Like most, the loading dies used in this example have the standard ⅞–14 threads. Since the ⅞–14 die has a thread pitch of 14 turns for every inch, it can be determined how much progression or reach the die will make for every full turn. This is done by dividing one by 14. The quotient of this division is a decimal fraction of .071″. This is slightly more than ¹/₁₆″. By using six-inch calipers to measure the second, or longest case, Jim finds that the oversized number two case is about .030″ longer than the close-fitting number one case. This measurement is taken on both cases from the base to the midpoint of each case shoulder. To relate this difference to die adjustment, Jim divides .030″ by .071″. This gives a quotient of .423 and means that the die can be adjusted for case 1 from case 2 by turning it down about four-tenths (.4) of a turn.

In order not to oversize case 1 accidentally, he unscrews the sizing die two full turns, places the number two (long) case in the shell holder, and runs the long case completely into the sizing die. Case 2 is extracted and examined. No contact has been made between the smoked case shoulder and the

die. The die is screwed down into the press one-quarter of a turn, or about .018″ closer to the long case shoulder. This gradual lowering of the die is repeated until contact is made between the case shoulder and the die, indicated by a smudge mark on the smoked case shoulder. Then the die is backed out of the press one-eighth of a turn. Case 2 is removed and case 1 reinserted. Jim now proceeds to make contact between the number one case shoulder and the die by adjusting the sizing die downward. This is done by turning the die down toward the case shoulder in one-eighth-turn increments. One-eighth of a turn is equal to .009″. The case is now about .030″ to .040″, or four adjustments, away from contact using one-eighth-turn changes. As no contact is made even after the second adjustment, the die is very close to the case shoulder. The adjustment increment is decreased to one-sixteenth of a turn, or .004″. After a few more tries and case inspections, positive contact is made with the number one case shoulder. This can be seen by a smudge over the entire case shoulder. To ensure positive resizing and to overcome the spring action of the brass case, the sizing die is further tightened one-sixteenth of a turn downward.

As each of the small die adjustments is made with

Each of these three cases was fire-formed in the same gun. The case on the left shows the shoulder area as it should be smoked for die adjustment. The middle case has been re-chambered in the gun—note the even, but light contact. The case on the right has been resized in a properly adjusted die. Shoulder contact is firm, but not overdone.

the ram in the "up" position, we would automatically know when the limit of die adjustment has been reached. This would happen when the shell holder makes contact with the die body. Quite often, the final die adjustment results in a slight space between the shell holder and the base of the sizing die. Sure enough, there is a small gap between the shell holder and the base of the die after the last die adjustment just described. To ensure that the sizing die is aligned properly with the ram and shell holder, a metal washer is placed between the shell holder and the bottom of the die. The metal washer acts as a shim. The reason for this last

step is to place some upward force on the die before the lock ring is set. This helps ensure that each cartridge case is not only properly sized, but also properly aligned in relation to its base.

After the setting and tightening of the die lock ring, the sizing die is removed from the press and cleaned of candle soot. After cleaning, the die is reinserted into the press. Make sure that it returns properly to the preset position. Now the decapping rod, expander button, and decapping pin assembly is reinserted about halfway back into the die. The thread size and pitch for the decapping rod is 1/4–28. This means that each turn of the rod will ad-

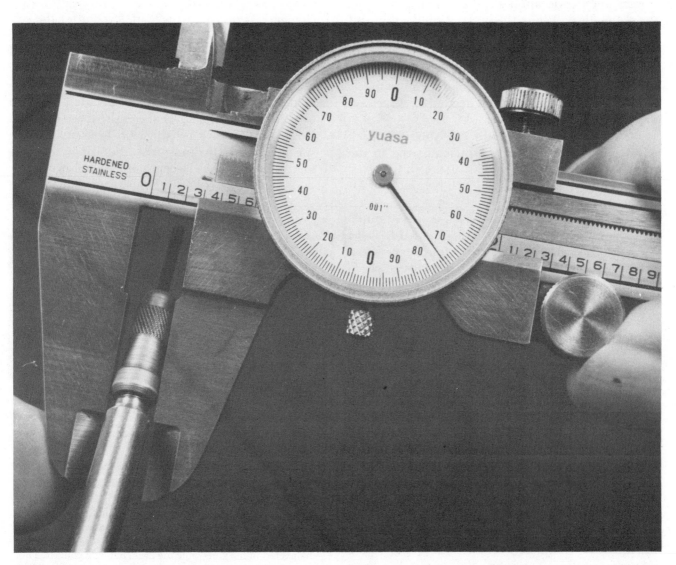

Before sizing, measure the expander ball with your calipers. This expander has a diameter of 0.275 inches. This is correct for 0.277 caliber bullets such as the .270 Winchester.

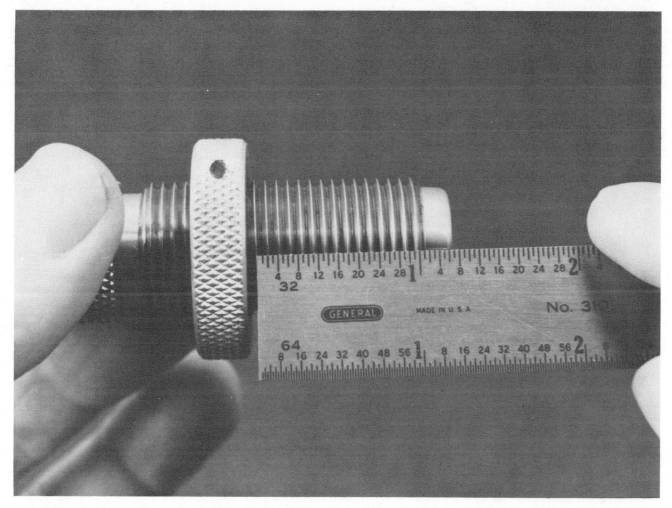

This is a standard ⁷/₈–14 die thread setup. If you don't have a thread gauge, you can use this method to find thread pitch. Measure between the threads, but count the thread crowns within one inch. Otherwise, you will count an extra thread as seen here. Other common threads for dies are ¹/₄–28, ³/₈–24, ⁷/₁₆–20, and ⁹/₁₆–18.

vance the decapping pin and expander ¹/₂₈″ (.036″) into the die body.

Next, Jim runs the clean number one case fully into the die and past the expander button. The decapping rod is screwed down into the die until the decapping pin enters the flash hole and makes contact with the spent primer in the case. The case is backed partly out of the die and the decapping rod is turned down one-half turn (.018″). The case is returned fully into the die. This adjustment is repeated until the spent primer is ejected. The decapping rod is tightened another one-half turn for positive depriming. Then the expander rod is set with the locking ring and jam nut while the case is still fully inserted into the die. The sizing die is

now precisely adjusted for this particular rifle chamber.

Again, if any fired cases from the test rifle had been available, this procedure could have been simplified—any such case could have been used for the die adjustment.

The procedure just described is a modified method of full-length resizing and varies slightly from most instructions. It offers the important advantage of easy chambering for hunting cartridges that can still be reloaded the maximum number of times. This causes less working of the brass case at the shoulder area and less stretching between the case head and wall. The same procedure should be used for belted cartridge cases as well. They receive

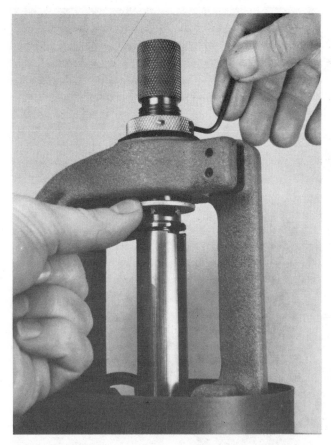

If there is any gap between the shell holder and die after adjustment, use a washer to take up the space and apply some force against the die before setting the lock ring. This helps keep the die aligned with the ram.

the same benefits from this technique. The belt is still there for added case strength, but headspacing is achieved with the case shoulder, not the belt. Full-length resizing is recommended for all high-powered hunting cartridges.

It is best to have 150 or more fired cases of the same brand and head stamp, all fired in the same rifle. This is usually not the circumstance, however. The next best alternative has been presented here. For our purposes, the advantage of collecting cases from the same rifle is minimal. The extra investments in time, effort, and money for fireformed brass are considerable. Furthermore, such practice would be contrary to objective 8: to determine that ammunition which best achieves the other seven objectives with the least expense of time, labor, materials, and money for testing. Using brass fired in another rifle is satisfactory for our needs as long as

the normal chamber tolerances in the described procedures for case sorting and die adjustment are observed and followed. The use of once-fired brass from any other firearm is not a compromise to your objective standards.

Now that the final adjustments to the sizing die have been made, work continues. Before lubricating the remaining cases, each case neck is wiped with a rag soaked in powder solvent to remove powder residue. A solvent such as Hoppe's #9 is good for this job. A case neck lubricating brush, dipped in solvent, is useful in removing the residue inside the case neck. All remaining selected cartridge cases are lubricated inside the neck with a neck brush and sizing lube. The case bodies and outside necks are lightly lubricated by rolling them in groups of five to ten cases on a lubricating pad. Then they are each resized, using the adjusted die. Each case is installed in the shell holder. The press handle is moved smoothly through the entire travel of its movement. This helps to give consistent, uniform sizing. Slow, steady sizing of brass also prevents bent case necks. Bent necks will not hold a bullet straight and true. They are a source of imprecision.

After each case is resized, it is removed from the shell holder, inspected, and placed in a box reserved for sized cases. During resizing, Jim finds that two cases will not easily enter the shell holder. One case has a rim that is too thick. The other has an extractor groove that is too large in diameter. Each of these cases is discarded and placed in the scrap brass can with the other rejects. Now there are 150 cases left.

## Trimming and Cleaning

After all the cases are resized, a check is made to see if case trimming is needed. Jim consults the maximum case length dimension in one of his reloading guides. It is found that the maximum length for .270 Winchester cases is 2.540″. The six-inch calipers are adjusted and locked to this measurement. After attempting to pass a few of the resized cases through the jaws of the calipers, it is found that some cases go through easily, but others do not. Some cases are longer than 2.540″ and they will not pass through the calipers. This clearly indicates that the cases must be trimmed to the correct overall length.

A case trimmer is mounted in the vise. One of the long cases is placed in the case trimmer and the trimmer blade setting is adjusted to that case. Next, Jim readjusts and locks the calipers to a setting of 2.530″, which is .010″ shorter than the maximum length. This measurement is the case "trim length." By using the fine adjustment on the case trimmer, the case is alternately trimmed and checked for length against the preset calipers. After reaching what appears to be the correct trim length with this first case, the trim setting is locked. Another long case is inserted into the trimmer. This case is also trimmed and measured with the calipers. The case is within a few thousandths of 2.530″. The third case is trimmed and it, too, is within the tolerance of 2.530 ± .002″. All of the other cases are run through the trimmer, then placed in a separate box. Some of the cases are short enough that the cutting blade does not trim any metal from them. Many cases do require some trimming, however. Jim can feel the cutter removing metal as he turns the crank and can also see the bright metal on the case mouth when it is removed from the trimmer. Every tenth case is checked while trimming to see that the trimming tool remains in adjustment.

After all cases are trimmed to length, a deburring tool is used to remove rough metal from the case mouths. Care is taken to remove only the burr from the outside of each case mouth. On the inside edge of each case mouth, a slight chamfer is cut to smooth bullet seating and prevent scraping of the bullet's soft metal base. All the trimmed cases are deburred and chamfered.

After trimming, deburring, and chamfering, a small brush is used to loosen primer residue from the primer pockets. This is done before final cleaning and facilitates priming. It is much easier to "feel" the primers as they are seated if primer pockets are clean.

There are three more case inspections to be performed before priming may begin. These are for primer flash hole diameter, case and neck concentricity, and neck wall thickness. Some handloaders consider these inspections unimportant. They are not unimportant, just different.

The simplest way to find if a primer flash hole is undersize is to use a drill bit as a "go" gauge. Since all the brass was successfully deprimed with a .070″ decapping pin, this concern can be eliminated since .070 is an acceptable hole size. The chief concern is now with primer holes that may be too big. Jim knows that the primer flash holes in his cases should be approximately .080″ in diameter and no larger than about .086″. A #44 drill bit has a diameter of .086″ and is well suited as this "go" gauge. He attempts to pass a #44 drill bit through each of the selected cases. It is found that no primer flash holes are large enough to permit entry of the drill. All of the cases are acceptable. If any cases had been found to have flash holes equal or larger than the drill bit, they would have been discarded.

During flash hole inspection, it is found that two cases have a fairly rare defect. The primer flash hole is not centered properly in the base of the cartridge head. These two cases are crushed and tossed into the scrap brass can. This will ensure that they won't be used in the future. Although safe for use, the flash hole defect would affect our confidence. With a seated primer, such cases could not be distinguished from others. Such cases could also break the decapping pin during future resizing. There are now 148 cases that have passed inspections.

Next, a flat surface is used to roll and inspect the cases for obvious signs of neck and body out-of-roundness and out-of-center conditions. By shimming one end of a piece of glass, Jim creates a flat surface that will allow the cases to roll easily, but slowly. A large, glass-framed picture will work fine.

Each of the selected cases is placed on the glass and allowed to roll from one end to the other. Cases that wobble at the neck or base are not true or concentric. They are off center and must be discarded. No such cases are found. This is a welcome surprise, since a few such cases usually appear during this test.

Lastly, the case mouths are inspected to find if any case necks have off-centered diameters. This results in a thick case neck wall on one side and a thin neck wall on the other. When this condition exists, the result is an off-center case throat. Bullets cannot be seated true in such cartridge cases. Some of our cases appear to have abnormal necks, but they are not as bad as they seem at first. Using the calipers, a few measurements are taken on these case necks. It is learned that the wall thickness seldom varies more than .004″ per side. The average thickness of each neck wall is about .015″. Two cases are found to have greater differences. These are discarded, leaving 146 cases.

If we were loading for a rifle designed for

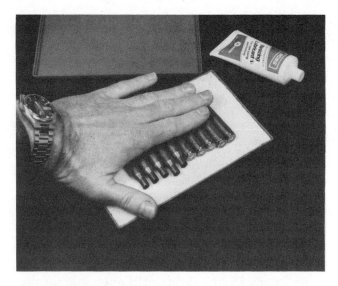

Cases must be lubricated lightly before resizing. Light lubrication can't be seen, only felt.

greater precision than Jim's, we might consider truing the case necks. This is done with a special tool to remove some of the surface and thickness irregularities of the case necks. But this solution presents other problems as well. Jim's hunting rifle has plenty of space for neck expansion. Such time and expense would not benefit him in a measurable way. He decides to use all of the cases as they are and discard only those with obviously bad neck walls.

The cases are now ready for final cleaning. All of the selected cases are dumped gently into a metal cooking pan. Solvent is poured into the pan until all the cases are covered. Any solvent that will cut grease is acceptable as long as it doesn't react chemically to brass. Gasoline, Naphtha, kerosene, lacquer thinner, paint thinner, methyl ethyl ketone (MEK), and many other solvents all do a good job of cutting grease. Naphtha is one of the best: it rapidly removes grease and some oxides with very little agitation of the cases required; it does not evaporate quickly; it can be used many times; it's cheap; and it washes away quickly with mild detergent. However, naphtha is no longer sold as commonly as it once was and you may find it difficult to purchase in small quantities. Naphtha is also flammable and must be stored in a proper metal container. This is true of most solvents, however. When using flammable solvents, ensure that there is no smoking and

no open flames near the cleaning area. Have a fire extinguisher nearby, nevertheless.

There are several commercially prepared brass-cleaning solutions available. Some do a good job. Some are nonflammable. Some react too strongly with brass, however. Experiment with some rejected brass before using such cleaners on your selected cases.

After soaking and agitating the cases in solvent for a few minutes, Jim pours off the solvent into its container and refills the pan with hot water. A tablespoon of household liquid detergent is added and the cases are agitated gently until the detergent is dissolved. The cases are soaked for a short while, after which the detergent solution is poured off. Fi-

Sizing and depriming. Use smooth, slow, unbroken strokes for good sizing. A jerky, broken motion causes stuck cases, inconsistent sizing, and bent necks—all sources of imprecision.

Precision Handloading

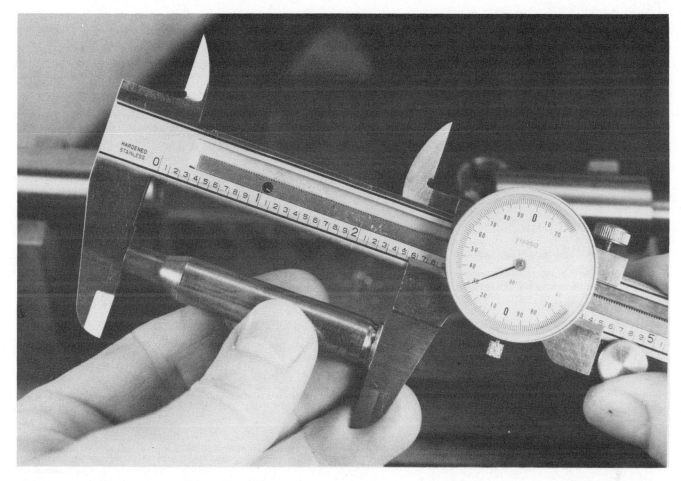

Checking case length with your calipers is the best way to know if trimming is needed. The calipers are also needed to adjust the trimmer and maintain adjustment within a couple of thousandths.

nally, the cases are rinsed with warm water, three or four times, until all traces of detergent are gone and the rinse water remains clear. The rinse water is then poured off and the cases are removed and blown dry with compressed air. They are placed on a towel or newspaper for complete drying.

An oven can be used to speed case drying, but only if the temperature is set and verified to be between 150 and 200 degrees Fahrenheit. Annealing of the brass can occur at temperatures not much above this.

## Weighing Cases

After all the cleaned cases are thoroughly dry, weight sorting may begin. This procedure further selects cases by eliminating those cases whose weight falls outside an acceptable range. In other words, cases are eliminated that are either too light or too heavy. This procedure is used to help meet objectives 1, 4, 5, and 7. Sorting cases by weight helps to ensure that all case volumes are equal. Heavy cases have less internal volume. Light cases may have too much volume. Cases with unequal volumes develop uneven pressure even with carefully weighed powder charges.

Grading cases by weight is not difficult as long as some objectivity is used. You must determine what you wish to accomplish by weight grading. It's really very simple. Exclude all cases from handloading that are too light or too heavy, using factory case weights as a standard. You need to do this because light and heavy cases are a source of imprecision.

Even once-fired cases may need trimming. Trim long cases so they are 0.010 inch shorter than the maximum permitted length. If crimping is important, as with handgun ammunition, all cases must be identical in length.

Here's the fastest, best way to sort cases by weight. First, select 20 percent of the remaining cases at random. Take them from the group that has survived all other inspections. Weigh them individually on your powder scale and record their individual weights. Next, add the weights for a total and divide by the sample number for an average weight. Now decide what weight deviations you will accept above and below the average weight. This will be your standard for case weight. This standard is used for sorting cases by weight.

After determining the standards, set the powder scale for the lowest weight permitted and weigh all of the cases. Cases that do not raise the scale pointer to zero or higher fall below the accepted low weight and should be separated. They are good cases, but too light for the standard. Now set the scale for the highest permitted weight. Again, weigh each remaining case from the surviving group. Cases that raise the indicator needle past the zero point are too heavy. They must also be separated. All remaining cases fall within the range of weight accepted as the standard. These cases will be the cases used for handloading. Now, let's apply this procedure to our example for better understanding.

After taking a 20 percent sampling of the 146 remaining cartridge cases that passed through the sizing, depriming, cleaning, and inspection procedures, Jim weighs each of the sample cases and records their individual weights. All the sample case weights are added and then divided by the number of sample cases. Their average weight is found to be 197.3 grains. He reviews the individual weights to find the lightest and heaviest cases. The lightest case is 193.5 grains. This is 3.8 grains, or about 1.9 percent below the 197.3 average. The heaviest case weighs 200.9 grains. This is 3.6 grains, or 1.8 percent above the average weight. These deviations seem small, but they are important. They can be improved with a stricter standard.

Jim decides to tighten weight standards by permitting only a 1.5 percent deviation above and below the average case weight. This is a 3 percent range of acceptable weight. He multiplies the average case weight of 197.3 grains times .015 (1.5%).

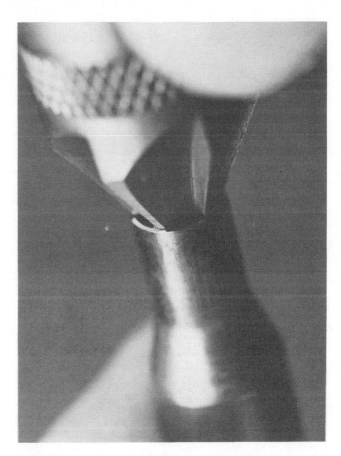

The inside edge of the case mouth should be deburred and given a slight chamfering. This makes bullet seating easier.

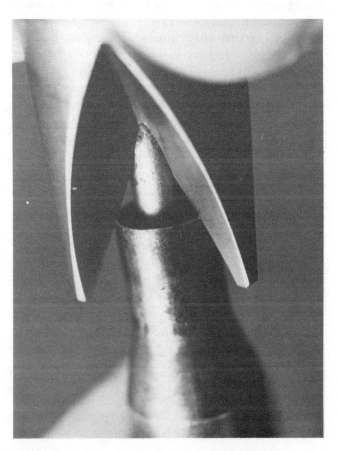

The outside of the case mouth should only be deburred slightly. Don't remove any more metal than necessary.

This figure rounds off to 3.0 grains. Three grains of deviation will give a tightened and improved weight tolerance. This means that the lightest case weight acceptable will be 194.3 grains. The heaviest will be 200.3 grains. Any cases lighter than 194.3 or heavier than 200.3 grains will be rejected.

The zero setting on the powder scale is verified again. The scale is set at the minimum case weight of 194.3 grains. Each case is weighed. All acceptable cases must be heavy enough to raise the pointer back to zero or higher. Any cases that don't raise the pointer to zero are too light. Eleven cases fail to do so. They are segregated, labeled, and stored away. These are good cases for other uses, but not this one.

Next, the scale is set and locked at 200.3 grains, the maximum allowable case weight. All the cases that passed the first weight test are reweighed, and 23 fail to qualify and must be culled from the select

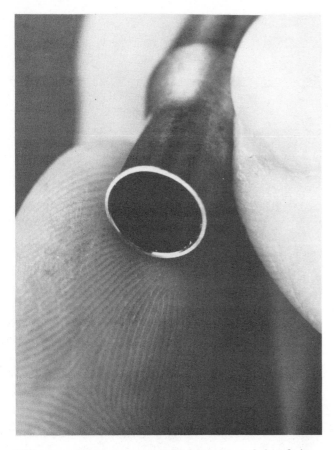

This shows the correct amount of deburring and chamfering for any type of brass case. Very little metal is removed so as not to weaken the case.

explained in a moment. This standard is needed to accomplish objective 4, greater consistency. It should also now be obvious why a minimum of 150 cases is needed to start any "handloading by objective" project.

In the above example of case weight sorting, Jim set a weight standard for the brass available to him. That is one way to achieve objective 4. But it should be understood that this standard is not one that applies directly to the ammunition he will use as a factory standard. He merely sorted cases by a standard that would help you learn the method easily. In truth, ammunition makers sometimes produce cartridge cases that fit within a 3 percent total weight range for a given lot of brass. But this is not always true. Each lot of factory brass is different. Weighing factory cases is the only way to know what the lot standard is. This requires dismantling factory ammunition. Jim completely disassembles ten cartridges from one box of the factory ammunition. Great care is taken to keep the components separated by individual cartridges. He weighs the ten cases and records their individual weights. It is determined that factory cases average 198.6 grains with this lot of brass. The lightest case weighs 197.1 grains, which is only a 1.5-grain or 0.8 percent deviation. This is very close, indeed. The heaviest case weighs 201.9 grains, however. This is a 3.3-grain, or 1.7 percent deviation, and this is the one that

group. Each of these cases raised the pointer above the zero mark. Each is heavier than the maximum allowable weight. These cases are also segregated, labeled, and stored for other uses. Now, only 112 cases remain.

The 55 rejected cases from the sorting, inspections, and weighings represent a 33 percent rejection rate. The remaining 112 cases all fit into a range of 194.3 to 200.3 grains. This is a ± 1.5 percent deviation from the average weight. It is a 3 percent range of acceptable weight. These are close standards, although achievable with several varieties of used brass. The 33 percent rejection rate is acceptable for this testing. The ability to achieve such standards for case weight tolerance with various lots of brass speaks highly of the manufacturing standards of U.S. ammunition makers. All things considered, Jim now has better brass than that used in the factory ammunition. This will be

Dirty primer pockets are a source of imprecision. They can cause inconsistent seating of the primer. This changes the quality of ignition from one shot to the next.

Precision Handloading

The wire brush scrapes the bottom of the primer pocket clean. It does not harm the walls of the pocket. The walls are critical for good primer fit.

This is how the primer pocket should look after brushing. There is another cleaning step which will remove even the traces of residue seen here.

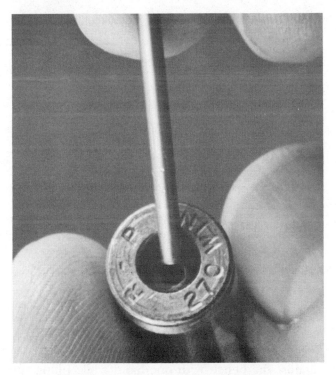

Use a drill bit to find oversize flash holes. The largest holes in U.S. cartridges are .080 inch. A #44 bit is .086 inch and should not pass through the case. If it does, scrap the case.

This primer flash hole was punched off-center. It will work but there will be a doubt as to how well. This case may also bend the depriming pin in the sizing die. Scrap it.

At the Loading Bench

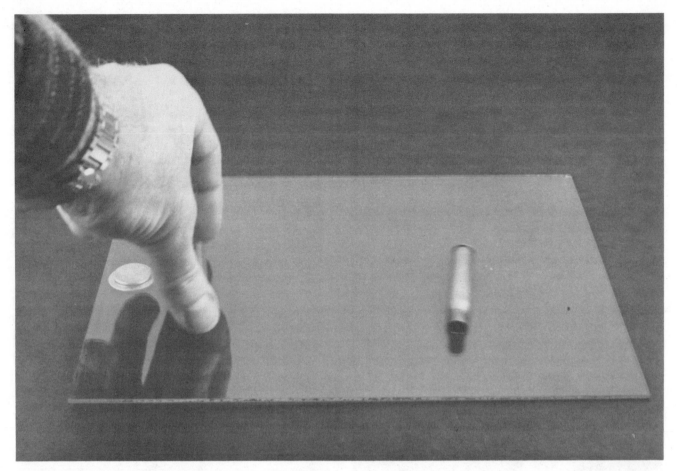

Rolling cases is a positive way to check for out-of-round and out-of-balance conditions. Out-of-round is the most serious condition and can hurt precision results.

counts. Under such circumstances, you can assume that further inspection of this factory lot of cases would have no better than a ± 3.3-grain deviation, or 6.6 grains range. This factory weight range is 3.3 percent of average weight. It is not as good as Jim's 3.0 percent range. He has achieved an important part of objective 4, greater consistency.

## Priming

The carefully chosen, prepared, and selected brass cases are finally ready for priming. A box of CCI primers is brought out. Jim then puts on his safety glasses because the next actions present some chance for injury.

After removing the top of the primer flip tray, the sliding cover of the primer box is opened to expose 50 primers. The tray cover is placed over the box of primers and while holding the tray cover and primer box together, they are flopped so that the primer tray cover is on the bottom. As the primer box is removed, 50 primers remain on the tray cover, some up and some down. Next, Jim mates the bottom portion of the primer flip tray to the top. The whole assembly is flipped over again and the tray cover is removed. After a little back and forth jiggling, each primer turns face down, exposing its anvil and paper cover. The tray cover is placed back on the tray, and the assembly is flipped over once more on the bench and the tray is removed. All the primers are now lying face down on the smooth surface of the tray cover. They are ready for loading into the primer feeding tube.

Wearing gloves, Jim holds the tray cover firmly against the bench with one hand while filling the primer tube with the other. After the primer tube is filled, it is placed into the priming tool. The retaining pin is removed, allowing the primers to fall into position. The cartridge shell holder is removed from the loading press and placed into the priming tool with the correct size primer-seating rod. Jim proceeds to seat a primer into the pocket of each selected case with equal force. As each case is primed, it is removed from the primer tool and placed head up in a clean loading tray. One hundred of the 112 cases are primed. After priming these test cases, the priming tool is removed from the bench vise, temporarily. The primer feed tube is inspected for any stuck primers and the retaining pin is replaced. Jim then verifies that he has

used and can account for every primer. Remember, if any portion of a box is used, these primers must be accounted for also. An empty box should be discarded. Any partially filled box of primers should be placed back into storage.

Next, all cartridge case heads are inspected to see that their primers are fully seated and below the surface of the head. If this is not obvious, place the case on a flat surface, head down. If the case rocks, the primer is protruding from the case head. In such a situation, first attempt to seat the primer fully. If that fails, the case should be carefully deprimed and the primer pocket measured for cor-

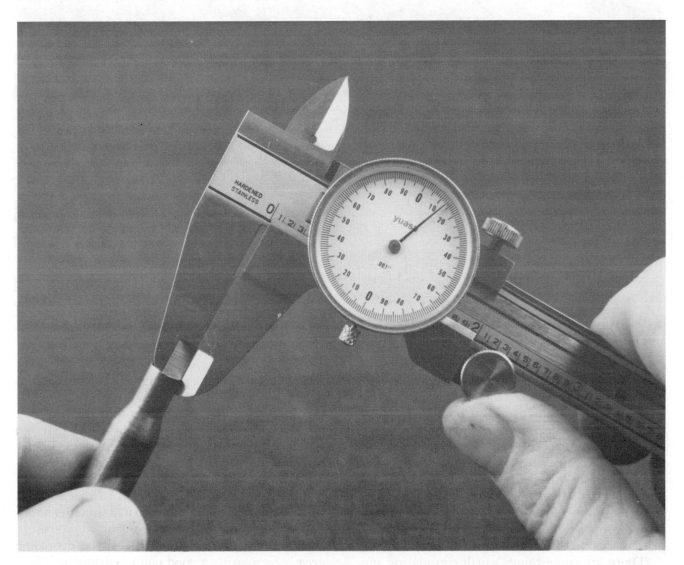

Calipers can be used to measure case neck thickness as seen here. Other, more precise instruments are made for this job, but the calipers tell us all we really need to know about this area of concern. Wall thickness should not vary more than 0.004 inch from one side to the other.

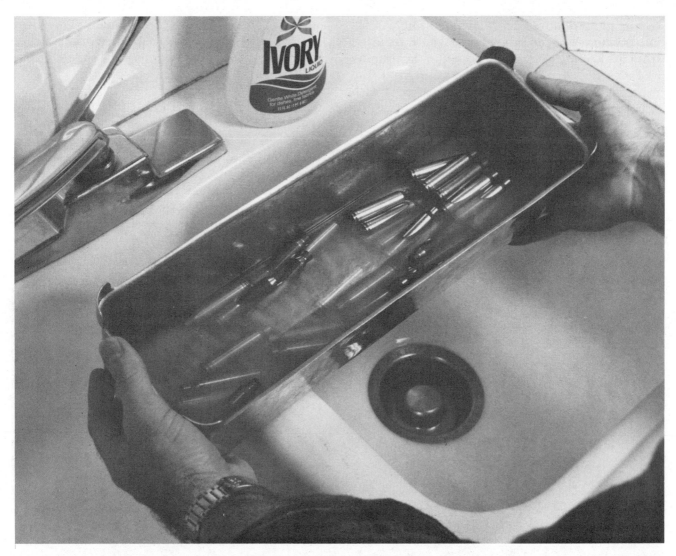

After the solvent bath to remove sizing lube, a detergent bath is needed to remove the solvent. This bath also removes brass tarnish and makes final inspection easier. Be sure to rinse all detergent away before drying the cases.

rect depth with the end of the six-inch calipers. Any primer pocket should be from .125″ to .130″ deep. Primers are about this deep also, but they compress slightly during the seating operation. Cases with shallow primer pockets must be discarded. They are a source of inaccuracy. Keep in mind that this is the last chance to reseat a primer and still observe the important safety rule, "never seat a primer in a loaded round." After all the primers have been seated properly, it's time to charge the primed cases with powder.

There are some things worth considering now for better understanding of powder charges and handloading by objective. For instance, since our method requires range testing to be performed under as nearly identical conditions as possible, it is best if all range firing can occur during a morning or afternoon on the same day. However, different shooters become fatigued at different rates. Therefore, it is good to fire no more rounds than you believe you can tolerate at a single sitting. The use of hearing protection can help you to extend your shooting time. Fatigue and such bad shooting habits as flinching, loss of breath control, nervousness, and lack of attention to detail can be overcome greatly by wearing a good pair of earmuffs.

We all get tired at some point while shooting and there must be a reasonable limit to what we should try to do in one day. If such limits are not observed, all your preparations can be wasted due to a bad day at the range. The general guideline for light- to medium-recoiling firearms, such as the .270 Winchester, is about 70 to 80 rounds maximum at any one shooting session. This takes into account all the proper techniques, equipment, adjustments, and the necessary comforts while shooting. Since Jim has not fired the new rifle and has not yet zero-adjusted its telescopic sight, his situation is thus compounded, which is not uncommon.

Considering these factors, Jim's range firing should be split into two sessions. During the first session, he should adjust and zero the sights on the rifle while firing factory ammunition. Some trigger adjustment may be necessary and this should be performed prior to actual handload testing. This plan will allow the shooter plenty of time to become acquainted with the procedures, personnel, and rules at the range. Just as important, he will have time to zero the rifle and scope properly with fac-

tory ammunition without having to worry about anything else.

During the second session at the range, Jim would fire a few factory rounds and the tested handloads to establish his results. The second trip would be the most condensed shooting session, but also the most interesting and rewarding one.

For the purposes of this book, however, the two sessions will be treated as one to avoid confusion. The rifle will be fired with factory ammunition and the handloads and pressure-test rounds tested during a single range firing session. It is understood that you may have already zeroed your own firearm. If so, you can also meet your objectives with one trip to the range. Now let's get on with the business of loading the cartridges in our example.

Jim reviews the *Du Pont Handloader's Guide* and the *Sierra Bullets Reloading Manual;* these are the publications that fit his chosen handloading components. He looks for the maximum recommended charge weight for the powder chosen—Du Pont

When drying cases with compressed air, keep a rag between you and the nozzle. The cases may be clean, but the air may be dirty or force foreign matter into your skin.

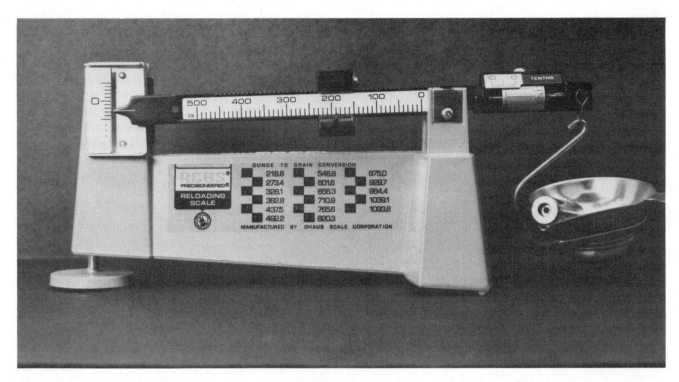

This scale is set for 194.3 grains. Whatever your standard, weigh the cases individually and separate those that don't measure up. Case weight is important to precision.

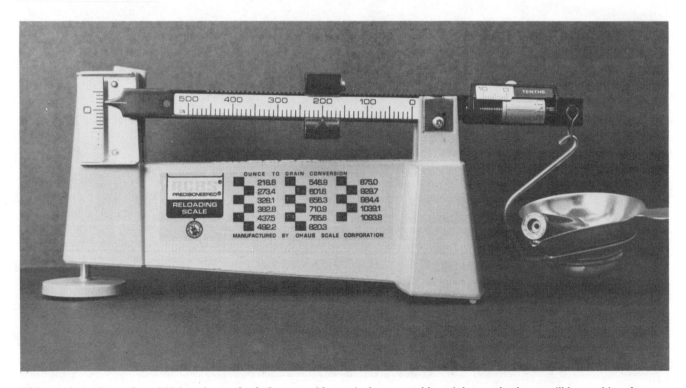

This case is too heavy for a 200.3-grain standard. Cases outside particular acceptable weight standards can still be used in other handloads, which have different parameters.

IMR 4831. The *Du Pont Guide* shows that a Remington 130-grain bullet can be loaded with up to 59.0 grains of IMR 4831 powder, but also indicates that this charge weight may require some compression. The *Sierra Bullets Reloading Manual* shows a maximum suggested charge weight of only 57.1 grains of IMR 4831 for the Sierra 130-grain bullet. Sierra also shows a recommended beginning charge weight of 52 grains of IMR 4831.

Knowing that guns vary, Jim decides to test charge weights from 52.0 through 60.0 grains. This will be done in ½-grain powder increments for successive loads. As each heavier load is fired, inspec-

tions and observations will be made for signs of excessive chamber pressure. Firing can be halted if or when too much pressure occurs. This is the best way to work up a handload. It will cover all ranges of loading and still be safe per objective 7, pressure.

The range of charge weights will be 9 grains, or 15 percent of the maximum charge weight. This is good because at least a 10 percent reduction from maximum charge weight is an accepted guide for most initial handload workups. Half-grain increases in propellant charges are changes of less than 1 percent of the mid-range loading weight. This is also good. It will determine precisely where

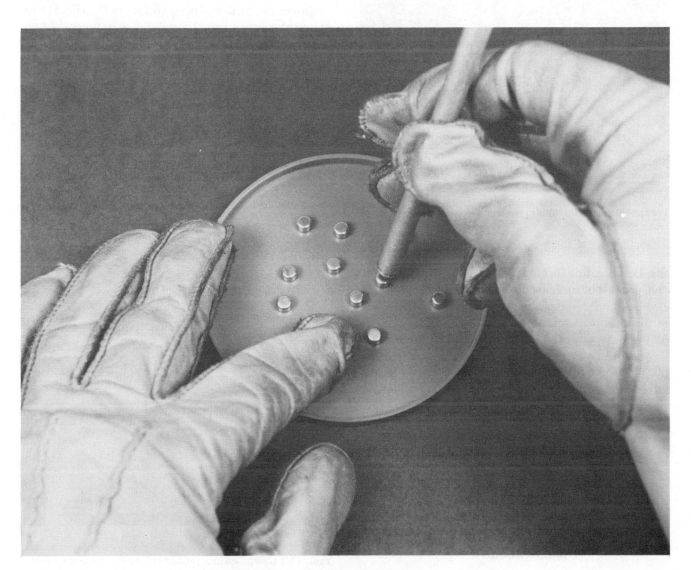

Primers *are not* positively 100 percent safe to handle; there's always the chance of an accident. Always wear safety glasses or goggles when handling primers. Leather gloves provide extra protection.

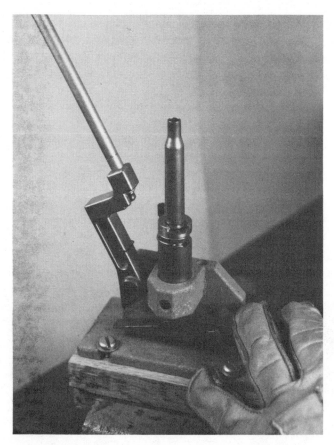

For consistent results, apply consistent force when seating primers.

cases with powder and seating the bullets—the making of a dummy round. A dummy round consists of only two components—a case and a bullet. It is a primerless, powderless case with a carefully seated bullet, which cannot be fired. A dummy round is used to speed the process of bullet seating for loading now and in the future. Now is the time to make it. Any of the cases that were eliminated due to incorrect weight may be used for the dummy round.

The sizing die is removed from the loading press and placed back into its container. We are now ready to use the bullet-seating die. Jim checks this die for any damage, then loosens the lock ring and removes the bullet-seating rod from the die. He inspects the seater plug to make sure of a good fit between the chosen bullets and the seater plug. After the die body is cleaned, the plug and rod are rein-

the best loading occurs. More will be said about charge weight increases in Chapter 6.

The handload data list is retrieved and Jim writes in the charge weights that he will test. They start at 52.0 grains, opposite load No. 1, and continue with 0.5-grain increases through the maximum load of 60.0 grains, opposite load No. 17. It should be realized that some of the heavy loads may never be fired if excessive pressure signs or diminishing target precision are observed. If so, those loads would be taken apart, the charges reduced to what has been found best, and the bullets reseated. Nothing will be wasted. Jim enters the date the loadings are prepared and the number 5 is entered in the column labeled, "no. rds" (number of rounds).

**Dummy Round**

Only one more job is required before filling the

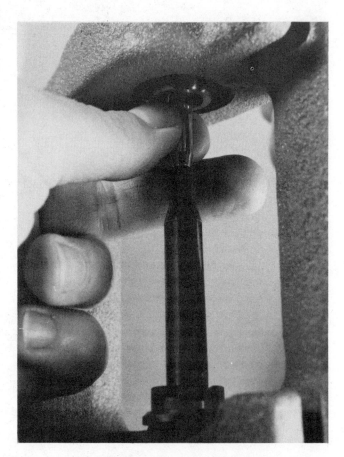

Guide the bullet into the seating die as you carefully raise the ram. This action captures the bullet between die and case. If you use other seating devices, like straight-line seaters, you have to adjust the method to the tool.

stalled into the die, with the plug in the uppermost position. For the time being, the seating die is left on the bench. The shell holder is placed back into the loading press. The dummy case is placed in the shell holder and raised to the top of the press stroke.

After ensuring that the bullet-seating rod is raised to the highest position in the seating die, Jim screws the seating die into the press until contact is felt between the die and the case mouth. He backs the die out of the press one-eighth of a turn (.009″) and adjusts the lock ring. Before the lock ring is tightened, the dummy round is removed and one or more steel washers are placed between the base of the seater die and the shell holder. The ram is raised in order to place some upward force on the seating die and properly align it as the lock ring is tightened. The washers act as shims to ensure contact between the shell holder and the seater die base. This is done for essentially the same reason as with the sizing die. The lock ring set screw is tightened to lock the adjustment. After the ram force on the die base is relaxed, a check is made to see that the lock ring is set properly but with enough freedom to permit removal of the seater die from the press. The washers are then removed. The dummy case is replaced and the bullet-seating adjustment proceeds. Jim lowers the ram and the cartridge case, partially inserts one of the component bullets into the case neck, and gently raises the ram and case back to the top position of the die. While the seating die holds the bullet in line with the case mouth, he turns the seater screw and plug down until contact is made with the bullet. At this point, we must pause again to make some more pertinent calculations.

Jim knows that the bullet-seater rod has a 1/4–28 thread. This means that the rod is 1/4″ in diameter and has 28 threads per inch of its length. It takes 28 turns to move the seater plug one inch. The bullets must also be seated at least 1/4″ into the case throat. This is for good bullet alignment and cartridge strength. A quarter-inch is also 1/4 of 28 turns of the seater die. This means that seven full turns of the seater die will move it up or down in the press exactly 1/4″. Therefore, the bullet-seater plug and rod must be screwed down about seven full turns to start. After such adjustment, he seats the bullet to this depth, removes the cartridge and brings the rifle to the loading bench.

While keeping the muzzle elevated, Jim slowly and carefully pushes the dummy round into the chamber of the rifle. This is done to keep the case head in contact with the bolt face as it is closed. If any bullet contact with the barrel is made before the bolt is fully closed, the cartridge will be withdrawn and the bullet seated deeper into the case. On the first try, contact is felt. Without forcing the bolt, the cartridge is carefully removed so as not to separate the case from the bullet and leave the bullet in the barrel.

Next, the seater plug is screwed down one turn (.036″). The bullet is "reseated" and placed into the chamber again. Once more, the fit is too tight. This checking, adjusting, and seating procedure is repeated until the dummy round can be fully chambered and the bolt closed and opened without pulling the bullet loose during extraction.

With the bench clear of powder, Jim lights a candle and smokes the bullet in the dummy round. This is done in the same manner as when adjusting the sizing die, described earlier. The bullet is smoked to find out how much contact or clearance exists between the bullet and the barrel lands. The rifling marks on the bullet are measured with the six-inch calipers. In this case, the marks are about .075″ long. Jim divides .075″ by .036″ to get a quotient of 2.1. This means that the bullet-seater plug must be screwed down about two full turns to seat the bullet to where it just touches the lands. This is done and the bullet is reseated and resmoked. Again, the round is carefully rechambered. After removing the round this time, it is found that minimal contact between the bullet and barrel lands now exists. Since he wants a bullet clearance of 1/16″ (0.63″), he calculates that the seater plug must be screwed down one and three-quarter turns more (.063 divided by .036 = 1.75 turns). This is done, the seater ring locked, and the bullet fully seated into the dummy round. Jim now labels the dummy round with an indelible marker. This identifies which bullet the dummy round contains and the bullet weight. He writes "Sierra #1860-130 grain" on the case. The dummy round can be used again to quickly reset the bullet-seating die should the die be disassembled for cleaning or used to seat other bullets. For now, the die is left in the press as we must finish the job of loading cartridges.

The dummy round is measured for overall length. The COAL (cartridge overall length) is

3.205″. This length is satisfactory. It is less than the maximum specified COAL for the .270 Winchester, which is 3.340″ maximum. The length of this handloaded dummy round leaves proper space in the rifle magazine and helps to satisfy handloading objective 6, correct functioning. The COAL is entered on the handload data list and Jim is now ready to charge the cases with powder, seat the bullets, and complete loading.

### Powder Charging and Bullet Seating

To prevent errors, leave all primed cases mouth down in the loading tray, except for those already loaded and those being loaded. To begin, the first row of five cases is turned mouth up. Next, a can of Du Pont IMR 4831 powder of the correct lot number is taken from storage. Jim zeroes the powder scale and sets it to read 52.0 grains. This is the correct weight for load No. 1. Now he secures the powder measure in the bench vise and fills the powder

trickler with powder. Some powder is then poured slowly into the scale pan until the indicator begins to move. The trickler is used to add powder into the pan until a balance is achieved at 52.0 grains. This occurs when the scale indicator reaches zero.

While looking down through the hopper on the powder measure, he turns the charging handle until the hole in the powder drum is visible. The 52.0 grains of powder in the scale pan is poured into the hopper. Now the charging handle is placed halfway between the "pick up" and "throw" positions. This closes the mouth of the metering drum but prevents powder from falling out of the measure. Next, Jim closes the adjustment screw on the measure drum until firm contact is made with the powder charge itself. This removes air space and adjusts the drum to the powder charge. In this position, the powder measure will throw a charge slightly lighter than the one used to set the measure.

Turning the handle slightly, Jim pours the first charge in the measure into case 1. This case is placed in the loading tray. Next, the powder hop-

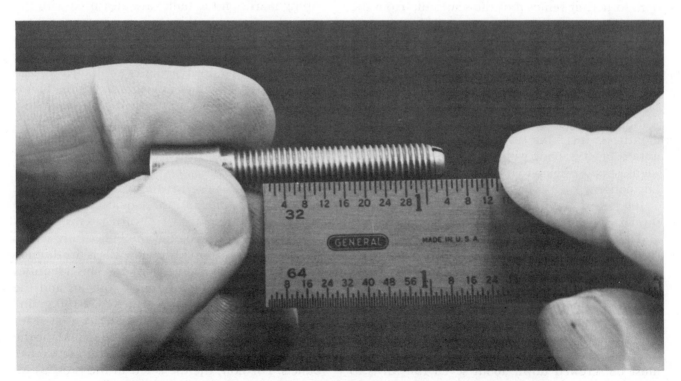

This is a bullet-seating plug. Bullet-seating adjustments are made with the screw threads. Shown is a ¼–28 thread. Twenty-eight complete turns are needed to move the seater one inch. One turn moves it ¹⁄₂₈ or 0.036 inch.

per is filled and a charge is thrown into the scale pan. After the pan is placed back onto the scale, the powder trickler is used to bring the weight up to exactly 52.0 grains. This charge is dumped into case 2, using a powder funnel. The same procedure is used with the other three cases on row one. As soon as these cases are filled, Jim inspects to see that each case received a charge. He seats a bullet in each case, using the adjusted seating die in the loading press. He places a check mark by load No. 1 on his handload data list to signify completion of that load number.

Before the next loading is begun, the powder meter screw is opened slightly to increase the charge weight. The powder scale is set to 52.5 grains for load No. 2. The next row of five empty cases is turned mouth up and they receive the second charge weight. Bullets are seated in these cases also. This procedure is used to handload all the test cartridges. Jim has 17 test loads of five rounds each. He prepares a total of 85 handloaded cartridges. As each load number is completed, the five cartridges

are placed into a cartridge box. Their location in the box is cross-referenced to their load number on a piece of paper. This is to prevent confusion and errors. After all the test cartridges are loaded, the powder scale is reset to zero (0.0 grains) to verify that the scale was not moved out of calibration during use.

As during case inspection, each completed round is rolled on a glass surface to see if any bullets were seated crookedly. If any bullets are found to be seated poorly, the round must be disassembled and the components placed into another, better case. Bent case necks cause most bullet-seating problems.

After this final loading test, verify that all cartridges have been placed correctly into their box in the same order that they appear on the handload data list. Pour the unused powder from the trickler and powder measure hopper back into the factory can and replace the cap. The powder canister and unused bullets are put back into storage along with the unused primers. Two more things are still needed to complete the loading bench chores.

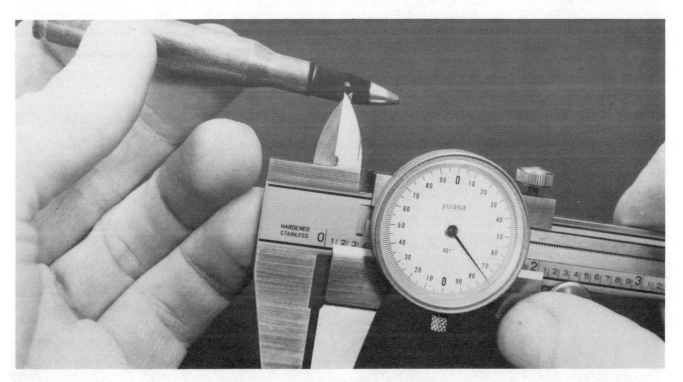

By using the barrel land marks on a dummy round, exact seating adjustments can be made. The mark here shows .075 inch of contact. This plus the clearance is used to adjust the bullet-seater plug.

## Pressure-Test Rounds

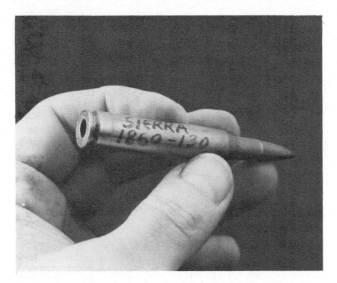

A dummy round is used to adjust the bullet-seater quickly. Powderless and primerless, a dummy round is a two-component cartridge; the bullet is simply loaded into a sized case. Every dummy round should be marked to show the exact bullet it holds.

There are still ten disassembled factory cartridges with which to deal. These were the rounds used to determine the weight standards for factory cases, factory bullets, and factory powder charge weights.

Using the loading tools, Jim reassembles five of the factory cartridges back into their original condition. He is careful to reseat the bullets to their original depth. The other five sets of factory cartridge components will be used in a different way. They will be used to assemble the pressure-test rounds.

At some point in testing, relative handload pressure must be determined. This is done by comparing handload case expansion against expansion due to factory ammunition pressure. This can be done with closely matched cases that have been sized in the same sizing die. Jim must load the five remain-

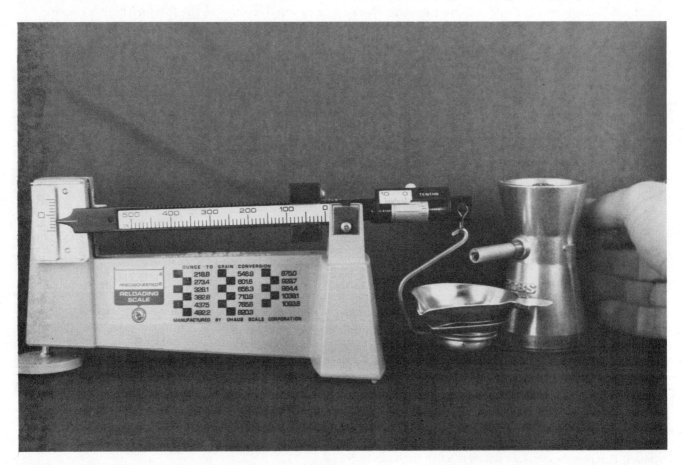

A powder trickler drops powder granules one at a time. This is the fastest way to reach exact weight for test ammunition.

ing sets of factory bullets, primers, and powder into five of the selected cases for handloading. This is a practical way to compare handload pressure fairly against factory pressure. This is explained fully in Chapter 8.

Jim uses the priming tool to carefully prime these five selected cases with the five factory primers. After doing this, each factory powder charge is carefully placed into one of the selected cases. Finally, he reseats the factory bullets into these cases. The factory bullets are carefully reseated to thesame depth as they were seated in the factory cases. These five specially prepared pressure-test cartridges will be used to achieve objective 7, proper, consistent, and safe pressure. In addition, these five pressure-test rounds will also help achieve objective 4, consistency. These five cartridges are also placed into the cartridge box and labeled appropriately on the piece of paper enclosed therein. They must also be cross-referenced with the handload data list.

Inspect the first completed round carefully. Verify that seating depth is correct. Measure the cartridge overall length (COAL) and enter this on the handload data list.

### Case Head Diameter

There is still one more thing to do before work at the bench is completed.

Case head diameter measuring remains to be done. At random, five of the handloaded cartridges are selected and their case head diameters measured with a micrometer, one at a time. After each is measured it is replaced in its box before the next cartridge is checked. In this way there should be no possibility of rounds being put back into the wrong spaces.

The average case head diameter for this batch of handloads is 0.4656″. This figure is entered on the handload data list in the "Case" block at the top of the sheet.

The boxes of carefully prepared handloads and pressure-test rounds can now be put away until it's time to go to the range. The loading bench is tidied

Use a consistent system or routine when charging the cases. Make sure that all powder gets into the case. If you're not sure, empty the case completely and start again.

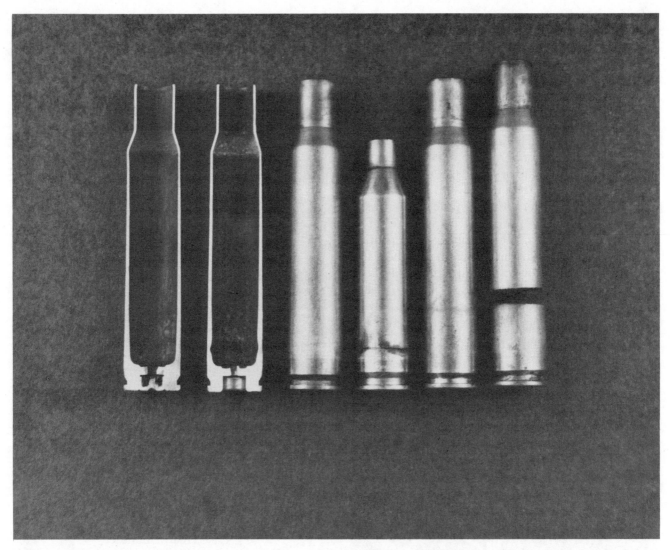

The two cut-away cases show normal (left), and stretched condition (right). The complete cases show different degrees of head separation from incipient to actual. Different brands will stretch at different points. This condition is almost always due to improper sizing or bad chamber fit. High pressure is seldom the cause.

up and all the equipment is returned to its storage area.

At last, Jim can take off his safety glasses. The lengthy job of preparing handloads for testing is now complete.

### Equipment for Handloading

Safety glasses
Firearm
Reloading press with shell holder and ram
Reloading dies

Powder scale (with approximate 500-grain capacity)
Powder measure
Powder trickler
Powder funnel
Case neck brush
Case pad
Case loading blocks
Case trimmer
Deburring (chamfering) tool
Calipers (vernier or dial—read to 0.001")
Micrometer (read to 0.0001")
Primer flip tray

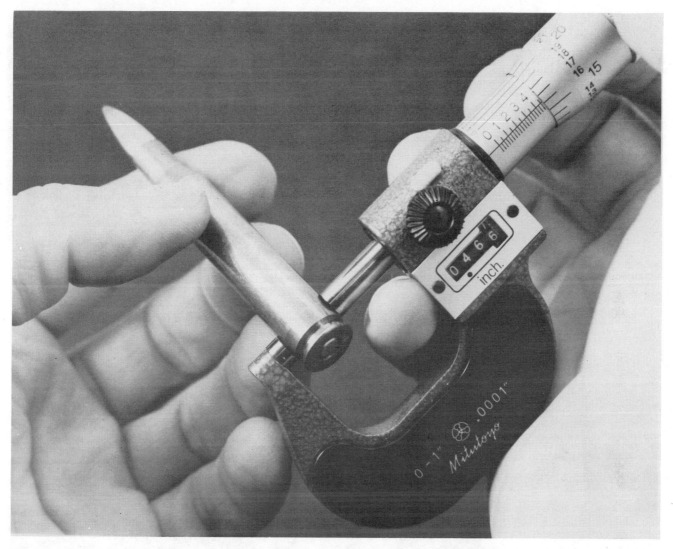

Measuring sized case heads with a micrometer. The case should be measured at three points and averaged. Use at least five cases for an overall average. This measure will be used to compare pressures. Enter the average diameter on the handload data list.

Primer pocket cleaner
Priming tool (hand- or bench-type)
Bullet puller
Metal cleaning tray (for washing cases)
Cartridge boxes
Desk calculator (with mean and standard deviation functions)
Flat surface (plate glass) 6″ × 12″ or larger

## Materials and Supplies for Handloading

Brass cases

Powder
Primers
Bullets
Factory ammunition
Patches and cleaning rods
Gun oil and grease
Case sizing lubricant
Rags
Solvent (Naphtha, M.E.K., lacquer thinner, etc.)
Powder solvent
Detergent (liquid)
Note paper

Candle
Matches
Newspaper (for case drying)
Handload data list
Precision graph
Velocity graph
Pressure graph
Targets
Labels

During and after loading, be sure to record the exact location of all test rounds. They should be placed into containers in the same sequence as needed for range firing. This helps prevent mistakes and loss of data.

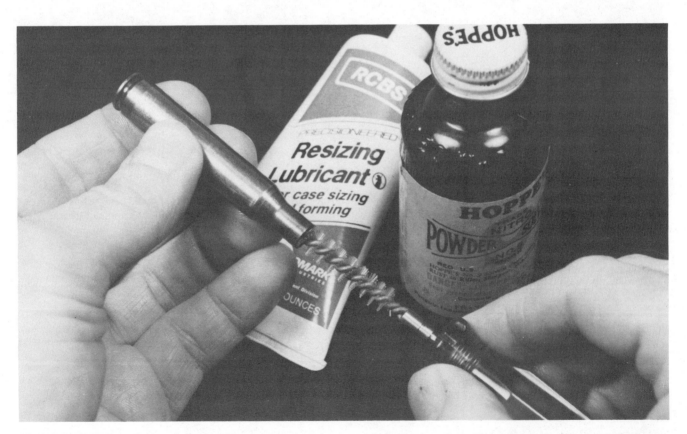

After cleaning the inside and outside of the neck with a powder solvent, grease the inside of the neck with a brush. The lube will be removed before loading.

# Chapter 5

# At the Range

In the last chapter you "observed" Jim as he prepared handloaded ammunition at the loading bench. In this chapter you will follow him to the shooting range and learn the range requirements needed to meet the intermediate objectives. Range procedures will be conducted in three basic phases: preparation for firing, firing, and actions after firing—all with safety in mind.

We are approaching the point where our efforts will begin to produce positive, visible results. So that those efforts won't be wasted, certain actions must occur at the shooting range, actions that are critical in achieving intermediate objectives 1, 2, 4, and 7.

In one respect, the procedures offered in this chapter are among the easiest to grasp. If you follow a good checklist and use good shooting techniques, you will make definite progress in meeting your objectives.

In another respect, this chapter can be difficult

for some handloaders. That's because one skill is required here that cannot be achieved by studying a text and tables—that is the skill of shooting. More precisely, you must be reasonably competent on the range and also be able to use the basic aids of the benchrest shooter.

If you feel that bench shooting is not one of your stronger talents, I recommend doing one of two things: find a competent shooter who is willing to fire your handloads in your gun using the procedures outlined in this chapter; or improve your own benchrest shooting skills before firing your test loads. To begin self-improvement, first read a good book on the subject, Warren Page's *The Accurate Rifle*, for instance. Next, find a good instructor who is willing to teach you. Listen to him and practice what you learn. The skills are not difficult to acquire. A session or two at the shooting bench should prepare you adequately. A .22 rimfire rifle and a 50-yard range are all that's needed to learn the skills of benchrest shooting.

For the purposes of this text, at least, it is assumed that the reader is reasonably experienced and competent at the shooting bench. The following pages divide range shooting into three broad categories: before firing; during firing; after firing.

## Before Firing

Several things must be considered before any range shooting can begin: selection of the shooting facility itself; the necessary equipment and supplies; and something that we'll call weather decision, for want of a better name.

Whether you use a public facility or construct your own shooting range, there are a number of points worthy of discussion for successful results and ease of operation. These points are: range availability, location, access, cost, size, facilities, layout, procedures, and safety.

One of the greatest problems shooters have is finding a place to shoot. Land use, public opinion, legalities, and costs have combined to make shooting more difficult for all of us. But where shooting facilities do exist and you have some choice, it is important that the following concerns be investigated. They can save you time, labor, and money. This is a direct concern of intermediate objective 8, expense. And, it makes sense.

First is location. If two shooting facilities are similar, the closest one is probably the better choice.

Second is the matter of access. Not only should entry to a shooting range be easy, but you also must be able to use the range at your convenience.

Most public ranges charge a fee. Private clubs require membership or both a fee and membership. If you plan to use the range only once, the membership fee may be excessive. If you will use the range several times during the year, individual usage fees may be of greater concern. Compare the costs.

Observe the types of shooters using the ranges. Sometimes the shooting may not be compatible with your own requirements for testing. For example, if the range authorities allow more than one type of shooting to go on simultaneously, you may find it difficult to test your handloads properly. In addition, some ranges may have restrictions that make testing difficult or impossible.

Range size is a factor, too, not in regards to the number of shooting positions, but rather to range depth. A 100-yard range is satisfactory for most high-powered rifle shooting. A 25- to 50-yard range is big enough for handgun testing. But extra space is required for driveways, parking, buildings, windbreaks, backstops, trenches, and the necessary separation of the range from adjoining private property.

The range itself should be laid out along a shooting line that coincides with the prevailing winds of the area. This direction line can be determined in a number of ways. The National Weather Service, local Chamber of Commerce, local newspapers, and almanacs supply this information. Another simple way for determining range layout is to look at an aviation chart for the area. Airport runway direction is shown on these charts. Most runways will follow the prevailing wind direction. If the range is constructed along the direction of these winds, your chances for crosswind interference on any windy day are reduced. Crosswind makes shooting and testing difficult. A range that is aligned with the prevailing winds will receive mostly tailwinds or headwinds, which cause far fewer shooting problems than crosswinds. Sometimes natural terrain is also used to advantage as a windbreak. Hills and valleys can provide natural silencing as well. But the winds are your first concern.

If the range is 200 yards or more in depth, there should be a safe access road for target changing by car. The time it takes to walk 400 yards or more round trip for a target change is frustrating for other shooters, and may have a negative effect on your own shooting.

Any shooting range must have a backstop and public ranges should have overhead baffles. This is a good idea for any range. Baffles prevent overshooting of the target backstop and accidents beyond the range property.

A shooting range should include some type of target backboard or frame for easy target placement, and at the same level as the shooting bench. As for target frame designs, there are many and most are adequate; however, any target frame should be made of wood and paper products only. This is for the safety of the shooter and all others

A large, well-run public range is an asset for local shooters. It can provide recreation and training for thousands of people every year. This is Elm Fork Shooting Park near Dallas, Texas. Note the overhead baffles to prevent over-shooting the target backstop.

on the range. Metal frames and targets can cause bullet deflection and accidents.

Parking should be far enough from the firing points so as not to interfere with the shooter's concentration. It's also nice when the parking lot is situated so that cars and trucks don't throw dust on the shooting area.

The firing points may be open, covered, or even enclosed in a shooting house. But the benches at each shooting point must always be solidly built. Benches should be about 33 inches high and their chairs or stools should be adjustable for shooters of different heights.

If the shooting range is private and you're there alone, operating procedure is of less concern than at a public range. But a shooting facility hosting more than one shooter at a time must have an enforced range procedure. This is for two reasons. Reason number one is safety. Reason number two is the operating needs that occur when more than one shooter is using a range. The more shooters, the greater the need for an enforced procedure. Furthermore, range procedures can't be enforced for the safety, comfort, and pleasure of others unless a designated person is appointed and present during all firing activities. This safety person must not be bound by any other duties and responsibilities. Range safety is always the most important consideration, whether the range contains one shooter or a thousand shooters. The need for safety is always there. It just becomes more obvious as the number of shooters increases. The same is true of range operating procedures. Good, simple range procedures are essential.

The preceding considerations are basic to range evaluation, and most, if not all, of these prerequisites should be a part of the range you choose. Range planning and construction is an involved subject filling volumes on civilian and military bookshelves. This kind of information is available from the National Rifle Association, the branches of the military, and the different shooting organizations. Range construction is beyond the scope of this book but range selection is the prerogative of the handloader.

Next comes equipment and supplies you'll need at the range. Each of these items is included in the checklist at the end of this chapter. Making a checklist is the best method I know to ensure that you have all the things you need to conduct your firing properly. The list is self-explanatory and I won't bore you by repeating all of the items one by one.

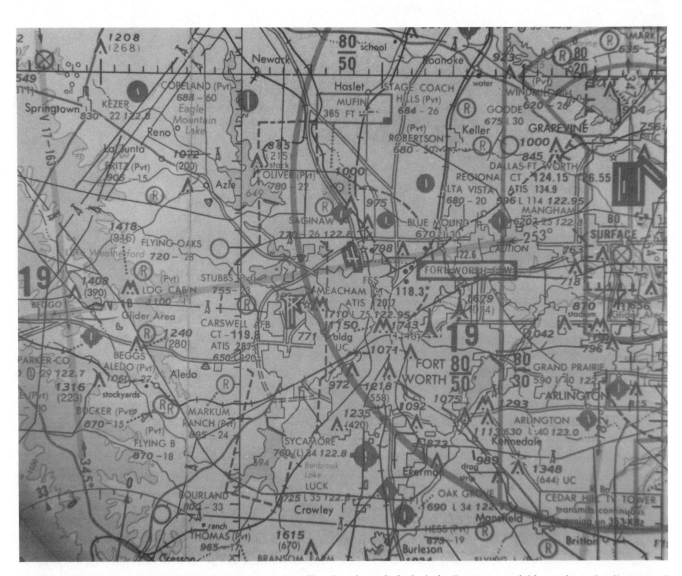

This sectional air chart used for navigation shows runway directions in each dark circle. Runways are laid out along the direction of prevailing winds in the area. Shooting ranges should be, too.

Precision Handloading

A safety official is an absolute must when two or more shooters are using the range. The range officer keeps things moving and under safe control so that everyone gets the most from his time on the line.

Rather, each item will be discussed as it is used by Jim, who will soon be joining us again.

Weather conditions are of vital importance to the range shooter. He is basically concerned with four weather factors: wind, temperature, visibility, and precipitation. These four things determine if range firing can be conducted successfully, while obtaining good, correct data. Every shooter will have to make his own "go" or "no go" decision regarding weather.

Wind is the most difficult weather factor to contend with when firing for precision. But wind can be tolerated up to a point. In fact, you must learn to live with a little wind because there is always some of it, even on calm days. The important thing is to recognize how much wind is too much and how much wind is tolerable. It is also important to understand how wind affects shooting at various distances, more than you might think.

A ten-mile-per-hour crosswind will deflect a 30-caliber 150-grain bullet, fired at 2,800 feet per second, almost 1 inch in the first 100 yards. A crosswind of 20 mph will push the bullet sideways twice as much—nearly 2 inches. A 50-grain 22-caliber bullet with the same velocity would be deflected almost twice as much as the 30-caliber bullet, given the same crosswinds. A 300-grain .375-caliber bullet would be deflected less than either of the above two bullets, but almost as much as the 30-caliber bullet. These examples indicate the measurable effect of crosswind on bullets and the relative effects of crosswinds on bullets of different weights.

If shooting distances are increased to 200 and 300 yards, the effect of the crosswind becomes remarkable. For example, that same 30-caliber bullet, which drifted off-line 1 inch at 100 yards, will be deflected nearly 4 inches at 200 yards by a 10-mph wind. This is four times greater, although the distance has only doubled. At 300 yards, the deflection will be almost ten times as great. Crosswinds affect lighter bullets traveling at slower speeds even more dramatically.

If you think the ten-mile wind effect at 100, 200, and 300 yards is bad, think about this. A 20-mph wind doubles the ten-mile effect. A 30-mph wind triples the effect at each yardage. A 30-mph crosswind will deflect the 30-caliber bullet about 2.5 inches at 100 yards. At 200 and 300 yards, the wind causes deflections of 10.5 and 24.6 inches respectively. Those figures are also fourfold and tenfold increases. This is far too much for precision shooting. For this reason, consider 100 yards to be about the greatest usable distance for testing handloads under any wind condition.

Interestingly, 100 yards is about the minimum range needed to see the effects of small loading differences on target precision. Except for some sight adjustment concerns, expect to do most target work with a high-powered rifle at 100 yards, and the crosswind influence should be no more than 12 to 15 mph. If winds are gusty, cut the allowable wind velocity to 6 or 7 mph. Gusty winds are not only much harder to judge, but they also create an additional problem. They cause extra motion for the shooter sitting at the bench. If you restrict your test firing to 100 yards, and under the maximum wind tolerances, you can develop good data on slightly windy days. If the wind exceeds these tolerances, don't go to the range for testing. You will only waste ammunition, time, effort, and money. You will set your project behind schedule if time is a factor.

Some shooters may ask, "Why test outdoors at all if wind is so important?" That's a good question and I'll try to answer it. First, few of us have access to covered or underground ranges. We must use outdoor ranges. Second, under reasonable wind conditions, there is a method to eliminate the effect of wind from your test data. In Chapter 6, you will learn how targets can be measured to compensate for and eliminate wind effects.

The next area of weather concern is temperature. Temperature extremes, both heat and cold, can have negative effects on shooting results. Heat can be exhausting to shooters not used to it, and it bothers all shooters to some extent. But the effects of heat on the shooter can be overcome if firing positions are shaded and the shooter goes about his business in a calm manner, with rest and water breaks.

Besides fatigue, heat produces target mirage, which is an optical effect caused by temperature differences in the atmosphere. Mirage makes precision shooting difficult because the target appears to move.

On a 100-yard grass range, a hot day may cause little mirage. On a sandy, reflective surface range, the mirage effects can be considerable, even at 100 yards. This is not conducive to the type of shooting required to achieve your objectives. At ranges of 200 yards and more, mirage is almost always a factor, regardless of ground cover or temperature.

Hot days and overheated barrels can cause a telescopic sight picture to become distorted. The effect is very much like a mirage, and results in poor shooting. This is another reason why shooting must be conducted at a pace to prevent excess barrel heat. On a warm day, the shooting pace must be slowed.

The effects of cold temperatures on shooting are less pronounced than those of heat. Mirage is less a factor on cold days. But midday sunshine seems to multiply the mirage effect in winter. Extreme cold can tire the shooter also. But both of these situations are extremes. A cold, calm, clear day presents the most nearly ideal conditions for good precision shooting. If the shooter dresses properly, excellent results can be achieved.

A third weather factor is visibility. Precision shooting is difficult, if not impossible, under poor visibility conditions. If you can't see the target, you can't hit it.

The greatest visibility concern is diminished light, but fog, haze, smog, dust, and smoke can add to visibility problems.

Don't start shooting too early or too late. You may have difficulties with dim light and fog when starting too early. If you start shooting too late, you can run out of time and fail to test all your handloads under the same circumstances.

Precipitation is the fourth weather factor to consider. Rain, snow, and sleet are a source of ballistic concern and shooter concern. Studies have been made on the effects of rain on the bullet's flight. The conclusions indicate that rain has little, if any, effect on exterior ballistics. The greatest problem caused by rain, snow, or sleet is interference with the shooter's concentration. All these forms of precipitation cause problems of sight picture distortion, discomfort, target damage, and nuisances at the shooting bench. Each problem has a negative effect on good shooting. Use a rainy or snowy day for other chores, not shooting.

The above four weather factors—wind, temperature, visibility, precipitation—can be listed in any order of importance. They are all factors to consider before firing test ammunition. If any one is too great, don't shoot. You'll waste the time you've already spent. In addition, you may have to load more test ammunition and refire. All of this defeats objective 8, expense.

Try to find a 100-yard grass range, oriented with the prevailing winds of the area. Use it on calm, clear days, under the coolest, brightest conditions possible. That's asking for a nearly optimum situation, but if you restrict your testing to the best environment, you will obtain the best results. Good results can be obtained under less than these ideal conditions but that requires some experience. The ideal situation is only mentioned as a standard for comparison. Sometimes, you'll hit it lucky.

The subject of weather brings another question to mind: "Which time of the year is best for handload testing?" The answer, ideally, is to test when weather conditions are most like those during your hunting situation. For instance, if the handloaded ammunition is going to be used for hunting in the fall, you may find that similar weather conditions

Good facilities, good schedules, and conscientious officers are needed for success in organized shooting. When the elements are all there, membership grows and top-notch shooters emerge. This photo shows a match in progress at the Dallas Pistol Club, Carrollton, Texas.

exist in your area in the late winter or early spring. Furthermore, if a handload is developed in the months of March, April, or May, it will be prepared well in advance of the coming fall hunting season. You will have one less preparation to make before that big hunt.

Late winter and early spring shooting sessions provide another bonus. Most outdoor shooting ranges have much less traffic then. This slack period can provide a real plus for the handloader. Fewer shooters and lower restrictions often make testing easier and provide better results.

### During Firing

One of your first concerns at the range is sight adjustment. Most high-powered hunting rifles are equipped with telescopic sights. Therefore, this section discusses procedures at the range that fit scope-sighted rifles. If your rifle or handgun is equipped with metallic sights, changes in procedures should be obvious. If your firearm is equipped with both metallic sights and a telescopic sight, you may wish to sight it in with the metallic sights first as security in case of scope damage. This is a good idea. It could save a long-awaited and expensive hunting trip.

Chances are the metallic sights were zeroed at the factory. That doesn't mean the factory adjustment is right for you, however. Follow the manufacturer's instructions for the rifle or handgun to adjust the sights properly. If instructions aren't available, just remember this: move the rear sight in the same direction you wish to move bullet strike on the target. If you want your shots to hit more to the right, move the rear sight to the right. It's that simple. The same holds true for elevation, both up and down adjustments. If you want a higher point of impact on the target, raise the rear sight higher. Take a shot or two at 25 yards to see where the bullets hit. They'll strike about the same height at 100 yards. The horizontal point of impact will be in the same direction from the center of the target, but four times as far if the sight is out of zero. All of the above pertains to metallic or iron sights only.

Mounting a telescopic sight is also done best by following the instructions of the scope maker and the mount maker. First check that the scope reticle (cross hairs) is centered in its vertical and horizontal travel. Do this by halving the total number of turns for both reticle adjustment screws. Turn the screw left or right until it stops. Now turn the screw in the opposite direction until it stops, but carefully count the number of turns or clicks required to complete its movement. Divide the turns or clicks by two. Now turn the adjustment screw back in the opposite direction this amount of turns or clicks. The reticle is now centered. Do the same for the other reticle as well.

Place the scope mount and the rings on the rifle securely, according to the maker's instructions. Then mount the scope where you get full field of view. This means that the scope eyepiece is completely filled with an image and without dark spots. This adjustment is made by simply sliding the scope forward or backward through loose rings. This adjustment should also provide maximum eye relief. This means that the scope eyepiece is far enough away from your eye for good safety. A scope that's mounted with too little eye relief can give you a nasty cut when the rifle recoils.

Ensure that the verticle reticle (horizontal adjustment) is aligned with the rifle bore center as the scope rings are tightened. This is important for good sight-to-bore alignment.

Focus the reticle with the eyepiece. A correct focus gives a clear image of the field of view and the reticle.

Next, use a collimator or simply bore sight, to bring the crossed reticle center and barrel center close to the same point of aim. Bore sighting can be done on bolt action rifles by removing the bolt. Look down the bore and align it while supporting the rifle on sandbags. Next, adjust the scope mount until the cross hairs align with the same point of aim. This is the coarse adjustment. The reticle adjustment screws are used to make fine adjustments. If an excess amount of adjustment is required, something's wrong. Verify that the correct scope mounts and rings have been installed on the rifle. If the mounts are correct and the scope elevation reticle must be adjusted near or beyond its vertical limit, use a brass or steel shim under the mount on the rifle. This should be done by bringing the centered reticle close to the point of target alignment. The elevation and windage adjustments should be used for fine adjustment only after rough adjustment has brought bullet impact within 2 inches of the desired impact point on a 25-yard target. This is roughly equivalent to 8 inches on the same target at 100 yards.

While still on the subject of telescopic sights, in recent years the trend has been to higher and higher scope mounts. There are several reasons for this but not many good ones. The best scope mount on a sporting rifle is the lowest mount that still allows bolt opening and closing. There are a lot of reasons for this also, all good ones. They have to do with accuracy, ballistic calculation, and best shooting results. Unfortunately, a low scope mount usually requires removal of the iron sights. The tradeoff is worth it for most shooters.

The rifle bore and chamber should be cleaned of grease and oil with a gun solvent and then wiped dry with a clean patch. Don't lubricate the chamber or the bore after this cleaning. The rifle is now ready for precision firing. Next, the bench must be prepared for shooting.

You will need some aids for bench shooting:

a. A seat or chair of the correct height (rigid or adjustable)
b. A forearm rest or sandbags to support the forend portion of the gun stock
c. A rear stock rest or sandbags for the toe portion of a rifle or the butt of a handgun

d. The right size screwdriver or coin for scope adjustment. Metallic sights may require special tools.

e. A good pair of shooting glasses, hearing protection, a hat or cap or sun visor, targets, thumbtacks or loaded stapler, and a pair of binoculars or spotting scope if your rifle scope is 6X or less. A pair of 7X binoculars provides easier viewing of the target than a 7X rifle scope. It can often eliminate walks to the target area. A spotting scope of 20X–32X is very nice but not necessary, if you proceed carefully.

If the rifle has not been zeroed, begin sight adjustment at a range of 25 yards. It is much easier to bore sight and rough zero a rifle at 25 yards before firing it at 100 yards. Your chances for striking the paper target with the first setting are much greater at the short range. A 25-yard range is very convenient for another reason also. When zeroed at 25 yards, most high-powered rifles will strike near the same point of impact on that target out at 100 yards. That's a ballistic fact. This means that if you zero your rifle at 25 yards first, you should be very close to the mark when you fire at 100 yards. Very little, if any, adjustment will be required.

The first round that strikes the 25-yard target is used as a reference for further adjustment. Remember that four times as much scope adjustment is required for a point-of-impact change at 25 yards as at 100 yards. This is true for both windage and elevation adjustments. Another way to remember this is that every one-inch change in bullet strike at 25 yards gives a four-inch change at 100 yards. In addition, most modern, high-velocity hunting rifles should be zeroed at 100 yards so bullet impact is about 2 or 3 inches above the point of aim while still aligned horizontally with this point. A two- or three-inch-high point of impact at 100 yards should hit close to the point of aim at 200 yards. Bullet strike generally will be below this point at greater ranges. This sighting technique provides a longer point-blank range for shooting. It takes advantage of the flat shooting characteristics of high-powered rifles; there's less need to compensate for bullet drop.

Where the bullet will strike above the aiming point can be calculated precisely once the velocity of the ammunition is known. For your testing, anything between 2 and 3 inches is fine. Once zero has

been accomplished at the 25-yard range, place a target at 100 yards. Now zero the rifle and scope carefully with the factory ammunition you will use as your standard of comparison. A fine adjustment can only be made after the handload is chosen, exact velocities known, and appropriate ballistic tables have been consulted. If the bullet strike is about 2 or 3 inches high at 100 yards, the rifle is properly zeroed with factory ammunition.

All of the above should be in order before you fire the test handloads. If your rifle has already been zeroed with factory ammunition, so much the better. If not, you should plan on spending a separate afternoon at the range. This ensures that scope mounting, zeroing, and any other necessary rifle adjustments are made before your test firing and data gathering. This includes settings and trigger adjustments as well. Retain a minimum of 15 unfired factory cartridges for comparison during the period of handload testing. This requirement plus the need for zero and pressure-test rounds usually takes about two boxes (40 cartridges) of factory-loaded ammunition.

During handload testing, we will be after three vital pieces of information about the handloads and the factory ammunition: first, we want to find which handloads achieve the highest precision; second, which handloads produce the greatest velocity; and third, compare pressure developed by the handloads against factory ammunition.

There are two basic methods for this kind of testing. The first method is to fire factory and handloaded ammunition for precision and pressure, in the meantime measuring bullet velocity on a chronograph.

The second method requires two trips to the range. Handloads are tested for precision and pressure on the first trip, but not velocity. After the most precise handloads are determined, more ammunition is prepared and chronographed along with factory ammunition for velocity data during a second testing period on another day. Both methods have advantages and disadvantages.

The first testing method involves measuring handloads for velocity while shooting for precision; however, this method has its disadvantages. For instance, unless you have one of the modern chronographs that uses light-sensitive sensors, you must replace circuit screens after every shot. Once a screen is broken by a bullet, it must be discarded since it will no longer conduct electricity. This requirement interrupts good benchrest shooting techniques and the ability to collect precision data. Even if you have a modern, light-sensitive chronograph, the necessity of recording and resetting the machine after each shot is not conducive to the best target shooting.

Furthermore, even if your chronograph automatically resets and records shots by itself, you may still encounter problems trying to fire for target precision while recording velocity data. Unless you have had a good deal of experience operating the chronograph under similar circumstances, you may find this method a bit cumbersome. On the positive side, chronographing test loads while firing for precision is beneficial in two ways: one is that you can obtain all your data (targets for precision, cases for pressure, and chronograph readings for velocity) in a single session at the range. The second is that your velocity readings will be taken on the same day, under the same shooting and weather conditions, and with the same exact cartridges as your precision targets, which will be measured and compared for the best accuracy potential. This last fact is a decided

The view from the bench shows the bullet path over the chronograph screens to the target. With some screens, several targets can be posted to save time. Note the sandbag arrangement. Sandbags can be made at home using empty lead shot canvas bags, or something similar.

Precision Handloading

advantage for sure, comparative results. It is such an advantage, this method is recommended if: (a) you are able to do both things—shoot well and operate a light-sensitive chronograph; or (b) you have a helper to record velocity data and change screens.

In the second testing method, a separate shooting session for precision and pressure data is required. You fire your test handloads for best target precision and relative pressure only on the first trip. Some factory ammunition is also fired for precision. The chronograph is not used during this session. After that, targets and cases are measured and graphed (as will be described in Chapters 6 and 8). From this information, a few selected test loads are duplicated. A second trip is made to the range. The duplicate handloads and more factory ammunition are fired through the chronograph for velocity.

The disadvantages of this method are that you're not determining precision and velocity results under the same exact conditions of weather and atmosphere, or with the same exact ammunition. You will be comparing precision and velocity for similar, but not the same, cartridges. Different factors of shooting and weather conditions will exist. Second, and of lesser importance, you'll have to make a second trip to the range, set up your equipment, and refire more ammunition. This usually requires buying another box of factory ammo. All of this adds to the cost of your handloading project and detracts from loading objective 8. This is the objective that stresses a minimum expenditure in time, labor, materials, and money for testing.

On the positive side, the second method has some points that make it a superior method for some shooters. First, you can concentrate on your best bench shooting techniques to develop positive data in the form of precision targets while carefully observing pressure in the handloads. Secondly, and of importance to many shooters, you may be able to accomplish objective 2 without the need to purchase a chronograph or borrow one for a whole day. Since you will be testing only a few rounds for velocity, you may be able to use a chronograph from a shooting club or have a friend fire your selected handloads the next time he sets up his own equipment. This possibility is more in keeping with objective 8, even though excellent, inexpensive chronographs are now available.

For the purpose of instruction in this text, our range procedure will be explained as if we are firing for precision and velocity on the same day as in the first method explained above. The seen, felt, and heard observations for pressure will be made at the beginning of firing for each new load. You can use a micrometer for a quick check of cartridge head expansion if you already know what expansion occurs with factory loads.

The second method of handload testing, as offered here, requires little change in procedure. Shooting for precision and pressure is separated from chronographing for velocity into two separate firing periods on separate days. Pressure checks must be made regardless of which method is used. With the assistance of our friend, Jim, who has been waiting patiently, let's begin firing. Again, we'll watch his every step.

After arriving at the range, Jim checks the weather. The wind is calm. The air is cool, lighting conditions are good, and no rain or snow is falling. He reports to the range house, gets permission to shoot, pays the fee, and chooses a firing point, or is assigned one. On an earlier trip, his rifle had been sighted-in with factory ammunition, so he's all set.

He organizes his shooting aids on the bench and removes the rifle from its case. The sling has been left at home. A sling only gets in the way for this type of shooting. He then opens the bolt on the gun to deactivate it — standard range procedure. The rifle is placed on sandbags. The front bags go under the forend a little behind the front swivel stud. Other bags go near the toe of the stock but forward of the rear swivel stud. Clearance for recoil is made between bench and rifle with additional sandbags. Jim raises or lowers the chair, according to the position of the gun. This coincides with aligning the scope on the target downrange.

Rough alignment of the scope reticle and target frame center is made with the front support. Fine sighting is made by squeezing the rear support with the nontrigger hand.

Jim prepares the first target. The following information is written in the top right corner of the target face:

> Warm Up Rounds
> .270
> 7–11–82 (the date of firing)
> Old Ammunition

A note is made of the temperature, wind velocity and direction, and any other observations of interest. Barometric pressure, range conditions, and so forth may be used for final decisions.

At the next signal for cease-fire, Jim picks up his target and stapler, stands up, and moves to the rear of the bench into the "ready" area.

After the firing line has been declared closed for safety, he walks downrange and posts his target on the target stand, being careful that the target is aligned vertically and at about the same height as his rifle on the bench. A small fluid level can be used to check that the target is properly aligned. Satisfied with the target placement, Jim returns to the firing line and obtains permission to align the chronograph screens. He does so and returns to the "ready" area. (Note: the positioning, alignment, and electrical connections for most chronographs should be made prior to starting time at public ranges whenever possible.) Jim remains in the "ready" area until the signal for shooters to return to the firing line is given. Sitting at the bench while other shooters are downrange is a breach of range safety and courtesy. Imagine being down at the target area, and noticing a shooter in position on the firing line with his rifle pointed in your direction. This is very unnerving and certainly unsafe, to say the least.

Only after all shooters have returned from the target area to the "ready" area are the signals given to return to the firing line and commence firing. Jim must now begin to use correct bench shooting techniques and all his shooting skills in earnest. He is about to begin collecting the data that will satisfy his purpose—to develop the best possible ammunition for his shooting needs.

As the firing line is activated, Jim replaces his hearing protectors and shooting glasses and begins the final preparations prior to firing.

After removing the rifle bolt and inspecting the chamber and bore for obstructions, he replaces the bolt and checks that the scope is set for the highest power, if it is a variable power-type. Next, the bench seat is adjusted for the most comfortable firing position. Inconsistent shooting methods, changing positions and rifle supports, different sight pictures, fatigue, hunger, alcohol, medication, breathing rate, and stress all have bad effects on good shooting. The best possible circumstances should exist on any visit to the range, especially this one.

Before a shot is fired, Jim reviews the sequence of steps that he wishes to perform during the day's shooting. This sequence requires some dry fire practice, firing some warm-up rounds, firing the pressure-standard rounds, the handloaded rounds, and factory ammunition.

Jim closes the bolt on an empty chamber and dry fires the rifle several times before shooting at the posted target. This is to ensure that the rifle is properly positioned and not subject to unequal forces. This can be detected during the dry firing practice by observing the scope reticle as the trigger is pulled and the striker released.

You can do this yourself by looking through the scope to see if any extreme vibrations cause the reticle to jump away from the target center in the sight picture. If the scope reticle jumps too much, undue force has been exerted somewhere on the rifle. Check its position and your own position. A certain amount of vibration will occur due to striker or hammer fall and trigger over-travel. The trick is to ensure that the small vibration occurs in the same direction and with the same force each time the trigger is pulled. The butt of the rifle should be held against your shoulder with only enough firmness to prevent injury, but with no unequal side force exerted on the stock.

Once Jim is satisfied that his shooting position is correct, the chronograph is switched on to see if it is operating properly. He chambers the first of the warm-up cartridges, closes the bolt, releases the safety and develops a good, comfortable sight picture. This is essential.

When ready to fire, Jim takes a deep breath, releases some of the air, and holds the rest. Trigger force is gradually increased while concentrating on the sight picture. When the gun goes off, it is almost a surprise.

After recovering from the rifle's recoil, Jim checks to see that the chronograph registered the velocity of the round. This velocity is recorded on a piece of paper under the heading, "Warm-Up Rounds."

A visual check is made to see if the bullet registered on the target. Because the warm-up rounds may have lower velocity, he wisely has posted a second target below and touching the first. This will pick up bullet holes that might be lost due to low bullet strike. This should be done for the initial handloads as well. He confirms that the first shot is sighted, that the velocity reading is entered on a notepad, and that no excess pressure signs were ob-

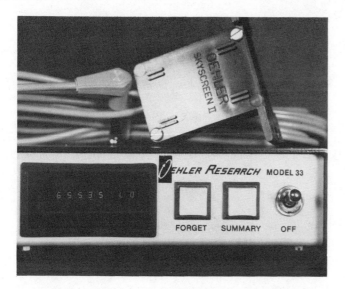

The only way to measure bullet velocity accurately is with a chronograph. Anything else is purely guesswork. There are accurate, inexpensive chronographs on the market today.

served. Each of the other four warm-up rounds is fired, using a shooting pace that is slow enough for proper barrel cooling, and careful enough to ensure good results and positive collection of data.

As he fires, he records each velocity, then turns the chronograph off to conserve battery life. He opens the rifle, removes the bolt, and dry brushes the bore with a bronze brush and wipes the bore clean with a dry patch, being careful that no solvent or oil is on either the brush or the patch. The dry brushing is only done to ensure that each group of ammunition is fired with the same beginning bore condition.

Jim picks up another target and writes the following information on it:

Pressure-Test Rounds
.270
7–11–82
Factory Components in Selected Cases

He retrieves his stapler and waits for the next cease-fire to remove the warm-up target and post the pressure-test target. This procedure is used for each of the preliminary groups of cartridges to be fired, as well as the handloads and factory ammunition. After posting each new target, Jim returns to the "ready" position and waits for permission to return to the firing line. (Note: with some chronograph sensors, it is possible to post multiple targets at one time. This can save steps, energy, and time.)

When ready to begin firing of the pressure-test rounds, Jim resumes his good shooting position and turns on the chronograph. Each velocity for the pressure-test ammunition is recorded. The date fired is entered on the handload data list, along with any other computation features the chronograph may provide. These may be such features as average velocity, extreme velocity spread, standard deviation, and so forth. These data can be recorded in columns 10 through 13 of the handload data list. If not, this data can be calculated after firing from the individual recordings.

As Jim fires the pressure-test cartridges and the first of the handloads, he is careful to examine the fired cases of each group for signs of excessive pressure. The pressure-test cartridges are fired first. This sequence provides a standard of comparison before the handloaded cartridges are fired.

After firing the pressure-test cartridges, Jim has a good idea of the effects that factory pressure will have on his once-fired, selected cases. As he fires and records the velocity for each of the test handloads, he is alert for signs of abnormal pressure. In addition to heard and felt observation, he checks cases for badly flattened primers, cratered primers, loose primers, ejector marks on the case head, uneven and excessively enlarged case bodies, and case ruptures. Any such sign might indicate too much pressure and signal an end to further handload testing. If any doubt exists, the micrometer can be used to compare case head expansion at the range. The suspect cases would be compared in size to those of the pressure-test cartridges. Such measurement would show when factory pressure is equalled or exceeded in the test handloads. This technique will be explained in Chapter 8.

Jim is careful to identify each of the targets used when firing the handloaded ammunition. Each target is numbered to correspond with the individual handload numbers. A typical target identification note might read:

Load#1
.270—130 grain
7–11–82
52.0/IMR 4831

Each target must be identified correctly so that precision measurements will properly correspond to the handloads.

The same basic procedure is used for target identification, firing, velocity recording, and data entry for the warm-up rounds, pressure-test rounds, handloads, and factory ammunition.

Although taking precautions to prevent excess pressure, Jim doesn't lose sight of objectives 2 or 7. Objective 2 is "To achieve equal or higher bullet velocity with handloaded ammunition than that of factory-loaded ammunition." Objective 7 is "To achieve proper, consistent, and safe pressure in the handloaded ammunition." These two objectives must be balanced to achieve successful handloaded ammunition.

During firing, we can observe pressure signs to help ensure that handloads remain within safe pressure limits. Pressure signs are practical and satisfactory methods for safe development of handloads. Observation experience is one of the best pressure "detectors" available to the handloader. Measurement of case expansion, explained in Chapter 8, is another comparative method using actual measurements. Such measurements are not actual pressure recordings. They are relative comparisons of pressure effect. In addition, factory pressure may or may not be maximum. Case head measurement only shows when handloads develop less, equal, or more pressure than factory ammunition. Head measurements should be used with the seen, felt, and heard observations to achieve objectives 2 and 7. It is unlikely that objective 2 will be reached with pressure that is lower than factory pressure. Careful balancing of both measurement and observance comparisons is needed to meet objectives 2 and 7. The use of both comparison methods, together, is a positive way to achieve both objectives.

After Jim completes firing all of his warm-up rounds, pressure-standard rounds, handloads, and factory ammunition, while noting the effects, changes, and observances on the handload data list, he will have accomplished three basic things. These things contribute greatly to the complete and satisfactory achievement of the handloading objectives. Jim will have three vital pieces of information obtained during firing: a measurable target for each group of ammunition, a measured velocity for each round of ammunition fired, and a fired cartridge case that can be used to help determine relative pressure achieved. These three pieces of information will soon allow him to discover which

When working up a load for any high-pressure cartridge, it's wise to measure case expansion occasionally. This gives the shooter a good idea of the kind of pressure his handloads are creating, compared to factory standard ammunition.

handloads are most precise, fastest, and what relative pressure was reached during firing. The chosen factory-loaded ammunition will be used as a basis of comparison to find just how well the objectives have been accomplished.

The targets will be measured scientifically and the results displayed on a graph to compare precision. The velocity recordings will also be displayed on a graph. This will provide a visual basis for velocity comparisons. The fired cases will be measured and those measurements will be displayed on a graph, too. This graph will compare the relative pressure of factory ammunition and handloaded ammunition. The methods for these measurements and comparisons will be explained in Chapters 6, 7, and 8. The use of this data to achieve the objectives will be shown and explained in Chapter 9.

## After Firing

After all firing is complete, Jim turns off the chronograph one last time and puts away the firearm. He wipes fingerprints off the gunmetal with an oily rag and places the rifle back into its carrying case. All records and targets are assembled, except for those still downrange. He checks to ensure that all fired cartridge cases are placed back into their correct locations in the ammunition box and that all appropriate notations have been made on the handload data list. He collects all his equipment, materials, and supplies and waits for the next cease-fire to retrieve the last of the targets. If necessary, he reports to the range office before leaving.

In the next chapter, we will watch our friend as he collects and records the data he will use to achieve his objectives and results.

---

## Actions at the Shooting Range

1. Decide if weather conditions are suitable. Wind is the most important factor.
2. Report to range office for permission to shoot.
3. Put on hearing protectors and shooting glasses.
4. Choose a firing point (if not assigned).
5. Place equipment, materials, and supplies on bench during firing period. Open action of firearm and leave open between shots.
6. During next cease-fire, post first target(s).
7. Erect and align chronograph screens.
8. Review written sequence of events you must perform: bore inspection, dry fire practice, warm-up rounds, pressure rounds, handloads, factory rounds.
9. Turn on chronograph.
10. Load and fire:
    a. observe heard and felt pressure signs
    b. record velocity from chronograph (individual rounds)
    c. observe case for visual pressure signs; measure against pressure-test cases
11. Turn off chronograph and deactivate firearm.
12. Dry brush and wipe bore (from chamber to muzzle only).
13. At next cease-fire, retrieve old target(s) and post next target(s). Verify target number matches load number.
14. Wait for permission to resume firing.
15. Repeat steps 9 through 14 until all firing is complete.
16. Collect and remove all materials, equipment, and supplies from your firing point. Verify that all data is recorded.
17. At next cease-fire, retrieve last fired target(s).
18. Report end of firing to range official or range office.
19. Depart.

---

## Equipment, Materials, and Supplies Needed for Test Firing

**Equipment**
Firearm and protective case
Benchrest and bench seat
Seat cushion
Forearm rest or sandbags
Rear stock rest or sandbags
Spotting scope or binoculars
Hand tools (for firearm and sight adjustments)
Stapler
Shooting glasses
Hearing protection (ear muffs or plugs)
Target stand
Hat, cap, or sun visor
Suitable carrying boxes or cases
Cleaning rod, tips, brushes, and guide
Counter chronograph
Screen (sensor),
Mount, and stand
Thermometer
Barometer
Wind Gauge
0–1″ Micrometer (accurate to 0.0001″)

**Materials and Supplies**
Ammunition (factory and handloads)
Cleaning accessories (solvent, patches, cloth rag)
Lubricants
Targets
Extra staples, or supply of thumb tacks
Spare batteries for chronograph
Spare screens for chronograph
Handload data list
Notepad for velocity data

# Chapter 6
# Precision

We are about to begin the most fascinating part of our search for the perfect cartridge; ideally, the one that fills our shooting needs best and gives us the greatest confidence in our shooting. The actions taken by our handloading friend, Jim, will now become much clearer. You will see how those actions and data will be used to make measurable and meaningful comparisons when evaluating ammunition. Let's begin this chapter by reviewing what we have accomplished so far.

First, we learned about handloading by objective. We learned how to develop a plan of objectives to achieve our purpose. Next, we studied the objectives and chose components to accomplish them. Attention was given to handload records and the actions needed at the loading bench for meeting each objective. Finally, Jim fired the test handloads at targets and measured their velocities. Each of the fired cartridge cases was placed back into its con-

tainer and kept for further measurements. All of which brings us to this point.

With that review, we're ready to begin using our data to achieve objective number 1. But in order to do this, we must become involved, to a slight extent, with the science of statistics. For that reason, let's digress from our discussion of handloading for a few moments and switch to the subject of statistics, because a basic understanding of that science is needed to use our data correctly and finish the job we've set out to do. We will return to handloading and the present concerns of precision and accuracy shortly.

Statistics is the science that collects, organizes, summarizes, presents, and analyzes data to make conclusions and decisions. Statistics uses mathematics and probability to find order and regularity among things. By knowing what order and regularity already exist, it is possible to predict results that may occur under other conditions. The employment of statistics fits handloading very well. You will soon see how it applies.

Statistical data can be collected by using all of the possible examples of a group or by using a small part of that group. Data that contains all possible examples is called population data. Data that consists of a smaller portion of a group is called sample data. The sample method of collecting data is the right one for handloaders. It allows us to use small samples of data chosen from all of the possible combinations available to us. We can use this data to predict what will probably happen if the same samples, or other samples, are used again.

A sample of handload data is any one of our groups of five test cartridges. Each of these groups has been given a load number. Using this sample data approach to handloading, we can draw probable and reasonable conclusions about the results we would achieve if all possible handloads were tested. Using sample statistics helps us because we can draw conclusions without actually having to load and fire so many shots. The use of sample data for handloading also helps us meet objective number 8 with an "absolute minimum of time, labor, materials, and money." Sample data is a practical use of statistics for handloading. The individual groups of handloads will become samples that Jim

The handloader should be a good benchrest shooter for best results. This kind of shooting is not difficult to learn. The idea is to remove all possible external factors so as to judge only the merits of the handloads.

will organize, summarize, and analyze to reach conclusions and decisions. In this chapter, we will discuss how to collect and store the handloading data needed to do this. This data will be presented as curves or lines of probability. These curves will consist of sample data collected from Jim's targets. The data curves will show the relation between powder weight and precision. We will analyze the data. It will help us establish the best handload to accomplish our shooting needs. It will allow us to achieve our final result.

Before this statistical business gets too heavy, let me explain in simple terms what will happen now. Jim will measure his five-shot targets for precision data. With these data measurements, he will plot points on a graph, then connect the data points to construct probability curves. These curves will tell us what can be expected from his handloads and the factory loads. This knowledge is needed to accomplish objective number 1, "To achieve equal or better precision with handloaded ammunition than with factory-loaded ammunition."

I hope this explanation serves for the time being. As we go along, everything I've said should become clear and understandable with a practical explanation and example. Now let's learn how to measure targets.

### Target Measurement

The first operation we must undertake for the collection of precision data is that of target measurement. Target measurement is a subject open to some debate. The important thing to remember, as handloaders, is what our objectives are and what method best serves our purpose.

There are many methods used for target scoring and measurement, but any method falls within one of two basic categories—precision and accuracy. A target can be measured or scored to find the precision or the accuracy of the shots. *Precision* refers to grouping or how close the bullet holes are to each other. The ability of a shooter to place bullets closely together on a target is dependent on the ammunition, the gun, and his skill. If the shooter can keep his shots close together and can also place that group of bullets on the point of aim, he has achieved *accuracy*. This example is the best way I know to describe the difference between precision

Although there are many books on statistics available, not all apply to practical handloading uses.

and accuracy, and can be seen in the accompanying illustration. As you may have guessed, accuracy is dependent on precision, and precision must be present before accuracy can be achieved. Again, there are several methods used for target measurement. Some are for precision and some are for accuracy. The following may help you understand this important concept.

The popular methods of target measurement are used because they serve the shooter, the organization, or the type of competition. Some shooting games use the bull's eye-type of target. The scoring of bull's eye targets is a measure of accuracy. Other games require counting the number of times a target is hit, for example, the silhouette games. They are also a measure of accuracy. But accuracy is not a factor in all types of target competition. For instance, benchrest rifle shooting is based on the precision capabilities of a shooter, his firearm, and his ammunition. A benchrest shooter's success depends on how closely together he is able to place all bullets. The scoring of benchrest targets is not a scoring of accuracy; it is a measure of precision. The object of the game is to put all the bullets into the same hole. That is precision, pure and simple. Since one of the objectives of our data search requires knowing the precision capabilities of our ammunition, we must choose a method of target measurement based on precision. Methods of precision target measurement range from simple to

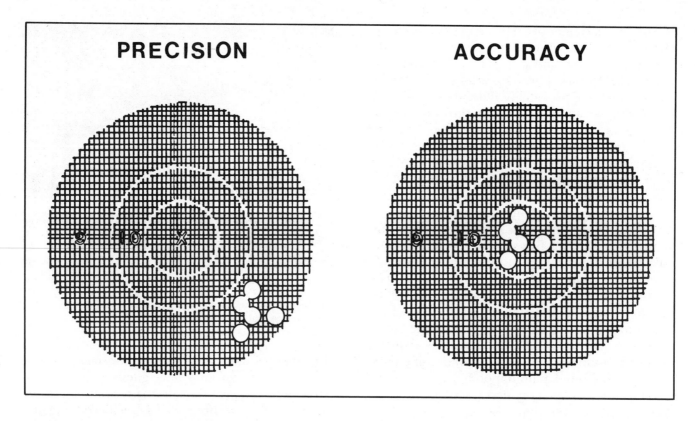

# PRECISION      ACCURACY

The difference between precision and accuracy. Precision deals with the grouping of shots; accuracy with where the group is on the target in relation to the aiming point.

complex. The next statements are included to help make the concepts of precision and accuracy and their measurement more understandable.

Science defines precision as the extent to which a set of measurements in a sample agree with their mean. Mean, as used here, is another word for average. Therefore, precision depends on how much the measurements within a given sample differ from their own average value. This tells us that precision in shooting is the ability to place bullets closely together on a target. Notice that this definition of shooting precision makes no reference to striking a specific point on the target. That's because precision is related to the size of the group and not the location of that group on the target. This concept is very important in the attainment of accuracy.

Accuracy is defined as the extent to which a given measurement agrees with the standard value for that measurement. This means that accuracy depends on how much a measurement differs from a

separate, standard value. Accuracy in shooting is dependent not only on the precision of the firearm and ammunition and their ability to put bullets closely together on a target, but also on the shooter's ability to adjust and place those same bullets on a specific point of the target. Shooting accuracy is not only a measure of repeatable, mechanical precision, but also the shooter's ability to use the precision effectively on a target.

***Overall methods*** of target precision measurement are visual comparison, extreme spread, mean spread, mean radius, standard radius, and figure of merit.

*Visual Comparison*—a subjective judgment of precision using no measuring devices such as a ruler or calipers. One group of shots is merely compared visually to one or more other groups.

*Extreme Spread*—a measurement of the center-to-center distance of the two bullet holes that are farthest apart in the group. Opinions vary as to the use of this method and its application. For that reason, it is difficult to define and use. Extreme spread is sometimes called overall spread or group diameter.

*Mean Spread*—the average dimension of a shot group. It is found by adding the largest and smallest dimensions of a shot group and dividing by two. It is an average of the worst and best group dimensions. Like the extreme spread, mean spread is subject to interpretation and use.

*Mean Radius*—the average distance of all bullet holes from the mathematical center of a shot group. Mean radius distance is found in three basic steps: first, find the horizontal center of the group and draw a vertical line through it. Next, find the vertical center of the group and draw a horizontal line through that point. The mathematical center of the group is where the two lines cross. Then measure the distance of each bullet hole from the group center. Lastly, add these radial distances, or deviations, and divide by the number of holes. The resulting figure is called the mean radius, although mean radial deviation or average radial deviation is more appropriate.

*Standard Radius*—identical to mean radius except for using the standard deviation calculation rather than simple averaging of the radial distances.

*Figure of Merit*—a refinement of the mean spread method described earlier. It consists of adding the horizontal distances between the centers of the far left and far right bullet holes to the vertical distance between centers of the highest and lowest bullet holes. The sum is divided by two to obtain an average. This overall method is used primarily for measuring very small shot groups.

**Vertical methods** of target precision measurement are extreme vertical spread, average vertical deviation, and standard vertical deviation. These methods of target measurement are concerned only with vertical shot dispersion. They are important to handloaders for measuring precision.

*Extreme Vertical Spread*—the vertical, center-to-center distance of the highest and lowest bullet holes in the target group. This method is also called vertical spread.

*Average Vertical Deviation*—similar to the mean radius method of target measurement but uses only the vertical factor of bullet deviation from the group's vertical center. The vertical center for the group is found first and a horizontal line is drawn through that point. The vertical distance of each bullet hole above or below this line is measured. The sum of these distances is divided by the number of holes to determine the average vertical deviation, or AVD.

*Standard Vertical Deviation*—identical to mean vertical deviation in every respect except that it uses the standard deviation calculation instead of a simple average for the result. Abbreviated, it is SVD.

Both average and standard vertical deviation measuring methods will be explained and illustrated fully as we proceed.

There are other methods of precision target measurement, but those just explained are the most useful to handloaders and shooters for comparison. Of these, the last two, average vertical deviation and standard vertical deviation, are best suited to handloaders and their projects.

Average vertical deviation (AVD) and standard vertical deviation (SVD) are nearly identical methods of target measurement. They differ in only one respect, which will be explained later. Both methods are adequate for handloaders and can be used easily and quickly with good results. Both methods can be illustrated with the same target example. Only the final calculation differs according to the method chosen. The only equipment necessary to use either method is a sharp pencil and a ruler with $1/50$-inch graduations. Dial calipers and a calculator make the job faster and easier, however.

Actual methods of precision target measurement will be described next. We'll call on Jim to give us a hand. Since both AVD and SVD methods are identical until the end of the calculation, both methods can be shown in one example.

The object of target measurement is to determine the precision quality of a handload since it ultimately controls overall accuracy. In order to make this example more realistic, actual data developed and gathered during the range testing will be used. The target is the first target fired with handloaded ammunition. That target corresponds to handload No. 1 on the handload data list. The target data that is needed for comparison will be measured and entered on the handload data list under the precision columns labeled: Data 1—Standard Vertical Deviation; Data 2—Extreme Vertical Spread; and Data 3—Height Above Aiming Point.

Jim gathers a ruler, piece of white paper, desk stapler, sharp pencil, six-inch dial calipers, and a calculator. The calipers and calculator aren't absolutely essential, but they speed the job along with less chance for error. The paper is stapled to the back side of the target so as to cover all the bullet holes. He lays the target right side up on his desk and carefully marks an X at the center of each bullet hole on the white backing paper. Next, a horizontal reference line is drawn across the target directly through the center of the highest bullet hole. This line can be seen on the precision data illustration as line AA. The target is ready for some serious precision measurement.

The first step is to find the target's vertical center. To begin, Jim measures the distance of each bullet hole below the horizontal reference line. It is easier to do this with the target turned sideways. Since the reference line is drawn directly through

Which target indicates the best precision? Which handload is best? Visual comparison is not enough. Target measurement is the only way to know for sure.

Precision Handloading

the top hole, the first vertical distance is always zero. Therefore, when measuring a target of five shots, it is only necessary to measure four distances. Jim measures the distance of the second, third, fourth, and fifth bullet holes below the reference line and writes the individual measurements on the target face. The last bullet hole measurement also represents the extreme vertical spread of the shot group. Data 2 on the handload data list is this measurement. The fifth and lowest hole is 1.44″ below line AA. This measurement is written in the appropriate block opposite load No. 1 over in the Data 2 column, Extreme Vertical Spread.

We must still find the vertical center of the group. To do this, add each vertical distance measurement to arrive at a sum of 3.04″. This is divided by the number of shots—3.04″ divided by 5 gives a quotient of 0.608″. This is rounded off to the nearest one-hundredth of an inch for a final figure of 0.61″. This distance identifies the location of the group's vertical center. At this point, Jim must draw the vertical center line. This is done by making a tick mark that is 0.61″ below the horizontal reference line on both sides of the target. The two tick marks are connected to form the vertical center line, BB. The vertical center line is used to develop the other two data items.

The first data developed with the center line is

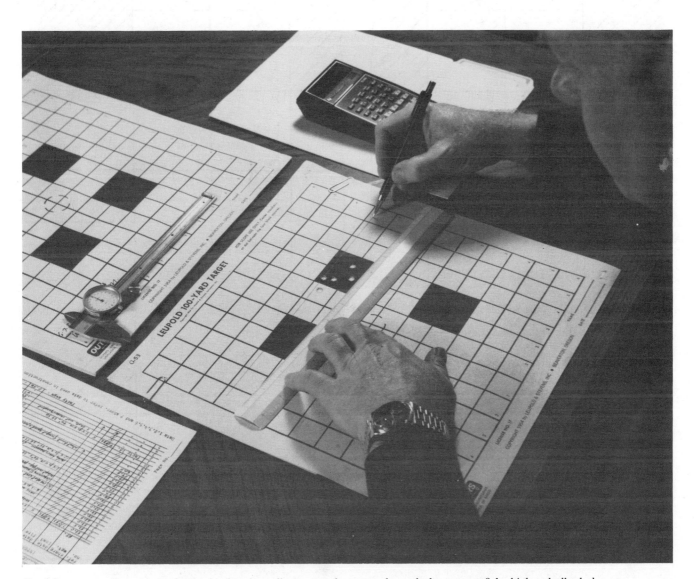

Precision target measurement begins by drawing a line across the target through the center of the highest bullet hole.

# Precision Data

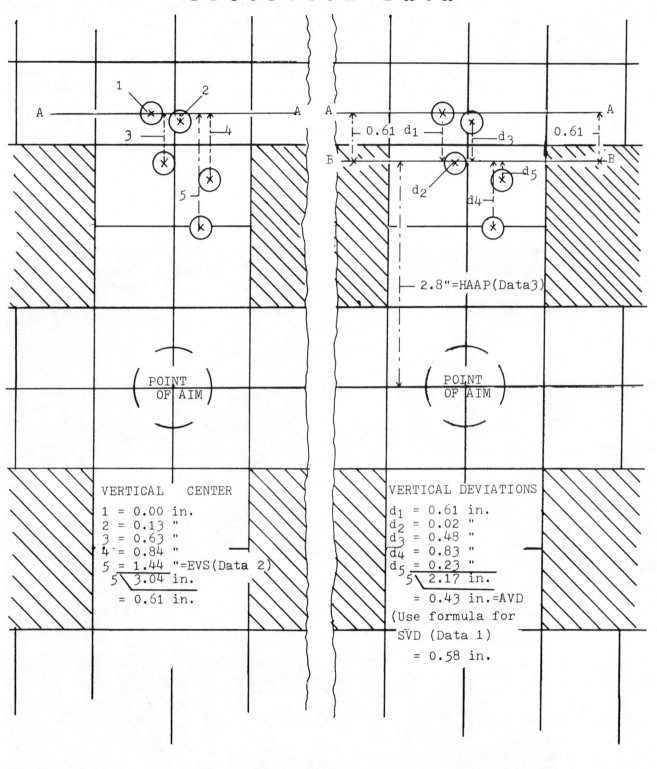

VERTICAL   CENTER

1 = 0.00 in.
2 = 0.13 "
3 = 0.63 "
4 = 0.84 "
5 = 1.44 "=EVS(Data 2)
5 ⟌3.04 in.
  = 0.61 in.

VERTICAL DEVIATIONS

$d_1$ = 0.61 in.
$d_2$ = 0.02 "
$d_3$ = 0.48 "
$d_4$ = 0.83 "
$d_5$ = 0.23 "
5⟌2.17 in.
  = 0.43 in.=AVD
(Use formula for
SVD (Data 1)
  = 0.58 in.

0.61 $d_1$       $d_3$       0.61

$d_2$       $d_5$

$d_4$

2.8"=HAAP(Data3)

( POINT
  OF AIM )

( POINT
  OF AIM )

Measuring a target to determine precision.

Data 3, Height Above Aiming Point, which is the distance of the group center above or below the point of aim. The point of aim on this target is the center of the target face. The vertical center line is drawn through the center of the target group. Therefore, the distance from the center line to the target center is the height above the aiming point. Jim measures this distance and finds that it is 2.8″. He enters this figure on the handload data list under Data 3 and opposite load No. 1.

The last data needed is Data 1, Standard Vertical Deviation. The vertical deviations are the distances of each bullet hole above or below the center line. This information is also found by using the vertical center line. Jim measures the vertical distances of each bullet hole above or below the center line. These vertical distances or deviations are also written on the target face.

Now, Jim has a choice to make. He must decide if average vertical deviation or standard vertical deviation is to be used for comparison. If the decision is to use AVD, the only step needed is merely to divide the sum of vertical deviations by the number of holes in the group. Since the sum of vertical deviations is 2.17″ and the number of holes is 5, AVD is equal to 0.43″, rounded off. This data can be substituted for Data 1 on the handload data list. As stated earlier, AVD is a satisfactory method of

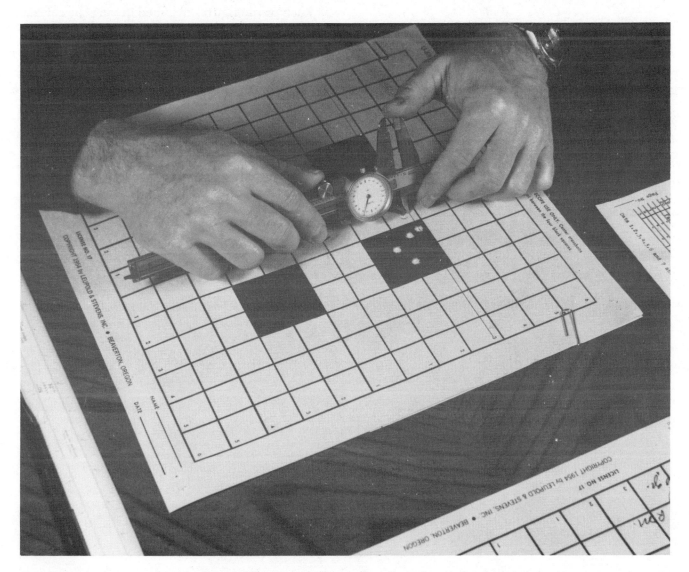

Shot groups can be measured with a ruler, but most handloaders prefer calipers for speed and consistency.

handload precision comparison. Jim, however, chooses to use the more accepted method of statistical comparison called standard deviation. Although he prefers to use a calculator with the standard deviation function, he will help us calculate the SVD of this example target so that we get a better understanding of standard deviation and how to use it.

Standard deviation is the statistician's method for determining how far data differs from its own average. This method for determining standard vertical deviation consists of inserting deviation factors into the formula as follows:

$$SVD = \sqrt{\frac{\Sigma\,(d_n)^2}{N-1}}$$

where:
$\Sigma$ = sum of the squared deviations
$d_1, d_2, d_3, \ldots, d_N$ = individual vertical deviations
N = number of bullet holes

Using this formula, Jim substitutes the measured deviation distances above and below the vertical center line into the formula. (See the accompanying illustration for elaboration.) In the illustration, you can see how the formula works with the inclusion of the known data figures. In the second step, each of the measured deviations has been put in and the number of rounds fired (5) has been substituted in place of N. In the next step, each of the deviation distances has been squared. The number of shots has been reduced by one, to obtain the divisor of four. The sum of all the squared deviations is divided by 4 to give a quotient of 0.34 in steps 4 and 5. The square root of this resulting figure is the SVD. In the last step, SVD is found to equal 0.58″.

Each of the figures obtained during the calculation must be rounded off to two places. This is because the answer can only be as accurate as our measurements. Jim's measurements have only been made to the nearest one-hundredth of an inch with the calipers. As the last step in precision target mea-

---

### STANDARD VERTICAL DEVIATION

$$SVD = \sqrt{\frac{\Sigma\,(d_n)^2}{N-1}}$$

where: $\Sigma$ = sum of the squared vertical deviations
$d_1, d_2, d_3, \ldots, d_N$ = individual vertical deviations in inches
N = number of bullet holes

Example: Load No. 1 for .270 Winchester, 130-grain bullet

Step 1. $\quad SVD = \sqrt{\dfrac{(d_1)^2 + (d_2)^2 + (d_3)^2 + (d_4)^2 + (d_5)^2}{N-1}}$

Step 2. $\quad = \sqrt{\dfrac{(0.61)^2 + (0.02)^2 + (0.48)^2 + (0.83)^2 + (0.23)^2}{5-1}}$

Step 3. $\quad = \sqrt{\dfrac{0.37 + 0.00 + 0.23 + 0.69 + 0.05}{4}}$

Step 4. $\quad = \sqrt{\dfrac{1.34}{4}}$

Step 5. $\quad = \sqrt{0.34}$

Step 6. $\quad SVD = 0.58 \text{ in}$

The formula for finding the standard vertical deviation. The figures are rounded off to two places.

Precision Handloading

surement, Jim writes the resulting standard vertical deviation for load No. 1 in the appropriate space on the handload data list. He enters 0.58 under the column, Data 1—Standard Vertical Deviation. All target measurements for the first handload are now complete.

Although measuring and calculating precision data is interesting, it soon becomes tedious when dealing with multiple targets. A great portion of the measurement and calculations can be eliminated by using one of the small, inexpensive calculators with averaging and standard deviation functions. If you use such a calculator, you can usually obtain the three items of precision data by merely completing the first step of target measurement as described earlier. It is only necessary to draw the horizontal reference line (AA) through the top bullet hole and measure the distance of the other four holes below that line. The distance of the lowest bullet hole below the line is equal to extreme vertical spread, or Data 2. Now key the five hole distances below the horizontal line AA. Remember that hole #1 is always 0.00″. The calculator can perform all the other mathematical drudgery. Press the average or "mean" key on the calculator to find the average distance. This figure represents the vertical center of the group and its location below line AA. The distance from the group center to the aiming point

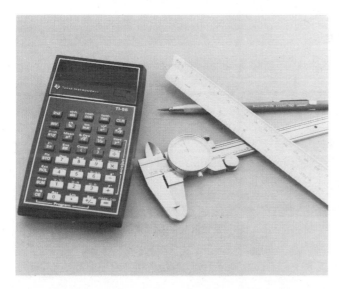

Only a ruler, graduated in 1/50-inch marks, and a sharp pencil are needed for precision target measurement. Calipers and a calculator make the job much easier and faster, however.

is Data 3, Height Above Aiming Point. Only one more precision data item is required. Using the calculator, Data 1—SVD is obtained by simply pressing the standard deviation key. The correct standard vertical deviation will appear in a fraction of a second. With the use of the calculator, the handloader can measure and compute the precision data for 10 targets in about one hour.

If you don't have a calculator with arithmetic mean and standard deviation functions, it is easier for you to compute Data 1 by using average, rather than standard vertical deviation. AVD is easier to compute than SVD. There is less chance for error with AVD when using a pencil or a simple calculator. The use of AVD will yield data results similar to those of SVD. Although AVD data is smaller than that computed with SVD, the overall result in probability curves is about the same. You will suffer no serious disadvantage by using AVD rather than SVD.

Standard deviation is the statistician's method for expressing uniformity. It has the advantage of being a slightly better comparing device than simple averaging, and it is less subject to statistical error when groups of varying size samples are used. Standard deviation gives the user a better feel for how far data differs from the average. Again, AVD is easier to calculate with pencil and paper than SVD. If your calculator has the standard deviation function, SVD is quicker than AVD. The choice is yours.

Now that we have a better grasp of how to go about measuring targets for precision, let us rejoin our friend, who has been measuring all of the other targets while we've been discussing statistics.

Jim continues to develop Data 1, 2, and 3 for each of the other sixteen test handloads and the targets fired with factory ammunition. All of the precision data is shown on the partially completed handload data list. Next, this data must be plotted on a graph so that he can see the results.

### Precision Graph

The precision data stored on the handload data list is used to make a display or precision graph, which will be used to make our objective decisions. Similar graphs will also be made for velocity and pressure data later. Each will include data developed from the test handloads and from the factory ammunition used as a standard for comparison. The graphs will allow us to interpret and compare the data against our handloading objectives. The graphs will also help Jim choose the best result that satisfies his shooting need. This will be done by eliminating those handloads whose data is inferior to that of the factory ammunition. Handloads that give data equal to or better than factory ammunition will be retained for a later, final decision.

The type of graph that best suits our purpose is a simple, two-axis linear graph. The horizontal axis is used to show the range of powder charge weights. The vertical axis is used to locate and show the size of the data corresponding to the samples. Data locations are indicated above their corresponding charge weights with a point or dot. After all data points are plotted, a line will be drawn to connect them, approximately. This line, or curve of probability, allows us to see what results would occur if the handloads were retested, or if any other charge weights within the range were tested.

Since the precision data includes three categories, the vertical axis will be used to locate three

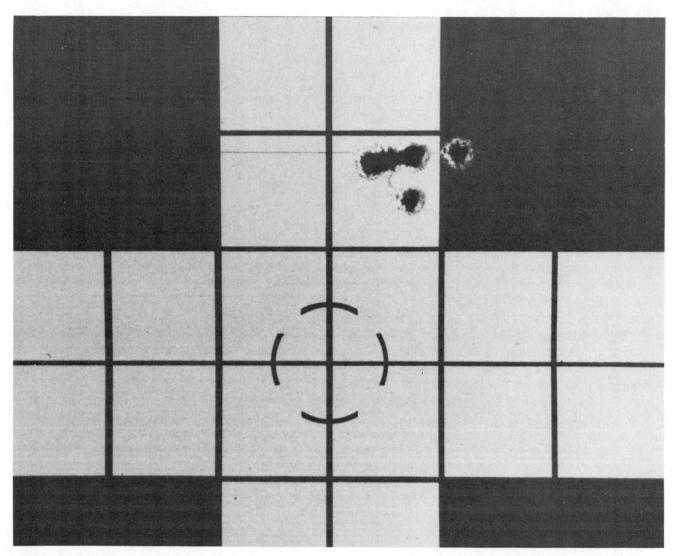

This is an example of good handload precision in a hunting rifle at 100 yards. It is load #3 from the text example (.270 Winchester). Your goal is to find ammunition with the least vertical dispersion. Notice how close the five holes are to the pencil line through the highest hole. Some width is understandable when you are concentrating on vertical precision without regard to wind. Each grid is one inch square.

All benchrest shooters are handloaders. Their game demands the utmost in precision loading techniques to stay competitive. Here, a top-notch shooter, Harold Henderson of Houston, demonstrates the tools unique to his sport—straight-line sizing and seating dies.

items on the graph. The numbers on the vertical scale correspond to Data 1, 2, and 3. In addition to the three data categories displayed, corresponding reference lines will be drawn. These lines will locate the data results for the factory ammunition. Again, factory ammunition will be used as the standard for comparison.

Let's stop dwelling over this explanation and call on our fellow handloader to put it all into practical use. The precision graph is made from Data 1, 2, and 3 on the handload data list. These data are the standard vertical deviation, the extreme vertical spread, and the height above the aiming point.

Each of these data was collected from the individual test target measurements.

First, Jim writes in the caliber, bullet, and powder information at the top of a blank precision graph. (See illustration.) These entries help identify the graph. In this case, the caliber is .270 Winchester, the bullet is a 130-grain Sierra, and the powder is IMR 4831. Next, he fills in the blanks for the charge weights located along the horizontal axis at the bottom of the graph. The entries here range from 52.0 through 60.0 grains. This is the range of weights for the propellant used in the test handloads in this instance.

CALIBER 270 WIN BULLET WGT. 130 gr.   HANDLOAD DATA

| FIREARM: mfgr. WIN | FACTY STD CARTRGE | CASE: mfgr REM (R-P) | BULLET: wgt 130 gr | POWDER: mfgr DuPONT |
|---|---|---|---|---|
| model 70 XTR | mfgr REM | avg wgt /97.3 ±3.0 gr | mfgr SIERRA | mfgr no. IMR4831 |
| barrel length 22 in | mfgr no. R270W2 | trim length 2.530 in | mfgr no. 1830 | lot no. P8JTY29-74 |
| twist rate 1:10 in | lot no. L25UD2452 | c.o.a. length 3.205 in | lot no. 40520 | PRIMER: mfgr CCI |
| TARGET: mfg/no. LEUP G-53 | bullet wgt 130 gr | sized head 0.4656 in | type SPIT., F.BASE | mfgr no. 200 |
| RANGE: dist. 100 yd | | | clearance 1/16 in | lot no. L25L |

| LOAD no. | charg wgt. gr. | date load | date fire | no. rds | INTERNAL AND EXTERNAL FACTORS (wind velocity, direction, temperature, precip., visibility, ch. pressure observations, other.) | PRECISION Dat1 Std Vert Dev. in. | Dat2 Extm Vert Sprd. in. | Dat3 HtAb Aim Pt. in. | VELOCITY Dat4 Std Vel. Dev. fps. | Dat5 Extm Vel. Sprd. fps. | Dat6 Avg Vel. fps. | no. rds rcrd | PRESSURE Dat7 Case Head Exp. in. |
|---|---|---|---|---|---|---|---|---|---|---|---|---|---|
| 1 | 52.0 | 7/5/82 | 9/9/82 | 5 | 4-6 fr 4:00@12:30, 94°F, 29.72 dry | 0.58 | 1.44 | 2.8 | | | | 5 | . |
| 2 | 52.5 | | | | exceptional group, but slow | .22 | 0.59 | 1.9 | | | | | . |
| 3 | 53.0 | | | | " | .16 | 0.41 | 1.7 | | | | | . |
| 4 | 53.5 | | | | very mild pressure | .55 | 1.34 | 2.1 | | | | | . |
| 5 | 54.0 | | | | 6-12 fr 4:00, 94°F, 29.62, Osmk | .28 | 0.75 | 2.8 | | | | | . |
| 6 | 54.5 | | | 4 | one shot lost thru another hole | .41 | 1.13 | 3.0 | | | | | . |
| 7 | 55.0 | | | 5 | beginning of primer flattening | .37 | 0.80 | 3.9 | | | | | . |
| 8 | 55.5 | | | | exceptional grp, good grp, trust | .50 | 1.14 | 3.7 | | | | | . |
| 9 | 56.0 | | | | exceptional grp, good grp, trust | .18 | 0.45 | 3.8 | | | | | . |
| 10 | 56.5 | | | | | .44 | .18 | 3.8 | | | | | . |
| 11 | 57.0 | | | | 2-4 fr 4:00, 94°F, 29.56 ↓ | .57 | 1.44 | 3.5 | | | | | . |
| 12 | 57.5 | | | | | .70 | 1.48 | 3.4 | | | | | . |
| 13 | 58.0 | | | | fairly heavy pressure, trust | .63 | 1.60 | 3.4 | | | | | . |
| 14 | 58.5 | | | | 2-4 fr 4:00, 94°, 29.52 ↓ | .59 | 1.23 | 4.1 | | | | | . |
| 15 | 59.0 | | | | | .59 | 1.45 | 3.9 | | | | | . |
| 16 | 59.5 | | | | | .90 | 2.33 | 3.4 | | | | | . |
| 17 | 60.0 | | | | limit of useful speed + pressure | .63 | 1.62 | 3.5 | | | | | . |
| 18 | .. | | | | | . | . | . | | | | | . |
| 19 | .. | | | | | . | . | . | | | | | . |
| 20 | .. | | | | | . | . | . | | | | | . |
| 1 | facty ld. | 9/9/82 | | 5 | 2-4 fr 4:00, 94°, 29.56 | 0.93 | 2.68 | 4.5 | | | | 5 | . |
| 2 | " | | | | 2 shots not chronographed | .25 | 0.59 | 4.2 | | | | 3 | . |
| 3 | " | | | | | .59 | 1.53 | 4.0 | | | | 5 | . |
| 4 | " | | | | | .47 | 1.27 | 4.7 | | | | | . |
| 5 | " | | | | | | | | | | | | . |
| | facty avgs = | | | | | 0.56 | 1.52 | 4.4 | | | | | |

Data 1, 2, 3, 4, 5, 6 and 7 above, refer to data used in construction of the PREC., VEL. and PRESS. graphs

A partially completed handload data list, through "Precision" data.

We are now ready to plot the standard vertical deviation data points for Data 1, using the following method:

1. Locate the charge weight and Data 1 measurements corresponding to load No.1.
2. Above that weight on the horizontal scale, plot the location of the Data 1 (SVD) measurement for load No.1. Use the vertical scale to determine the location of the point above the corresponding charge weight. Place a dot at that point.
3. Repeat the above procedure for each of the other loads on the handload data list.

After plotting all the data points for Data 1, Jim has to draw a smooth line through the points that *approximate* the pattern that the data points indicate. This is done by holding the graph sheet horizontally at eye level. Turn the graph so that the plotted points appear to cluster along an imaginary curve. Be careful not to connect the individual points to form a jagged line, but instead draw a smooth curve that *approximates* the line formed by the points themselves. Jim discovers that this Data 1 line crosses some points, misses others, and passes between other pairs of points, as in the illustration.

After drawing the Data 1 line, we must show the standard of comparison, factory ammunition results. Standard 1 data is the average SVD found for the factory ammunition. This data is given in the factory average block at the bottom of the Data 1 column on the handload data list. It should be obtained from at least three five-shot groups of the same ammunition.

A line is drawn across the chart at the average factory SVD level. This becomes the Standard 1 line. All points on the Data 1 curve below the Standard 1 line indicate better precision than factory ammunition. All points on the Data 1 curve above the Standard 1 line indicate worse precision than with factory ammunition. At the point where the two lines cross, handload and factory precision are the same.

Next, the Data 2, Extreme Vertical Spread, curve is plotted. He does this using the same method he applied for Data 1. An approximate curve is drawn for this data also. The Data 2 points are circled so they won't be confused with the Data 1 points. Jim also plots and draws the Standard 2 line (average factory EVS level) for comparison. The data is the extreme vertical spread for the handloads and the factory ammunition. It is of value as a second source when verifying handload precision. Extreme vertical spread is similar to, but not the same as, standard vertical deviation. By comparing Data 1 to Data 2, confidence in the overall data can be strengthened.

In this example, Data 1 and Data 2 indicate that handload precision is best when using about 53.0 grains of powder. At this weight, handload precision is superior to factory ammunition. As propellant charge weight is increased, precision erodes at a slow, but fairly constant rate until it equals factory precision at approximately 57.5 to 58.5 grains. Above 58.5 grains, handload precision is inferior to that of factory ammunition. This is obviously an important fact and will be used in choosing the best handload, based on our eight objectives.

The last category of data to be entered on the precision graph is that of Data 3, Height Above Aiming Point. This data is of importance when determining which handloads most nearly duplicate the bullet strike location of factory ammunition. It is also useful for sight alignment. Propellant characteristics can be compared to those of factory ammunition with Data 3. Factory ballistics can sometimes be duplicated, if so desired, using this data.

Jim plots the Data 3 points using the Data 3 scale and draws in the approximate curve which is labeled Data 3. He also draws the standard reference line for Data 3 as determined with the factory standard targets. This line is labeled Standard 3.

The completed precision graph is shown in the last illustration. The use of this precision graph will be discussed later, after the velocity and pressure graphs are also completed.

There are still two types of data that we must account for. These are the velocity recordings and the cartridge cases from his testing. They will be used to develop data and construct graphs for velocity and pressure. We will learn how to do this in the next two chapters.

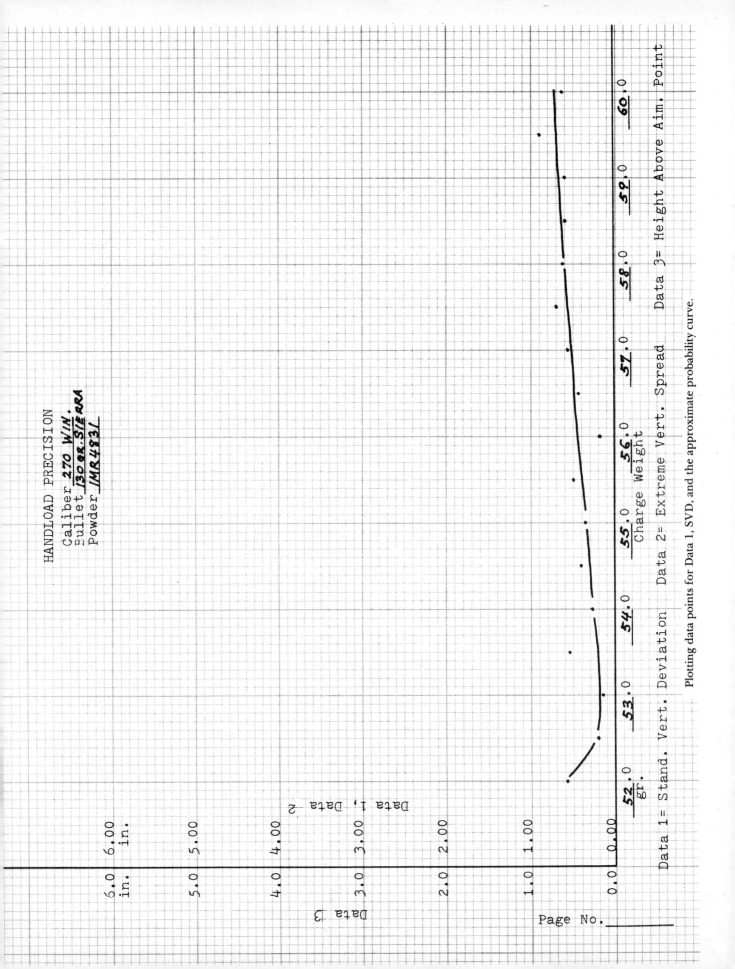

HANDLOAD PRECISION

Caliber *270 WIN.*
Bullet *130gr. SIERRA*
Powder *IMR 4831*

Charge Weight
gr.

52.0  53.0  54.0  55.0  56.0  57.0  58.0  59.0  60.0

Data 1, Data 2

0.00  1.00  2.00  3.00  4.00  5.00  6.00
in.

Data 3

0.0  1.0  2.0  3.0  4.0  5.0  6.0
in.

Page No. _____

Data 1= Stand. Vert. Deviation    Data 2= Extreme Vert. Spread    Data 3= Height Above Aim. Point

Plotting data points for Data 1, SVD, and the approximate probability curve.

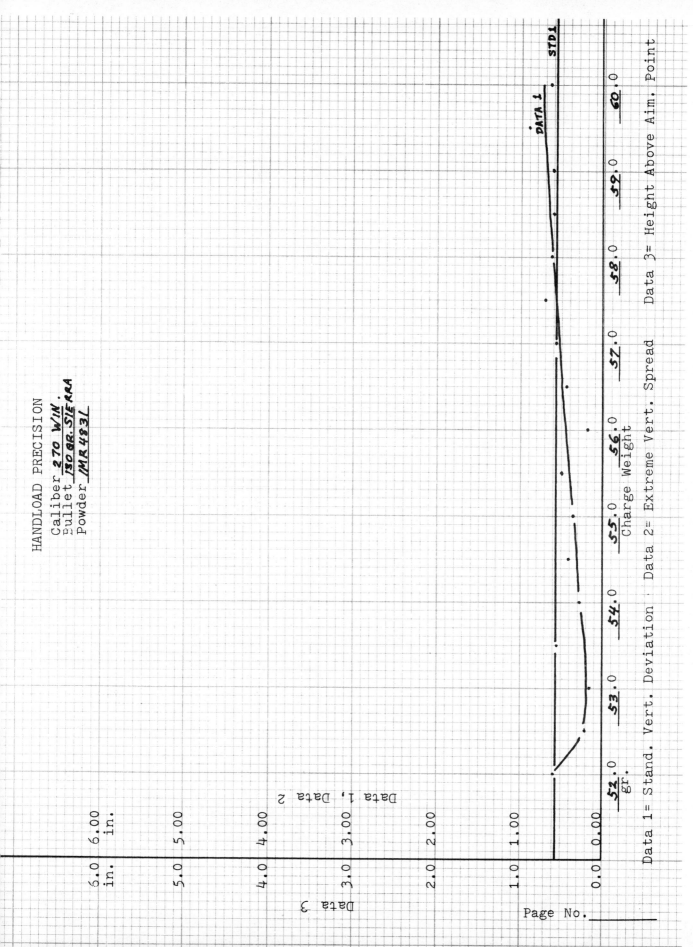

HANDLOAD PRECISION

Caliber _270 W/N._
Bullet _130 GR. SIERRA_
Powder _IMR 4831_

The Standard 1 line is put in (average factory ammunition SVD level).

Data 1= Stand. Vert. Deviation ; Data 2= Extreme Vert. Spread    Data 3= Height Above Aim. Point

Charge Weight
gr.

Page No. _____

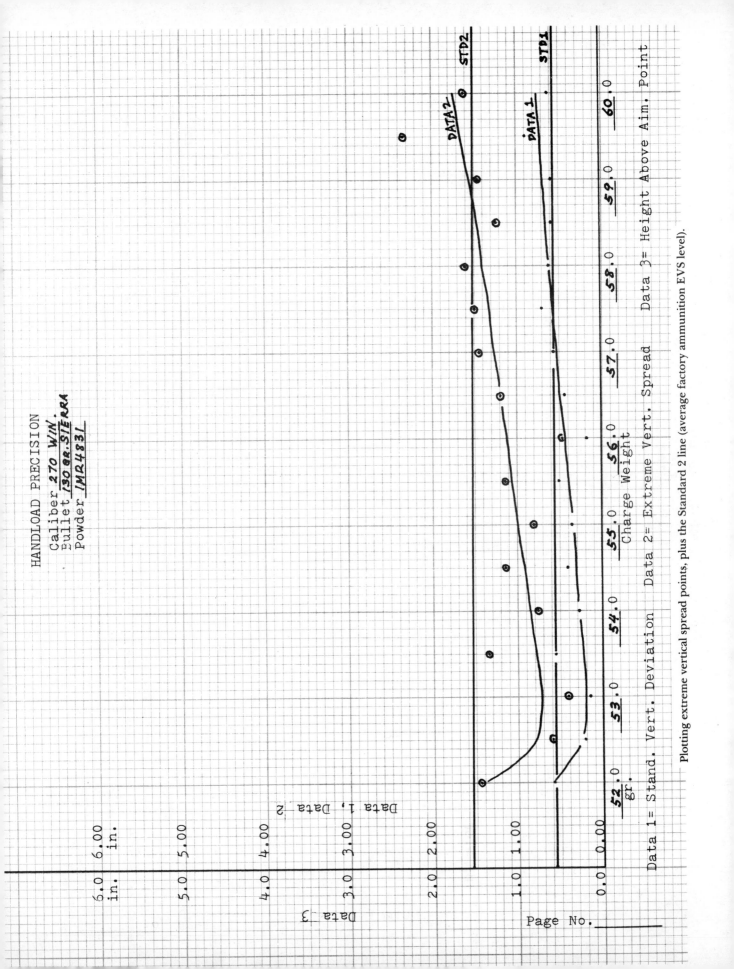

HANDLOAD PRECISION

Caliber _270 WIN._
Bullet _130 GR. SIERRA_
Powder _IMR 4831_

STD 2

STD 1

DATA 2

DATA 1

60.0

59.0

58.0

57.0

56.0

55.0

54.0

53.0

52.0

Charge Weight

gr.

Data 1, Data 2

Data 3

6.00 in.
5.00
4.00
3.00
2.00
1.00
0.00

6.0 in.
5.0
4.0
3.0
2.0
1.0
0.0

Page No. _____

Data 1= Stand. Vert. Deviation     Data 2= Extreme Vert. Spread     Data 3= Height Above Aim. Point

– Plotting extreme vertical spread points, plus the Standard 2 line (average factory ammunition EVS level).

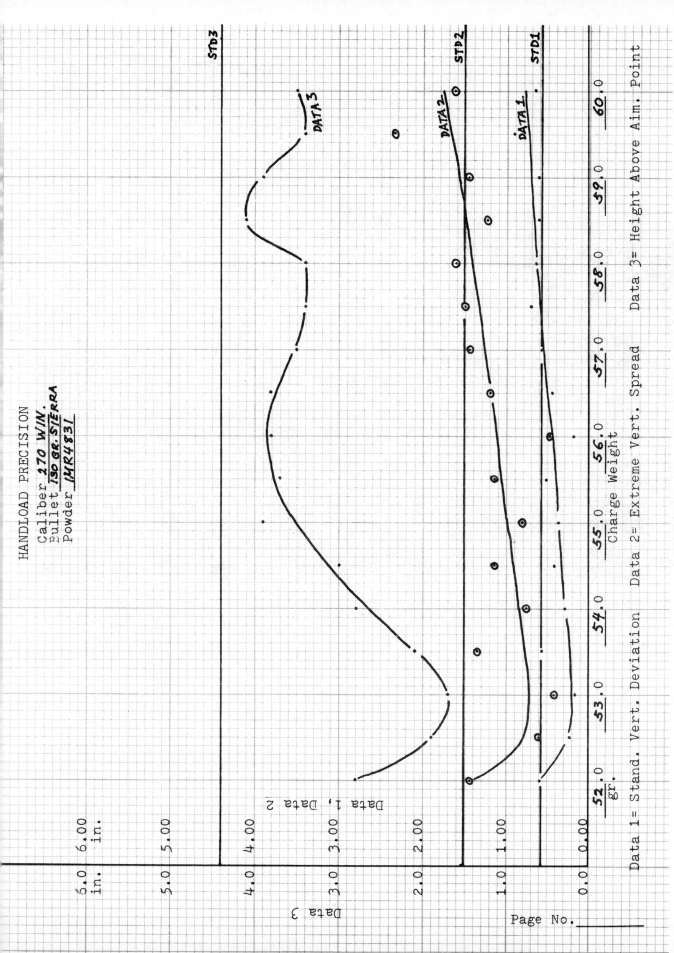

HANDLOAD PRECISION

Caliber _270 WIN._
Bullet _130 gr. SIERRA_
Powder _IMR4831_

Plotting the height above the aiming point data, plus the Standard 3 line (average factory ammunition HAAP level).
A completed precision graph.

Data 1 = Stand. Vert. Deviation    Data 2 = Extreme Vert. Spread    Data 3 = Height Above Aim. Point

Page No.

A club shooting match demanding the highest precision—benchrest competition. These typical shooters are precise-type people, shooting precise equipment, and getting precise results. As a group, they are also among the friendliest, most talkative, helpful, and enthusiastic people in the American shooting fraternity. (Central Texas Benchrest Shooters, Inc., at Howard Dietz Range, New Braunfels, Texas.)

# Chapter 7
# Velocity

It is now time to think about velocity as a factor in handload development. Most modern, metallic ammunition is made to deliver high bullet velocity. High velocity can be a desirable attribute in ammunition and firearms. But questions concerning velocity often arise where shooters gather, questions such as: What is high velocity? How is velocity measured? Why strive for high velocity?

These questions have been asked by shooters and handloaders for many years. Each deserves a proper answer. The best way to answer the first question is to define and explain the term *velocity*. Velocity, or linear velocity, is the time rate of change of position of a body in reference to a specified direction. Similarly stated, velocity can be considered to be the time rate of linear motion in a given direction. Speed, quickness, rapidity, and celerity are all synonyms of velocity. They are similar, but not exactly the same as bullet velocity.

Bullet velocity is most commonly measured by the number of feet, yards, or meters that are traveled in a one-second interval of time. The distance traveled per second is a measurement that enables us to compare the velocity of one bullet against that of another.

High velocity is a relative term without exact meaning. What constitutes high velocity to one shooter may be considered low velocity by another. Also, former high-velocity cartridges may now be judged relatively slow with respect to improvements in guns and ammunition. Today, most contemporary shooters would agree that a high-velocity rifle cartridge is one whose bullet is propelled at a muzzle velocity of about 2,500 feet per second or faster. Almost all high-velocity cartridges have been developed since the turn of this century when smokeless propellants were first introduced and perfected.

When one begins to speak of high velocity in reference to handgun cartridges, the term becomes less distinct. Only a few years ago, a high-velocity pistol or revolver cartridge was considered to be one whose bullet traveled 1,100 feet per second or faster. This is about the speed of sound, and considerably slower than a high-velocity rifle cartridge. The recent use of rifle-type cartridges in specialized handguns has resulted in some very impressive velocities. Some handguns are now capable of bullet velocities that rival those of high-powered rifles.

Bullet velocity can be measured at any point along the bullet's path from the cartridge case to the target. Velocity measurements inside the firearm's barrel are important for internal ballistic study and are used in the design of firearms and the development and further improvement of ammunition and propellants.

Velocity measurements taken outside the firearm are important for external ballistic study. These external measurements are determined with the aid of a chronograph, and are used to design better bullets and to determine the ballistic capabilities and effects of ammunition and bullets at various distances. Shooters and handloaders use chronograph readings to compare the relative ve-

After firing you have three valuable pieces of information: targets, velocity recordings, and cases. These items will provide the precision, velocity, and pressure data needed to make objective decisions later.

locity of one cartridge or bullet against another, and to estimate the effects of range on a given target. The velocity of a bullet at some point near the firearm muzzle is the one most commonly used and is referred to as muzzle velocity. In actuality, almost all muzzle velocity measurements are taken some distance away from the muzzle, due to chronographic equipment limitations and safety. Such measurements are referred to as instrumental velocity readings.

There are two ways to determine muzzle velocity—estimation and measurement. Estimation is simply a matter of referring to manufacturers' loading tables. In some cases, the estimate is correct and assumptions of performance are also correct. In all cases, however, the estimate is just a guess. Most are inaccurate to some degree. For some shooters, an estimate is enough for their needs. But an estimate is not factual; it is not sufficient data upon which to base objective decisions that affect your shooting confidence. We must have a better idea of relative bullet velocity to compare handloads with factory ammunition. An estimate won't do. We must have accurate velocity measurements for sound decisions.

## Measuring Velocity

The first device to measure bullet speed was developed in England in the 1700s. It is referred to as the ballistic pendulum. A ballistic pendulum is just what its name implies, a heavy wooden or metal object suspended so that it will move when struck by a bullet. The pendulum's movement is measured by a piece of tape attached to it. The tape is pulled through a slot. Before firing, any slack in the tape is removed. As the bullet strikes and moves the pendulum, the tape is pulled through the slot, and since the tape does not slip backward, the amount of movement due to bullet strike can be measured. By knowing the weight of the pendulum, the weight of the bullet, and the amount of movement, the energy of the bullet transferred to the pendulum can be accurately calculated. By knowing the energy of the bullet, its velocity can be found.

Although crude by modern standards, the ballistic pendulum worked and provided a great boost to the science of ballistics. With the advent of electric-

ity, far more precise methods of measuring bullet velocity were developed. These electrical devices are referred to as ballistic chronographs.

Ballistic chronographs vary considerably in the way they function. Although each device measures a period of time for a bullet to pass between two points and activate electrical sensing circuits, the physical methods used to trip the sensing circuits differ.

The period of time it takes for a bullet to pass two points of known distance from each other is the critical piece of information needed to measure bullet velocity. Once this is known, simple calculations to find velocity are made and much useful knowledge can be developed. All this knowledge falls into the category of exterior ballistics. By knowing velocity and bullet shape, accurate estimates of trajectory, bullet drop, remaining energy, and maximum range of any ammunition can be made. Such information is invaluable to the shooter, the hunter, and to the military.

The most useful, precise, and popular bullet velocity-measuring instruments are known as ballistic counter chronographs. These instruments "count" the time required for a bullet to pass over a measured distance. The time of flight over that distance is used to determine average velocity between the "start" and "stop" points along the bullet's path. This measurement is called instrumental velocity. In practice, the bullet starts a clock by first passing through a triggering device and then stops the clock as it passes through a second such device. These triggering devices are commonly referred to as chronograph screens and they are of two basic varieties: electromechanical and photoelectric.

The older, electromechanical screen is an electrical fuse in the chronograph system that completes a circuit. As the bullet passes through the "start" screen, the electrical circuit is broken, triggering the counter mechanism in the chronograph. The counter "counts" or measures the amount of time that elapses until the bullet passes through the second or "stop" screen, which also stops the counter. The elapsed time of the bullet's flight through the two screens is recorded and used to determine the bullet's velocity. Electromechanical screens are quite positive but generally require replacement after every shot.

The photoelectric chronograph sensor is a newer

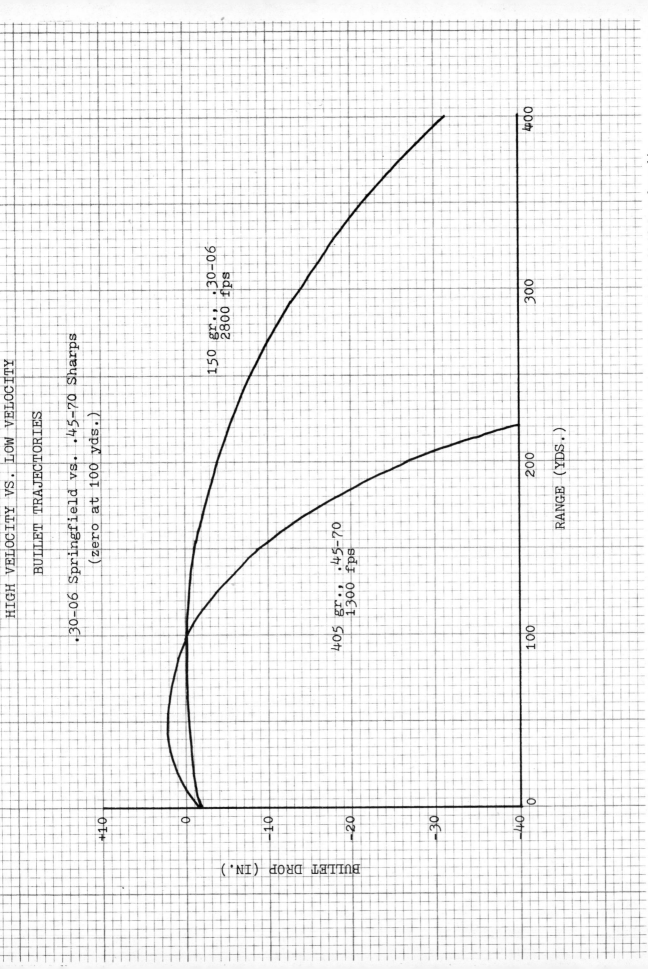

HIGH VELOCITY VS. LOW VELOCITY

BULLET TRAJECTORIES

.30-06 Springfield vs. .45-70 Sharps

(zero at 100 yds.)

150 gr., .30-06
2800 fps

405 gr., .45-70
1300 fps

BULLET DROP (IN.)

+10

0

-10

-20

-30

-40

RANGE (YDS.)

0     100     200     300     400

Notice the rainbow trajectory of the .45-70 bullet out to 100 yards, compared to the much flatter-shooting .30-06. In order to hit with the old .45-70 at 220 yards, the shooter would have to hold at least three feet over the target because of bullet drop. At 2,800 fps, the .30-06 offers a 200-yard advantage.

ballistic research development. The photoelectric sensors use the shadow of the bullet in flight to stop and start the time counter. What's more, these sensors do not require replacement between shots. This is a big advantage for several reasons: first, all rounds in a series may be fired without leaving the shooting bench. This allows precision shooting to be accomplished at the same time as velocity determination for easier, faster handload data gathering. Also, this type of chronograph is practical to use on public shooting ranges. Lastly, because there is no need to replace conducting screens, the photoelectric sensors reduce costs.

Not long ago, chronographs were economically unfeasible for individual handloaders. Today, an individual or group of shooters can purchase a good, basic chronograph at an amazingly small price. This welcome change is due principally to the development of the integrated circuit, and the practical use of several other technological advances by a few dedicated shooters and inventors. As a result, thousands of handloaders now enjoy the benefits of chronographing. Until modern, inexpensive chronographs were made available to individual shooters, bullet velocity was only a "guess" or a "promise." Handloaders guessed at their bullet velocity and ammunition manufacturers promised what velocity their ammunition would deliver. The new chronographs have shown that both the guesses and the promises were often wrong.

At the present time, there is only one precise, practical way for the shooter to know how fast his bullets are traveling. That is with the use of a ballistic counter chronograph. Knowing bullet velocity is essential to meeting objective 2 and our overall project result.

Among beginning shooters, the question is often asked, "Why is high velocity desirable?" This is an interesting question for several reasons. Seventy-five years ago, the same question would have received a prompt, positive reply from experienced shooters of the day. They knew very well why higher bullet velocity was so desirable. Most of these fellows had experience with both black powder guns and the then relatively new smokeless, high-velocity firearms. They understood the problems of black powder guns such as low velocities and arcing bullet trajectories. They also appreciated the ad-

vantages of the modern guns and ammunition. Most of the slow, black powder guns and cartridges could only provide short-distance accuracy in the hands of the average shooter because there was a great deal of bullet drop from the muzzle to the distant target. Correct range estimation and a knowledge of trajectory were required for shooting accuracy past 150 yards with the old guns. Smokeless powder changed that.

With the adoption of the .30-06 Springfield cartridge by the U.S. military in 1906, the modern, high-velocity cartridge became a reality for American soldiers and sportsmen. No longer did the hunter have to pass up distant shots. He could aim directly at the target, at ranges of 300 yards and more, and be reasonably sure of a humane, one-shot kill. And the soldier could be much more effective on the battlefield. The accompanying illustration clearly shows the difference in trajectory between the .30-06 Springfield and the old .45-70 Sharps cartridge. The superior, flat trajectory of the high-velocity, modern cartridge is obvious. This characteristic contributes greatly to shooting accuracy at longer ranges. Guns and ammunition both took a giant step with the development of smokeless propellants. These new propellants gave arms makers the ability to drive bullets safely at high velocities resulting in increased accuracy at long range. That is one very good reason why high velocity was, and is, so desirable.

Another benefit of high bullet velocity is that greater velocity increases bullet energy. Bullet energy, or kinetic energy, is the energy developed by a bullet in motion. The graph illustration shows that increases in bullet velocity provide more than equal increases in energy. If a bullet's velocity is doubled, its kinetic or moving energy is not just doubled, it is quadrupled. For instance, if a 150-grain bullet has a muzzle velocity of 1,400 fps, its kinetic energy is approximately 653 ft-lbs. If the same bullet's velocity is doubled to 2,800 fps, as in the .30-06, approximately 2,611 ft-lbs of kinetic energy is developed. This also means that relatively small increases in bullet velocity have a greater effect on bullet energy than one might first suppose. If the same 150-grain bullet can be safely pushed from 2,800 to 3,000 fps by handloading, the resultant energy becomes 2,997 ft-lbs. The handloader would receive a 14.8

This shows the relative aiming points for a vital hit using the .45-70 Sharps and the .30-06 Springfield at 220 yards if both guns are zeroed at 100 yards.

percent increase in bullet kinetic energy by increasing velocity only 7.1 percent. All of this can be explained with the formula for kinetic energy:

$$KE = \frac{1}{2}mV^2 \text{ where:}$$

$$m = \text{bullet mass} = \frac{\text{bullet weight in grains}}{7000 \times 32.174}$$

and V = bullet velocity in fps

I've just tried to explain the two most important reasons for achieving higher bullet velocity: greater long-range accuracy and greater energy. But other factors are also related. Two such factors affected by bullet velocity are power and momentum.

Power is the amount of work accomplished in a given time. This can be restated as the amount of energy transferred in a unit of time. When kinetic energy is increased by increasing velocity, power is increased also.

Momentum, a subject of some controversy in ballistics, is the product of bullet mass times velocity. Again, an increase in velocity increases momentum directly. Momentum has some relevance when discussing "knockdown" capabilities of different cartridges in the silhouette shooting games, and penetration of big game animals in the field.

The preceding illustrates the effect that velocity can have on bullets. Not all shooting requires high velocity by any means. But velocity is definitely an objective for Jim in this text example.

He definitely wants the greatest velocity feasible, so long as the other loading objectives are realized. From his graph of precision results, he understands that at some point velocity increases may be accompanied by a loss of precision plus excessive chamber pressure.

Because the handload shot groups began to enlarge past the factory standard with more than 57.5 grains of powder, Jim hopes that the handloads have equalled or exceeded the factory velocity before this point. Fortunately, he has recorded the chronographic measurements and saved the fired cases. We will soon know what degree of success has been achieved.

As you recall, Jim shot for precision and velocity results on the same day. We have the information now to find all of the velocity data on the handload data list and build a velocity graph of the handloads for intelligent decision-making. We will do this shortly, but first, a few more simple calculations are necessary.

Although some chronographs available to handloaders now have the ability to sense, record, calculate, and display all of the data items noted under the "Velocity" heading of the handload data list, the use of a simple chronograph is assumed in this text to show the individual calculations for data suited to our purposes. Any chronograph will serve for your velocity measurements as long as it yields positive readings of bullet velocity for each round and is used correctly. This is what chronographs are supposed to do. With simple chronographs, you will have to jot down the individual velocity recordings after each round is fired. This is good practice even when using the sophisticated instruments, for if you or the chronograph computer should make a mistake, it is possible to lose all the data held in memory for a complete handload number. Jotting down individual round recordings after each round is fired should become a standard practice. It helps to ensure that no valid data is lost. As long as a handloader collects the individual velocity measurements, he can compute the other required data at another time.

There are four items of importance to us under the heading of "Velocity" on the handload data list: Data 4, Standard Velocity Deviation; Data 5, Extreme Velocity Spread; and Data 6, Average Velocity. The number of rounds recorded is also included under this heading as a control factor, but this information is not used in the construction of the velocity graph. With the exception of Data 4, all velocity calculations are simple and quick to perform. And Data 4, Standard Velocity Deviation, is also a snap if you have a calculator with the standard deviation function.

The velocity calculations will be demonstrated using figures taken from actual firing and chronographic readings for load No.1. Five instrumental velocity readings were obtained:

Round 1—2,678 fps
Round 2—2,688 fps
Round 3—2,695 fps
Round 4—2,747 fps
Round 5—2,696 fps

The first velocity determination is already performed, which is to determine and enter the number of rounds and velocity recordings on the handload data list. The second calculation is also simple. That calculation is for Data 5, Extreme Velocity Spread.

Extreme velocity spread is the difference between the highest velocity recorded and the lowest. In this case, the lowest velocity corresponds to round 1 (2,678 fps) and the highest velocity to round 4 (2,747 fps). By subtracting the velocity of round 1 from that of round 4, Jim determines that the extreme velocity spread in this group of handloads is 69 fps. He enters the figure 69 under the column labeled Data 5 and opposite load No.1.

Data 6, Average Velocity, is the next calculation. The average velocity is simply the arithmetic mean or average of all five velocity recordings for load No.1. This is determined by adding the five velocities and dividing the sum by the number of rounds recorded. Jim adds the velocity recordings to obtain their sum:

$$
\begin{array}{r}
2,678 \text{ fps} \\
2,688 \text{ fps} \\
2,695 \text{ fps} \\
2,747 \text{ fps} \\
\underline{2,696 \text{ fps}} \\
13,504 \text{ fps}
\end{array}
$$

He then divides the sum of velocities by the number of rounds recorded to determine the average velocity:

$$
\text{Average velocity} \ = \ \frac{13,504}{5} \ = \ \begin{array}{l} 2,700.8 \\ \text{or } 2,701 \text{ fps} \end{array}
$$

The figure 2,701 is entered under Data 6 of the velocity columns opposite load No.1.

The last velocity data calculation to be performed is to find the standard velocity deviation, or Data 4. Again, as with precision data, you have a choice of methods. You may opt to use the less complex calculation for average velocity deviation

---

### STANDARD VELOCITY DEVIATION

$$
\text{Standard Velocity Deviation} \ = \ \sqrt{\frac{\Sigma \ (v_n)^2}{N - 1}}
$$

where: $\Sigma$ = sum of the squared velocity deviations

$v_1, v_2, v_3, \ldots, v_N$ = individual velocity deviations (from the average velocity) in feet per second

N = number of velocity recordings

Example: Load No. 1 for .270 Winchester, 130-grain bullet

Substituting the individual deviations, measured from the average velocity of load number 1, is done as follows:

Step 1. Standard Velocity Deviation $= \sqrt{\dfrac{(v_1)^2 + (v_2)^2 + (v_3)^2 + (v_4)^2 + (v_5)^2}{N - 1}}$

Step 2. $\qquad\qquad\qquad = \sqrt{\dfrac{(23)^2 + (13)^2 + (6)^2 + (46)^2 + (5)^2}{5 - 1}}$

Step 3. $\qquad\qquad\qquad = \sqrt{\dfrac{529 + 169 + 36 + 2116 + 25}{4}}$

Step 4. $\qquad\qquad\qquad = \sqrt{\dfrac{2875}{4}}$

Step 5. $\qquad\qquad\qquad = \sqrt{718.75}$

Step 6. Standard Velocity Deviation $= 26.809513 = 27 \text{ fps}$

The formula for finding Standard Velocity Deviation.

rather than standard velocity deviation. We will use the calculation for standard velocity deviation. The formula for standard velocity deviation, which is similar to the standard vertical deviation, developed earlier for our precision data, is:

$$\text{Standard Velocity Deviation} = \sqrt{\frac{\Sigma \, (v_n)^2}{N-1}}$$

where: $\Sigma$ = sum of the squared velocity deviations
$v_1, v_2, v_3, \ldots, v_N$ = individual velocity deviations (from the average velocity)
$N$ = number of velocity recordings

The formula for standard velocity deviation is used exactly like the one for precision data, except that the deviations are for individual velocities rather than for shot group dispersion. Since Jim already knows the average velocity is 2,701 fps for this group of shots, he merely subtracts each velocity reading from 2,701, disregarding the minus signs that result from subtracting velocities greater than the average. The resultant velocity deviations are calculated as follows:

$$
\begin{aligned}
v_1 &= 2{,}701 - 2{,}678 = 23 \text{ fps} \\
v_2 &= 2{,}701 - 2{,}688 = 13 \text{ fps} \\
v_3 &= 2{,}701 - 2{,}695 = 6 \text{ fps} \\
v_4 &= 2{,}701 - 2{,}747 = -46 \text{ fps} \\
v_5 &= 2{,}701 - 2{,}696 = 5 \text{ fps}
\end{aligned}
$$

These deviations, without signs, could be averaged at this point to determine average velocity deviation rather than standard velocity deviation. As stated before, we will use standard velocity deviation so that we can see how it is calculated. The velocity deviations are inserted into the formula (see illustration).

This illustration shows the use of the standard deviation calculation for developing Data 4. In step 1, all the symbols are entered. In step 2, the symbols are replaced by actual deviations calculated earlier. You must also include the number of velocity recordings (5) for the factor N. Although the velocity deviation for round number four resulted in a negative figure, deviations can only be expressed as absolute numbers without positive or negative signs. Even if he had entered a negative sign, the squaring of the velocities within the formula would automatically eliminate the negative sign.

In step 3, the squares of the deviations are shown. In step 4, the sum of the squared deviations

is divided by 4 to give a quotient of 718.75, step 5. Jim determines the square root of 718.75 and rounds the resulting figure off to the nearest whole number. These calculations result in a standard velocity deviation for handload No.1 of 27 fps. This figure is entered opposite load No.1 under the velocity column labeled Data 4 on the handload data list.

Jim now proceeds to calculate and list all of the velocity data for the other handloads and factory ammunition used as the standard. When the velocity data is complete, he is ready to show us the velocity results graphically.

Three items of velocity data are needed to construct the velocity graph. Each of these data can be presented on the handload velocity graph similar to the way pertinent data was plotted on the precision graph.

As with the precision graph, these three velocity items will be judged against factory ammunition data lines, which will be labeled on the graph as lines Standard 4, Standard 5, and Standard 6.

Standard velocity deviation is a statistical way of stating the amount of velocity deviation within a group of shots. Velocity deviation is the amount of velocity difference of an individual round from the average velocity of the group. By using the formula for standard deviation, as described during precision graph construction, the velocity characteristics of any handload number can be compared directly with any other handload and the factory-loaded ammunition.

Extreme velocity spread of individual groups is simply the difference in speed of the fastest and slowest rounds within a group. Extreme velocity spread is a data item related to standard velocity deviation. It, too, is a measure of general tendency. These two data items, Data 4 and Data 5, result in very similar graph curves that differ only in their magnitude or height. They tend to support each other and give us added confidence in their validity.

The third velocity data item is obviously important. Data 6 is the average velocity of the five shots in any given group and is easily calculated by dividing the sum by the number of rounds.

Incidentally, conversion of all instrumental velocity readings to an estimated muzzle velocity would needlessly complicate data storage. It is easier to use instrumental velocity for all data storage and display. The differences in instrumental and

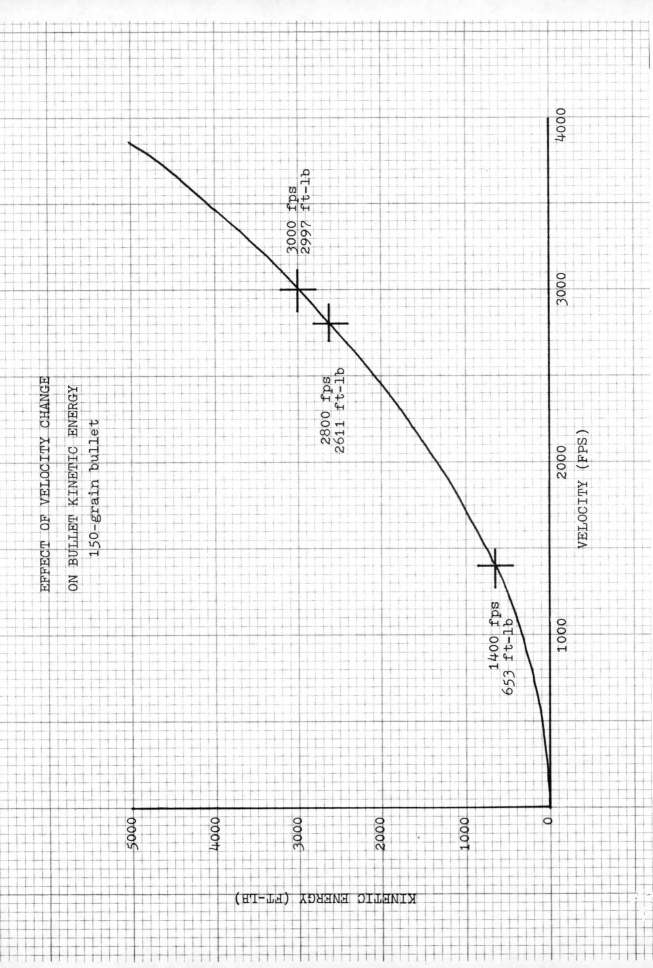

The effect of velocity change on bullet energy is diagrammed. In addition to accuracy, greater velocity results in more energy. There's a bonus: for every 1 percent increase in velocity, the energy increase is 2 percent.

muzzle velocity are very small. The only muzzle velocity that is of importance to the shooter is the estimated velocity of the chosen handload. After determination of the best handload, the instrumental velocity for that handload can be converted to an approximate muzzle velocity by a simple calculation shown in Chapter 10. The estimated muzzle velocity can then be used for further ballistic calculations with the chosen handload.

### The Velocity Graph

Jim is ready to start constructing the velocity graph. The first step is to plot all of the Data 4, Standard Velocity Deviation, points and draw an approximate Data 4 curve using the freehand method as explained in the discussion of precision graphs in Chapter 6. Then a horizontal Standard 4 line (factory average) corresponding to factory-loaded ammunition is drawn. This will allow us to compare the standard velocity deviation of his handloads against that of the factory ammunition. This can be seen on the graph example. Jim uses the same technique for constructing the Data 5, Extreme Velocity Spread, approximate curve and its related Standard 5 line. Observe that the two resulting curves for Data 4 and Data 5 are similar in general shape, but the extreme velocity spread curve is at a higher level, even though both curves are plotted using the same scale for their magnitude.

With both data, notice that most of the data points lie below their respective Standard 4 and Standard 5 lines. This means that most of the handloads were more uniform in velocity and less subject to wide variations in shot-to-shot spread than the factory ammunition. These findings are due in some part to the careful selection and sorting of brass for handloading, the adjustment of the sizing die, bullet clearance, and Jim's ability as a handloader to fill each cartridge case with identical weights of propellant. Although skeptics might argue that such differences are minor and of little importance for most shooting, the fact remains that the differences do exist. Where precision is involved in competitive shooting, almost all shooters use carefully handloaded ammunition.

The differences in velocity between handloads and factory ammunition are interesting. Of equal interest should be the fact that some of the handloads have velocity deviations and spread that are greater than those of the factory ammunition. This is an important fact for handloaders to understand, as the graph shows clearly that handloaded ammunition, even when loaded with extreme care, is not always superior to factory products. Information such as that displayed on this velocity graph is invaluable for making any intelligent handloading decisions.

The last data item on the handload velocity graph to construct is Data 6, Average Velocity. Again, use the data from the handload data list to plot the Data 6 line and the Standard 6 line. Interestingly, it is not necessary to draw a curve connecting the Data 6 points. The Data 6 points represent a straight line function. This is a characteristic of single-based propellants and can be quite useful when estimating velocities for additional charge weights within and without the range of tested weights.

From the velocity graph, Jim sees that he can equal factory ammunition velocity by using 54.5 grains of the tested propellant. He also notices that higher velocities have been achieved with all handloads of greater charge weight. At this point, the handload velocity graph is complete.

There is only one more thing to do before we can use this information and make the selection; we must graph the results of case head expansion to see and compare the pressure of factory and handloaded ammunition.

CALIBER _270 WIN_ BULLET WGT. _130_ gr.          HANDLOAD DATA

| FIREARM:mfgr. _WIN_ | FACTY STD CARTRGE | CASE:mfgr _REM (R-P)_ | POWDER:mfgr _DuPONT_ |
|---|---|---|---|
| model _70 XTR_ | mfgr _REM_ | avg wgt _197.3±3.0_ gr | mfgr no. _IMR4831_ |
| barrel length _22_ in | mfgr no. _R270W2_ | trim length _2.530_ in | lot no. _P8IJY29A-74_ |
| twist rate _1:10_ in | lot no. _L25UD2452_ | c.o.a. length _3.205_ in | PRIMER:mfgr _CCI_ |
| TARGET:mfg/no. _LEUPG-53_ | bullet wgt _130_ gr | sized head _0.4656_ in | mfgr no. _200_ |
| RANGE:dist. _100_ yd | BULLET:wgt _130_ gr | | lot no. _L25L_ |
| | mfgr _SIERRA_ | | |
| | mfgr no. _1830_ | | |
| | lot no. _40520_ | | |
| | type _SPIT., F.BASE_ | | |
| | clearance _1/16_ in | | |

| LOAD | | | | INTERNAL AND EXTERNAL FACTORS | | PRECISION | | | | | VELOCITY | | | | | PRES-SURE |
|---|---|---|---|---|---|---|---|---|---|---|---|---|---|---|---|---|
| no. | charg wgt. gr. | date load | date fire | no. rds | wind velocity, direction, temperature, bar. pres., precip., visibility, ch. pressure observations, other. | Dat1 Std Vert Dev. in. | Dat2 Extm Vert Sprd in. | Dat3 HtAb Aim. Pt. in. | Dat4 Std Vel. Dev. fps. | Dat5 Extm Vel. Sprd fps. | Dat6 Avg Vel. fps. | no. rds rcrd | Dat7 Case Head Exp. in. |
| 1 | 52.0 | 7/8/82 | 9/10/82 | 5 | 4-6 fr 4:00 @ 12:30 94°F 29.72 day | 0.58 | 1.44 | 2.8 | 27 | 69 | 2,701 | 5 | . |
| 2 | 52.5 | " | | | exceptional group, but slow | .22 | 0.59 | 1.9 | 4 | 10 | 2,748 | | . |
| 3 | 53.0 | " | | | " " " | .16 | 0.41 | 1.7 | 11 | 31 | 2,769 | | . |
| 4 | 53.5 | " | | | avg wind pressure | .55 | 1.34 | 2.1 | 12 | 28 | 2,791 | | . |
| 5 | 54.0 | " | | | 6-12 fr 4:00, 94°, 29.62, dry, brisk | .28 | 0.75 | 2.8 | 18 | 43 | 2,826 | | . |
| 6 | 54.5 | " | | → | | .41 | 1.13 | 3.0 | 13 | 33 | 2,870 | | . |
| 7 | 55.0 | " | | 4 | one shot lost thru another hole | .37 | 0.80 | 3.9 | 17 | 44 | 2,909 | | . |
| 8 | 55.5 | " | | 5 | beginning of primer flattening | .50 | 1.14 | 3.7 | 20 | 55 | 2,941 | | . |
| 9 | 56.0 | " | | | exceptional grp, good adj, brisk | .18 | 0.45 | 3.8 | 25 | 71 | 2,980 | | . |
| 10 | 56.5 | " | | | | .44 | 1.18 | 3.8 | 15 | 34 | 2,998 | | . |
| 11 | 57.0 | " | | | 2-4 fr 4:00, 94°F, 29.56 ↓ | .57 | 1.44 | 3.5 | 17 | 38 | 3,016 | | . |
| 12 | 57.5 | " | | | | .70 | 1.48 | 3.4 | 9 | 26 | 3,045 | | . |
| 13 | 58.0 | " | | | fairly heavy pressure, brisk | .63 | 1.60 | 3.4 | 12 | 32 | 3,075 | | . |
| 14 | 58.5 | " | | | 2-4 fr 4:00, 94°, 29.52 ↓ | .59 | 1.23 | 4.1 | 26 | 60 | 3,123 | | . |
| 15 | 59.0 | " | | | | .59 | 1.45 | 3.9 | 11 | 29 | 3,142 | | . |
| 16 | 59.5 | " | | | | .90 | 2.33 | 3.4 | 11 | 28 | 3,179 | | . |
| 17 | 60.0 | " → | → | → | limit of useful speed & pressure | .63 | 1.62 | 3.5 | 18 | 47 | 3,189 | ↓ | . |
| 18 | . | | | | | . | . | . | | | | | . |
| 19 | . | | | | | . | . | . | | | | | . |
| 20 | . | | | | | . | . | . | | | | | . |
| 1 | facty ld. | 9/8/82 | 9/8/82 | 5 | 2-4 fr 4:00, 94° 29.56 | 0.93 | 2.68 | 4.5 | 19 | 52 | 2,917 | 5 | . |
| 2 | " | " | → | → | 2 shots not chronographed | .25 | 0.59 | 4.2 | 26 | 50 | 2,870 | 3 | . |
| 3 | " | " | | | | .59 | 1.53 | 4.0 | 19 | 48 | 2,823 | 5 | . |
| 4 | " | " | → | | | .47 | 1.27 | 4.7 | 16 | 40 | 2,813 | → | . |
| 5 | | | | | | | | | | | | | . |
| | | | | | facty avgs = | 0.56 | 1.52 | 4.4 | 20 | 48 | 2,856 | | |

Data 1, 2, 3, 4, 5, 6 and 7 above, refer to data used in construction of the PREC., VEL. and PRESS. graphs

A partially completed handload data list, through "Velocity" data.

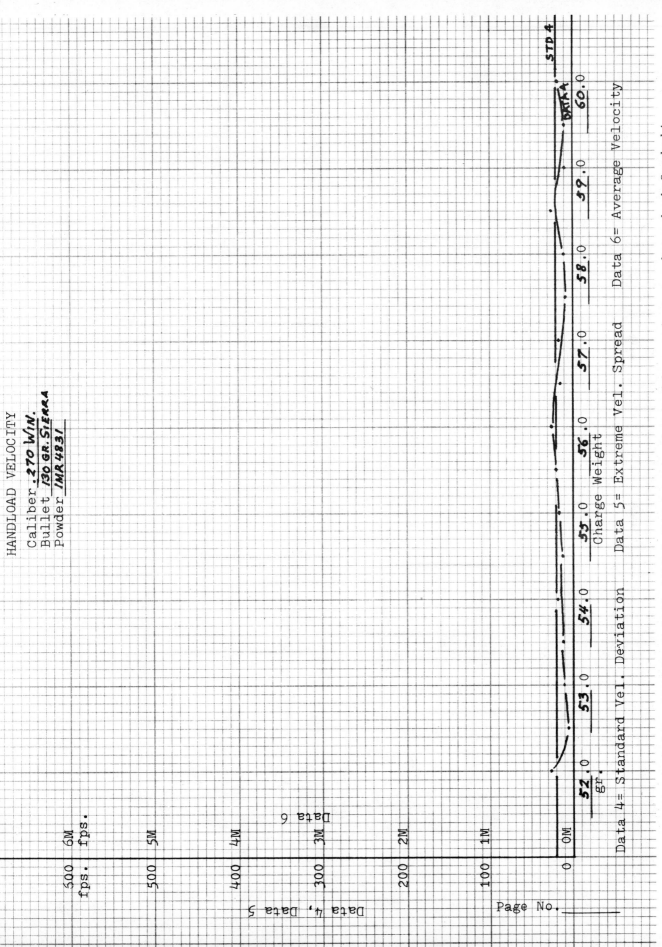

HANDLOAD VELOCITY

Caliber .270 WiN.
Bullet 130 GR. SIERRA
Powder IMR 4831

Data 4= Standard Vel. Deviation    Data 5= Extreme Vel. Spread    Data 6= Average Velocity

Charge Weight

A velocity graph with Data 4, Standard Velocity Deviation, points plotted and the approximate curve drawn, plus the Standard 4 line for factory ammunition indicated.

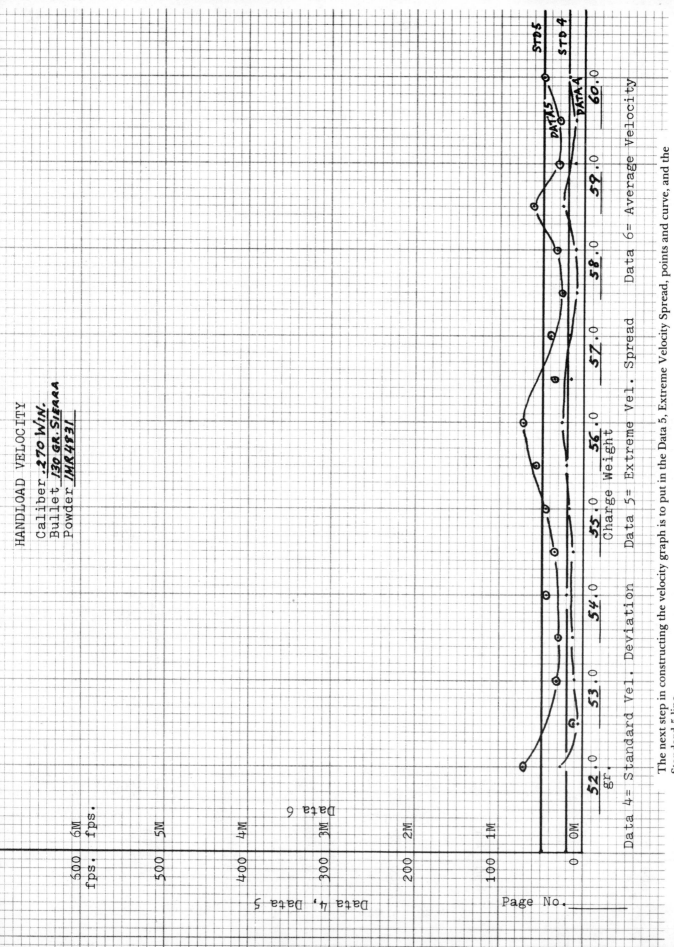

HANDLOAD VELOCITY

Caliber .270 WIN.
Bullet 130 GR. SIERRA
Powder IMR 4831

Data 4= Standard Vel. Deviation    Data 5= Extreme Vel. Spread    Data 6= Average Velocity

The next step in constructing the velocity graph is to put in the Data 5, Extreme Velocity Spread, points and curve, and the Standard 5 line.

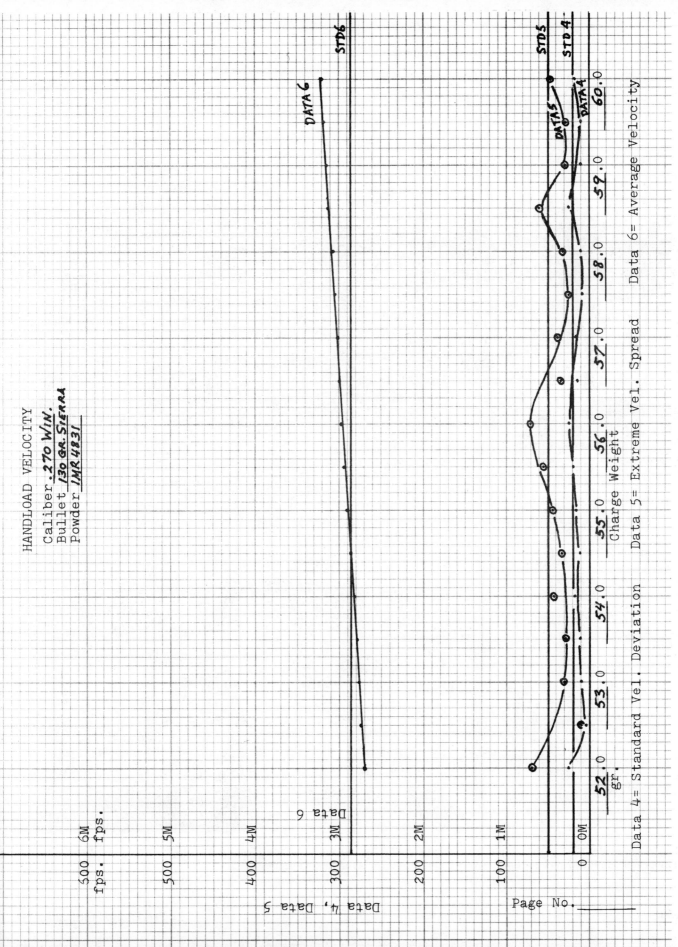

HANDLOAD VELOCITY

Caliber .270 WIN.
Bullet 130 GR. SIERRA
Powder IMR 4831

Data 4= Standard Vel. Deviation    Data 5= Extreme Vel. Spread    Data 6= Average Velocity

With the addition of the Data 6, Average Velocity, points line (as it turned out), and the Standard 6 line, the velocity graph is complete. All velocity data is now shown.

This is a good idea when chronographing a handgun or rifle. Tie a string to the "start" sensor. Use the string to separate the sensors and gun for correct instrumental velocity measurement before testing begins.

# Chapter 8
# Pressure

With precision and velocity findings out of the way, Jim has progressed well past the halfway point in his efforts to find the best ammunition for his needs. Very soon all the pieces of this handloading puzzle will be assembled in a way that provides everything needed for the final decision. He has only one more data area to wrap up; he must know how much pressure his handloads produce—whether they develop less, more, or the same pressure as the factory ammunition. He must know if there is enough pressure to do the job. Conversely, too much pressure would be unsafe and cause excessive wear on the gun.

First, let me say a few things about this mysterious thing called pressure. The most misunderstood aspect of handloading is surely that of pressure, which can be a help or a hindrance, depending on the circumstances, but it is essential to the functioning of ammunition and firearms. Understanding, controlling, and using pressure is important for all shooters and handloaders. This discussion will explain pressure in terms relative to handloading for a better understanding, and give methods for using and controlling pressure to achieve better shooting.

In order to understand pressure as it relates to shooting, we must realize that the pressure inside the chamber of a firearm is that of a fluid dynamic system: fluid, because the expanding gas from the burning propellant is a fluid medium; dynamic, because the system moves the bullet. A fluid dynamic system involves the physical concepts of force, area, and pressure.

Force is an influence that, when applied to a movable object, will cause that object to move. If an object, such as a bullet, is not held back by other factors, and the force is continually applied, the object will accelerate. The force acting on that object or bullet is measured in pounds. Force is a part of pressure.

Area, or surface area, is the number of unit

squares equal in measure to the surface included within a set of lines. Area is measured in square inches. Area is also a part of pressure.

The concept of pressure combines force and area. Pressure is the amount of force applied to a unit of area. Another way to show this is the formula for pressure:

$$P = \frac{f}{A} = \frac{\text{force}}{\text{area}} = \frac{\text{pounds}}{\text{square in.}} = \frac{\text{lbs}}{\text{in.}^2} \text{ or psi}$$

where: P = pressure
      f = force
     A = area

Since force is measured in pounds and area is measured in square inches, pressure is measured by the number of pounds of force applied to a square inch of surface area. A chamber pressure of 50,000 psi means that a force of 50,000 pounds is exerted on each square inch of surface area in contact with the burning, pressurized gas in the chamber of the firearm.

An important point to remember is that pressure and force are two different factors and should not be confused. For instance, the same chamber pressure may be generated within two different cartridges of different case size. The larger case will be subjected to more internal force because it has more internal surface area for the gas pressure to act against. Perhaps the following example will explain this better: the .222 Remington cartridge has about 2.1 square inches of inside chamber area. The .375 H & H Magnum cartridge has about 5.4 square inches of inside chamber area. Both cartridges operate at about 50,000 psi during peak pressure. This means that each cartridge has a force of 50,000 pounds acting on each square inch of surface. The .222 Remington must contain a total force of about 105,000 pounds. The larger .375 H & H Magnum must contain internal forces of about 270,000 pounds. The larger cartridge must contain over two and a half times the amount of force held by the smaller cartridge. This fact must be considered in firearms design, the alteration of case dimensions, and even some handloading projects.

Another reason for knowing about pressure is to understand the pressure effects of different propellants and their proper and safe use.

The black powder cartridges and firearms of

Case inspection for signs of high pressure is just as necesary for handguns as for rifles. As always, use the powder and bullet makers' data as a guide. Start at least 10 percent below the maximum recommended charge weight.

long ago were built to operate at much lower pressures than those reached today with modern, smokeless propellants. Using smokeless propellant in black powder cartridges and firearms can be dangerous. Likewise, the use of incorrect propellants in any firearm is a bad practice. If pressure exceeds the design capacity of the gun or the cartridge, something will break. The effect can be disastrous. Pressure and force limits must be understood and respected by the handloader to avoid injury to himself, others, and the firearm.

Some determination of chamber pressure should be made when developing any new handload, but finding chamber pressure in a firearm is not as simple as finding the tire pressure of an automobile. The latter is static or non-moving, but chamber pressure is a dynamic or moving pressure that occurs in a very short span of time.

Precision Handloading

In a ballistic laboratory, chamber pressure can be found by using a pressure gun and metal "crusher" slugs. When the pressure-test cartridge is fired, the "crusher" is compressed by the force exerted on it from the pressure in the chamber. The amount of compression is used to find chamber pressure by comparison to some standard of reference.

Some ballistic laboratories also use a newer and more direct method of chamber pressure measurement called the transducer method. This method measures the amount of electrical current generated in a crystal from the chamber pressure. The transducer, or "pick up" unit, is attached to the firearm chamber and pressure readings are taken electronically.

The two pressure-finding methods explained here are beyond the ability of most handloaders. Other, more feasible, methods are needed for determining chamber pressure. Fortunately, such methods exist and they are practical for our needs.

Handloaders have two methods available to them for comparing and controlling chamber pressure: observation of result and case head expansion. Both methods use a standard of comparison which is usually a factory-loaded cartridge. Since the true or absolute pressure developed in a gun with factory-loaded ammunition is not actually known by the handloader, the factory cartridge serves as a standard of relative pressure, without specific numerical value. But its importance as a standard is still valuable.

A handloader does not know if a factory round develops 35,000, 45,000, or even 55,000 pounds of pressure in his gun. But if the factory ammunition can be assumed to develop safe and correct pressure, handloads may be compared to it using the observation of result and the case head expansion methods.

## Observation of Result

One method used by handloaders to compare chamber pressures is that called observation of result. This technique, along with the proper use of a good loading table and some experience, is a fairly good means for keeping handloads in the safe pressure range. Observation of result will not tell you when you have reached a pressure of 50,000 psi, but it can tell you, reasonably well, if your handloads are performing safely or if you are approaching an unsafe level of pressure in the firearm. It is a very basic, subjective method of finding relative chamber pressure and is used by handloaders as well as ballistic technicians as a guide and complement to other means of pressure determination. The method requires that the handloader have some experience with the firearm, the cartridge, and the components for positive determination, however.

The observation of result process for finding chamber pressure consists of heard, seen, and felt sensations. It begins as soon as the cartridge is fired. The first two observations that you should make are those you feel and hear as the firearm recoils and the muzzle blast is heard. Recoil greater than that produced by the factory cartridge probably indicates higher pressure. A muzzle blast that is louder and sharper than that produced by factory ammunition may also indicate higher pressure. Both of

A good example of oversizing, probably caused by excessive headspace and too much of the wrong propellant. The results are a marked case head due to brass extrusion into the bolt face, a flanged primer, and an enlarged primer pocket. Also, the case is split.

CALIBER 270 WIN BULLET 130 gr.        HANDLOAD DATA

| FIREARM: mfgr. WIN | FACTY STD CARTRGE | CASE: mfgr REM (R-P) | BULLET: wgt 130 gr | POWDER: mfgr DUPONT |
|---|---|---|---|---|
| model 70 XTR | mfgr REM | avg wgt 197.3±3.0 gr | mfgr SIERRA | mfgr no. IMR4831 |
| barrel length 22 in | mfgr no. R270W2 | trim length 2.530 in | mfgr no. 1830 | lot no. P81JY29A-74 |
| twist rate 1:10 in | lot no. LZ5UD2452 | c.o.a. length 3.205 in | lot no. 40520 | PRIMER: mfgr CCI |
| TARGET: mfg/no. LEUP G-53 | bullet wgt 130 gr | sized head 0.4656 in | type SPIT, F. BASE | mfgr no. 200 |
| RANGE: dist. 100 yd | | | clearance 1/16 in | lot no. L25L |

| LOAD no. | charg wgt. gr. | date load | date fire | no. rds | INTERNAL AND EXTERNAL FACTORS — wind velocity, direction, temperature, bar. pres., precip., visibility, ch. pressure observations, other. | PRECISION Dat1 Std Vert Dev. in. | Dat2 Extm Sprd in. | Dat3 HtAb Aim Pt. in. | VELOCITY Dat4 Std Vel. Dev. fps. | Dat5 Extm Vel. Sprd fps. | Dat6 Avg Vel. fps. | no. rds rcrd | PRES-SURE Dat7 Case Head Exp. in. |
|---|---|---|---|---|---|---|---|---|---|---|---|---|---|
| 1 | 52.0 | 7/6/82 | 9/10/82 | 5 | 4-6 fr 4:00 @ 12:30 94°F 29.72 dry | 0.58 | 1.44 | 2.8 | 27 | 69 | 2,701 | 5 | 0.0034 |
| 2 | 52.5 | | | | exceptional group, but slow | .22 | 0.59 | 1.9 | 4 | 10 | 2,748 | | .0036 |
| 3 | 53.0 | | | | | .16 | 0.41 | 1.7 | 11 | 31 | 2,769 | | .0037 |
| 4 | 53.5 | | | | | .55 | 1.34 | 2.1 | 12 | 28 | 2,791 | | .0037 |
| 5 | 54.0 | | | | avg mild pressure | .28 | 0.75 | 2.8 | 18 | 43 | 2,826 | | .0037 |
| 6 | 54.5 | | | → | 6-12 fr 4:00, 94°, 29.62, dry, brisk | .41 | 1.13 | 3.0 | 13 | 33 | 2,870 | | .0039 |
| 7 | 55.0 | | | 4 | mg shot lost thru another hole | .37 | 0.80 | 3.9 | 17 | 44 | 2,909 | | .0038 |
| 8 | 55.5 | | | 5 | beginning of primer flattening | .50 | 1.14 | 3.7 | 20 | 55 | 2,941 | | .0038 |
| 9 | 56.0 | | | | exceptional grp; good grp'd, brisk | .18 | 0.45 | 3.8 | 25 | 71 | 2,980 | | .0040 |
| 10 | 56.5 | | | | | .44 | 1.18 | 3.8 | 15 | 34 | 2,998 | | .0041 |
| 11 | 57.0 | | | | 2-4 fr 4:00, 94°F, 29.56 ↓ | .57 | 1.44 | 3.5 | 17 | 38 | 3,016 | | .0042 |
| 12 | 57.5 | | | | | .70 | 1.48 | 3.4 | 9 | 26 | 3,045 | | .0042 |
| 13 | 58.0 | | | | fairly heavy pressure, brisk | .63 | 1.60 | 3.4 | 12 | 32 | 3,075 | | .0043 |
| 14 | 58.5 | | | | 2-4 fr 4:00, 94°, 29.52 ↓ | .59 | 1.23 | 4.1 | 26 | 60 | 3,123 | | .0042 |
| 15 | 59.0 | | | | | .59 | 1.45 | 3.9 | 11 | 29 | 3,142 | | .0043 |
| 16 | 59.5 | | | | | .90 | 2.33 | 3.4 | 11 | 28 | 3,179 | | .0045 |
| 17 | 60.0 | | → | → | limit of useful speed + pressure | .63 | 1.62 | 3.5 | 18 | 47 | 3,189 | → | .0041 |
| 18 | | | | | | | | | | | | | |
| 19 | | | | | | | | | | | | | |
| 20 | | | | | | | | | | | | | |
| 1 | facty ld. | 9/3/82 | | 5 | 2-4 fr 4:00, 94° 29.56 | 0.93 | 2.68 | 4.5 | 19 | 52 | 2,917 | 5 | 0.0038 |
| 2 | " | | | → | 2 shots not chronographed | .25 | 0.59 | 4.2 | 26 | 50 | 2,870 | 3 | .0038 |
| 3 | " | | | → | | .59 | 1.53 | 4.0 | 19 | 48 | 2,823 | 5 | .0032 |
| 4 | " | | | | | .47 | 1.27 | 4.7 | 16 | 40 | 2,813 | → | |
| 5 | | | | | | | | | | | | | |
| | | | facty avgs = | | | 0.56 | 1.52 | 4.4 | 20 | 48 | 2,856 | | .0038 |

Data 1,2,3,4,5,6 and 7 above, refer to data used in construction of the PREC., VEL. and PRESS. graphs

A completed handload data list, through "Pressure" data.

these perceptions are judgments influenced by several factors such as hearing protection, shooting conditions, shooting position, and clothing.

Another observation occurs when you go to open the bolt or action and it sticks or is abnormally hard to open. It could mean excessive chamber pressure. Some shooters call this observation "stickiness." The chamber pressure can be great enough to squeeze a part of the brass cartridge case into a recess of the chamber or the bolt face. This brass extrusion causes extra friction and may even be sheared off as the action is opened. Greater force is required to open the action and eject the cartridge case. This same condition can be felt in pump and lever action rifles as well. In semiautomatic firearms, high pressure can result in failures to extract or eject the cartridge case fully. Low pressure can also cause a failure to extract and eject, but this is usually accompanied by less recoil when the gun is fired, and can be felt at the shooter's shoulder.

Once the gun's action is opened and the cartridge case is removed, attention should be shifted to the brass case itself and your observations become visual. The condition of the primer and the case head ought to be the first areas of concern.

A completely flattened primer may indicate high pressure. I say "may indicate" as none of these observations are positive evidence by themselves. They are merely indications of such. Some primers are made with thin, soft cup material and are flattened easily, even with mild pressure. This can happen with different lot numbers of the same brand and stock number. Flattening will occur easily with any primer when there is some amount of headspace between the bolt face and the cartridge case, which allows the case to gain a running start against the bolt after the primer has already popped out of its pocket. A smashed, flattened primer with a flange around its border could signal this condition, even at mild pressure. With straight-walled cases, as used in revolvers, even normal pressure usually results in such flattened primers.

Primer "cratering" is another indicator used in finding excessive chamber pressure, but "reading" primer craters requires some experience with the given firearm for positive pressure determination. Cratering is caused by the primer being squeezed or extruded into the space between the firing pin hole and the firing pin on the bolt face. Some firing pins fit loosely and permit the primer to crater easily.

Also some primer cup material is very soft and easily extrudes into the firing pin hole. A slightly overlong chamber, or the type of action, can also accentuate primer cratering and flattening effects. If the chamber is correct, the sizing die is adjusted properly, the factory ammunition does not show cratering or abnormal flattening, and you are using maximum charge weights in your handloads, a flattened, cratered primer may indicate high pressure.

Another indicator of too much pressure is a bright mark on the base of the cartridge case head. This head mark usually occurs with guns in which the ejector pin is mounted in the bolt face. Brass is squeezed into the ejector pin hole under high pressure. This bright spot is where brass was sheared off the case as the action was opened. The bright mark on the case head shows where extrusion occurred, and often indicates excessive pressure for that chamber.

Another observation is a leaking primer pocket. This can be due to a primer that is undersized (very rare), a primer pocket that is too large, or high pressure. However, an abnormally small primer or an enlarged pocket will always let gas escape, even at mild pressure. But if you know that the primer pocket was a tight fit before firing, a gas leak at this location is a very good sign of high pressure.

Don't be misled by case head separation and case body splits. Although both types of damage are generally related to pressure, they can occur at low pressure as well. For instance, case head separation is almost always a result of excessive headspace. The head separates because the case stretches in length beyond its elastic limit. It can happen if the chamber or headspace of the gun is too large, or the cartridge case shoulder is pushed back too far during the sizing operation, or both. Case head separation may occur on first firing of factory ammunition, but it happens more often after the second or third reloading. This kind of damage to the case head will be kept to a minimum or eliminated by following the procedure for sizing die adjustment that was explained in Chapter 4.

Another poor indicator of pressure is a split case. A split may occur almost anywhere on a case and for any one of several reasons, almost none of which have a direct bearing on chamber pressure. Splits are caused by metal fatigue, a bad fit of cartridge and chamber, or both. Case splits are not reliable indicators of relative chamber pressure.

Most of these observations are subjective and not positive indicators in themselves. Some can occur at low pressure and tend to confuse our evaluation of pressure. The best way to use these indicators or observations is to keep them in perspective considering the circumstance. For instance, if you are firing handloads that begin at the lower levels of recommended charge weight for the powder and bullet you are using, and the rifle has performed properly with factory ammunition, the appearance of a well-flattened primer would not be a positive sign of high pressure. If you follow the published loading recommendations properly, you should still be within the safe pressure range. But if you've reached a point in your load work-up where recoil feels greater than when firing factory ammo, muzzle blast is very sharp, the primer is extremely flattened and possibly cratered, a shiny mark appears on the case head where it touches the ejector pin, and the bolt handle has become difficult to open, you have probably exceeded good, safe chamber pressure in that firearm. You should not fire any more of those handloads, or any handloads with even greater powder charges! You will have to be content with less powder, less pressure, and lower velocity. The firearm has reached its limits with that handload. Two or more of the above indicators may be positive signs of excessive chamber pressure.

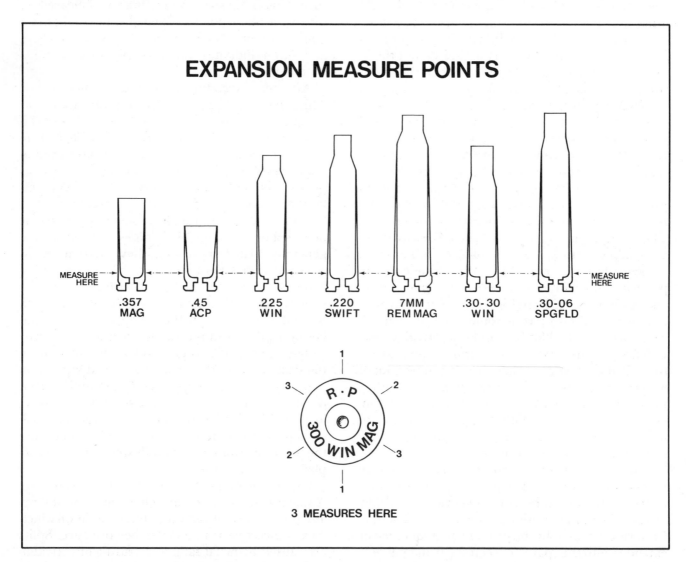

Because cases do not expand equally in all directions, three measurements should be taken and averaged to arrive at the most accurate figure.

All of the above observations of result, when coupled with shooter experience and good use of loading tables, provide a quick method for observing relative chamber pressure when firing handloads and factory ammunition. These indicators have been used since the brass case was invented and have played an important role in the development of arms and ammunition. But remember, they must be used in conjunction with some standard for comparison, and preferably by a shooter who is fairly experienced in their use. Any pressure observations that are significant should be listed opposite the appropriate load number on the handload data list in the column titled "Internal and External Factors." Do not neglect this chore.

### Case Head Expansion

The second procedure that handloaders employ for finding relative chamber pressure is the case head expansion method. The measurement of case head expansion is not subjective, as are the observed result techniques; instead, it is an objective method that measures the result of pressure in a very similar manner to that of the measurement of the copper crushers used in ballistic laboratories. Case head expansion measurement is susceptible to method abuse and interpretation, however.

The only special equipment required to measure the expansion of case heads is a one-inch micrometer that measures to four places or .0001″. Calipers, which are only correct to three significant places, cannot be used for this method of pressure-finding. There are a number of methods and techniques for measuring case heads, but only one such method is satisfactory for our use.

Briefly stated, the method involves measuring case heads before and after firing. The difference in size represents the amount of expansion due to pressure in the case when fired. Expansion greater than that of the pressure-test or pressure-standard ammunition indicates that higher pressure occurred than with the standard.

To begin, remove the bullets, powder, and primers from five factory cartridges (note: this was done by Jim in Chapter 4). These components will be used in the pressure test as pressure-standard rounds for comparison. Load these components into five of the selected, sorted cases used for hand-

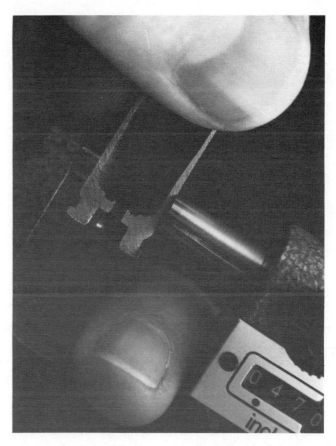

After cutting a sample case in half, you can easily see where the web of the case head is drawn into the thinner wall portion. This is where resizing and controlled, measurable expansion occurs.

loading. These five rounds can be called the pressure-test rounds. After firing some warm-up ammunition, fire the pressure-test rounds. Find their average head expansion. This is done by subtracting the average resized head diameter from the expanded heads. The average resized head diameter is already known. This dimension was determined earlier and is on the handload data listing in the "Case" block in the space for "sized head." The difference in the expanded case head and the sized head is the expansion measurement used as a standard of comparison here. It relates to factory pressure.

This measurement is then entered in the Data 7, Case Head Expansion, column and opposite the factory load reference number near the bottom of the handload data list. Again, these case head measurements must be taken with a one-inch microm-

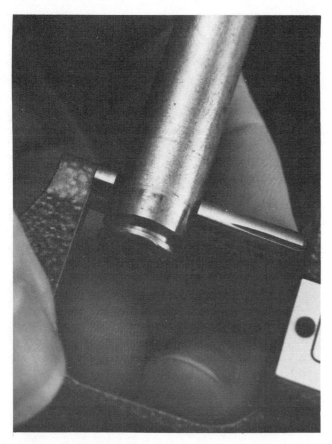

Another way to find the exact location for expansion measurements on most cases is to examine a case as it is withdrawn from the sizing die. The die will always leave a mark on the case where the lowest point of sizing occurs. Measure here, as seen in the photo.

are made from the same selected brass cases and are sized in the same sizing die, comparison of expansion between handloads and factory pressure-test components is valid. The amount of head expansion from resized to fired cases is measured and entered in the appropriate block under the Data 7 column and opposite the appropriate load number.

The only problem with this method, in theory, is that the factory pressure-test components are not fired in their original cases. This is not as much of a problem as might be assumed. Testing has shown that the pressure and velocity results achieved with factory-assembled rounds is very close to that achieved when the same factory components (bullet, powder, and primer) are placed in a resized, once-fired case of the same brand and head stamp as the factory ammunition. The results are certainly close enough for the needs of the handloader when the objectives are safety and relative chamber pressure comparison.

There are two items of concern when actually measuring case heads. First, make sure you measure each case in the right spot, and second, make sure your measuring technique is consistent and thorough.

The correct area for case head expansion measurement is where the cartridge case web, or base, is drawn into the thin wall of the case body. This is usually the point where the sizing die makes the lowest contact with the case as it is fully inserted into the die. On most rimmed and rimless cartridge cases, this point is about one-quarter of an inch above the base of the rim. On belted-type cases, the measurement location is generally about one-tenth of an inch above the top edge of the belt. This can be seen on the illustration. If you are in doubt about this location on the brass you're using, there are two methods to find the point of measurement. First, you can cut a cartridge case completely in half from neck to base. This will let you look inside and see where the web of the head is drawn into the wall of the case body. Near this point, you can find where expansion and resizing occur. This must be done with a once-fired and resized cartridge case.

Another, easier way to find the correct spot for head measurement is to examine a case as it is drawn from the sizing die. You should be able to find the lowest point on the case body where sizing occurred. This area is the only place where there is enough case strength to remain resistant to the

eter that reads to four significant places. Such a measurement can be made during range testing and can be used as a comparison while firing the test handloads to know when factory pressure has been achieved with handloaded ammunition. Keep in mind that some factory ammunition is loaded below the maximum pressure level. It is entirely possible that your handloads may surpass the factory pressure slightly and still be well within safe pressure limits; the opposite is also possible.

Case head expansion, like observation of result, is only a method that indicates relative pressure. Common sense, caution, proper use of loading tables, starting with the lowest recommended charge weights and working up, and experience should all be employed when developing any handloaded cartridge.

Since all handloads and the pressure-test loads

pressure of combustion but not too resistant to allow a good expansion measurement. This exact spot must be determined for each situation and each type of cartridge case. This is true for both standard bottle-necked rifle cartridges, and straight-walled rifle and pistol cartridges, regardless of the type of rim. On belted magnum rifle cases, the expansion measurements are taken in the same relative position with the case wall and web, but the location is often more difficult to define. With belted cases, you must also be careful to keep the micrometer anvil slightly above the top edge of the belt. The corner of the belt can cause interference with the micrometer thus giving incorrect readings. This concern can be easily recognized and avoided. A micrometer with blade anvils can help in this situation. A standard micrometer can almost always be used as well.

With belted cases, expansion measurement is made very near the belt itself. Be careful that you don't obtain a bad measurement by including the small radius at the corner of the belt. It can be seen near the anvil of the micrometer. A blade-type anvil can be helpful for this kind of case.

Since case heads seldom expand evenly in all directions, you must also measure each case head in more than one spot to find an average size for each individual case. The illustration shows the three points of measurement to obtain this average. Start at a recognizable point, such as the dash in the head stamp "R-P." Turn the case about 60 degrees and take a second measurement. Do this a third time and you will automatically measure the case in three equally spaced locations. These figures should be written down and averaged to determine that case head expansion. Then add all five case averages for that load number and find their average head expansion as well. This method has the advantage of providing a smooth, consistent expansion figure when dealing with more than one group of cases in a load work-up. The difference in the average head expansion for each group of cartridges minus the average resized case head diameter is the head expansion entered under Data 7.

An advantage of the method detailed here is the ability to recover data if errors should occur. For instance, if you should forget to calculate the average-sized head dimension before firing, you need only to resize a few of the fired cases to find the resized dimension. If you work uniformly, cases should resize to near identical dimensions each time they are sized again. Your work may continue without a loss of data.

As with precision and velocity data, it is possible to calculate average and standard deviation for case head expansion. Such a calculation for measuring pressure uniformity is not needed because better data already exists. Data 4, Standard Velocity Deviation, is easily the most consistent indicator of pressure uniformity. There are, in fact, several good reasons for not using standard expansion deviation in addition to the time-consuming and difficult calculations. First, it is a fact that the deviations are so small that they conflict with manufacturing tolerances for the cartridge cases themselves. The result is scattered data, which is difficult to show graphically. Secondly, in each case where this has been attempted, case head deviation diminishes as propellant charge weight and pressure increase. This does not mean that higher pressures give more consistent pressure results. In several situations, the velocity deviation increased as expansion deviations decreased. This doesn't make sense but there is a reason for it. As the pressure of com-

The collection of pressure data requires a lot of measuring. Each case is measured at three locations around the head for an average expansion. Then the five cases of each load are averaged. This average, less the resized head diameter, is the average expansion—Data 7 used to graph the pressure results.

bustion expands the cartridge case, expansion decreases while uniformity increases, due to the unyielding confines of the steel chamber. All of this is to say that cartridge case head measurements are sufficient for relative pressure findings. Pressure uniformity is best compared by using the standard velocity deviation, Data 4.

During this discussion, our handloading friend, Jim, has collected his cases and completed his case head expansion measurements. He has entered the data in the proper slots in the pressure column on the handload data list. Now we are all anxious to see the results of his labor. Let's watch as he converts

the data for relative pressure into a graph to help with his final decision.

The handload pressure graph is not a graph of pressure readings. It is so named only for the sake of simplicity. Rather, it is a graph of comparison between case head expansion of handloads when compared to case head expansion from factory-loaded components. The handload pressure graph shows *expansion due to pressure* rather than actual pressure. The vertical axis for Data 7 is a scale of case head expansion. The plotted points for Data 7 consist of head diameter expansion measured in inches instead of pounds per square inch.

As stated before, case head expansion is one of the two practical ways for handloaders to compare handload pressure with that of factory pressure. Observation of pressure results is a useful tool for safety at the range. Case head expansion is a more useful tool when actually comparing pressure of handloaded ammunition and factory ammunition. Case head expansion results can also be displayed graphically.

By knowing the average resized case head diameter, it is possible to measure the amount of case head expansion due to different pressure from different powder charge weights. It is also possible to measure the case head expansion of a resized case if the primer, powder, and bullet from a factory cartridge are placed into a test case as used for the handloads. In this manner, it is possible to compare, although indirectly, the relative chamber pressures developed in handloads versus the factory standard. Consequently, one can discover if a handload develops relatively more, less, or about the same pressure as the factory-loaded cartridge used as the standard.

The handload pressure graph is constructed in the same basic manner as the precision and velocity graphs, except that there is only one paired set of data on the graph. These are Data 7 for the handloads and the Standard 7 line (factory average) for the factory ammunition. These data are the only pertinent items needed for relative pressure determination. Again, simple plotting.

After measuring and averaging the fired cartridge cases for the test handloads and the pressure-test rounds, Jim has entered the expansion measurements in the final column on the handload data list. Next, each of the Data 7 points is plotted on the pressure graph. After plotting all of the points, Jim finds that pressure, like velocity, is a straight line function when shown graphically. That is, pressure increases occur in the same proportion as like increases in propellant charge weight. This is true when dealing with single-based propellants. Double-based propellants generally show a slight to moderate curve when their pressure results are displayed graphically.

In addition to plotting the Data 7 points, Jim also draws the Standard 7 line. This line has a value on the Data 7 scale of .0038″. It represents the average of case head expansion in the pressure-test rounds. The pressure-test rounds were composed of factory bullets, primers, and powder when placed into the same brass as sorted for handloading. From the handload pressure graph, it appears that handload pressure is equal to factory pressure when about 54.5 to 55.0 grains of propellant are used. This coincides very closely with the data results shown on the velocity graph. This means that the factory propellant and handload propellant are similar.

The handload pressure graph indicates that charge weights above 55.0 grains cause pressure greater than that of the factory ammunition. This does not necessarily mean that handloads using more than 55.0 grains are unsafe. It only means that such handloads produce more pressure than the factory ammunition used in this testing.

At this point, Jim has accumulated four important, vital documents:

1. Handload data list
2. Handload precision graph
3. Handload velocity graph
4. Handload pressure graph

These four documents will soon allow him, selectively and intelligently, to eliminate, isolate, and choose the best ammunition that satisfies his handloading objectives. The method for doing this will be explained in the next chapter.

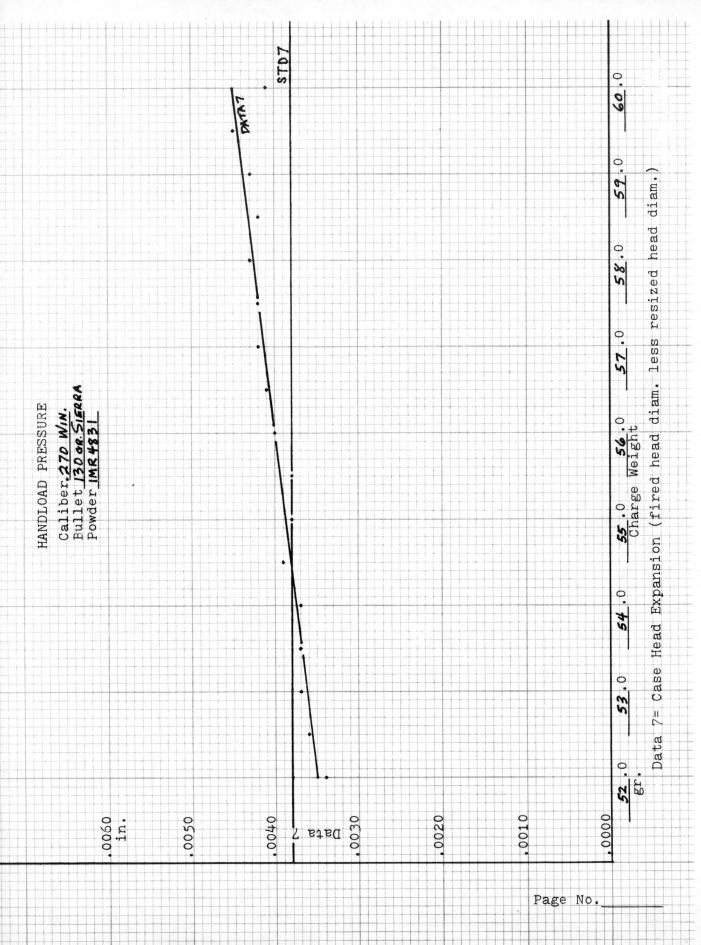

HANDLOAD PRESSURE

Caliber 270 WIN.
Bullet 130gr.SIERRA
Powder IMR 4831

Data 7 = Case Head Expansion (fired head diam. less resized head diam.)

A completed handload pressure chart. Only two pieces of data need be plotted.

# Chapter 9
# Using Handload Data

As stated in the preceding chapter, Jim has completed the collection and display of all the handloading data. He is now ready to use this important information to make the final decision. All the objectives that were proposed for this handloading project must be considered as we begin comparing the data and before making the final choice. An overlooked objective could invalidate that decision.

Since the handloading objectives are so vital to Jim's decision, let's take a moment briefly to review those objectives.

First, we learned that Management by Objective was a good way to manage a handloading project and that MBO entails four steps involving results, planning, activities, and time.

Next, we learned that there is an objective-setting process. It is used to help establish the specific objectives. In doing so, five questions, which must all be answered positively, are asked: is the objective worth setting, practical, attainable, clearly stated, and compatible with the expected result?

Eight objectives were set for this project. These were detailed in Chapter 2, but to summarize, Jim wanted to achieve equal or better precision, velocity, consistency, performance, and pressure with handloaded ammunition as opposed to factory ammunition. Also important was the ability to duplicate the chosen load at any time in the future. In addition, he wanted handloads that would feed through the action of his rifle flawlessly. Finally, he wanted to accomplish all this with the least expenditure of time, labor, materials, and money for testing loads.

If you have followed Jim's progress, you will probably agree that these objectives have more meaning now than when they were first set, and that they can fit other shooters' needs for similar hunting ammunition. But, remember, your individual shooting requirements must be considered when setting objectives. Different situations and circumstances call for different objectives.

Our friend has four important documents to

consult: handload data list, precision graph, velocity graph, pressure graph. He will consider the objectives and then use the process of elimination to find the best ammunition for his particular needs.

Some of the objectives have already been achieved. Due to the decisions prior to loading (Chapter 3), the work at the loading bench (Chapter 4), and the shooting at the range (Chapter 5), Jim has already satisfied two of the objectives.

Objective 5 has been fulfilled—the ability to duplicate any of the handloads because all the necessary data is recorded on the handload data list. Everything he needs to know regarding components, precision, velocity, and pressure is there,

listed according to the specific handload numbers.

Objective 8 has also been achieved. The methods explained and used in Chapters 2 through 8 will let Jim achieve the other seven handloading objectives with the "least expense of time, labor, materials, and money for testing."

There are six handloading objectives that have not yet been reached; actually, they may be, but we don't know for sure at this point. If the remaining objectives can be realized with any handload, they can be identified positively with the four informative data records.

First, the handload precision graph is studied. You can follow the analysis with the illustration.

After the accumulation and display of all handload data is complete, the shooter can begin to make his final decision as to the best load.

From this graph, it can be seen that any point on the Data 1 curve above the Standard 1 line represents a handload that is less precise and less accurate than the factory cartridge. The same thing can be said for the relationship of Data 2 and the Standard 2 line. Both Data 1 and Standard 1 are standard vertical deviation data. This was all explained in Chapter 6. These deviation curves show that handload precision and factory precision are about equal where 57.5 grains of propellant are used.

Data 2 and Standard 2 are the extreme vertical spread data. They show very similar results. Vertical spreads are about the same at 58.5 grains.

Since we are trying to gain equal or better precision with the handloads than with factory ammunition, it is obvious that handloads containing more than 57.5 grains of propellant should be eliminated. This decision eliminates load numbers 13 through 17. The data indicates that probably none of these loads are capable of factory ammunition precision. These load numbers may be identified and eliminated from further consideration by drawing a line through their corresponding numbers on the handload data list.

For the present, all handloads with 57.5 grains or less propellant can be considered satisfactory for the precision requirements of objective 1. Each of these loads indicates equal or greater precision than that of the factory ammunition.

Data 3 and Standard 3 (height above the aiming point) are not necessary for achieving any of the eight objectives. This data is plotted on the graph for the other reasons explained in Chapter 6. It is useful for duplicating factory ammunition and sight-setting.

Jim now turns his attention to the handload velocity graph. This graph is used to further the selection process. The Data 6 curve is examined first. This curve (essentially a straight line) represents the average velocity readings of the handloads. It is matched against the Standard 6 line, which represents the average factory load velocity.

All points on the Data 6 curve below the Standard 6 line represent handloads that are slower than the factory ammunition. The average factory velocity was 2,856 fps.

Objective 2 states that the handloaded ammunition must achieve "equal or higher bullet velocity" than that of the factory-loaded ammunition. The handloads with less than 54.5 grains of propellant

do not meet this requirement and must be scratched from the handload data list. Load numbers 1 through 5 are thereby eliminated.

A total of seven handloads are still in contention. They represent charge weights that range from 54.5 through 57.5 grains of propellant. The choices can be trimmed further by using Data 4 and Data 5. Data 4 is standard velocity deviation and Data 5 is extreme velocity spread. Both of these data represent uniformity of velocity. In addition to helping achieve objective 2, they assist in achieving objectives 3, 4, and even objectives 6 and 7.

All points on the Data 4 curve above the Standard 4 reference line represent handloads whose velocities are less uniform than the factory ammunition velocity. This situation occurs at several points. However, only those points between the still existing range of possible charge weights (54.5–57.5 grains) are of any consequence. Only handloads 6 through 12 are left; however, according to the Data 4 curve and Standard 4 line, load numbers 8 and 9 should be eliminated because their velocities are more unstable than the factory velocity. By using Data 5 and the Standard 5 line, which represent extreme velocity spread, these handloads can be confirmed as having relatively poor uniformity. Jim draws a line through handload numbers 8 and 9 on the handload data list.

The process of elimination leaves only five of the tested handloads still capable of satisfying all of the precision and velocity requirements. These are load numbers 6, 7, 10, 11, and 12. At the same time, we must not forget that Jim is looking for the very best loading that satisfies all eight of his objectives. Further "weeding out" must take place before that final and best choice can be made.

All of the remaining handloads may still satisfy the objectives; the final choice should be predicated on which one does it best. At this point, the objective that is of greatest concern is velocity. Objective 2 can be achieved in a more satisfactory manner if the selected load also produces the highest velocity. This thinking would indicate that load No.12 (57.5 grains) should yield the best results in regard to precision and velocity. But there is still one major area of concern: pressure with respect to safety and uniformity as stated in objectives 4 and 7. The handload pressure graph will help us with this final, important decision.

The handload pressure graph, which consists of

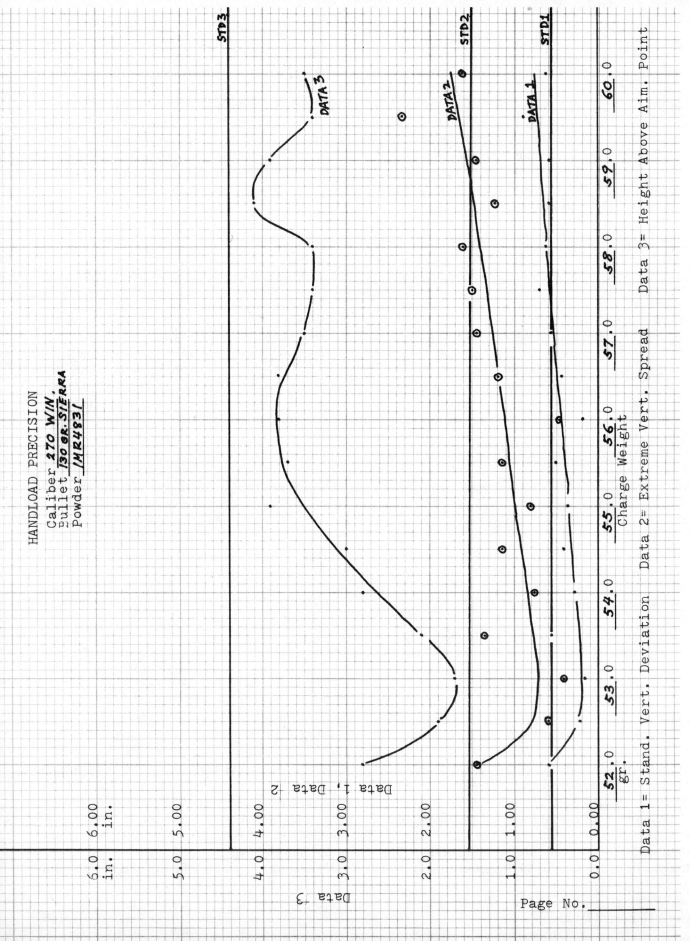

A completed handload precision graph.

CALIBER 270 WIN BULLET WGT. 130 gr.     HANDLOAD DATA

| FIREARM:mfgr. WIN | FACTY STD CARTRGE | CASE:mfgr REM (R-P) | BULLET:wgt 130 gr | POWDER:mfgr DUPONT |
|---|---|---|---|---|
| model 70 XTR | mfgr REM | avg wgt /97.3±3.0 gr | mfgr SIERRA | mfgr no. IMR4831 |
| barrel length 22 in | mfgr no. R270W2 | trim length 2.530in | mfgr no. 1830 | lot no. P81JY29A-74 |
| twist rate 1:10 in | lot no. L25UD2452 | c.o.a.length 3.205in | lot no. 40520 | PRIMER:mfgr CCI |
| TARGET:mfg/no. LEUP G-53 | bullet wgt 130 gr | sized head 0.4656 in | type SPIT. F.BASE | mfgr no. 200 |
| RANGE:dist. 100 yd | | | clearance 1/16 in | lot no. L25L |

| LOAD no. | charg wgt. gr. | date load | date fire | no. rds | INTERNAL AND EXTERNAL FACTORS — wind velocity, direction, temperature, bar. pres., precip., visibility, ch. pressure observations, other. | PRECISION Dat1 Std Vert Dev. in. | Dat2 Extm Vert Sprd in. | Dat3 HtAb Aim Pt. in. | VELOCITY Dat4 Std Vel. Dev. fps. | Dat5 Extm Vel. Sprd fps. | Dat6 Avg Vel. fps. | no. rds rcrd | PRES-SURE Dat7 Case Head Exp. in. |
|---|---|---|---|---|---|---|---|---|---|---|---|---|---|
| 1 | 52.0 | 7/8/82 | 9/8/82 | 5 | 4-6 fr 4:00 @ 12:30 94°F 29.72 dry | 0.58 | 1.44 | 2.8 | 27 | 69 | 2,701 | 5 | 0.0034 |
| 2 | 52.5 | | | → | exceptional group, but slow | .22 | 0.59 | 1.9 | 4 | 10 | 2,748 | | .0036 |
| 3 | 53.0 | | | | | .16 | 0.41 | 1.7 | 11 | 31 | 2,769 | | .0037 |
| 4 | 53.5 | | | | very mild pressure | .55 | 1.34 | 2.1 | 12 | 28 | 2,791 | | .0037 |
| 5 | 54.0 | | | | 6-12 fr 4:00, 94°F, 29.62, dry | .28 | 0.75 | 2.8 | 18 | 43 | 2,826 | | .0039 |
| 6 | 54.5 | | | 4 | | .41 | 1.13 | 3.0 | 13 | 33 | 2,870 | | .0038 |
| 7 | 55.0 | | | | no shot thru another hole | .37 | 0.80 | 3.9 | 17 | 44 | 2,909 | | .0038 |
| 8 | 55.5 | | | 5 | beginning of primer flattening | .50 | 1.14 | 3.7 | 20 | 55 | 2,941 | | .0040 |
| 9 | 56.0 | | | | exceptional grp, good except ht | .18 | 0.45 | 3.8 | 25 | 71 | 2,980 | | .0041 |
| 10 | 56.5 | | | | | .44 | 1.18 | 3.8 | 15 | 34 | 2,998 | | .0041 |
| 11 | 57.0 | | | | 2-4 fr 4:00, 94°F, 29.56 ↓ | .57 | 1.44 | 3.5 | 17 | 38 | 3,016 | | .0042 |
| 12 | 57.5 | | | | | .70 | 1.48 | 3.4 | 9 | 26 | 3,045 | | .0043 |
| 13 | 58.0 | | | | fairly heavy pressure, truob | .63 | 1.60 | 3.4 | 12 | 32 | 3,075 | | .0043 |
| 14 | 58.5 | | | | 2-4 fr 4:00, 94°, 29.52 ↓ | .59 | 1.23 | 4.1 | 26 | 60 | 3,123 | | .0042 |
| 15 | 59.0 | | | | | .59 | 1.45 | 3.9 | 11 | 29 | 3,142 | | .0043 |
| 16 | 59.5 | | | | | .90 | 2.33 | 3.4 | 11 | 28 | 3,179 | | .0045 |
| 17 | 60.0 | | → | → | limit of useful speed + pressure | .63 | 1.62 | 3.5 | 18 | 47 | 3,189 | | .0041 |
| 18 | . | | | | | . | . | . | | | . | | . |
| 19 | . | | | | | . | . | . | | | . | | . |
| 20 | . | | | | | . | . | . | | | . | | . |
| 1 | facty ld. | 9/8/82 | | 5 | 2-4 fr 4:00, 94° 29.56 | 0.93 | 2.68 | 4.5 | 19 | 52 | 2,917 | 5 | 0.0038 |
| 2 | " | | → | → | 2 shots not chronographed | .25 | 0.59 | 4.2 | 26 | 50 | 2,870 | 3 | .0034 |
| 3 | " | | → | | | .59 | 1.53 | 4.0 | 19 | 48 | 2,823 | 5 | .0032 |
| 4 | " | | | | | .47 | 1.27 | 4.7 | 16 | 40 | 2,813 | → | .0032 |
| 5 | | | | | facty avgs = | 0.56 | 1.52 | 4.4 | 20 | 48 | 2,856 | 48 | .0033 |

Data 1, 2, 3, 4, 5, 6 and 7 above, refer to data used in construction of the PREC., VEL. and PRESS. graphs

Load numbers 13 through 17 are scratched from the handload data list because they cannot equal factory ammunition in regard to precision.

case head expansion data, relates directly to chamber pressure. The greater the charge weight, the greater the pressure, and the greater resulting expansion, as shown on the graph. All points on the Data 7 line that are above the Standard 7 reference line represent pressure that is relatively greater than that of the factory cartridge. The fastest of our remaining handloads is load No.12 with 57.5 grains of propellant. Load No.12 indicates a greater chamber pressure than that of the tested factory ammunition. Jim's chief concern is whether or not load No.12 is unsafe. That is a relevant concern and one which must be answered before the final selection can be made.

Although the handload pressure graph is a good display of case expansion and relative pressure, its data must be viewed in regard to the observations that occurred during range testing. Therefore, the observations that were heard, felt, and seen while firing the ammunition are important factors. Any questionable observations indicating possible pressure problems should be noted on the handload data list immediately after firing. With this handload, no greater resistance was felt when opening the bolt than with factory ammunition. The condition of the cases after firing seemed fine, as did the appearance of the primers. Actually, no difference in resisting force at the bolt handle was noticed after firing any of the 17 test handloads. Only slight primer changes were observed across the entire range of loads. No excessive case strain or stretching signs could be seen during firing or later, when measured. No case head stretch marks were seen under close examination. No splits or cracks occurred at the neck, shoulder, or wall area of any case. No ejector marks appeared on any of the handload case heads. Lastly, after the fired handloads were resized, deprimed, and then reprimed, no enlarged primer pockets were found.

All of the above observations merely serve to confirm that chamber pressure remained safe, even though greater than that of factory ammunition. This is due partly to the moderate case dimensions, the rifle used in this example, the very slow, progressive burning rate of the propellant that was used, and the bullet weight that was chosen. If a faster-burning powder or a heavier bullet had been used, higher pressures might have been attained.

Case head expansion with handload No.12 exceeded that of the factory ammunition. This handload probably developed greater chamber pressure than the factory ammunition components. Results showed that the factory ammunition used in this project developed mild chamber pressure and moderate bullet velocity. As the notes on the back of the handload data list state, the test rifle should have developed factory instrument velocity of about 3,061 fps. The factory ammunition only developed 2,856 fps. That is 205 fps less than expected. The factory ammunition used as a standard for this test apparently was loaded conservatively. Conversely, handload No.12 demonstrated relatively firm chamber pressure and good velocity. It is interesting to note that this handload developed an average velocity of 3,045 fps, very close to the anticipated factory velocity of 3,061 fps.

Jim still has to choose among five handloads. This is a predicament because each of these handloads will satisfy his objectives, so far. Loads 6, 7, 10, 11, and 12 are all capable of precision as good or better than that of the factory ammunition and each handload can equal or better factory velocity. Handloads 6 and 7 are the remaining loads at the low end of the charge scale. Both represent fine precision and equal the factory velocity at the same pressure. Either would be an excellent choice for many handloaders. They are the best choices for the shooter concerned most with a high degree of precision and long barrel and case life.

At the other end of the charge scale, loads 10, 11, and 12 remain. Each of these handloads is also capable of precision that can equal or better factory ammo performance. Although these loads all show slightly higher pressure than the factory ammunition, they do produce greater velocity; considerably greater velocity, in fact—load No.12 is nearly 200 fps faster. This difference can give the hunter a measurable advantage in long-range accuracy and bullet energy.

Although Jim is concerned with precision and accuracy, he knows that factory precision is quite good, and any of the five remaining handloads are at least that good. The velocity gains with loads 10, 11, and 12 are more important to him than the precision gains with loads 6 and 7. Of these, load No.12 (57.5 grains) is the fastest and also shows very consistent uniformity in regard to velocity and pressure. Furthermore, he knows that load is safe in his rifle.

For all of these reasons, Jim decides that load No.

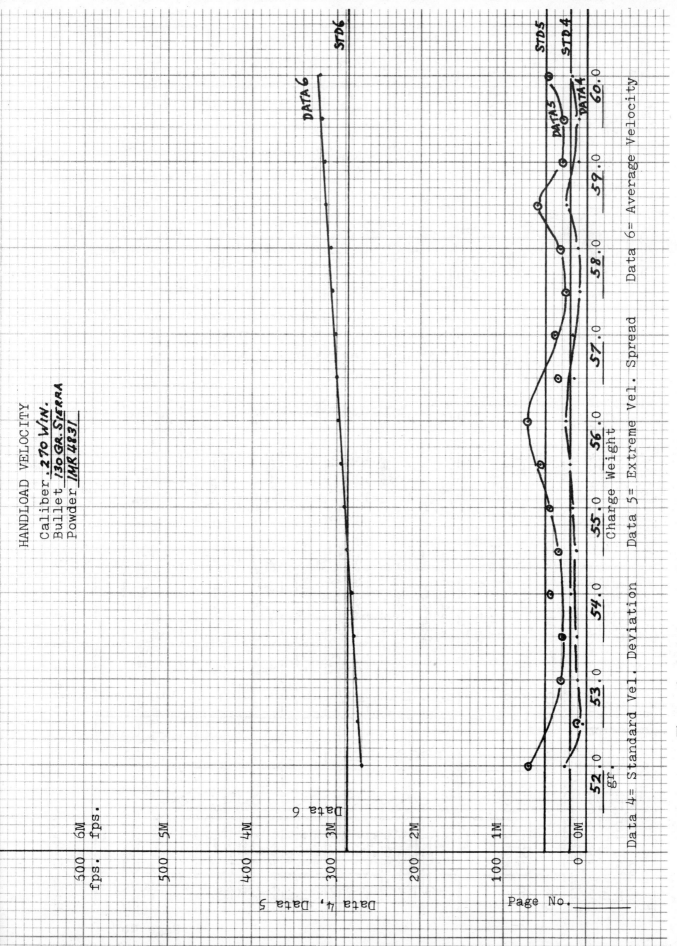

The completed velocity graph will be consulted in the decision-making process. It diagrams vital data.

CALIPER 270 WIN BULLET WGT. 130 gr.          HANDLOAD DATA

| FIREARM: mfgr. WIN | FACTY STD CARTRGE | CASE: mfgr REM (R-P) | BULLET: wgt 130 gr | POWDER: mfgr DuPONT |
|---|---|---|---|---|
| model 70 XTR | mfgr REM | avg wgt/97.3 ±3.0 gr | mfgr SIERRA | mfgr no. IMR4831 |
| barrel length 22 in | mfgr no. R270W2 | trim length 2.530 in | mfgr no. 1830 | lot no. P915Y29A-74 |
| twist rate 1:10 in | lot no. L25UD2452 | c.o.a. length 3.20 in | lot no. 40520 | PRIMER: mfgr CCI |
| TARGET: mfg/no. LEUP G-53 | bullet wgt 130 gr | sized head 0.4656 in | type SPIT. F. BASE | mfgr no. 200 |
| RANGE: dist. 100 yd | | | clearance 1/16 in | lot no. L25L |

| LOAD no. | charg wgt. gr. | date load | date fire | no. rds | INTERNAL AND EXTERNAL FACTORS — wind velocity, direction, temperature, bar. pres., precip., visibility, ch. pressure observations, other. | PRECISION Dat1 Std Vert Dev. in. | Dat2 Extm Vert Sprd in. | Dat3 HtAb Aim. Pt. in. | VELOCITY Dat4 Std Vel. Dev. fps. | Dat5 Extm Vel. Sprd. fps. | Dat6 Avg Vel. fps. | no. rds rcrd | PRESSURE Dat7 Case Head Exp. in. |
|---|---|---|---|---|---|---|---|---|---|---|---|---|---|
| 1 | 52.0 | 7/8/82 | 9/8/82 | 5 | 4-6 fr 4:00 @12:30, 94°F 29.72 dry exceptional group, but slow | 0.58 | 1.44 | 2.8 | 27 | 69 | 2,701 | 5 | 0.0034 |
| 2 | 52.5 | | | | | .22 | 0.59 | 1.9 | 4 | 10 | 2,748 | | .036 |
| 3 | 53.0 | | | | | .16 | 0.41 | 1.7 | 11 | 31 | 2,769 | | .037 |
| 4 | 53.5 | | | | may mild pressure | .55 | 1.34 | 2.1 | 12 | 28 | 2,791 | | .037 |
| 5 | 54.0 | | | | 6-12 fr 4:00, 94°F, 29.63, break | .28 | 0.75 | 2.8 | 18 | 43 | 2,826 | | .037 |
| 6 | 54.5 | | | 4 | no shot lost thru another hole | .41 | 1.13 | 3.0 | 13 | 33 | 2,870 | | .039 |
| 7 | 55.0 | | | | | .37 | 0.80 | 3.9 | 17 | 44 | 2,909 | | .038 |
| 8 | 55.5 | | | 5 | beginning of prime flattening | .50 | 1.14 | 3.7 | 20 | 55 | 2,941 | | .038 |
| 9 | 56.0 | | | | exceptional grp, good grp, break | .18 | 0.45 | 3.8 | 25 | 71 | 2,980 | | .040 |
| 10 | 56.5 | | | | | .44 | 1.18 | 3.8 | 15 | 34 | 2,998 | | .041 |
| 11 | 57.0 | | | | 2-4 fr 4:00, 94°F, 29.56 | .57 | 1.44 | 3.5 | 17 | 38 | 3,016 | | .042 |
| 12 | 57.5 | | | | | .70 | 1.48 | 3.4 | 9 | 26 | 3,045 | | .042 |
| 13 | 58.0 | | | | fairly heavy pressure, break | .63 | 1.60 | 3.4 | 12 | 32 | 3,075 | | .043 |
| 14 | 58.5 | | | | 2-4 fr 4:00, 29.52 | .59 | 1.23 | 4.1 | 26 | 60 | 3,123 | | .042 |
| 15 | 59.0 | | | | | .59 | 1.45 | 3.9 | 11 | 29 | 3,142 | | .043 |
| 16 | 59.5 | | | | | .90 | 2.33 | 3.4 | 11 | 28 | 3,179 | | .045 |
| 17 | 60.0 | | | | limit of graceful speed + pressure | .63 | 1.62 | 3.5 | 18 | 47 | 3,189 | | .041 |
| 18 | | | | | | | | | | | | | |
| 19 | | | | | | | | | | | | | |
| 20 | | | | | | | | | | | | | |
| 1 | facty ld. | 9/8/82 | | 5 | 2-4 fr 4:00, 94° 29.56 | 0.93 | 2.68 | 4.5 | 19 | 52 | 2,917 | 5 | 0.0038 |
| 2 | " | | | | 2 shots not chronographed | .25 | 0.59 | 4.2 | 26 | 50 | 2,870 | 3 | .0038 |
| 3 | " | | | | | .59 | 1.53 | 4.0 | 19 | 48 | 2,823 | 5 | .0032 |
| 4 | " | | | | | .47 | 1.27 | 4.7 | 16 | 40 | 2,813 | | |
| 5 | " | | | | | | | | | | | | |
| | | | | | facty avgs = | 0.56 | 1.52 | 4.4 | 20 | 48 | 2,856 | 48 | .0038 |

Data 1, 2, 3, 4, 5, 6 and 7 above, refer to data used in construction of the PREC., VEL. and PRESS. graphs

Load numbers 1 through 5 are eliminated because they are too slow.

CALIBER 270 WIN BULLET WGT. 130 gr.        HANDLOAD DATA

| FIREARM: mfgr. WIN | FACTY STD CARTRGE | CASE: mfgr REM (R-P) | BULLET: wgt 130 gr | POWDER: mfgr DuPont |
|---|---|---|---|---|
| model 70 XTR | mfgr REM | avg wgt 197.3±3.0 gr | mfgr SIERRA | mfgr no. IMR4831 |
| barrel length 22 in | mfgr no. R270W2 | trim length 2.530in | mfgr no. 1830 | lot no. P15Y29A-74 |
| twist rate 1:10 in | lot no. L25UD2452 | c.o.a. length 3.2o5in | lot no. 40520 | PRIMER: mfgr CCI |
| TARGET: mfg/no. Lvup G-53 | bullet wgt 130 gr | sized head 0.4656 in | type SPIT., F.BASE | mfgr no. 200 |
| RANGE: dist. 100 yd | | | clearance 1/16 in | lot no. L25L |

| LOAD no. | charg wgt. gr. | date load | date fire | no. rds | wind velocity, direction, temperature, bar. pres.; precip., visibility, ch. pressure observations, other. | PRECISION Dat1 Std Vert Dev. in. | Dat2 Extm Vert Sprd in. | Dat3 HtAb Aim. Pt. in. | VELOCITY Dat4 Std Vel. Dev. fps. | Dat5 Extm Vel. Sprd fps. | Dat6 Avg Vel. fps. | no. rds rcrd | PRES-SURE Dat7 Case Head Exp. in. |
|---|---|---|---|---|---|---|---|---|---|---|---|---|---|
| 1 | 52.0 | 7/1/82 | 9/9/82 | 5 | 4-6 fr 4:00 @ 12:30, 94°F, 29.72 dry | 0.58 | 1.44 | 2.8 | 27 | 67 | 2,701 | 5 | 0.0034 |
| 2 | 52.5 | | | | exceptional group, hot flow | .22 | 0.59 | 1.9 | 4 | 10 | 2,748 | | .0036 |
| 3 | 53.0 | | | | " | .16 | 0.41 | 1.7 | 11 | 31 | 2,769 | | .0037 |
| 4 | 53.5 | | | | " | .55 | 1.34 | 2.1 | 12 | 28 | 2,791 | | .0037 |
| 5 | 54.0 | | | 4 | very mild pressure, 6-12 fr 4:00, 94°, 29.63 (dry) | .28 | 0.75 | 2.8 | 18 | 43 | 2,826 | | .0037 |
| 6 | 54.5 | | | 5 | | .41 | 1.13 | 3.0 | 13 | 33 | 2,870 | | .0039 |
| 7 | 55.0 | | | | no shot lost thru another hole | .37 | 0.80 | 3.9 | 17 | 44 | 2,909 | | .0038 |
| 8 | 55.5 | | | | beginning of primer flattening | .50 | 1.14 | 3.7 | 20 | 55 | 2,941 | | .0038 |
| 9 | 56.0 | | | | exceptional grp, godoglod brush | .18 | 0.45 | 3.8 | 25 | 71 | 2,980 | | .0040 |
| 10 | 56.5 | | | | | .44 | 1.18 | 3.8 | 15 | 34 | 2,998 | | .0041 |
| 11 | 57.0 | | | | 2-4 fr 4:00, 94°F, 29.56 ↓ | .57 | 1.44 | 3.5 | 17 | 38 | 3,016 | | .0042 |
| 12 | 57.5 | | | | | .70 | 1.48 | 3.4 | 9 | 26 | 3,045 | | .0042 |
| 13 | 58.0 | | | | fairly heavy pressure, brush | .63 | 1.60 | 3.4 | 12 | 32 | 3,075 | | .0043 |
| 14 | 58.5 | | | | 2-4 fr 4:00 194°, 29.52 ↓ | .59 | 1.23 | 4.1 | 26 | 60 | 3,123 | | .0042 |
| 15 | 59.0 | | | | | .59 | 1.45 | 3.9 | 11 | 29 | 3,142 | | .0043 |
| 16 | 59.5 | | | | | .90 | 2.33 | 3.4 | 11 | 28 | 3,179 | | .0045 |
| 17 | 60.0 | | | → | burst of wind, sprct pressure | .63 | 1.62 | 3.5 | 18 | 47 | 3,189 | ↓ | .0041 |
| 18 | : | | | | | : | : | : | | | : | | : |
| 19 | : | | | | | : | : | : | | | : | | : |
| 20 | : | | | | | : | : | : | | | : | | : |
| 1 | facty ld. | | 9/9/82 | 5 | 2-4 fr 4:00, 94°, 29.56 | 0.93 | 2.68 | 4.5 | 19 | 52 | 2,917 | 5 | 0.0038 |
| 2 | " | | | → | | .25 | 0.59 | 4.2 | 26 | 50 | 2,870 | 3 | .0038 |
| 3 | " | | | | | .59 | 1.53 | 4.0 | 19 | 48 | 2,823 | 5 | .0032 |
| 4 | " | | | → | | .47 | 1.27 | 4.7 | 16 | 40 | 2,813 | → | |
| 5 | " | | | | 2 shots not chronographed | | | | | | | | |
| | | | | | facty avgs = | 0.56 | 1.52 | 4.4 | 20 | 48 | 2,856 | | .0038 |

Data 1, 2, 3, 4, 5, 6 and 7 above, refer to data used in construction of the PREC., VEL. and PRESS. graphs.

Load numbers 8 and 9 are passed over because of their unstable velocities, compared to factory ammunition.

12, with 57.5 grains of propellant, is the best handload for his shooting needs. He believes that he has achieved his result and can gain the greatest shooting confidence with this handload and that this selection is the one that best fulfills his objectives and purpose.

**Handloading objective 1** has been achieved. Using uniform methods of target measurement, a handload was chosen that equalled or surpassed factory ammunition precision. The selected handload will produce target precision that is equal to, if not slightly better than, the factory average. The precision graph shows us that 57.5 grains will yield standard vertical deviation of only about .55 inches, which is very good and is equal to factory ammunition performance. This will also result in group sizes whose extreme vertical spread should be no more than 1.5 inches.

**Handloading objective 2** has been achieved. Under equal weather and wind conditions, over a reliable chronograph, the selected handload produced considerably higher bullet velocity than that of the factory ammunition. This is a meaningful improvement over the standard.

**Handloading objective 3** has been achieved. Using available information, ballistic data, and testing, equal or better bullet performance was realized. Besides being equal to, or better than, factory ammunition in terms of precision, the handload is also nearly 200 fps faster. The greater ballistic potential of this handload is evident, which can be confirmed easily with available manufacturer's information. The killing ability of the handload bullet is considered equal to that of the factory ammunition bullet at similar velocity. The increased velocity of the handload should yield better results.

**Handloading objective 4** has been achieved. Using target data, chronograph data, component identification, control of handload cartridge dimensions and weights, statistical calculations, and graphic displays, greater consistency in handloaded ammunition was achieved in regard to precision, velocity, pressure, and bullet performance. This achievement is even more obvious if different lots of factory cartridges, including similar loadings from different ammunition manufacturers, are compared. The selected handload is capable of greater consistency in all the above aspects of cartridge performance, and it can be assembled at different times and will retain that consistency.

**Handloading objective 5** has been achieved. By using the component information on the handload data list for cartridge loading requirements, and the recorded data concerning precision, velocity, and pressure, the chosen handload can be duplicated at any time as long as the same sizing die is used.

**Handloading objective 6** has been achieved. The selected handload complies with correct cartridge dimensions and component usage, and passed all function and firing tests. Therefore, the selected handload did achieve correct functioning in the firearm in regard to ease of chambering and extraction of cases.

**Handloading objective 7** has been achieved. The selected handload was subjected to audible, tactile, and visual observations during and after firing, and its case head was measured for expansion. The load was found to produce proper, consistent, and safe chamber pressure in the test rifle. Although somewhat greater than that of factory ammunition, pressure was judged safe in the tested firearm. The propellant and the charge weight used comply with handloading guides furnished by the propellant manufacturer and the bullet manufacturer.

**Handloading objective 8** has been achieved. The best possible ammunition that will fulfill this handloader's shooting needs has been developed, and it accomplished all of the first seven objectives with the least expenditure of time, labor, materials, and money for testing.

So there you have it—a successful handload development that can be used with the greatest confidence by our handloading, hunting friend. He now has superior ammunition that can be expected to produce the best possible results in his shooting situation. He has achieved this by adhering to the proven methods of handloading as presented here.

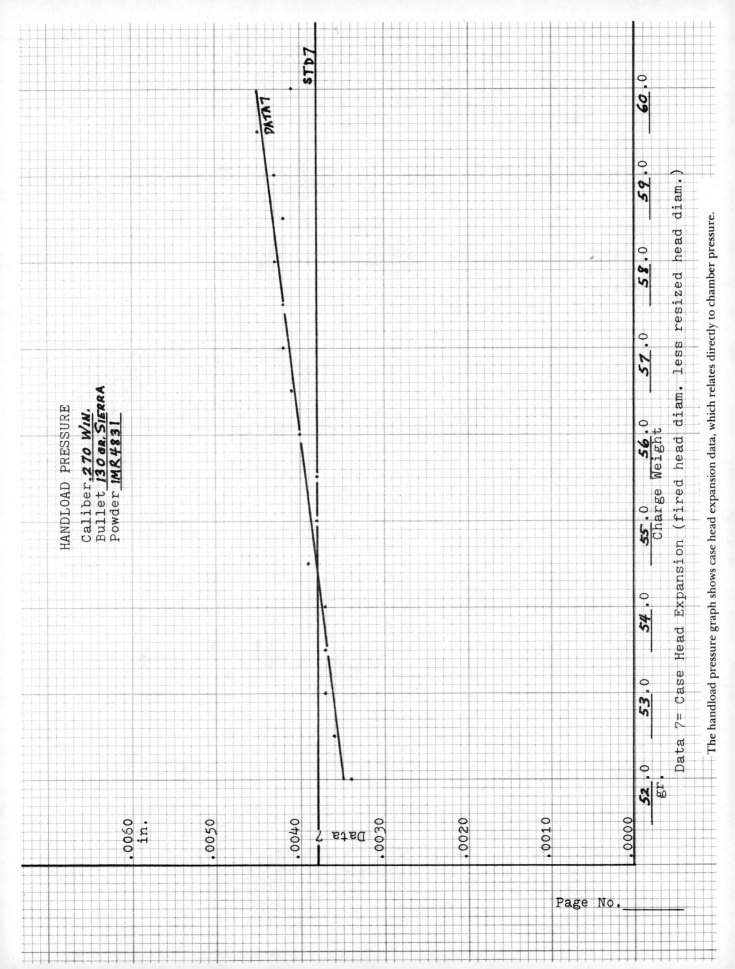

HANDLOAD PRESSURE

Caliber .270 WIN.
Bullet 130 GR. SIERRA
Powder IMR 4831

Charge Weight

Data 7= Case Head Expansion (fired head diam. less resized head diam.)

The handload pressure graph shows case head expansion data, which relates directly to chamber pressure.

Page No. _____

CALIBER 270 WIN BULLET WGT. 130 gr.          HANDLOAD DATA

| FIREARM | FACTY STD CARTRGE | CASE | BULLET | POWDER |
|---|---|---|---|---|
| mfgr. Win | mfgr REM | mfgr REM (R-P) | wgt 130 gr | mfgr DuPont |
| model 70 XTR | mfgr no. R270W2 | avg wgt/97.3±3.0 gr | mfgr SIERRA | mfgr no. IMR4831 |
| barrel length 22 in | lot no. L25UD2452 | trim length 2.530 in | mfgr no. 1830 | lot no. P817Y29A-74 |
| twist rate 1:10 in | bullet wgt 130 gr | c.o.a. length 3.205 in | lot no. 40520 | PRIMER:mfgr CCI |
| TARGET:mfg/no. LeupG-53 | | sized head 0.4656 in | type SPIT.,F.BASE | mfgr no. 200 |
| RANGE: dist. 100 yd | | | clearance 1/16 in | lot no. L25L |

| LOAD no. | charg wgt. gr. | date load | date fire | no. rds | INTERNAL AND EXTERNAL FACTORS — wind velocity, direction, temperature, bar. pres., precip., visibility, ch. pressure observations, other. | PRECISION Dat1 Std Vert Dev. in. | Dat2 Extm Vert Sprd. in. | Dat3 HtAb Aim Pt. in. | VELOCITY Dat4 Std Vel. Dev. fps. | Dat5 Extm Vel. Sprd. fps. | Dat6 Avg Vel. fps. | no. rds rcrd | PRESSURE Dat7 Case Head Exp. in. |
|---|---|---|---|---|---|---|---|---|---|---|---|---|---|
| 1 | 52.0 | 7/31/82 | 9/19/82 | 5 | 4-6 fr 4:00 @ 12:30, 94°F, 29.72 dry | 0.58 | 1.44 | 2.8 | 27 | 69 | 2,701 | 5 | 0.0034 |
| 2 | 52.5 | | | | exceptional group, but slow | .22 | 0.59 | 1.9 | 4 | 10 | 2,748 | | .0036 |
| 3 | 53.0 | | | | | .16 | 0.41 | 1.7 | 11 | 31 | 2,769 | | .0037 |
| 4 | 53.5 | | | | very mild pressure | .55 | 1.34 | 2.1 | 12 | 28 | 2,791 | | .0037 |
| 5 | 54.0 | | | | 6-12 fr 4:00, 94°F, 29.63 dry | .28 | 0.75 | 2.8 | 18 | 43 | 2,826 | | .0037 |
| 6 | 54.5 | | | 4 | no shot lost thru another hole | .41 | 1.13 | 3.0 | 13 | 33 | 2,870 | | .0039 |
| 7 | 55.0 | | | 5 | beginning to show flattening | .37 | 0.80 | 3.9 | 17 | 44 | 2,909 | | .0038 |
| 8 | 55.5 | | | | exceptional grp, good optd, trust | .50 | 1.14 | 3.7 | 20 | 55 | 2,941 | | .0038 |
| 9 | 56.0 | | | | | .18 | 0.45 | 3.8 | 25 | 71 | 2,980 | | .0040 |
| 10 | 56.5 | | | | | .44 | 1.18 | 3.8 | 15 | 34 | 2,998 | | .0041 |
| 11 | 57.0 | | | | 2-4 fr 4:00, 94°F, 29.56 | .57 | 1.44 | 3.5 | 17 | 38 | 3,016 | | .0042 |
| (12) | 57.5 | | | | | .70 | 1.48 | 3.4 | 9 | 26 | 3,045 | | .0042 |
| 13 | 58.0 | | | | fairly heavy pressure, truck | .63 | 1.60 | 3.4 | 12 | 32 | 3,075 | | .0043 |
| 14 | 58.5 | | | | 2-4 fr 4:00, 94°, 29.52 | .59 | 1.23 | 4.1 | 26 | 60 | 3,123 | | .0042 |
| 15 | 59.0 | | | | | .59 | 1.45 | 3.9 | 11 | 29 | 3,142 | | .0043 |
| 16 | 59.5 | | | | | .90 | 2.33 | 3.4 | 11 | 28 | 3,179 | | .0045 |
| 17 | 60.0 | | | | limit of useful speed + pressure | .63 | 1.62 | 3.5 | 18 | 47 | 3,189 | 5 | .0041 |
| 18 | . . | | | | | . | . | . | | | . | | . |
| 19 | . . | | | | | . | . | . | | | . | | . |
| 20 | . . | | | | | . | . | . | | | . | | . |
| 1 | facty ld. | 9/19/82 | | 5 | 2-4 fr 4:00, 94°, 29.56 | 0.93 | 2.68 | 4.5 | 19 | 52 | 2,917 | 5 | 0.0038 |
| 2 | " | | | | 2 shots not chronographed | .25 | 0.59 | 4.2 | 26 | 50 | 2,870 | 3 | .0038 |
| 3 | " | | | | | .59 | 1.53 | 4.0 | 19 | 48 | 2,823 | 5 | .0032 |
| 4 | " | | | | | .47 | 1.27 | 4.7 | 16 | 40 | 2,813 | | . |
| 5 | " | | | | | | | | | | | | |
| | facty avgs = | | | | | .56 | 1.52 | 4.4 | 20 | 48 | 2,856 | | .0038 |

The handloader feels that the velocity gains provided by loads 10 through 12 are more important than the precision gains with loads 6 and 7, which are dropped from contention. Among the remaining three loads, No. 12 is the fastest, and since it satisfies all the other objectives as well, it is his final choice.

# Chapter 10
# Completing the Project

Everything done so far in this book has focused on achieving one or more of the eight handloading objectives used in the example. Each of those objectives has now been reached. The purpose for handloading, to develop the best possible ammunition for our shooting needs, and our reason for handloading, to gain the greatest confidence in our shooting, have also been satisfied. There are only a few things that still need to be done. One is to make more of the chosen handload; another is to discuss some of the concerns for good shooting results.

Right about now we should step back, catch our breath, and think about what comes next. Now that Jim and we have positively identified the best handload that will satisfy the purpose and reason for this handloading project, the next logical step is to load up a batch of that ammunition. You'll recall that we planned for this eventuality. Therefore, a supply of components is available to us: cases, powder, primers, and bullets in correct proportion that can

be used to duplicate the selected handload for present and future needs. I suggest that components chosen for such a specific requirement be completely used up to make more cartridges once the best combination is found. This should be done within a reasonable period of time. A long delay can cause memory and records to lose detail and perspective. Furthermore, unused components might be accidentally switched to another project and be lost should you want to make more of the favored handloads at a later date. Therefore, the components should be used now to complete this project while everything is fresh in your mind.

Loading your supply of ammunition requires the same basic procedures described in Chapter 4, except that several time-consuming steps can now be eliminated. There is no longer a need to document your actions; no lists, charts, or graphs are needed. There is no need to adjust the reloading dies, measure targets, or set up and dismantle the chronograph. All of these things were only required for establishing the best handload. That has already been done. All you have to do is reload cases and store the ammunition.

After you've loaded your ammunition, be sure to carefully box, label, and store it so that no confusion, loss, or deterioration occurs. Label the handloads with all the information needed to identify them. This should consist of at least the caliber, bullet weight, bullet make, powder, charge weight, primer, and the date that it was loaded. Be sure to reference the handload data list as to which handload was chosen. Your final decision should be written into the conclusion notes on the back of the handload data list. Make a notation explaining why you chose the load. These reasons can help satisfy questions that may arise later.

After you have made more of the selected handloads, zero the sights on your rifle. This should be done to get the maximum accuracy out of your ammunition and gun. The ballistic tables provided by most bullet makers are excellent guides for this job. Consult their data and use the appropriate table for your bullet and velocity to help set your sights. But before you make the final zero, keep the following considerations in mind: adjustments, modifications, cleaning, and lubrication.

Many handloads are developed with rifles and handguns that may need attention to reach their full potential. For example, the firearm may be equipped with sights that will be changed before intended use. Or, some trigger adjustment may be needed for better precision. And, the stock may require modification, bedding, or repairs before use in competition or in the field.

Any of the above changes to the firearm, although seemingly minor, may have a big effect on bullet strike. This affects accuracy. Therefore, any such alteration should be made prior to the final zeroing; if not, you may find that you'll have to do it again later.

In regard to the final zero point, consider the intended use of the gun. Some requirements dictate an exact zero if the gun will be used for paper target shooting at known distances. Other types of shooting may require a point of impact that differs from the point of aim, as is usually the case with high-velocity, scope-sighted hunting rifles.

The typical scoped big game rifle should be zeroed so that bullet strike at 100 yards is slightly

After loading a batch of the selected handloads, store them in a sturdy cartridge box and be sure to label the container in some detail, as shown here. You can reference the handload data list for more information about the load.

above the point of aim. The reason for this is to better utilize the flat shooting characteristics of modern firearms and thereby increase their range of accuracy; range estimation and target "holdover" judgments may be reduced or eliminated. The bullet should strike in the vital zone of the animal at all reasonable distances if the hunter holds the cross hairs in the center of the heart/lung area.

Exact zero for any cartridge depends on the bullet, muzzle velocity, and the near and far limits of range. All of this information can usually be found in the ballistic tables supplied by the bullet manufacturer. All you must supply is the muzzle velocity.

Data 3, Height Above Aiming Point, and Data 6, Average Velocity, found during range testing, are very valuable for two reasons. First, velocity must be known so the correct ballistic table can be used. Second, knowing the location of bullet strike (Data 3)

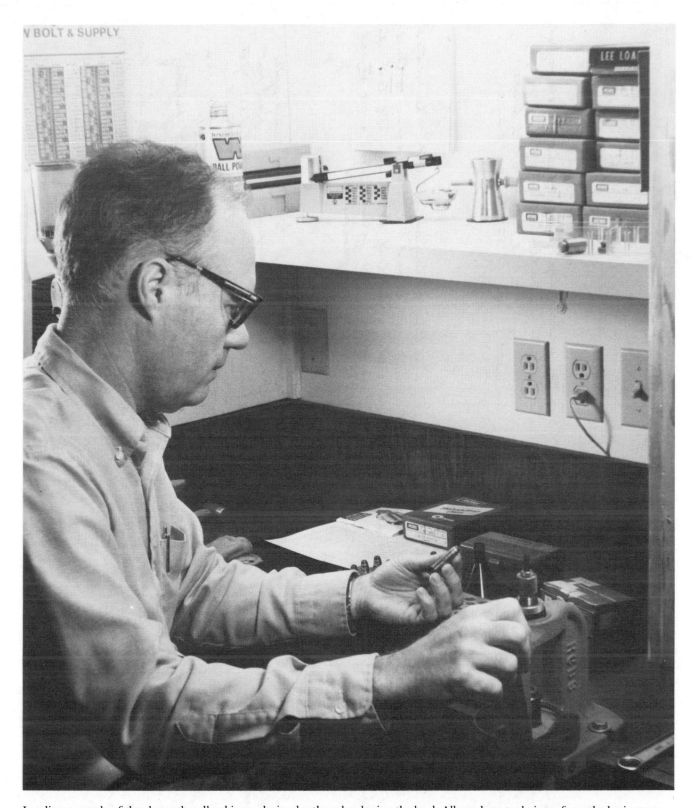

Loading a supply of the chosen handload is much simpler than developing the load. All you have to do is perform the basic steps of loading, beginning with case preparation. If your planning was correct, you should have plenty of the same components used for development.

Completing the Project

Caliber .270 WIN.     Bullet 130 GR. SIERRA     Powder IMR 4831

## NOTES

Planning: Use the stated objectives in the text. Factory cartridge to be used as comparison standard for precision, velocity and pressure. Factory bullet = 130.0 ± 0.2 gr.; diam = 0.2774 ± .0001 in.; Powder = 55.3 ± 6.3 gr.; dimension = 0.038 diam × 0.085 length (tubular grain); fired case to base of neck; Primer = Rem. std.; Case = 2.528 ± .002 length; unfired head diam = 0.4639 in., avg = 198.6 ± 3.3 gr. (3.3% range).

Loading: The #1830 Sierra bullet weight 130.0 ± 0.2 gr equalling factory weight std. When seated 1/16" from lands, its base is aligned with the bottom of the case neck. Load #8 just begins to touch the base of the bullet. Load #7 is only slightly compressed. Excellent density. All test rds. were loaded by weight to within 0.1 grain of stated charge. Once-fired cases were weighed by wgt to 197.3 ± 3.0 gr. This is a 3.0% avg range and exceeds the factory std.

Firing: Firing pressure was equalled in each of loads 6, 7 and 8. Residual ring after that no extreme pressure indications occurred at any charge weight. Read out of case capacity. Barrel cleaning was dry, brisk and then clean, dry patches after approx. every 25 rds. round. Very slight fouling was noticed with this combination. Factory ind. velocity = 2,856 instead of estimated 3,061 f.p.s. This test rifle was new and velocity further indicates mild factory pressure. Load #12 = 3,045. muzzle velo. for #12 is estimated to be 3,054 f.p.s., almost exactly what factory ammo. should produce in a 22" barrel.

Conclusions: Using the intermediate loading objectives as a basis for elimination, the best handload from a precision, velocity and pressure standpoint is #12 (5/15g). The powder measure enabled this at a setting of 5.290 (reference).

The reverse side of the handload data list and some typical comments that might be found there.

for the handload is helpful in making the final zero adjustment to the gun sights.

## Determining Muzzle Velocity

If you want to use ballistic tables accurately, you should calculate the muzzle velocity of your handloads. The velocity measured by a chronograph is instrumental velocity. There is a difference between muzzle velocity and instrumental velocity. Knowing the difference will help you understand the calculation and use the tables. The following explanation should help.

Chronographs do not measure muzzle velocity directly. They measure the time it takes the bullet to pass over a measured distance. This time period and the distance is used to compute velocity by means of a pair of sensing screens. The first screen starts the chronograph clock and the second screen stops it. The screens are separated at a known distance. The variable factor is "bullet time." This figure can be used to find velocity by dividing the time into the distance between screens. Remember that velocity is equal to distance divided by time ($V = {}^d/_t$). Some chronographs contain a computer to perform this calculation for you. They provide a direct readout of velocity. Other chronographs give only the time; you calculate the velocity. In any case, all chronographs use the same basic principle to measure time in order to calculate velocity.

The velocity computed from a chronograph's time measurement is the average velocity of the bullet as it passes between sensing screens. This is called instrumental velocity. It represents the bullet velocity near the midpoint between screens. Since a bullet begins to lose velocity after it leaves the gun muzzle, instrumental velocity is always less than muzzle velocity. Furthermore, the first sensing screen must be placed some distance from the gun's muzzle for safety and also to ensure that the muzzle blast doesn't damage the screen or cause a false recording. The distance from the muzzle to the midpoint between screens is where instrumental velocity is measured. This distance is used to calculate actual muzzle velocity.

If the chronograph "start" screen is placed ten feet from the muzzle, and the screens are ten feet apart, the instrumental velocity would be recorded at a point 15 feet from the muzzle. If the "start"

screen is ten feet from the muzzle and the screens are only five feet apart, the instrumental velocity is measured at a point $12\frac{1}{2}$ feet from the muzzle. These distances must be known to calculate muzzle velocity. Now let's learn how to do it.

Jim knows that the average instrumental velocity of the chosen handload was 3,045 fps. By using the bullet maker's ballistic table, he can calculate muzzle velocity. He will do this by:

1. Finding how much velocity is lost in 100 yards
2. Computing how much velocity is lost from the muzzle to the midpoint between the sensing screens
3. Adding this loss to his instrumental velocity to obtain muzzle velocity

First, the instrumental velocity is rounded off to the nearest 100 fps. This changes the figure to 3,000 fps. Now Jim locates the ballistic table for the bullet used, and that shows 3,000 fps data. (See illustration.) On the table, you can see that this bullet will lose 211 fps in the first 100 yards (3,000 − 2,789 = 211). But the velocity loss we are concerned with is that from the muzzle to the midpoint between the screens. This is only a fraction of the distance from the gun to the target. Jim placed his "start" screen ten feet from the muzzle and the "stop" screen five feet past that. Therefore, the measuring point for instrumental velocity was $12\frac{1}{2}$ feet from the gun's muzzle. Twelve and a half feet is $\frac{1}{24}$ of the 300-foot distance to the target. He must add $\frac{1}{24}$ of the 211 fps loss to the original instrumental velocity ($\frac{1}{24}$ of 211 is 8.8, and 3,045 + 8.8 = 3,053.8). The resulting figure rounds off to 3,054 fps. This is the muzzle velocity for Jim's handload. Since 3,054 fps is closer to 3,100 fps than 3,000 fps, he should use the ballistic table for 3,100 fps for further calculations. (See illustration.)

To be honest, this method for computing muzzle velocity is not technically correct. It is practical, however. There is a more complex method for this calculation that involves higher mathematics, but the difference in the results is negligible, usually less than one foot per second. The method just explained will provide a good estimate of muzzle velocity in order to use the ballistic tables with confidence. Incidentally, if Jim had spaced his screens ten feet apart for more precision, he would have to use different numbers. That arrangement would place the measuring point 15 feet from the muzzle or $\frac{1}{20}$ of 300 feet (100 yards), but the muzzle velocity should remain the same, of course.

That's the easiest and most practical way to find muzzle velocity. Knowing muzzle velocity lets you use ballistic tables accurately and make a proper, final zero adjustment.

## Cleaning and Lubrication

Another area of concern is cleaning and lubrication, principally that of the internal operating mechanism, trigger, cartridge chamber, and bore. The reason this point has been brought up is because so much confusion exists about gun cleaning that it is often difficult to know what is correct. Some writings tend to oversimplify the subject; others overcomplicate the topic. This can cause indecision and even neglect.

Although some shooters profess that all guns should be completely broken down, piece by piece, and cleaned yearly, this is not a good practice. It also involves a lot of work. Many fine firearms have suffered from needless disassembly. This doesn't mean that cleaning shouldn't be performed when necessary. Fortunately, most guns disassemble easily into a few basic parts or units. Such disassembly usually separates wooden parts from metal. Stocks and grips should have any dust, dirt, or oil removed from their surfaces. A small, stiff brush is helpful to clean out the stock where the action is bedded. Other than that, the best stock treatment is to leave it alone. Unless a stock is so badly damaged or weatherbeaten that refinishing is necessary, the best surface care is only a light buffing with a soft cloth to remove fingerprints.

Metal parts require a different sort of cleaning treatment. Most metal gun parts are blued or made of corrosion-resistant materials. This is fortunate and allows us to clean those parts in a simple, no-nonsense way. Using one of the aerosol solvents, it is possible to saturate a gun's action thoroughly in a few seconds. After the solvent has had a chance to

| (CROSSWIND) | (30 MPH) | .00 | 1.74 | 7.17 | 16.68 | 30.79 | 50.06 | 75.11 | 253.31 |
|---|---|---|---|---|---|---|---|---|---|
| **MAXIMUM POINT BLANK RANGE IS 390 YDS. SET ZERO AT 330 YDS.** | | | | | | | | | |
| VELOCITY FPS | | 3200. | 2979. | 2769. | 2564. | 2368. | 2181. | 2002. | 1339. |
| ENERGY FT-LB | | 2955. | 2562. | 2213. | 1898. | 1619. | 1373. | 1157. | 518. |
| DROP INCHES | | .00 | -1.68 | -7.28 | -17.40 | -32.80 | -54.40 | -83.30 | -305.93 |
| BULLET PATH | (100 YDS) | -1.50 | .00 | -2.41 | -9.35 | -21.57 | -39.98 | -65.70 | -275.60 |
| INCHES | (200 YDS) | -1.50 | 1.21 | .00 | -5.74 | -16.75 | -33.96 | -58.47 | -263.55 |
| (ZERO RANGE) | (300 YDS) | -1.50 | 3.12 | 3.82 | -.00 | -9.10 | -24.40 | -47.00 | -244.44 |
| | (400 YDS) | -1.50 | 5.39 | 8.37 | 6.83 | .00 | -13.02 | -33.35 | -221.68 |
| DEFLECTION | (10 MPH) | .00 | .60 | 2.49 | 5.80 | 10.73 | 17.46 | 26.23 | 89.16 |
| INCHES | (20 MPH) | .00 | 1.20 | 4.97 | 11.61 | 21.46 | 34.92 | 52.46 | 178.32 |
| (CROSSWIND) | (30 MPH) | .00 | 1.81 | 7.46 | 17.41 | 32.19 | 52.38 | 78.68 | 267.48 |
| **MAXIMUM POINT BLANK RANGE IS 380 YDS. SET ZERO AT 320 YDS.** | | | | | | | | | |
| VELOCITY FPS | | 3100. | 2884. | 2676. | 2475. | 2283. | 2100. | 1925. | 1280. |
| ENERGY FT-LB | | 2774. | 2401. | 2067. | 1769. | 1505. | 1273. | 1070. | 473. |
| DROP INCHES | | .00 | -1.80 | -7.76 | -18.58 | -35.06 | -58.21 | -89.23 | -330.25 |
| BULLET PATH | (100 YDS) | -1.50 | .00 | -2.67 | -10.19 | -23.38 | -43.23 | -70.96 | -298.80 |
| INCHES | (200 YDS) | -1.50 | 1.34 | -.00 | -6.18 | -18.03 | -36.55 | -62.94 | -285.43 |
| (ZERO RANGE) | (300 YDS) | -1.50 | 3.40 | 4.12 | .00 | -9.79 | -26.24 | -50.58 | -264.82 |
| | (400 YDS) | -1.50 | 5.84 | 9.02 | 7.34 | .00 | -14.01 | -35.89 | -240.35 |
| DEFLECTION | (10 MPH) | .00 | .63 | 2.60 | 6.08 | 11.26 | 18.34 | 27.57 | 94.41 |
| INCHES | (20 MPH) | .00 | 1.25 | 5.19 | 12.16 | 22.51 | 36.67 | 55.13 | 188.83 |
| (CROSSWIND) | (30 MPH) | .00 | 1.88 | 7.79 | 18.24 | 33.77 | 55.01 | 82.70 | 283.24 |
| **MAXIMUM POINT BLANK RANGE IS 370 YDS. SET ZERO AT 310 YDS.** | | | | | | | | | |
| Sierra Bullets | | | | | | | | | 517 |

Ballistic tables show velocity loss at various distances. The handloader uses the figure at 100 yards in calculating the actual muzzle velocity of his load.

Precision Handloading

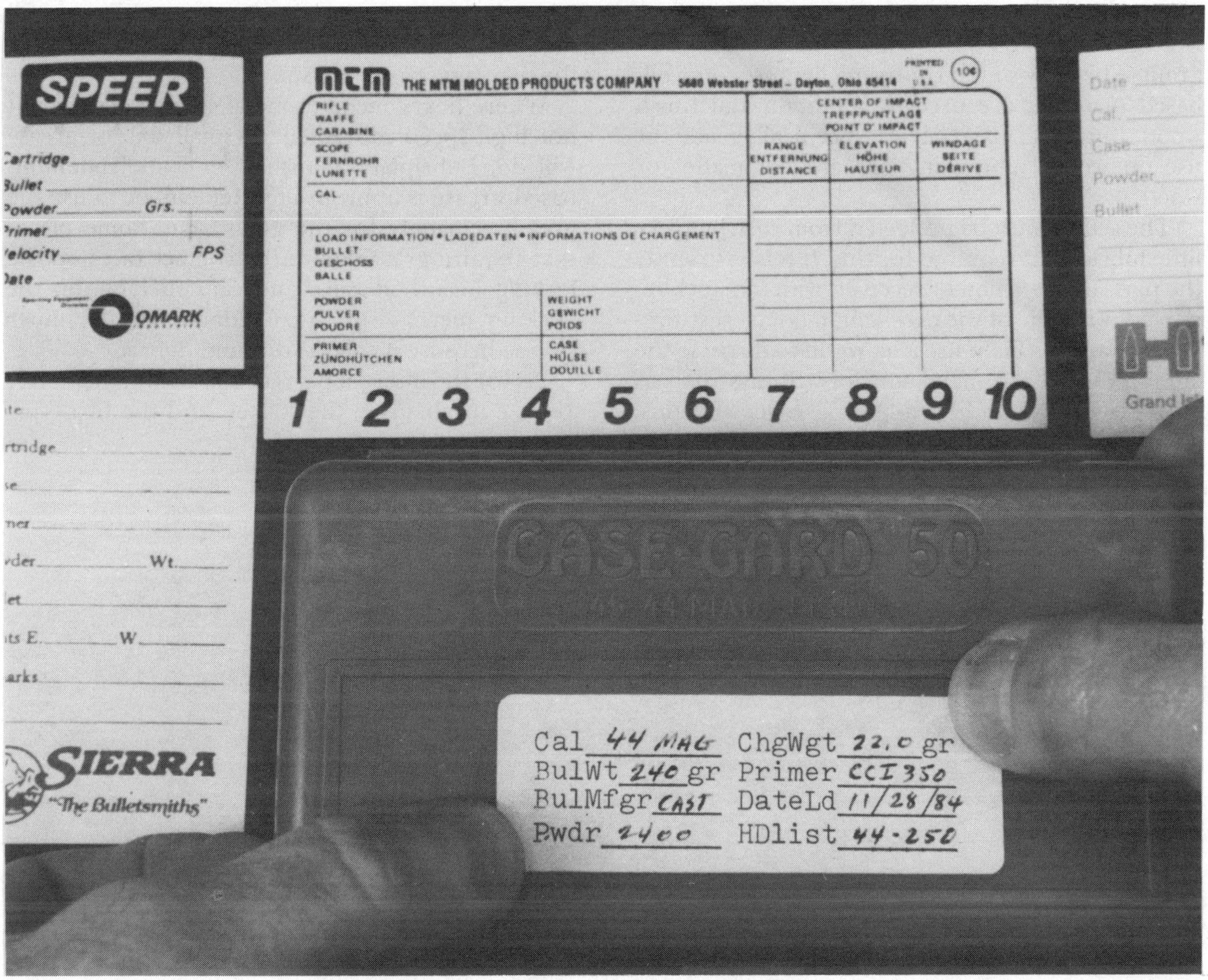

SPEER

Cartridge
Bullet
Powder_____ Grs.
Primer
Velocity_____ FPS
Date

OMARK

mtm THE MTM MOLDED PRODUCTS COMPANY    5680 Webster Street – Dayton, Ohio 45414    U.S.A.    PRINTED IN U.S.A. (106)

| RIFLE WAFFE CARABINE | | CENTER OF IMPACT TREFFPUNKTLAGE POINT D' IMPACT | | |
| SCOPE FERNROHR LUNETTE | | RANGE ENTFERNUNG DISTANCE | ELEVATION HÖHE HAUTEUR | WINDAGE SEITE DÉRIVE |
| CAL | | | | |
| LOAD INFORMATION • LADEDATEN • INFORMATIONS DE CHARGEMENT | | | | |
| BULLET GESCHOSS BALLE | | | | |
| POWDER PULVER POUDRE | WEIGHT GEWICHT POIDS | | | |
| PRIMER ZÜNDHÜTCHEN AMORCE | CASE HÜLSE DOUILLE | | | |

1 2 3 4 5 6 7 8 9 10

CASE-GARD 50

SIERRA
"The Bulletsmiths"

Cal 44 MAG     ChgWgt 22.0 gr
BulWt 240 gr   Primer CCI 350
BulMfgr CAST   DateLd 11/28/84
Pwdr 2400      HDlist 44-250

The specific type of label used is up to you. Some loaders make up their own; others use commercial labels. In either case, there should be sufficient room to list all pertinent data.

break through the powder residue and excess grease, blow the dirt and grime away with compressed air. Be sure that all lightly attached parts are removed so that they are not blown away. Wear safety glasses when you do this and keep a rag between your hand and the metal part. This cleaning method has three advantages: First, there is no need to disassemble and reassemble the mechanism completely; second, a fine collector's piece can be cleaned without risking any scratches or tool marks on the finished assembly or screw heads; and third, no adjustments after assembly are necessary.

The lubrication requirements for firearms are similar to that of other moving mechanisms; that is, some parts need grease, some parts need oil, and some parts don't need any lubrication. Where lubricant is needed, it is generally best to use grease for slow-moving parts and where heavy mechanical action takes place. Use light oil where fast movement and light action occurs. The real key to lubrication is to remember to use the lubricant only where it is needed. Lubricants are really a necessary evil and should only be used where required.

Let's discuss the major components in a rifle and their lubrication needs. First is the stock. This is simple. Don't put lubricating oil on any part of the stock. Make sure that adjacent metal parts don't transfer oil or grease to the stock. Grease and oil will eventually ruin wood. The wooden stock will deteriorate in time if oil is allowed to penetrate the wood grain. This may sound confusing because some oil-based materials are used to condition and finish wood. But those materials are specifically made for use on wood; lubricating oils are not made for wood.

The action must be protected from rust, but very little lubricant is required for this. It is best to spray the parts of the action or receiver, with the stock removed, with one of the excellent, modern rust-preventive sprays. Then use a blowgun to disperse the spray onto all the metal surfaces. Sprays such as WD–40, LPS–1, and Sheath are excellent for this.

They leave dry, non-oily, non-sticky film on all metal parts. The same treatment is also excellent for the trigger mechanism.

Where heavy metal-to-metal contact occurs, but not high-speed movement, a small dab of grease will do. Lubriplate, Gunslick, or a molybdenum-based grease is appropriate. Remember to use the grease sparingly for the gun's sake. Some places that require greasing are the contact faces on the locking lugs, bolt rails, and cam surfaces on the cocking mechanism. Again, don't use too much grease because it collects dirt and debris.

As for the internal parts of the action, the striker release mechanism, the striker, and the firing pin

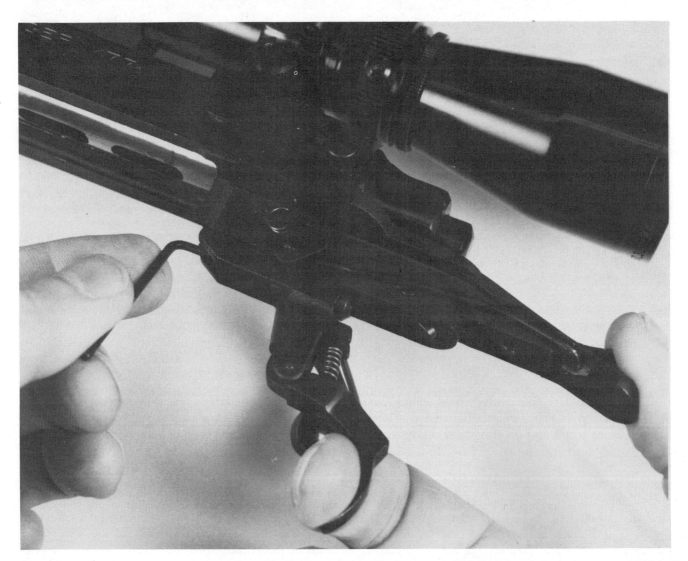

One adjustment you may wish to make before final zero is the trigger. Here, the overtravel adjustment is made on a Ruger Model 77 action. This reduces movement after the striker is released, increasing precision and accuracy.

Precision Handloading

mechanism in rifles must not be lubricated heavily. This also applies to the firing pin mechanisms in handguns and shotguns. Heavy use of grease and oil have a slowing effect on the speed of the mechanism. Lock times rise and accuracy drops. This can happen in any type of firearm. A dry, rust-preventive-type lubricant is much better than oil or grease.

Trigger mechanisms need a bit of light oil. Some benefit from the new Teflon- based lubricants. You may want to experiment to see what you like best.

The external metal surfaces require rust prevention only. This can be done by wiping off the gun with a lightly oiled or silicone-impregnated cloth. External moving parts, such as folding sights and sling swivels, need only a drop of light oil or rust preventive such as LPS–2. Thick oil or grease on the outside of the gun always rubs into the stock and makes the firearm messy to handle. Then the gun stains the carrying case, your clothes, and whatever it comes in contact with.

The most important areas of concern in regard to gun care are the chamber and bore. Here, again, let common sense be your guide. Noncorrosive primers, smokeless propellants, and nonfouling bullet materials have practically eliminated many of the old requirements for bore cleaning and bore care. I said "practically" eliminated, not "entirely" eliminated.

Bore care should be discussed in terms of how often the firearm will be used. If a gun is not to be used for over a year, I suggest a good, thorough cleaning of the chamber and bore. Use a bore solvent such as Hoppe's No. 9. Use a bronze brush and swab with solvent-soaked patches until all the metal and powder fouling in the bore is gone. If the patch comes out black, brown, or green, the bore is still fouled. Repeat the swabbing and brushing until the patch shows no further indication of fouling. After the bore is clean, dry it with a tight, dry patch. Finally, coat the bore sparingly with light oil and store the gun.

If the gun is to be used yearly or more often, a different approach to cleaning is called for. Most modern guns require very little chamber and bore care for rust prevention or accuracy. Modern cartridge components do not cause rust; they help prevent it. If a rifle or pistol bore gets wet, it is probably better to fire a round through the barrel than to clean the gun carefully as described here. Let me explain. Firing a smokeless cartridge in a gun does

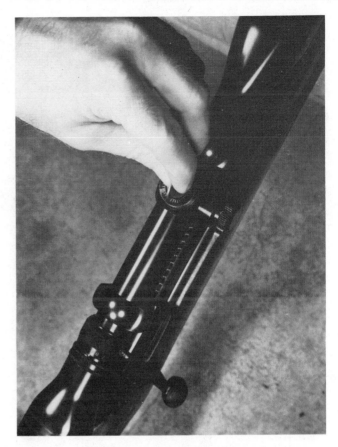

Some sight adjustment is usually required after the handload decision is made to convert precision into accuracy. Data 3, Height Above Aiming Point, from the precision graph is helpful for this final zeroing. Data 6, Average Velocity, and the ballistic tables will help you decide the best sight setting.

several things. First, water is eliminated by the heat of the burning gas, and second, the coating of primer and propellant fouling helps prevent rust for a considerable length of time. Further, the natural fouling is needed so that the bullet will perform in the same way as when the gun was zeroed for accuracy. Remember that the bore was fouled when the rifle was zeroed.

Let's discuss what happens if the chamber and bore are scrupulously cleaned and lubricated as if for long-term storage. Besides picking up lint and dust on the oil-plated bore surface, there is a good possibility that when cleaning is performed, excess solvent and oil will enter the action, bolt, and trigger. From there the oil will seep into the stock and ruin it in time. After a few rounds are fired, powder and residue will find their way past the chamber into the action, bolt, striker, and trigger areas. A

A small sampling of the many cleaning products and lubricants available for gun care. They are all good if used properly.

thick, black gummy substance usually forms. This eventually hardens and slows down the moving parts in the action. Slow lock time and even misfires result. The trigger may fail to operate, or even go off accidentally. Excessive, unneeded cleaning and lubrication can and do cause these mishaps to occur. Too much cleaning can even be unsafe. To stretch a point, recall how many stories you've heard of gun-related accidents that occurred while the gun was being cleaned. Also, something that occurs on a regular basis to many fanatic cleaners is the damage done to a good bore by an improperly used, poor-quality cleaning rod. And don't forget the loss of accuracy and missed shots due to the first round being fired through a clean, oily gun.

So what should you do? This is a good question. If a high-powered rifle is to be used at least annually, follow these chamber and bore care procedures. After every ten to 25 rounds, dry brush the bore with a clean, dry, properly-sized bronze brush. Be sure to use a good cleaning rod such as a one-piece steel rod. Push or pull the brush from the chamber, if possible. Use a chamber guide, if you have one. Slowly and gently, push or pull the brush completely through the length of the bore about four times. The muzzle should be pointing down to help prevent residue and bronze bristles from entering the receiver.

Then replace the brush with a jag point and push a clean, dry, and tight patch through the bore from

Precision Handloading

chamber to muzzle. This will remove the loose residue and any bits of bronze brush. Push a second patch through to clean up. Don't use solvent or oil if the gun will be used within six months or even a year. If you do, you can count on the next few rounds going somewhere other than where you expect. Furthermore, oil causes fouling to build up fast in some guns. If you use the dry brush method as described above, the bore will not rust. You can expect the kind of precision and accuracy that you nurtured from your handload with the first shot. If the gun is to be stored for the season, use a solvent such as Hoppe's No. 9. But remember to fire a few rounds to foul the bore before the gun is used again.

Although cleaning and lubrication have nothing to do with handloading, they do affect precision and accuracy, which are definitely areas of concern for handloaders.

Just one last word about final zero and sight

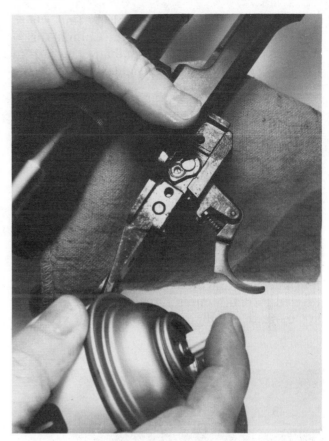

A good way to clean the metal assemblies on most guns is to spray the area with a cleaning solvent and then use a blowgun to blast the dirt away. It's quick, easy, and thorough.

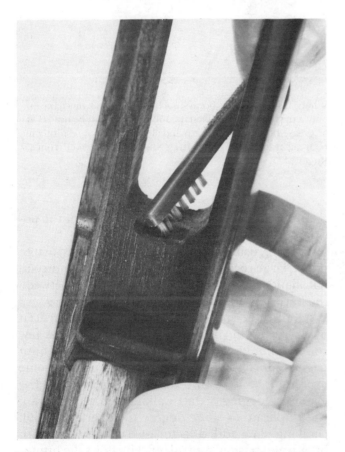

This is a situation where a small brush is invaluable. Debris, chips, and dirt in the stock can cause poor bedding, resulting in inaccuracy.

alignment. Many guns, high-powered hunting rifles in particular, often have a tendency to throw the first shot away from the other shots in a group. The amount varies with different guns, but can usually be minimized by good adjustment and good handloading. Some divergence still occurs, however. In most hunting situations, the first shot is the most important. Therefore, zero your rifle with "first shots" only. What this means is to fire a group of three or five shots to find the group center, but allow enough time between shots to let the barrel cool completely. The time needed can range from 15 to 45 minutes between shots on cold and hot days respectively.

Taking your time for a final zero is very important and necessary with many guns. Once the final zero is obtained, mark the elevation and windage adjustment screws on the sight. Replace the dust covers and don't touch the adjustment screws again.

Completing the Project

Use the appropriate ballistic table to find where shots should fall at different ranges. Commit this to memory or write it on a card and tape the card to the stock. Don't change the sights every time the hunting situation changes.

The last item of concern in completing the project is practice. The best gun and the best ammunition lose most of their potential if the shooter cannot perform well also. For that simple and obvious reason, you should practice. There is no other way to gain or maintain proficiency in any of the shooting sports without practice. Furthermore, practice, except for the formalized types of shooting sports, should be varied. A hunter should practice his shooting skills by creating various situations. For instance, practice firing in the standing, squatting, kneeling, and even prone positions. All may be needed in real hunting situations. Some positions are more demanding than others. You may find

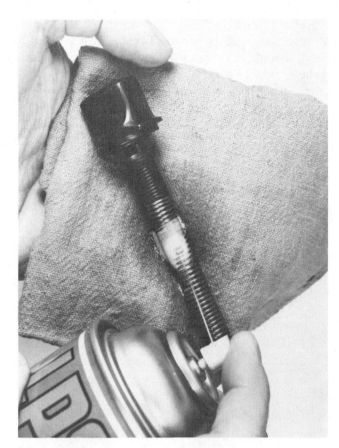

Where fast movement occurs, such as in the lock mechanism, only a dry, rust-preventive-type lubricant should be used. Oil or grease here could gum up and slow the action, resulting in poor accuracy and even misfires. Shown is the striker from a Ruger M77.

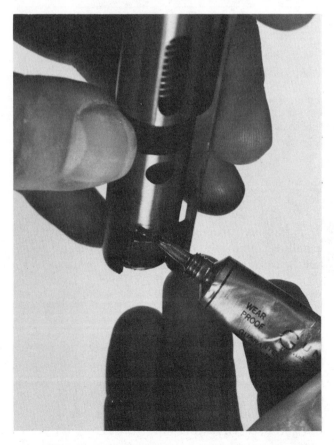

A small dab of grease is needed where heavy force and slow movement occur, for example, the contact surfaces on the bolt lugs.

that more practice is required with some of the positions than others.

Practice using improvised rests such as a tree trunk, large rock, or the roof of a car. Put your coat, hat, hand, or any other available cushion between the hard rest and the gun.

All of these shooting positions can be practiced by dry-firing in your home or at the range. A few rounds should be fired each year before any hunt begins. More realism can be experienced if some exercise is worked into the shooting practice. For example, jogging or fast walking before dry-firing will duplicate to some degree the exertion of hill climbing. The added factor of having to deal with breath and trigger control quickly shows the hunter what he may have to contend with afield. Some practice should be done while wearing the clothing

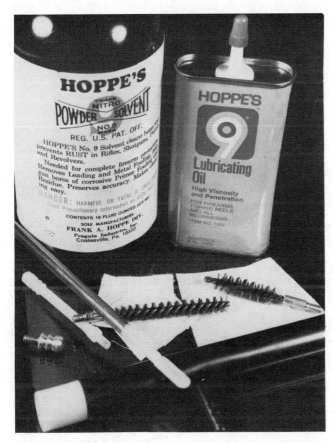

If the gun will not be used for a long time, before storing clean the bore of powder residue and any traces of metal (lead and copper). Then swab well with a solvent such as Hoppe's No. 9. After the bore is perfectly clean, run a lightly oiled patch through it. Always use a top-quality rod to prevent bore damage while cleaning.

to be used on the hunt. In other words, do all you can do to create realistic conditions.

Physical conditioning can also play a part in the success of hunting and marksmanship. Some hunting is easy. But often, the most exciting and memorable hunting experiences occur in difficult and physically demanding conditions of weather and terrain. The same is true of lengthy, demanding

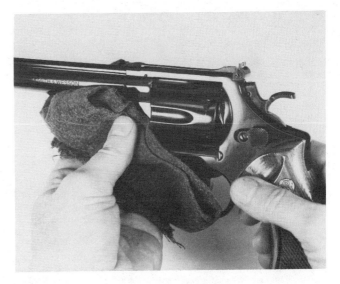

Simply wiping off the outer surface with a rust preventive medium is sufficient. This Smith & Wesson revolver is being wiped with a silicone-impregnated cloth. The silicones help remove fingerprints and prevent rust without the use of oil.

match target competition. Being in reasonable physical condition is always an aid to shooting success, whatever the circumstance.

There are many factors involved in hitting a distant target under difficult conditions, too many to recall and check off when the situation presents itself. Some shooting responses must be almost automatic, and this is learned through practice. The hunter may have all he can do to steady the rifle, develop a sight picture, and squeeze the trigger. Fortunately, the hunter or target shooter who uses the methods presented here to make his ammunition has two big factors resolved before he pulls the trigger on that once-in-a-lifetime shooting opportunity. He knows he will be firing the best possible ammunition for his shooting needs; and he has complete confidence in the capability of the ammunition and his chance for success.

Successful varmint hunters and other long-range shooters depend on high velocity and great precision, and have the experience to utilize the potential of their arms and ammunition.

Precision Handloading

# Chapter 11

# Handgun Cartridges: Loading and Testing

One major area of metallic cartridge loading is that of creating ammunition for the handgun. Handloading for handguns is a large area, indeed, and the methods presented in this book apply perfectly. This is because the principles of Management by Objective are the same regardless of the job. Only the specifics of job management differ, based on the purpose of the job.

Handguns and rifles are both forms of firearms but that's where the similarities end. Their construction, operation, and ammunition are suited to different roles and different purposes more often than not. Loading and testing handgun ammunition is different from that of rifles.

The methods for loading popular handgun cartridges differ from rifle loading for two reasons: first, the cartridges themselves are different, and secondly, the guns are different. For instance, centerfire handgun ammunition is generally shorter in length but wider in diameter than centerfire rifle ammunition. The most popular rifle calibers range from 5mm to 8mm in bullet diameter. Popular centerfire pistol and revolver calibers start at about 8mm and extend through the 11mm size. The bullet weights of many handgun cartridges are twice that of some rifle bullets in the 6mm and 7mm range. Yet the fastest production handgun cartridges generally achieve only about half the velocity of centerfire rifle cartridges.

With all of these cartridge differences, you might think that the objectives of handloading in regard to handguns would be very different from those for the rifle. This is not so. Depending on the shooting need, the various objectives as used for loading centerfire rifle ammunition fit the needs of handgun loading quite well. They only have to be altered to fit the exact shooting requirements, that is, hunting, target, home defense, military, and so forth.

The objectives of precision, velocity, pressure, uniformity, function, duplication, and costs are still valid and applicable.

The mechanics of loading handgun cartridges do differ from the loading of most rifle cartridges. The greatest differences in handgun and rifle cartridges are with the shape of the cases and the function requirements of the guns themselves. These differences are most obvious when comparing a bolt action rifle with a semiautomatic pistol.

Most high-powered rifles use a bottle-necked cartridge case and the rifle is designed to headspace on either the cartridge shoulder, belt, or rim. In contrast, most semiautomatic pistols fire cartridges with straight-walled cases. The pistol, more often than not, headspaces on the mouth of the case. Cartridges designed for revolvers headspace on the case rim. Additionally, rifles achieve their greater velocity with relatively slow-burning powder expanding slowly in a long barrel and acting against a bullet of high sectional density. The opposite is true of pistols. Most handguns, both pistols and revolvers, achieve their best results with a fast-burning powder in a short barrel, acting against a bullet of low sectional density. Incidentally, handguns are similar to shotguns in these last mechanics, and some shotshell propellants are often suitable for handgun cartridges.

The above points underline another difference between handguns and rifles; handguns are more critical than rifles in regard to powder burning rate. Their short barrels and actions depend on correct pressure, speed of operation, timing, and pressure duration to produce reliable functioning and best velocity.

With the new popularity of big game handgunning, the metallic silhouette shooting games for handguns, and modern, single-shot handguns, some of the differences between handguns and rifles have been reduced. Some high-powered rifle cartridges are now used in very specialized handguns. Numerous new cartridges have been developed for handgun hunting and handgun shooting games. They are not really handgun or rifle cartridges according to traditional classification. Rather, they are a new breed of cartridges, designed for ultra-high-powered handguns. Most of these cartridges have been designed for big game

hunting and long-range silhouette target shooting. This new category of cartridges also fits into the concepts of handloading by objective. But again, the objectives must be carefully tailored to fit the shooting need.

Understanding the big differences between handgun and rifle cartridges and the guns themselves is important for successful loading of either type cartridge. These differences and their distinctive operating needs first become apparent during the case preparation stage of loading, and continue throughout each handloading step.

With straight-wall revolver and pistol cases, three or four loading dies may be used to accomplish the same things done with two rifle dies. For instance, pistol die #1 generally resizes the case. Pistol die #2 expands the case mouth to accept the bullet and may also deprime the case. Pistol die #3 is used to seat the bullet and crimp the case mouth around the bullet. Depending on the cartridge and the die maker, these last two steps may be expanded into a fourth die, usually to separate the seating and crimping operation.

Different thoughts on handgun die making and use exist. But it is a fact that die sets for handguns generally contain one or two more dies than do rifle die sets so the job can be done correctly.

Many semiautomatic pistols depend on case length for headspacing. This means that it is very important to good target precision that pistol cases not only be the correct, specified length, but also the same length in regard to each other. This does not mean that the cases should be within five to ten thousandths of an inch of each other. They must be within *one* to *two thousandths* of an inch of each other—essentially the same length. This uniform length requirement is more important than obtaining the specified maximum case length as stated in different information sources. This is due to the handgun's critical need for equal lock time.

## Lock Time

Lock time is the time from when the trigger sear breaks hammer contact until the primer is struck, and occurs after the trigger is pulled, but before the burning gas starts pushing the bullet from the barrel. Consistency in lock time is important for precision and accuracy with handguns, as well as with rifles. It is during this time that the stored energy of the hammer, the trigger springs, and the shooter's grip and trigger pressure are released. If lock time differs from one round to the next, these energies acting on the gun will be of unequal duration. A short cartridge case can cause a lengthy lock time. When the trigger sear breaks contact with the hammer, a long lock time allows the inner and outer forces greater time to throw the firearm out of alignment with the target. These factors affecting lock time have an effect on rifles as well as handguns, but handgun precision is affected more by unequal lock time than rifles. Handguns are lighter, have a shorter sight radius and a shorter recoil radius.

If the hammer or firing pin of the handgun travels varied distances to reach the cartridge primer, the handgun will be pointing in a different direction for every shot. This simply means that it is more difficult to keep a handgun in correct sight alignment after the trigger is pulled than a rifle. The need for exact case length is more important for handguns than for rifles and it is even more important for pistols than for revolvers. This is always true for pistol cartridges that headspace on the mouth of the case. The .45 Automatic Colt Pistol cartridge is one of several that must be included in this category; the 9mm Luger is another.

Nowadays, you may have some difficulty finding pistol cases that are as long as the specifications suggest. For some reason, manufacturers are making them a tad shorter. With some cases, such as the .45 Auto, you may never find cases that are as long as the industry standards specify, but don't worry about it. Furthermore, most pistol cases don't stretch in length as do rifle cases, even after repeated loadings and firings. In fact, they may shrink a hair when resized. Don't be overly concerned. The most important requirement is that the cases be equal in length to each other so that uniform headspacing and equal lock time can occur. For this reason, it's a good idea when preparing once-fired, semiautomatic brass for the first time to trim the cases to a uniform length immediately after the sizing operation step. This will give a more square and true case mouth than if trimming is

Handgun cartridge crimps vary considerably. From left to right: the .38 wadcutter has little or no crimp. The .357 Magnum has a moderate crimp on the bullet cannelure. The .44 Magnum has a heavy, roll crimp over the shoulder of the lead slug. The .45 Auto has only a slight taper crimp.

done after the belling operation. Choose the shortest acceptable case length and then trim the others accordingly.

## Crimps

In addition to the equal headspace requirement, which can only be achieved with equal length cases, there is another important reason for equal case length—proper crimp.

Most revolver and pistol cartridges require a good crimp for optimum ignition and best ballistic results. A proper cartridge crimp is one that is tight enough to give good bullet "pull" and allow thorough ignition of the charge, yet one that is very uniform in regard to tension so that the chamber pressure is equal from one shot to the next.

There are two factors that must be present in order that proper, uniform crimping can occur: first, the cartridge cases must be exactly equal in length so the crimping die performs identically on all cases; second, the case mouth walls must be the same thickness. If different brands of cases and different head stamps are intermixed in the loading operation, nonuniform, poorly crimped cartridges

This shows the disparity of case length often found when loading the .45, 9mm, .380, and similar calibers. The gap between case and receiver is usually even greater than this due to tolerances in the gun. This amount of space does not help precision and accuracy.

will be produced. Even cases of the same brand and head stamp should be graded by case mouth thickness to within .002 to .004 inch average. Cartridges with nonuniform mouth thickness, even though carefully prepared and loaded with the best of components, will perform poorly. Some may achieve good velocity. Others will not. Precision will be poor also, resulting in poor accuracy and a loss of shooting confidence.

Revolver cartridges and some of the single-shot handgun cartridges also need proper crimping, but revolver requirements differ from those of semi-auto pistols. Revolvers, which use straight-wall pistol cases, headspace on the case rim and are not as dependent on case length uniformity for equal lock time. However, revolver cartridges do require crimps of equal tension for equal ballistic results. The only way to achieve consistent crimping is to have virtually identical case lengths and equal case thickness. This is true with any revolver cartridge, especially where high velocity is involved. The uniform case length requirement is important for revolvers, just as it is for pistols. In all but the slowest target revolver cartridges, where soft bullets, low velocity, fast powders, and no crimp are employed, a proper, uniform crimp is absolutely essential.

Regardless of the type of cartridge case, cleanliness is important. Handgun cases should be thoroughly cleaned before inspection and loading begin. For uniform sizing, any powder residue, grit, or remaining bullet sealant must be removed from the case mouth. This is not only important for sizing, but also for the expansion and belling steps. For these reasons, it is a good idea to wash all cases thoroughly in a solvent before and after sizing. The second solvent bath and detergent washing removes sizing lubricant before bullet seating.

As with rifle cases, uniform case volume is important to handgun cartridge reloading. Case weight, which was explained in detail in an earlier chapter, is the best indicator of case volume. A good standard is a weight deviation range of about 3 percent of the case weight. For example, if the case weight average of the .38 Special is 63.0 grains, minimum and maximum weights should be no more than 1.5 percent, or about 0.9 grains below or above 63.0. That's close, but it is needed for good results.

## Testing

Testing handgun cartridges also differs from that of rifle cartridge testing. Handgun testing involves range, target, bench, chronograph, and firearm functioning needs just like those of rifles. But each of these needs is subject to the conditions imposed by the handgun itself.

Beginning with range needs, most production handguns are designed to perform within a range of from ten feet to 50 yards. Some of the high-powered handguns are capable of good precision past 100 yards but they don't have the advantage of a shoulder stock, long sight radius, and bullet velocity of a rifle. The handgun may be capable of riflelike precision, but not the accuracy. Most shooters simply can't hold a pistol as steady as a rifle, even on a benchrest. For these reasons, the range requirements change for handguns.

Most handgun range testing can be done at 25 to 50 yards, depending on the velocity of the handgun and the type of sights installed on it. This distance is long enough to see the precision differences in loads while reducing the shooting skills required of the shooter.

A good guideline for handgun range distance, based on bullet velocity, is generally: for handguns whose muzzle velocities are below 1,000 fps, a 25-yard range is adequate. If the cartridge is expected to be faster than 1,000 fps, a 50-yard range may be better, but only after initial testing at 25 yards.

When working up loads for any handgun, it is best to start testing at short shooting distances and use large paper targets. Handguns are capable of good precision, but that usually happens in a very narrow range of charge weights. In addition, handguns have much greater variance in precision and accuracy over a range of charge weights as compared to rifles. This variance is often enough to cause complete misses and "lost" shots on standard pistol targets. Even a small difference of powder weight with some handgun cartridges can cause the bullet to strike off the target paper. This can happen with the largest of targets, and prevents any measurement of precision. There's a loss of data and a waste of time, effort, and materials.

These guidelines are subject to interpretation, however. For instance, the handgun may have either adjustable or fixed sights. Adjustable sights are needed for a precise zero even at 25 yards. A 50-yard range begins to press most shooters to the limit of their abilities even with guns equipped with good adjustable sights. Handguns with fixed sights are generally limited to 25-yard shooting, or less. One reason for range testing is to compare the precision of the test loads in the gun. If the shooter feels he will lose confidence in his own ability at 50 yards, he should plan on testing at 25 yards. Twenty-five yards is enough distance to see and measure the vertical deviation of shots with handgun ammunition. Furthermore, the type of handload may rule out the need for any testing past 25 yards. The handloader should consider all the factors relating to his shooting needs and intended use of the cartridge. If the handgun is equipped with a telescopic sight, the testing distance may be extended somewhat. But use caution and don't overdo it. A scope sight, regardless of its quality and power, does not make a handgun into a rifle.

Except for a few highly modified firearms, most handgun loads can be thoroughly tested for precision at 25 yards. Range testing at 50 yards and more should not begin until you can hit consistently at 25 yards, and the loads are showing some degree of

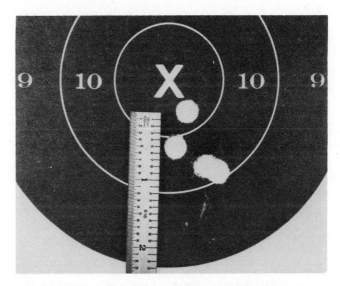

This is a good five-shot group at 25 yards with a pistol. Careful, consistent handloading can pay dividends for handgunners in both competitive shooting and hunting.

precision. Otherwise, you will become frustrated and waste precious time.

It is often best to test loads for handguns in two stages. First, try the broad range of test loads at a short distance. After that, narrow down the loads to the better ones. The shooting distance may be stretched also. This is the best and least expensive way to test handgun ammunition.

In addition to the size of the target for testing handguns, the shape of the target is important. The majority of handgunners use metal sights. Most of these sights have a square blade in front and a square notch at the rear. But most pistol targets are a simple, round bull's eye designed for scoring accuracy. These are almost useless for precision testing of loads. The best type of target for square, metallic sights, rifle or handgun, is a black square on a white background. The size of the square will vary, depending on the gun. This type of sight will be explained and shown in Chapter 12.

Handguns and rifles are tested differently at the shooting bench. For most handgun precision and velocity testing, there is only one good method for bench firing: get into a comfortable sitting position where the gun and your elbows can be comfortably, but firmly, supported. The handgun should be raised on sandbags to eye level and steadied with your hands. A two-handed hold is best, but some-

This is one way to support a handgun for bench testing. The device is adjustable for reach and height. This one is made of metal, but wood will work as well. Place sandbags on the rest and cover them with a piece of plastic or leather when firing revolvers. Otherwise, the gas and lead leaks at the barrel-to-cylinder gap will cut through the bag. And, there is abrasion caused by recoil, which will take the finish off the gun in short order. Therefore, covering the sandbags is a good idea whatever the handgun type.

times a singled-handed hold is needed for a good sight picture. The pistol or revolver should be supported by sandbags on at least two points for maximum rigidness. This will depend on the shape of the gun. The best points for support on most handguns are under the barrel, next to the front of the trigger guard, and underneath the trigger guard, next to the shooter's middle, fourth, and fifth fingers. These two support points, plus the shooter's hand hold, provide good vertical and lateral support. A third point of support can be the butt of the handgun grip.

After the sandbag rests are correctly placed, they should be covered with a soft cloth or a piece of leather to protect the gun's metal finish. It doesn't take long for sand grit to rub the finish away.

For safety, be sure that the gun's muzzle extends past any point on the bench or the rest where muzzle blast could cause damage. With revolvers, keep hands and clothing away from the cylinder and barrel gap. The gas leak on all revolvers will cut or burn anything soft.

Don't place a hand or finger between the bench and the butt of the pistol grip. Due to the nature of handgun recoil, you could receive a nasty bruise. I learned this fact a long time ago while testing a .44 Magnum revolver. I tried to support the butt of the revolver with the little finger on my left hand. The first round convinced me forever that this was not to be done.

This procedure for bench testing handguns will give you the best precision, but not the best accuracy. Let me explain. Bench testing as described here does let you find which loads are most precise, but there's a catch. The gun will not place shots in the same spot when fired offhand. Make sure you also zero sights with the chosen load using a normal hold and stance. Otherwise you will think your ammunition has gone bad.

There are other considerations when testing loads in handguns. One concern is that revolvers use multiple firing chambers or cylinder holes for successive shots. If firing five-shot groups, in a six-shot capacity revolver, you will be eliminating the use of one cylinder for each five-shot test group. For uniformity, you should load the five test rounds of each handload number in the same five cylinder holes for each successive shot group. This requires identifying the cylinder hole you wish to exclude during the testing procedure.

Identification of the excluded cylinder hole can be done in several ways. Some revolvers make this easy, due to the appearance of the mechanism itself or a stamped mark near one of the holes. Most guns do not have such handy reference points. Usually, you must identify the unused sixth hole with a scratch mark, some paint, or a piece of tape. Load a dummy round into the unused cylinder hole to equalize the weight and balance the cylinder. Be sure to place the dummy round into the same cylinder hole each time you reload. This method will offend some shooters because only five holes in the cylinder will be receiving all the stress. This could cause some uneven wear to the revolver with extensive, heavy testing. A simple answer is to load test rounds in groups of six and score all six shots. With six-shot revolvers, this method has the added advantage of providing extra data and slightly better statistical results.

When test firing semiautomatic pistols, there is another concern. This involves the relation of the pistol's slide action, the magazine, and the cartridges in the magazine.

With many semiauto pistols, the last round fired will strike the target at a different point due to the change in the magazine when the last round is chambered. The magazine follower makes contact with the slide mechanism, not another brass cartridge. This alters the functioning of the pistol slightly and often causes some loss of precision as the last round is fired. The simplest cure for this is to load one or more dummy rounds into the empty magazine first. Then load your test rounds. The dummy rounds will be at the bottom of the magazine. This procedure accomplishes two things: first, you will eliminate the last round "flier"; and, second, you will be firing the pistol with a fully loaded magazine. This is good because it will place full spring tension on the magazine follower. Many potential first-round malfunctions can be identified with this method. First-round malfunctions are the most serious kind for both hunting and defense purposes with semiautomatic pistols. If you don't use this method for testing handloads in semiauto pistols, it is possible to find a very precise loading and duplicate more of the same not knowing that load might cause malfunctions with a full magazine.

Semiauto pistols are dependent on the magazine for good functioning. Different magazines can cause a change in functioning. Use the same magazine for all load testing.

Another aspect of firing semiautoloading pistols deals with functioning and the recoil force of the ammunition.

Since semiauto pistols are generally made to work with a specific type ammunition, a special purpose handload may alter the pistol's ability to function reliably. A different bullet shape may cause poor feeding and chambering. Some modification to the feed ramp on the barrel's chamber and the receiver may be required, or perhaps a different bullet. Modification of the magazine may also be required. Light target loads in auto pistols may not generate enough recoil force for good extraction and ejection. Loading, chambering, and locking will also suffer. These problems can be doubly frustrating, especially if the most proven, precise load positively prevents proper pistol performance. Phew! That last sentence made my poor pencil poop out.

Light target loads in semiauto pistols often require experimenting with lighter recoil springs. The hammer and firing pin springs, which absorb some of the recoil energy, may have to be changed as well.

The last area of concern when testing handgun handloads is that of how the chronograph is used. Compared to rifle testing, the chronograph will be used differently with handguns, for example, the positioning of the sensing screens. Metallic sights on handguns are usually an inch or so closer to the barrel than the scope sight on a rifle. A modified screen setup procedure and different height gauges are needed for good sensitivity and safety. This is true with the older, electromechanical screens as well as the newer light-sensitive screens.

Next, with handloads that produce plenty of muzzle blast but velocity below 1,200 fps, you may need to place a sound baffle between the muzzle of the gun and the first sensing screen. This is because the sound shock from the muzzle blast can reach the first screen before the bullet arrives. This would trip the screen and start the clock prematurely. The second, farther screen may only sense the bullet. This condition causes a low velocity reading. It occurs with some photoelectric screens and subsonic bullets and usually happens when the first screen is mounted very close to the gun muzzle. Some chronograph testing should be done before testing handguns to see if this condition exists with your equipment. A number of the newer photosensing screens are also less sensitive to the blast effect and work quite well without any baffles.

This brings us to the end of the discussion about differences in testing rifles and handguns. To summarize, the use of MBO for handguns is identical to that for rifles. The handload data list and the precision, velocity, and pressure graphs are constructed in the same way for handguns as with rifle cartridge testing. With some handgun testing, there is the need to use a different vertical scale on the precision graph. That presents no problem. You may also want to stretch out the charge weights over the lower scale to get a longer curve. Just change the numbers to suit your personal, particular needs.

The purpose of this chapter is to make the job of handloading for handguns a little easier. I sincerely wish you the best of luck with your handgun loading. It is different but often more interesting than loading rifle cartridges. If you have your objectives clearly identified, use scrupulous methods, and you're willing to start over after a failure, you will be successful. Some revolver and pistol cartridges are simple to load and good results come easily; many are more difficult, however. Although they are centerfire-type cartridges, handgun ammunition is different from rifle ammunition and is affected more critically by small differences in loading. If you accept this fact and you're prepared to work with it, the rewards can be very gratifying.

A setup for finding precision and velocity data includes: a fixed, steady position for the gun, a properly aligned pair of chronograph screens, and the correct size target for precision shooting.

Precision Handloading

# Chapter 12

# Other Handloading Points

This chapter is a collection of other objectives and thoughts relevant to handloading that did not fit into the discussion until now. For simplicity, the material is divided roughly into two parts. The first part lists other objective points that relate to the given system of handloading. The last part contains points of interest for handloaders that are not necessarily related to objective planning.

As stated in Chapter 2, there are obviously other objectives than those established for handloading projects like the text example. That example used a modern, high-powered, big game hunting rifle cartridge. Other types of rifle and handgun shooting that would need similar objectives, for similar desired results, would be varmint and small game hunting. Some of the objectives listed in Chapter 2 might fit the specific needs of the military also. But one group of shooters that would probably want a different set of handloading objectives would be the target shooters.

Precision is certainly the most important objective for target shooting, both rifle and handgun competition. In big events, top shooters are very evenly matched. The precision quality of their ammunition is often the deciding factor in winning and losing. In some target matches, however, velocity is still a consideration. This is especially true in long-range target matches. Good velocity is needed for accuracy. Almost all such matches are measured on the basis of accuracy, rather than pure precision.

The choice of bullet would also be a different consideration for the target shooter. His choice would be made on the bullet's ability to maintain maximum target precision at acceptable velocity. The bullet's killing ability would be of no consequence whatsoever.

Different objectives are needed for ammunition used for personal defense. For instance, in a good cartridge for home defense use, precision may be a very small concern. Getting enough velocity and the correct pressure for good bullet expansion and reliable functioning of the gun would be the important objective points.

For some types of hunting, good accuracy combined with low velocity may be needed. As an example, in states permitting the use of rifles for taking wild turkeys, knowledgeable hunters have been making up special, low-velocity handloads for years. Shots at turkeys are normally fairly close, sometimes barely beyond shotgun range, and a full-velocity round would destroy too much of the bird with a solid hit. Another example might be varmint hunters in more populated areas. They would have need for accurate, low-velocity, subsonic ammunition to keep noise to a minimum.

## Rimfire Ammunition

There is one area of shooting that is often ignored by handloaders. That's the area of rimfire ammunition. The rimfire or .22 user cannot tailor ammunition to his needs but he does have the ability to choose brand, type, and lot number. There are enough differences among the many .22 rimfire offerings to warrant close comparison. Many of the methods discussed in this book can be used to find better ammunition for the smallbore, rimfire shooter, as well as the centerfire handloader.

If you want the best results in your .22 handgun or rifle, try this. Buy a few boxes of the various brands of ammunition that fit your needs. Use the handload data list to record your choices. Fire at least three groups of five rounds each for good data. Measure, record, and compare each of these five-shot groups for precision and velocity. Don't worry about pressure. You will probably find that one brand of ammunition performs best in your gun. Just make sure you know what your objectives are before beginning. The methods of target precision measurement and the use of velocity recordings as explained in preceding chapters will let you compare the results for .22-caliber ammunition, just as was done with centerfire ammunition.

## Raising Standards

Not too far removed from this matter of modi-fying ammunition is the topic of standards for handloading components, guns, sights, and factory-loaded ammunition. We've already used factory ammo as a standard for comparison when handloading. Remember that you're not locked into any inviolate standards; they can be raised after your initial selected load has been established. For instance, if you're not truly satisfied with your results, you can use a narrower range of powder charge weight and experiment further. Then, you may want to test loads past 100 yards to define your data and graphs better. There are many things you can do, and this is one of the fascinating aspects of handloading.

The propellant is one component you can control. If you're not happy with your first results, choose another brand. If you believe it is satisfactory, consider purchasing it in a larger bulk container. This will give you a good supply with better uniformity.

If your bullet fails to give the precision or hunting results you want, change. You might also try seating the bullet closer to the lands of the barrel, reducing clearance, and using a straight-line bullet seating die. All of these things may help, but proceed with only one change at a time and always decrease the charge weight slightly and watch for pressure changes.

The character of the bullet itself, particularly performance, is an area of great concern to handloaders. Bullet expansion, penetration, and integrity are all serious factors. They can only be positively determined with actual testing. If chosen properly, handloaded bullets from reputable manufacturers will perform comparably to factory-loaded bullets. This is a favorable comparison because U.S. ammunition makers almost always provide proper bullets that get the job done.

If you're still concerned about bullet performance, test your handload against the factory ammunition. It requires some effort but the knowledge reinforces confidence in your chosen handload.

When testing bullets, especially those for hunting, you have three objective considerations: penetration, expanded diameter, and retained weight. Each of these features is measurable after firing the bullet into suitable test material, which may be of sophisticated composition, or as simple as newspaper.

## Testing Bullet Performance

There are several materials used to test bullets. Some are difficult to obtain. Some are expensive. Some are not suitable for your needs. Newspaper is easy to obtain, costs nothing, and is a good test medium since only a relative comparison between factory and handload bullets is necessary.

First, collect newspaper. Lots of it. Make bundles that are ten inches high and tie them tightly both ways with a string. Build a wooden platform that's wide enough for your newspapers and about five or six feet long. Use sawhorses to support the platform and get it off the ground. Shim the whole assembly with small pieces of wood to align it with the firing point.

The day before you test bullets, take your newspapers to the site and soak them in water. A play pool or old bathtub is great for this. The paper needs to soak for several hours. This makes the newspaper more uniform and stops the bullet in less distance. The newspaper bundles swell and get much heavier, so do the soaking at the test site, if possible.

Set up a spotting target by the side of the test platform. This is so you can determine the impact point of each different cartridge and hit the newspaper bundles dead center each time on the first shot. This will require two rounds of factory ammunition and two rounds of handload ammunition for each test. Loading newspapers, firing, and walking back and forth to the target limits testing to about three or four comparisons in one afternoon, so don't try to test everything during one period.

Make sure you take a steel tape to measure bullet penetration after each shot. Put the recovered bullet in an envelope and label it as to caliber, bullet, range, and so forth.

After testing you have to weigh and measure the bullets for the other two concerns—retained weight and expanded diameter.

Measure the bullet diameters first. Use your calipers to measure the smallest and largest diameters across the mushroomed bullet face. Average these two measures. This is the expanded bullet size.

Before weighing each bullet, you should clean it for uniform comparison. This is no small job as the bullet will probably contain a sizable amount of finely ground newspaper and lead particles, all compacted tightly in every fold of the deformed

Degree of penetration is one of the important aspects of comparing bullet performance. Don't forget to measure for comparison as soon as the bullet is located.

bullet. A sewing needle will help you pick out the foreign material, but it is still a rather time-consuming job.

After weighing the cleaned bullet, divide the weight by its original weight and multiply by 100. This will give you the third measurement—percent of retained weight.

I've found that most good deer cartridges penetrate from 10 to 20 inches of wet newspaper. Powerful handgun cartridges go in 6 to 10 inches. This will give you an idea of how many newspaper stacks are needed.

Bullet testing in this way is a real chore but also fun. The results are interesting and useful for complete knowledge of your loading.

Firm guidelines for bullet performance are difficult to make, however, for three reasons: first, when two good bullets are compared fairly, the results are often very similar. Second, if results differ, one category of performance will usually be offset by another's gain. For instance, one bullet may not expand as much as another, but its penetration may be greater. Third, the subject of bullet testing is controversial in itself. Different shooters value performance criteria in different ways. Some shooters will argue that a different test material is needed. Others say that there is no adequate test material for bullets. They may be right.

The intended use of the bullet should always be kept in mind when comparing results. This is surely the most important consideration, but also a subject of controversy. One would think that actual hunt-ing results would give some finality to bullet choice. No way! If anything, hunters tend to fuel the fires of controversy over bullet selection even more. Hunting experiences are seldom scientific. Maybe that's the way it should be.

Bullet testing is very interesting but the results are subject to interpretation. The best bullet results are probably those that satisfy you. Bullet choice is largely a personal matter. Knowledge of bullet comparison results may be more important as a confidence factor rather than having any effect on shooting. You must make the decision that best suits your needs.

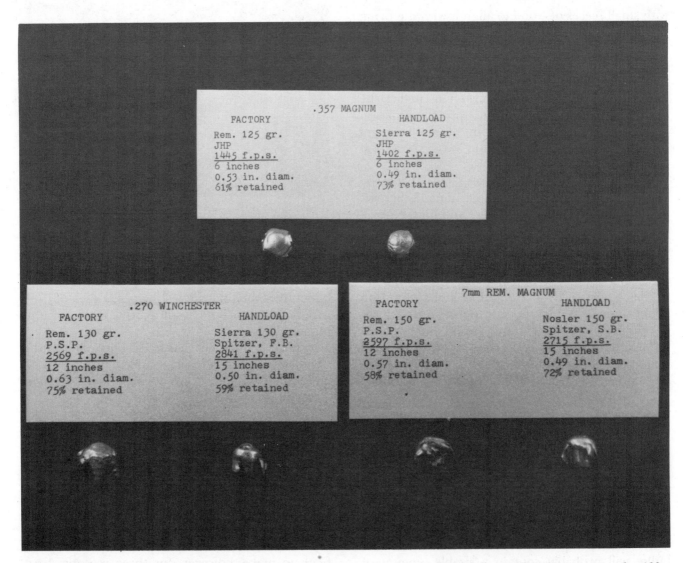

A few comparisons of factory and handload bullets after testing in wet newspapers. High-powered rifle bullets were tested at 100 yards, magnum revolver bullets at 25 yards. Data shows bullet and type, impact velocity, penetration, expanded diameter, and retained weight.

If you think a change in primers may help, try it. There are some handloaders who swear by magnum primers. They could be right. A good way to know is to test both kinds of primers using the measuring and comparing methods explained in this book. The tools of target, velocity, and pressure measurement can help you decide. Once you've made up your mind, consider purchasing primers in larger quantities. A carton of 1,000 is about minimum to ensure best uniformity and confidence if you do much loading.

The last component to consider in regard to standards is the cartridge case. You have great control over the quality of your ammunition depending on how you prepare your cases. Although the most important and basic aspects of case preparation have already been covered, more things can be done to make the case even better. For instance, you may elect to neck size rather than full-length size. If so, purchase a neck-sizing die for your cases. You can also use a dial indicator and V-blocks to check for crooked cases. Such inspection allows you to discard cases that have too much "run out."

Rolling cartridge cases will indicate any obvious signs of crookedness, but a dial indicator will show it conclusively in a measurable way. You can use the same setup to check completed rounds for bullet straightness. This is another positive way to increase the quality of your ammunition.

Using a neck reamer may help to even out neck thickness, uniformity, and bullet pull. A small lathe can be used to true the outside of case necks. It can also be used to true the case heads for exact head spacing, which may be an advantage where benchrest precision is required.

If your brass cases are straight and uniform in thickness, neck reaming and the use of a dial indicator probably won't help you much. But there is one quality control technique that you can still use with good results—weight selection.

Although we narrowed the range of case weights for handloading to 3 percent in our example, you can go further. You may wish to narrow the difference of weight in your cartridge cases to 2½ percent, 2 percent, or even 1 percent. You can go as far as you want if you have plenty of brass and your target precision and velocity priorities are that critical, as they are for most benchrest shooters.

Now let's consider the firearm itself. Certainly, its standards can be raised. Adjustments, modifica-

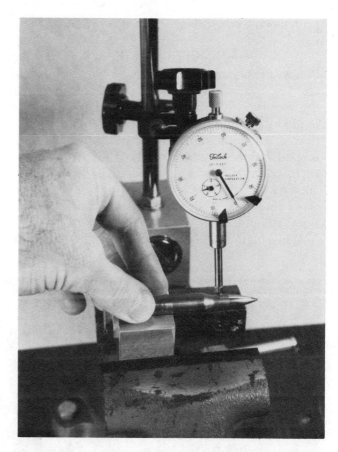

Here is one way to measure cartridge straightness. The cartridge is turned in the V-block while observing the dial. A crooked neck will cause the dial needle to move outside the reference marks. The test may be performed on case or cartridge. It's simple but effective.

tions, adapters, and corrections can be made to almost every component. A good deal of attention can be centered on the trigger mechanism. Adjustments to the trigger pull, creep, and overtravel may often produce better precision results. Sometimes changing a trigger may be justified. But make sure the type of trigger and the adjustments are correct for your shooting need. A target trigger on a hunting rifle is very dangerous; there is no advantage to such a modification.

Some rifles benefit from a simple adjustment of the tension on the guard screws. These are the screws that pull the action into the wooden stock. The use of fiberglass, or one of the plastic materials, to give more positive and complete contact between the metal and wooden parts of the gun can also help, not always, but sometimes. Consult a good gunsmith before trying to do this yourself. He can probably tell you if this expense is worth it for your rifle.

If you're not satisfied with the sights on your gun, switch to something better or more appropriate. Use caution here, also. Most guns come from the factory with sights that are adequate for the intended use, but most rifles benefit from the addition of telescopic sights. Handguns are sometimes scoped, but this can be carried to the extreme. One such example was a snub-nosed, .38-caliber revolver with a 4X scope mounted on top. That gun was completely useless for its intended purpose, home defense.

While on the subject of telescopic sights, consider the scope mount. It is just as important as the scope itself. On high-powered rifles, mounts should be set low and solid with absolutely no movement tolerated. This is vital. I have been told that the majority of complaints about telescopic sights can be traced to improper sight mounts. It has happened to me several times. The mount for any telescopic sight is a very important part of the gun.

If your gun is equipped with a scope, you can take advantage of it to test your bullets. A scope will allow you to shoot with precision at ranges of 200 and 300 yards, assuming it has ample magnification. With this ability, you can observe if your bullets are still stable and give good precision at long

This is a device to test cases for uniformity and straightness. The case is held and centered on the primer pocket and case mouth. As the case is turned, any crookedness will show up on the dial. Similar devices are available commercially.

range. Of course, factory ammunition should be the standard here, also.

To conclude this topic of standards, consider factory ammunition. As was mentioned earlier regarding .22 rimfire ammunition, you have a choice. Try comparing factory centerfire ammunition. Select several brands. Fire and measure a few groups of each. Using the measurement methods for precision and velocity, pick the best factory ammunition according to your objectives. Then review your results and correct any faults with your handloaded ammunition. In this way, you can be sure that you have absolutely the best ammunition for your shooting needs.

One last note about standards. Remember this, if you've already established a load that is better than factory ammunition, by your objectives, your handload should be the new standard. Use this ammunition for comparison if you try another bullet, powder, primer, or seating adjustment.

### Handloading Without a Chronograph

Now let's go to another subject—handloading without a chronograph. While a chronograph is essential for handloading by objective as described in this book, the extra investment for chronograph equipment is not mandatory for all handloading. Before deciding what can be done without a chronograph, consider the pros and cons to qualify your decision.

As normally used, chronographs are set up to measure bullet velocity near the muzzle of the firearm. Some shooters believe that knowing velocity will not only let them compare bullet speeds, but will also tell them how precise their shooting is. Don't believe it. Velocity deviations are just that and no more. A good standard velocity deviation may accompany poor target performance. Velocity alone should not be the deciding factor in choosing a handload. Only direct target measurement will show target precision.

Good, uniform velocity is one requirement for precision shooting, but it is not the only factor. Poor bullets will not develop true spin and uniform flight even when fired at equal velocities. Their target precision and accuracy potential will be poor even though they all leave the muzzle at the same speed. Furthermore, at some velocities, even though uni-

form, extra barrel movement occurs and the bullets do not group well on paper. The chronograph cannot measure precision.

Some good bullets show big differences in precision depending on their spin rate and the amount of barrel whip developed at different velocities. And although bullet spin is directly proportional to muzzle velocity, this knowledge alone does not ensure precise groups. Again, actual target measurement, as explained in the text, is the only true measurement of target precision and inherent accuracy. Velocity uniformity does not guarantee target precision; other things are involved.

So what does bullet velocity really tell us? Well, by knowing actual bullet velocity, it is possible to compare the speeds of different cartridges. This is important if greater velocity is an objective of the

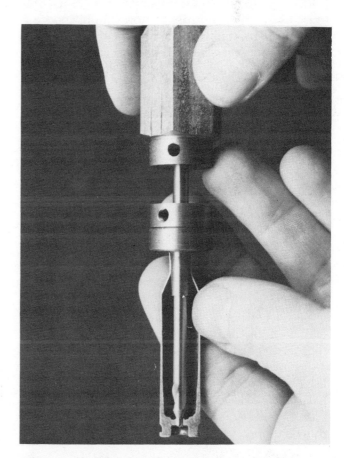

This is a homemade tool for correcting primer flash holes. The handle is equipped with a 4-inch No. 2 center drill. Twirling the tool removes metal burrs from the flash hole inside the case. The pilot on the drill is centered in the hole, while the collet and lock ring limit the cutting. The cartridge case has been opened to show how the procedure works.

shooter. Known bullet velocity, along with the appropriate exterior ballistic tables, also lets the shooter compensate closely for bullet drop at extreme shooting ranges and determine bullet energy at the various ranges. That's about all a chronograph can do for you, although that is considerable.

The handloader who is not concerned with velocity still has two major tools that he can use for comparison purposes. First, he can measure targets to determine the relative target precision and accuracy potential with each group of his handloaded cartridges. Second, he can measure case head expansion to find relative chamber pressure. Those are two of the three major areas of handload concern that can be measured without a chronograph. What this all boils down to is the requirement or need for velocity knowledge.

If knowing the actual velocity is a necessity, you must use a chronograph. If not, simply choose a loading that exhibits acceptable or desired precision without excessive case head expansion. If velocity is important to you, but a chronograph is not available, pick the loading with the heaviest propellant charge that shows acceptable precision and acceptable head expansion. You may still be equalling or bettering the factory-loaded ammunition velocity. It's that simple.

Since some people do better without the extra involvement of chronographing while shooting, they may develop better data by separating their precision shooting from chronograph work. After firing for precision and pressure, they should reload and fire four or five of the handloads and record the velocities. This can be done in a short period of time with very little extra work. These pieces of data can be used to construct a good velocity graph. All loading points in between the known velocities can be estimated by drawing a vertical line from any charge weight to the velocity line drawn between the recorded data. The only data you won't have is Data 4, Standard Velocity Deviation, and Data 5, Extreme Velocity Spread. But you can estimate Data 6, Average Velocity, confidently, using this short method.

### Refining Charge Weights

The next area of thought is that of charge weights, rather, increments of charge weight for powder. The increment is how much difference in propellant charge weight is used to separate each group of test handloads. This subject has been tossed back and forth for too long and needs to come to rest. I have my standards. Other shooters have theirs.

I believe that incremental charge weight differences depend on the middle charge weight to be used in any handload development. This means that if your test cartridges will be loaded with a maximum of 52.7 grains of powder, you will probably start loading at a point about 10 percent, or 5.3 grains less than the 52.7 maximum. This means that the middle or median of the charge weight range will be about 50 grains of propellant. This is the place to apply a standard that I refer to as the "rule of hundredths."

The "rule of hundredths" states that incremental charge weight increases should be made in amounts that equal one-hundredth of the mid-charge weight itself. This equals about 1 percent of the total charge weight near the median or middle of the charge range.

Since the example cited has a mid-charge weight of 50 grains, the incremental charge weight increase should be one one-hundredth of 50 grains or about 0.5 grains. Increases are applied to the starting charge weight of 47.4 grains and are added successively to each load number until the maximum charge weight is achieved. What you would have then would be load numbers whose charge weights begin with 47.4 grains, followed by 47.9, 48.4, 48.9, 49.4, 49.9, 50.4, 50.9, 51.4, 51.9, 52.4, and lastly, 52.7 grains. This gives a total of 12 different loads, all separated by 0.5 grains of powder, except the last two. You may wish to simplify this further by rounding off all weights to the nearest whole and half-grain. Then you would start at 47.5, 48.0, 48.5, 49.0, and so forth. In either case, you will find you've created 10 or 12 loads every time you use this method. That's good, too. This gives enough test data for solid, consistent, believable results. The data is better and easier to graph. Ten loads or 50 shots is not too much shooting to cause bad habits, either.

Incidentally, it takes about 10 or 12 load numbers to establish well-defined curves as explained in the chapters on precision, velocity, and pressure. The experts know what they are talking about when they suggest that we always start at least 10 percent below maximum charge and work up gradually.

There are exceptions to the neat "rule of hundredths," but the exceptions are created by equipment limits rather than by method logic. For instance, if a very small mid-range charge weight is used, you will have a problem in applying the rule. If you are loading a .38 Special cartridge for target shooting, your mid-range charge weight will probably be about 2.5 grains. The "rule of hundredths" would be difficult to apply. According to the rule, different test loads for this 2.5-grain example should be separated by only 0.025 grains of powder. Since almost all reloading powder scales are only accurate to 0.1 grains of weight, an obvious problem occurs due to equipment limitations. Only the analytical-type balance, as used in laboratories, could be used for such hair-splitting powder weights. Some shooters do this, however. It's that important to them.

If powder measures were capable of such precise accuracy, the small differences in charge weight would show measurable advantages, as they seem to do in some of my own experiments.

To overcome the conflict in the example given, there is only one practical option that I know of. That is to increase the small charge weight loadings to the nearest 0.1-grain weight. Under such circumstances, you must use extreme care to ensure that variations are less than 0.1 grains. This is especially true of your test loads. They must be exact for good, believable data. Charge weights in small- and large-capacity cases are still relative to their cartridge. A plus or minus 0.1-grain change with a 2.5-grain mid-charge is like a 2.0-grain difference in a cartridge using 50 grains of powder. Imprecision results in both such situations.

Once mid-charge weights reach about 5.0 grains, the weight limits, as explained, begin to have less effect. The "rule of hundredths" cannot be used precisely until mid-charge weights of 9.5 grains or more are used, however. The table labeled "Charge Weight Increments" shows proper charge weight increases better than any explanation.

Since very little has been said about powder choices, other than in the text example, a few comments and even some opinions are needed on this subject.

For most modern, high-powered rifles, I believe single-based propellants give slightly more predictable results when using objective loading techniques. I'm speaking chiefly of results where high velocities are desired. This is a factor in their favor.

The chief disadvantage of the single-based propellants is their coarse grain structure. This can cause some loading difficulty, especially with small-caliber cartridge cases. Furthermore, the single-based, tubular or stick propellants require weighing for each cartridge. Where small-caliber rifle cases must be loaded in quantity and individual weighing is unacceptable, you may be able to use single-based propellants with smaller grains or flakes, such as IMR 4227 or IMR 4320. But most likely the best alternative will be to use one of the double-based flake- or ball-type propellants. Metered charges with such propellants provide very uniform weights and often eliminate the need for individual weighing, once your testing has shown what's best. These propellants are very popular for most of the above reasons with benchrest and varmint shooters, where lots of shooting and lots of loading is done.

Typical handguns provide a near opposite set of requirements for the propellant-choice question. With nearly all pistols and revolvers, propellants of the double-based variety (nitrocellulose and nitroglycerin) are needed. This is because of their low sectional densities, short barrels, large bores, and barrel-to-cylinder venting as mentioned earlier. Handguns require that energy be developed quickly, and often in the cartridge case itself. With common handguns, the luxury of long barrels for gradual bullet acceleration is nonexistent. Velocity must be achieved quickly. Fast-burning propellants are a must. But even here there are some exceptions. One of the most popular powders for magnum handguns is IMR 4227. This is due to its uniform pressures and good precision. But it is an exception; H110, Blue Dot, and W-W 296 are more often used for this purpose.

Although the use of ball- and flake-type double-based propellants makes the chore of handloading handgun cartridges faster and easier, there is a catch. Handgun cartridges develop much of their energy and precision the instant that the bullet leaves the case. Because of this, they are even more dependent on the quality of loading than is the rifle cartridge. This means that handguns benefit more from individual charge weighing than do rifles. Powder measures load by volume rather than weight. You sacrifice finite accuracy for speed and convenience when using a powder measure.

When handloading for handguns, the process of case selection, case conditioning, bullet seating, and case crimping is of primary importance. This is especially true during initial workup. For this reason, a two-stage workup for handguns is suggested. First, fire a broader range of charge weights for testing. Next, narrow the range and experiment with closer charges. Then work on bullet seating, bullet crimping, and so forth.

As mentioned before, there is usually more than one propellant that will give nearly identical results in any given loading. This is true whether the firearm is a rifle, handgun, or shotgun. Knowing and employing any one of several appropriate component combinations will usually give excellent results. But always use the recommended procedure for choosing powders, as explained earlier. Consult the propellant maker's guide and then the bullet maker's data as secondary and additional confirmation. With handguns, your objectives may actually narrow the choice of propellants down to one or two that are best. With a few handgun cartridges, only one powder is best; they are that critical in this respect.

### Targets

Target selection is another not-so-obvious concern. Targets are, in fact, very important for good handloading. An improper target can prevent measurable precision. Anything less than acceptable will not provide measurable or believable target groups.

For rifles with telescopic sights, I believe the old Leupold and Stevens type G-53, 100-yard target design is best. You may alter target design slightly to accommodate your needs, but for most conventional-type scope sights, the Leupold and Stevens design is very near optimum. The design consists of four 2-inch black squares placed in the corners of a 6-inch white square. A 1-inch grid pattern runs throughout. This pattern leaves a 2-inch white cross in the middle of the target. You can see this in the illustration.

The white cross permits easy alignment of most scope sights on the target because the cross is wide enough to see some "light" on each side of the cross hairs. It helps with precise sight alignment.

The Leupold and Stevens-type target is very use-ful for our needs because it allows precise vertical and horizontal alignment of the sight, target, and eye. All of this is of the utmost importance in target alignment, shooting, and target measurement. You may use this target, or an adaptation, for most all telescopic sights. If range distance or reticle size change greatly, alter the target to suit your needs. Remember, precision must come first. Good targets definitely help precision.

The Leupold and Stevens-type target, or an adaptation, may be well suited for handgun cartridge development if a handgun is fitted with a scope sight. If the handgun uses conventional metal sights such as the blade- or post-type front sight and a notched rear sight, a different type of target should be used.

For precision handload testing in pistols and revolvers, you will need a target that makes best use of the sights on the gun. This requirement rules out the use of round, bull's eye-type handgun targets in almost all cases. For most handguns with conventional metal sights, a black square aiming point on a white background is usually best. The exact size of the black square depends on several factors. These include range distance, sight width, sight radius, shooting position, and the hand-to-eye distance of the shooter. The best method for finding the correct target size is described next.

After making sure the gun is empty and disabled,

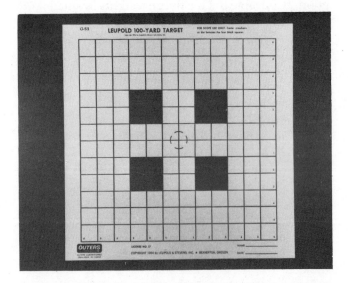

This is the best type of target for precision testing handloads in scope-sighted rifles. The black squares are placed in just the right locations to outline the scope reticle.

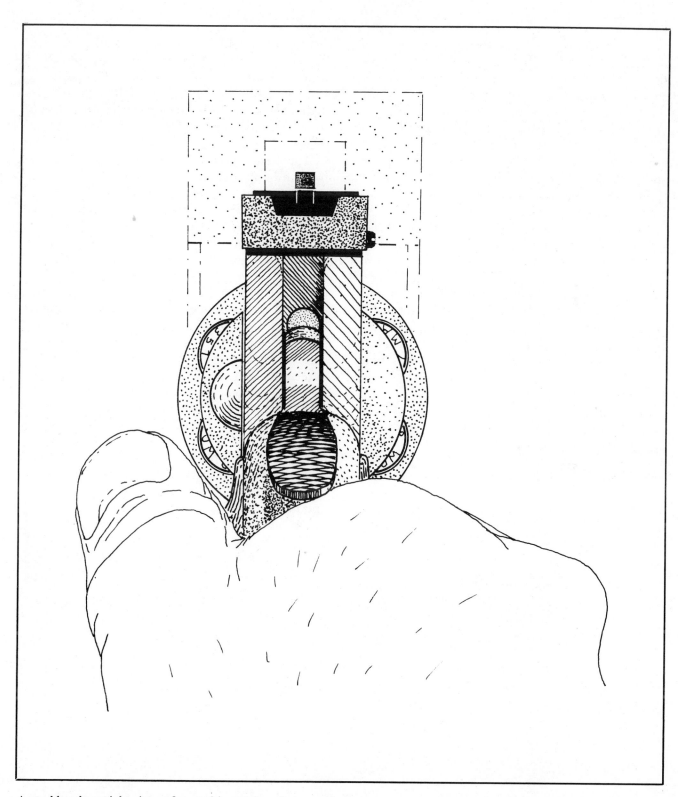

A good handgun sight picture for precision testing of ammunition.

put it on the rest just as if you were preparing to fire, sandbags and everything. Next, position yourself into a good shooting attitude for correct sight alignment. Have a helper place thumbtacks on the target paper to the left and right of the target center so that the inside corners of the rear sight on the gun intersect your line of sight and the paper target. The distance between the two thumbtacks should equal the size of the black square you will use as a target aiming point. In other words, the square should "match the notch" when viewed through the sight. The accompanying illustration may help clarify the use of the black target square.

You may also wish to make the aiming square in the shape of a rectangle whose height in the sight picture appears to be about equal to the depth of the notch in the rear sight on the handgun. This technique permits very positive sight alignment and sight picture, both horizontally and vertically. Again, the size of the black square will vary, depending on the various factors involved with range, the gun, and the shooter. This always requires some experimentation but the target has to be right for best precision.

You can accomplish the same results by placing various-sized black squares on a large piece of white paper. In this way you can make comparisons to get the optimum size square. Squares of 2, 3, 4, 5, 6, 8, and 10 inches will do for 25- and 50-yard pistol ranges. For most adjustable-sight handguns, you should find that a square of 3 to 5 inches wide is best at 25 yards. Then make the square larger or smaller in quarter-inch increments. You can really see the difference. I have a six-inch-barreled Colt Python with standard adjustable sights. I need a 4-inch black square target at 25 yards with this gun. My .45 ACP will align perfectly with a 3¾-inch black square. A Smith & Wesson Model 29 with an 8⅜-inch barrel also gets along quite well with a 3¾-inch square. Other guns and other shooters will need different sizes, though.

The described type of handgun target works well for handguns and even rifles where a square front sight post and square-notched rear sight are used. For metal sight of various shape, some alteration to the above procedure is needed.

The shape of the sight best determines the shape of the black aiming point on your target. The aiming points generally need to be the same shape as the front sight on the gun and should be as wide in the sight picture as the rear notch. Depending on front and rear sight shape, you may need a dot, square, post, triangle, diamond, or half-moon.

Both the shape and the size of the target must be determined through trial and error. You can do it quickly with some sample targets, as explained before. In any case, do what is necessary to provide a proper-sized and shaped target to satisfy fully the precision objective. Only you can be the best judge of the best target for your needs.

The last part of this chapter is not discussion, but rather a listing of conversion factors for weights and measures and a group of the mathematical formulas most helpful for handloading.

# CONVERSION FACTORS FOR WEIGHTS AND MEASURES

| Metric | Unit | U.S., Eng. & AVDP |
|---|---|---|

### Length

| | | | | |
|---|---|---|---|---|
| 2.54 cm | = | 1 in | = | 0.0833 ft |
| 0.3048 m | = | 1 ft | = | 0.3333 yd |
| 0.9144 m | = | 1 yd | = | 3 ft |
| 1.6093 km | = | 1 mile | = | 5,280 ft |
| 0.1 cm | = | 1 mm | = | 0.03937 in |
| 10 mm | = | 1 cm | = | 0.3937 in |
| 1000 mm | = | 1 m | = | 1.0936 yd |
| 1000 m | = | 1 km | = | 0.6214 mile |

### Weight

| | | | | |
|---|---|---|---|---|
| 0.0648 g | = | 1 grain | = | 0.0001428 lb |
| 28.350 g | = | 1 oz | = | 437.5 grains |
| 0.4536 kg | = | 1 lb | = | 16 oz or 7000 grains |
| 0.9072 ton | = | 1 ton | = | 2000 lb |
| 1000 mg | = | 1 g | = | 15.4321 grains |
| 1000 g | = | 1 kg | = | 2.2046 lb |

### Capacity/Volume

| | | | | |
|---|---|---|---|---|
| 16.387 $cm^3$ | = | 1 $in^3$ | = | 0.0005787 $ft^3$ |
| 0.4732 liter | = | 1 pt. (liquid) | = | 0.125 gal. or 16 oz. (liq.) |
| 3.7853 liter | = | 1 gal. | = | 4 qt. or 8 pt. (liq.) |
| 0.9464 liter | = | 1 qt. | = | 0.250 gal. |
| 0.000001 $m^3$ | = | 1 $cm^3$ or 1 ml | = | 0.0610 $in^3$ |
| 1000 $cm^3$ or 1000 ml | = | 1 liter | = | 1.0568 qt. or 0.2642 gal. |

### Velocity

| | | | | |
|---|---|---|---|---|
| 0.3048 meter/sec | = | 1 ft/sec | = | 0.6818 mi./hr |
| 1.6093 km/hr | = | 1 mi./hr | = | 1.4666 ft/sec |
| 3.6 km/hr | = | 1 meter/sec | = | 0.3645 ft/sec |
| 0.2777 meter/sec | = | 1 km/hr | = | 0.6214 mi./hr |

### Area

| | | | | |
|---|---|---|---|---|
| 6.4516 $cm^2$ | = | 1 $in^2$ | = | 0.0069 $ft^2$ |
| 929.0304 $cm^2$ | = | 1 $ft^2$ | = | 144 $in^2$ |
| 100 $mm^2$ | = | 1 $cm^2$ | = | 0.1550 $in^2$ |

### Pressure

| | | | | |
|---|---|---|---|---|
| 0.07032 $kg/cm^2$ | = | 1 $lb/in^2$ | = | 0.0680 atmosphere |
| 0.9671 atmosphere | = | 1 $kg/cm^2$ | = | 14.2207 $lb/in^2$ |
| 1.034 $kg/cm^2$ | = | 1 atmosphere | = | 14.70 $lb/in^2$ |

### Energy

| | | | | |
|---|---|---|---|---|
| 0.1383 kg-m | = | 1 ft-lb | | |
| | | 1 kg-m | = | 7.233 ft-lb |

## FORMULAS FOR HANDLOADERS

### FOR LOADING

Determining Propellant Requirements for Handload Testing

1. Median (average) Charge Weight × Number of Test Rounds = Weight of Propellant (grains)

2. $\dfrac{\text{Weight of Propellant (grains)}}{7000}$ = Number of Pounds Required

Determining Screw Thread Progression (Reach)

1. Determine Thread Pitch
   Example: $\frac{1}{4}$–20 screw has 20 threads per 1 inch length
2. Determine Progression per Screw Turn = Reciprocal of Thread Pitch
   Example: Pitch of 20 threads per inch yields 1/20 inch per turn so, 1 turn = 1/20 inch = 0.05 inch
3. Divide progression required by that progression per turn
   Example: If 0.35 inch progression is required, how many screw turns are required?
   $\dfrac{0.35}{0.05}$ = 7 turns

### FOR PRECISION AND ACCURACY DETERMINATIONS

Determining Minutes of Angle (M) Subtended on Target

1. $M = 60 \left[ \text{Tan}^{-1} \left( \dfrac{\text{group size in inches}}{\text{range in inches}} \right) \right]$
   where: M = number of minutes of angle subtended
   or 1 min = 1/60° = 1.047 inches at 100 yards
2. Minutes of Angle Subtended by a Target Group at 100 yds
   $M = \dfrac{\text{Target Group Size (inches)}}{1.047}$

Determining Standard Deviation (Target Precision or Velocity)*

$\text{s.d.} = \sqrt{\dfrac{\Sigma (d_n)^2}{N - 1}}$

where: s.d. = standard deviation (precision = inches, velocity = feet per second)

$d_n$ = vertical distance from reference line in inches (precision)
   or velocity deviation of individual round from average velocity in
   feet per second (velocity)

N = number of rounds in group

*See Chapters 6 and 7 for use of this formula.

### FOR EXTERNAL BALLISTIC DETERMINATIONS

Ballistic Coefficient of a Bullet

$C = \dfrac{W}{i\,d^2}$

where: C = ballistic coefficient (pure number)

W = weight of bullet in pounds = $\dfrac{\text{weight in grains}}{7000}$

i = form factor (usually 0.5 or 0.76 for spitzer)

d = diameter of bullet in inches

## Sectional Density of a Bullet

$$\text{S.D.} = \frac{W}{d^2}$$

where: S.D. = sectional density (pure number)

W = weight of bullet in pounds = $\dfrac{\text{weight in grains}}{7000}$

d = diameter of bullet in inches

## Bullet Energy (kinetic)

$$E = \frac{V^2 m}{2}$$

where: E = Energy (foot-pounds)

V = velocity in feet per second

m = mass of bullet in slugs = $\dfrac{\text{weight in grains}}{7000 \times 32.174}$

## Bullet Momentum

$$M = mV$$

where: M = bullet momentum in slug-feet per second

m = bullet mass in slugs = $\dfrac{\text{weight in grains}}{7000 \times 32.174}$

V = bullet velocity in feet per second

## Bullet Spin

$$\text{R.P.S.} = V \left( \frac{12}{\text{barrel twist}} \right)$$

where: R.P.S. = spin rate in revolutions per second

V = bullet muzzle velocity in feet per second

## Speed of Sound in Air

$$\text{MACH 1} = \sqrt{2400\,(460 + \text{temperature in °F})}$$

Examples:

MACH 1 at 30°F = 1084.4 feet per second
MACH 1 at 50°F = 1106.3 feet per second
MACH 1 at 70°F = 1127.8 feet per second
MACH 1 at 90°F = 1148.9 feet per second

## Temperature Conversion Formulas

$$C° = \frac{5(F° - 32)}{9} \qquad F° = \frac{9}{5} C° + 32$$

## Pressure, Force, Area

$$\text{Pressure} = \frac{\text{Force}}{\text{Area}} = \frac{f}{A}$$

$$\text{Force} = \text{Pressure} \times \text{Area} = P \times A$$

$$\text{Area} = \frac{\text{Force}}{\text{Pressure}} = \frac{f}{P}$$

# CHARGE WEIGHT INCREMENTS

Based on "Rule of Hundredths"
and Mid-charge Weights

| Mid-charge Weight | Charge Weight Increase (for each load from start) |
|---|---|
| 0.1 to 14.4 grains require | 0.1 grains (or less) |
| 14.5 to 24.4 grains require | 0.2 grains |
| 24.5 to 34.4 grains require | 0.3 grains |
| 34.5 to 44.4 grains require | 0.4 grains |
| 44.5 to 54.4 grains require | 0.5 grains |
| 54.5 to 64.4 grains require | 0.6 grains |
| 64.5 to 74.4 grains require | 0.7 grains |
| 74.5 to 84.4 grains require | 0.8 grains |
| 84.5 to 94.4 grains require | 0.9 grains |
| 94.5 to 104.4 grains require | 1.0 grains |

## GEOMETRIC FORMULAS FOR HANDLOADERS

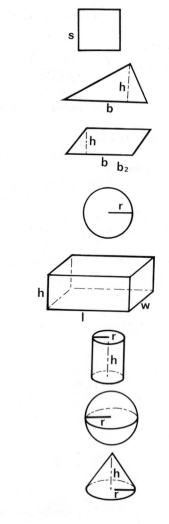

Area of square  $A = s^2$

Area of triangle  $A = \frac{1}{2} bh$

Area of parallelogram  $A = bh$

Area of circle  $A = \pi r^2 = (3.1416)r^2$
Circumference of circle  $C = 2\pi r$
Diameter of circle  $D = 2r$

Volume of rectangular box  $V = lwh$

Volume of cylinder  $V = \pi r^2 h$

Volume of sphere  $V = \frac{4}{3} \pi r^3$

Volume of cone  $V = \frac{1}{3} \pi r^2 h$

# Chapter 13

# Other Handloading Examples

Many thoughts on handloading have been expressed and discussed in the text. Most important were those of objective management introduced in Chapter 2. They are the basic tools for the handloading steps in this book. But a lot of pieces have to come together for success in any selective handloading project.

So that you can get a better feeling for handloading by objective, a few additional examples are presented here. They represent some of the favorite cartridges in the United States today, along with useful bullet loadings. Together with a bit of background history, use, and loading, comparisons like those made in the text example are included. This will reinforce the understandings of precision, velocity, and pressure data use for best load selection. The objectives mentioned in earlier chapters fit most of these examples.

While reading the following material, keep this important point in mind: each example shows the results of a specific combination of ammunition, handload components, and gun. Don't expect the same results, even if you duplicate the brands and models. It can't be done. Handloading results cannot be duplicated that way. You can't simply choose a load from these examples and expect the same results in your gun; there are just too many variables. You must work up your own handloads and use your own data for best results and safety. There is no specific recipe for any handload, only the method for handloading. Again, these examples are here for demonstration purposes only. Noting the successes and failures in each can be helpful when you have similar experiences. Now let's take a look at the examples and see what happened.

**Example 1—.243 Winchester**

This cartridge was introduced by Winchester in 1955. It was a development from the handloading efforts of several wildcatters (innovators). The basic 7.62×51mm NATO or .308 Winchester case is necked down to 6mm bullet size, .243 inches in diameter, hence the name. The .243 Winchester is considered a varmint-to-deer-sized-game cartridge. A bullet for deer hunting is loaded in this example. But the best use of this cartridge is probably with 70- to 90-grain varmint bullets. It's tops for that purpose.

In the example, handload precision was better than that of factory ammunition with most loads (see the handload data sheet). The lighter and the heavier loads were about equal to factory precision, except for the last, No. 13, which was considerably better than all others except for No. 7. Number 13 should be loaded and fired again for verification. Loads No. 3 through 10 and 13 all showed better than factory standard precision.

The handload reached factory velocity easily with load No. 4. All heavier charges produced even greater velocity. Uniformity was also better at all velocities with very little deviation. The best was load No. 10. This leaves loads No. 4 through 10 and 13, all of which gave better precision and velocity than the factory ammunition.

Pressure was different, as the graph shows. Handloads were equal to factory pressure at No. 4 and 10. Pressure was greater than the factory standard past load No. 10. None were found to be excessive, however.

Eight loads could have been chosen that accomplish all of the objectives. Number 13 was the best, but it should be retested since it is an extreme. The next choices were probably No. 10, owing to its very high uniformity of velocity, and No. 7, because of its extreme precision. This is a matter of individual choice based on individual needs. Instrumental velocity loss was about 11 fps for each of these selected loads. Add this figure to the recorded velocity to find muzzle velocity.

**Example 2—.270 Winchester**

This is the same example as that used in the text. It is reproduced here, together with the notes and all graphs, for ease of comparison.

The .270 Winchester is not a new cartridge, but it is still a great one. It has been available since 1925, and is essentially a .30-06 case, slightly lengthened and necked down for .277-inch-diameter bullets. The 130-grain bullet does everything well, but 100-, 110-, and 150-grain bullets may be better for varmints and heavier big game animals respectively, from marmots to moose.

**Example 3—7mm Remington Magnum**

The 7mm Remington Magnum has been around since 1962. It fires bullets ranging from 115 to 175 grains for everything from varmints to the largest North American game animals. The 140- to 160-grain bullets are very popular and the best for deer. The cartridge is similar in power and performance to the 7×61 Sharpe and Hart and the 7mm Weatherby Magnum, both of which were developed earlier. The Remington cartridge is more widely used, however, because it is more affordable to most shooters.

Precision was better than factory results at all loadings, and best around 62 to 63 grains of propellant in this gun. Precision began to deteriorate more rapidly after 64 grains of powder were used, but still beat the commercial ammo.

Achieving factory velocity was more difficult. Maximum recommended loading was required to equal factory velocity even though the data shows it was perfectly safe. Velocity uniformity was best at around 66 grains.

Pressure, along with velocity, did not equal that of factory ammunition until after 65.5 grains.

All in all, load No. 12 was best because it equalled factory velocity with excellent uniformity, equal pressure, and better precision.

Velocity in this rifle was disappointing with both factory ammunition and handloads. Energy was calculated to be 2,835 ft-lb. This is only 142 foot-pounds better than that developed by the .270 Winchester—hardly worth the extra recoil of the Mag.

CALIBER .243 WIN. BULLET WGT. 100 gr.     HANDLOAD DATA

| FIREARM: mfgr. Ruger | FACTY STD CARTRGE: mfgr WIN.-WESTERN | CASE: mfgr W-W SUPER | BULLET: wgt 100 gr | POWDER: mfgr DuPont |
|---|---|---|---|---|
| model M77 | mfgr no. X2432- | avg wgt 163.7±2.5gr | mfgr Hornady | mfgr no. IMR 4350 |
| barrel length 22 in | lot no. A5SL71-151 | trim length 2.035in | mfgr no. 2450 | lot no. P80AP07B6350 |
| twist rate 1:10 in | bullet wgt 100 gr | *c.o.a. length 2.728in | lot no. G-20881 | PRIMER: mfgr CCI |
| TARGET: mfgr/no. LEUP G-53 | | sized head 0.4667 in | type SPIRE PT., FLAT BSE. | mfgr no. 200 |
| RANGE: dist. 100 yd | | *SAMMI MAX = 2.710 in. | clearance 1/16 in | lot no. L25L |

| LOAD no. | charg wgt. gr. | date load | date fire | no. rds | INTERNAL AND EXTERNAL FACTORS (wind velocity, direction, temperature, bar. pres., precip., visibility, ch. pressure observations, other.) | PRECISION Dat1 Std Vert Dev. in. | Dat2 Extm Vert Sprd in. | Dat3 HtAb Aim Pt. in. | VELOCITY Dat4 Std Vel. Dev. fps. | Dat5 Extm Vel. Sprd fps. | Dat6 Avg Vel. fps. | no. rds rcrd | PRES-SURE Dat7 Case Head Exp. in. |
|---|---|---|---|---|---|---|---|---|---|---|---|---|---|
| 1 | 39.1 | 1/10/83 | 2/8/83 | 5 | 5 to 11:00, 54°F 30.25, clear | 0.47 | 1.12 | 1.9 | 8 | 21 | 2,649 | 5 | 0.0030 |
| 2 | 39.5 | " | " | " | #1 all → 6 (octa brass) | .58 | 1.53 | 2.6 | 13 | 36 | 2,659 | | .0029 |
| 3 | 39.9 | " | " | " | | .48 | 1.12 | 2.8 | 7 | 19 | 2,687 | | .0029 |
| 4 | 40.3 | " | " | " | | .41 | 0.93 | 2.9 | 15 | 43 | 2,723 | | .0031 |
| 5 | 40.7 | " | " | " | | .36 | 0.96 | 2.5 | 6 | 17 | 2,740 | | .0030 |
| 6 | 41.1 | " | " | " | | .48 | 1.03 | 3.0 | 16 | 38 | 2,754 | | .0029 |
| 7 | 41.5 | " | " | " | | .25 | 0.62 | 3.2 | 7 | 17 | 2,773 | | .0029 |
| 8 | 41.9 | " | " | " | | .41 | 1.01 | 3.5 | 16 | 44 | 2,803 | | .0028 |
| 9 | 42.3 | " | " | " | Very light cratering, erratic | .44 | 1.15 | 3.9 | 9 | 24 | 2,832 | | .0030 |
| 10 | 42.7 | " | " | " | chronol off during 1st round | .42 | 1.09 | 3.9 | 9 | 21 | 2,861 | 4 | .0031 |
| 11 | 43.1 | " | " | " | Cratering more pronounced, bar. light | .60 | 1.46 | 4.4 | 9 | 25 | 2,886 | 5 | .0032 |
| 12 | 43.5 | " | " | " | no pressure problems | .53 | 1.15 | 5.3 | 10 | 29 | 2,919 | | .0034 |
| 13 | 43.9 | " | " | " | | .18 | 0.445 | 4.7 | 13 | 30 | 2,954 | | .0033 |
| 14 | " | | | | | | | | | | | | |
| 15 | " | | | | | | | | | | | | |
| 16 | " | | | | | | | | | | | | |
| 17 | " | | | | | | | | | | | | |
| 18 | " | | | | | | | | | | | | |
| 19 | " | | | | | | | | | | | | |
| 20 | " | | | | | | | | | | | | |
| 1 | facty ld. | | 2/8/83 | 5 | | 0.54 | 1.25 | 3.8 | 14 | 29 | 2,726 | 5 | 0.0031 |
| 2 | " | | " | " | | .40 | 0.92 | 4.0 | 14 | 36 | 2,707 | | .0031 |
| 3 | " | | " | " | | .58 | 1.46 | 3.7 | 19 | 52 | 2,696 | | .0031 |
| 4 | " | | | | | | | | | | | | |
| 5 | " | | | | | | | | | | | | |
| facty avgs = | | | | | | 0.51 | 1.21 | 3.8 | 16 | 39 | 2,710 | | 0.0031 |

Data 1, 2, 3, 4, 5, 6 and 7 above, refer to data used in construction of the PREC., VEL. and PRESS. graphs

The handload data list for the .243 Winchester with a 100-grain bullet.

Caliber **.243 W.N.**    Bullet **100 gr. HORNADY**    Powder **IMR 4350**

## NOTES

**Planning:** Used the Test objectives. Dupont guide shows max. of 43.5/4350 about yield @ 2,980 f.p.s. in 22 in. barrel. I computed charge of 46.0/4831 will yield @ 3,010 f.p.s... Table of loading compressed charges is not worth 30 f.p.s. differ. Hornady recommends max. of 42.4/IMR4350 for 2900 f.p.s. use a range of 39.1 to 43.9 gr. for work up in 0.4 gr. increments. Fairly standard: bullet = 100.6 ± 0.3 gr.; powder = 40.0 ± 0.4 gr. (tubular); case = 165.2 ± 1.6 gr or 1.9% range (very good), 2.035 in = length, C.O.A.L. = 2.660 in.

**Loading:** Dupont IMR4350 gave excellent loading density with heavier charges. When seated for 1/16" clearance, the Hornady bullet base extends @ 0.15 in. below base of 7th case neck. No powder compression, but very little air space at 43.9 gr. charge. Powder is then about 1/8" above base of shoulder. Lower edge of bullet canelure is 0.070 in. above the trimmed case mouth. C.O.A.L. exceeds S.A.M.M.I. recs. of 2.710 in. but only by 0.020 in. Function is o.k. in test rifle. Top 8 seater screw is 0.623 in. above die body. Powder measure set at 3.71 for 43.9 gr. /4350. Sirt cases = 163.7 ± 2.5 gr. (3% range). Sirts to tightened after filled load is chosen to equal factory standard.

**Firing:** Pressure (expansion) curve was old... not straight-line. Factory pressure occurred at two points @ #5 and #10. #5 velocity equalled factory velo. This may be related to overage chamber in this gun, however. This has been observed before, too. No extreme pressure signs observed at any of the test loads. Very brushed barrel every 5 shots.

**Conclusions:** Estimated inst. velocity showed be about 2,909 f.p.s. (2960 - 40 = 2920 - 11 = 2409)

> barrel    inst.
> ↓         ↓

for factory ammo. It was only 2,710 which is 200 f.p.s. slower than expected. This is a very small loading, but gave good precision. Load #10 and #13 tie the two best choices. (#13 should be rejected because it is at extreme end of Test range. #10 shows best velo. uniformity. #7 shows it may give best precision. Tout it should be retested. Too. Without further testing, Load #10 would be my choice. Precision is equal to factory and bullet strike the same as factory. Velocity of #10 is 151 f.p.s. greater than factory and worth better uniformity. Precision of #10 is equal to factory.

---

Comments on the back of the handload data sheet concerning the .243 loads.

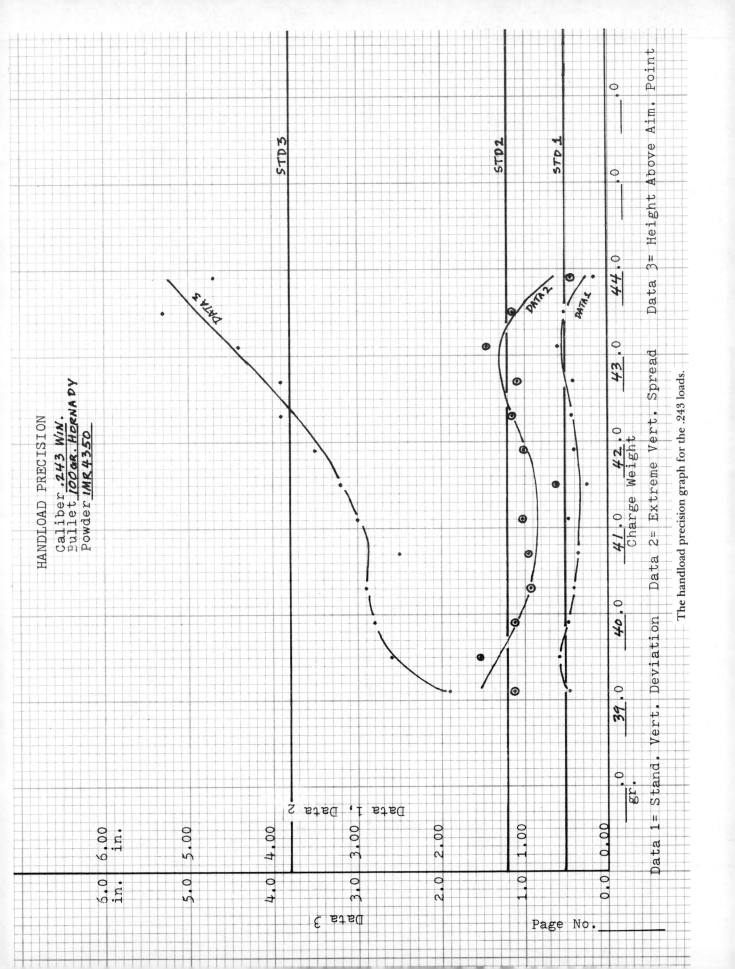

The handload precision graph for the .243 loads.

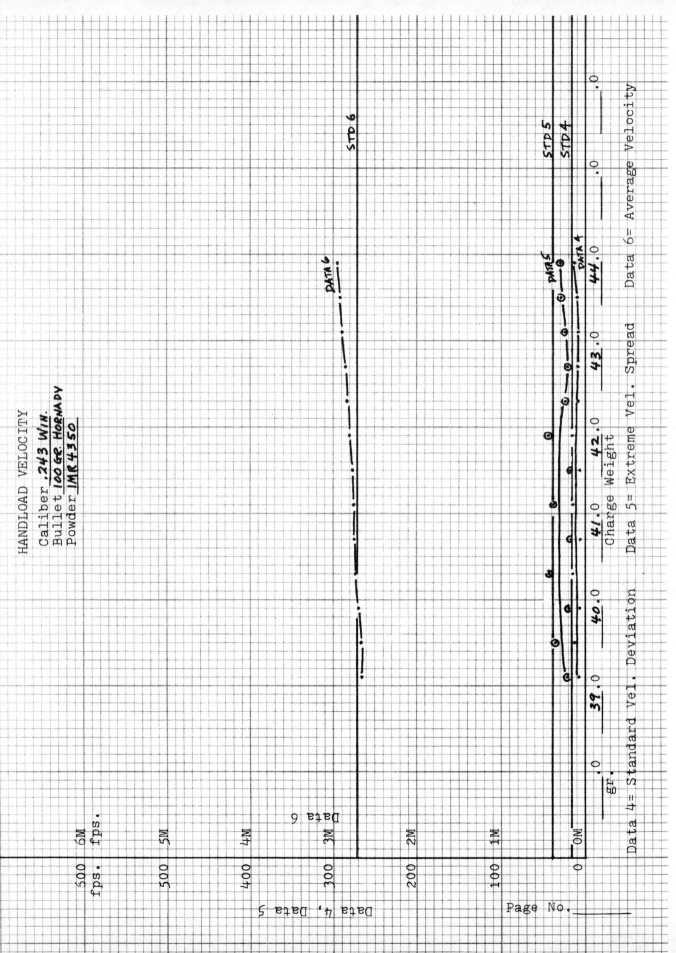

The handload velocity graph for the .243 loads.

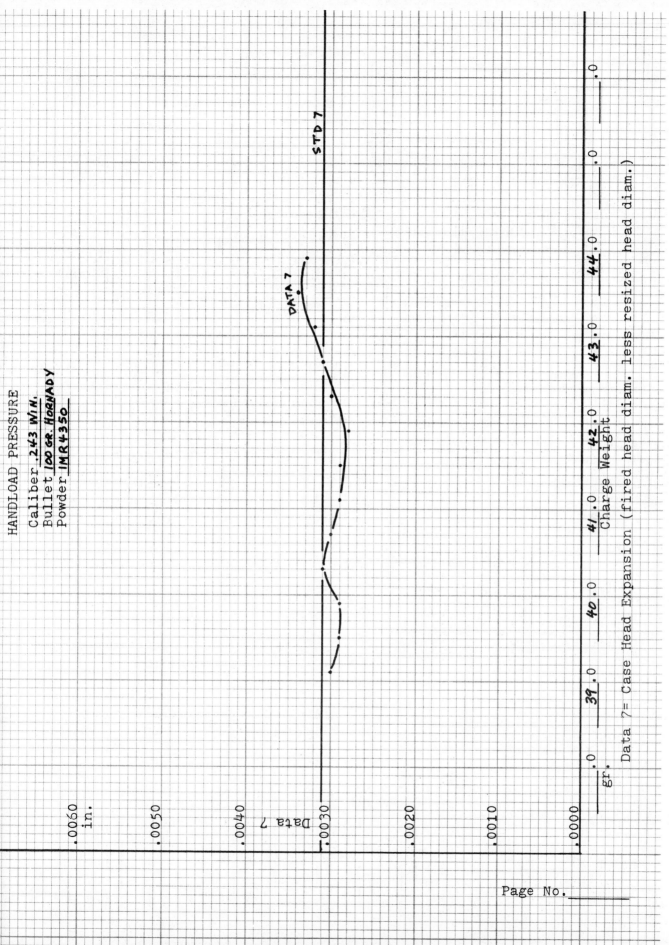

HANDLOAD PRESSURE

Caliber .243 WIN.
Bullet 100 GR. HORNADY
Powder IMR 4350

Charge Weight

Data 7= Case Head Expansion (fired head diam. less resized head diam.)

The handload pressure graph for the .243 loads.

Page No. _____

CALIBER 270 WIN BULLET WGT. 130 gr.          HANDLOAD DATA

| FIREARM:mfgr. WIN | FACTY STD CARTRGE | CASE:mfgr REM (R-P) | RULLET:wgt 130 gr | POWDER:mfgr DuPONT |
|---|---|---|---|---|
| model 70 XTR | mfgr REM | avg wgt 197.3 ±3.0 gr | mfgr SIERRA | mfgr no. IMR4831 |
| barrel length 22 in | mfgr no. R270W2 | trim length 2.530 in | mfgr no. 1830 | lot no. P8IJY29A-74 |
| twist rate 1:10 in | lot no. L25UD2452 | c.o.a.length 3.205 in | lot no. 40520 | PRIMER:mfgr CCI |
| TARGET:mfg/no. LEUP G-53 | bullet wgt 130 gr | sized head 0.4656 in | type SPIT., F.BASE | mfgr no. 200 |
| RANGE:dist. 100 yd | | | clearance 1/16 in | lot no. L25L |

| LOAD no. | charg wgt. gr. | date load | date fire | no. rds | INTERNAL AND EXTERNAL FACTORS (wind velocity, direction, temperature, bar. pres., precip., visibility, ch. pressure observations, other.) | PRECISION Dat1 Std Vert Dev. in. | Dat2 Extm Vert Sprd. in. | Dat3 HtAb Aim. Pt. in. | VELOCITY Dat4 Std Vel. Dev. fps. | Dat5 Extm Vel. Sprd. fps. | Dat6 Avg Vel. fps. | no. rds rcrd | PRES-SURE Dat7 Case Head Exp. in. |
|---|---|---|---|---|---|---|---|---|---|---|---|---|---|
| 1 | 52.0 | 7/1/82 | 9/10/82 | 5 | 4-6 fps 4:00 @12:30, 94°F, 29.72 dry | 0.58 | 1.44 | 2.8 | 27 | 69 | 2,701 | 5 | 0.0034 |
| 2 | 52.5 | " | | | exceptional group, but slow | .22 | 0.59 | 1.9 | 4 | 10 | 2,748 | | .0036 |
| 3 | 53.0 | " | | | | .16 | 0.41 | 1.7 | 11 | 31 | 2,769 | | .0037 |
| 4 | 53.5 | " | | | very mild pressure | .55 | 1.34 | 2.1 | 12 | 28 | 2,791 | | .0037 |
| 5 | 54.0 | " | | | 6-12 fps 4:00, 94°F, 29.62, dry, calm | .28 | 0.75 | 2.8 | 18 | 43 | 2,826 | | .0037 |
| 6 | 54.5 | | | | one shot lost thru another hole | .41 | 1.13 | 3.0 | 13 | 33 | 2,870 | 4 | .0039 |
| 7 | 55.0 | | | | | .37 | 0.80 | 3.9 | 17 | 44 | 2,909 | | .0038 |
| 8 | 55.5 | | | | beginning of primer flattening | .50 | 1.14 | 3.7 | 20 | 55 | 2,941 | 5 | .0058 |
| 9 | 56.0 | | | | exceptional grp, good, ogked, brush | .18 | 0.45 | 3.8 | 25 | 71 | 2,980 | | .0040 |
| 10 | 56.5 | | | | | .44 | 1.18 | 3.8 | 15 | 34 | 2,998 | | .0041 |
| 11 | 57.0 | | | | 2-4 fps 4:00, 94°F, 29.56 | .57 | 1.44 | 3.5 | 17 | 38 | 3,016 | | .0042 |
| 12 | 57.5 | | | | | .70 | 1.48 | 3.4 | 9 | 26 | 3,045 | | .0042 |
| 13 | 58.0 | | | | fairly heavy pressure, brisk | .63 | 1.60 | 3.4 | 12 | 32 | 3,075 | | .0043 |
| 14 | 58.5 | | | | 2-4 fps 4:00, 94°, 29.52 | .59 | 1.23 | 4.1 | 26 | 60 | 3,123 | | .0042 |
| 15 | 59.0 | | | | | .59 | 1.45 | 3.9 | 11 | 29 | 3,142 | | .0043 |
| 16 | 59.5 | | | | | .90 | 2.33 | 3.4 | 11 | 28 | 3,179 | | .0045 |
| 17 | 60.0 | | | | limit of useful speed + pressure | .63 | 1.62 | 3.5 | 18 | 47 | 3,189 | | .0041 |
| 18 | | | | | | | | | | | | | |
| 19 | | | | | | | | | | | | | |
| 20 | | | | | | | | | | | | | |
| 1 | facty ld. | 9/9/82 | | 5 | 2-4 fps 4:00, 94° 29.56 | 0.93 | 2.68 | 4.5 | 19 | 52 | 2,917 | 5 | 0.0038 |
| 2 | " | | | | 2 shots not chronographed | .25 | 0.59 | 4.2 | 26 | 50 | 2,870 | 3 | .0038 |
| 3 | " | | | | | .59 | 1.53 | 4.0 | 19 | 48 | 2,823 | 5 | .0032 |
| 4 | " | | | | | .47 | 1.27 | 4.7 | 16 | 40 | 2,813 | | |
| 5 | | | | | | | | | | | | | |
| | | | | facty avgs = | | 0.56 | 1.52 | 4.4 | 20 | 48 | 2,856 | | .0038 |

Data 1,2,3,4,5,6 and 7 above, refer to data used in construction of the PREC., VEL. and PRESS. graphs

The handload data list for the .270 Winchester with a 130-grain bullet.

Caliber .270 W.I.N.     Bullet 130 GR. SIERRA     Powder IMR 4831

<u>NOTES</u>

Planning: Use the stated objectives in the text. Factory cartridge to be used as comparison standard for precision, velocity and pressure. Factory bullet = 130.0 ± 0.2 gr.; diam = 0.2774 ± .0001 in.; Powder = 55.3 ± 6.3 gr.; dimension = 0.038 diam × 0.085 length (tubular grain); fired case to base of neck; Primer = Rem. std.; Case = 2.528 ± .002 length, unfired head diam = 0.4639 in., wgt = 198.6 ± 3.3 gr. (3.3 % range).

Loading: The #1830 Sierra bullet weight 130.0 ± 0.2 gr. equalling factory weight std. When seated 1/16" from lands, its base is aligned with the bottom of the case neck. Load #8 just begins to touch the base of the bullet. Load #17 is only slightly compressed. Excellent density. All test rds. were loaded by weight to within 0.1 grain of stated charge. One-fired cases were sorted by wgt to 197.3 ± 3.0 gr. This is a 3.0% wgt range and exceeds the factory std.

Firing: Factory pressure was equalled in even # loads 6, 7 and 8. Pressure rise after that, no extreme pressure obturations occurred at any change weight. Reduct of case capacity. Barrel cleaning was dry. Truck and two clean, dry patches after appx. every 20 # round. Very stable fouling was noticed with this combination. Factory inst. velocity = 2,850 instead of estimated 3,061 1.7/.12. This test rifle was new and velocity further indicates mild factory pressure. Load #12 = 3,045 muzzle velo. for #12 is estimated to be 3,054 f.p.s., almost exactly what factory ammo. should produce in a 22" barrel.

Conclusions: Using the intermediate loading objectives as a basis for elimination, the best handload from a precision, velocity and pressure standpoint is #12 (575g). The powder measure needed this at a setting of 5,290 (reference).

Comments on the back of the handload data sheet concerning the .270 loads.

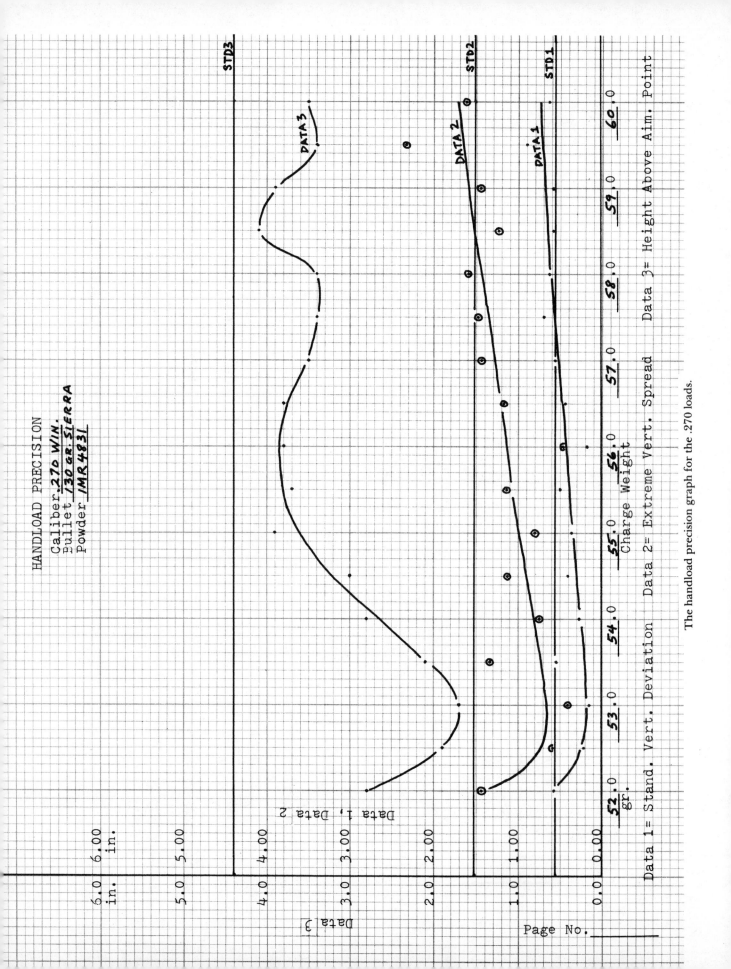

The handload precision graph for the .270 loads.

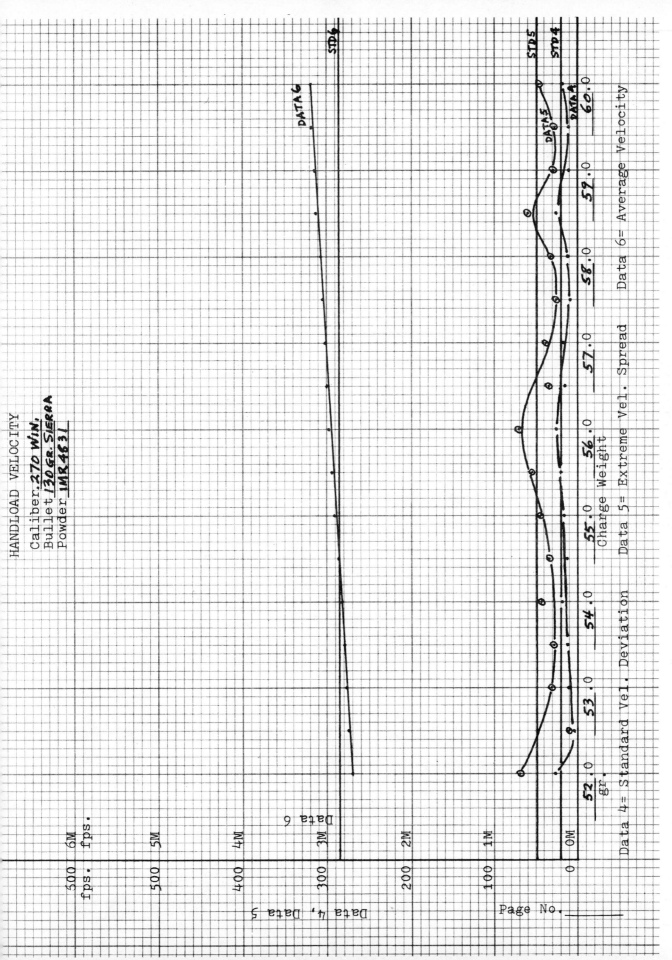

HANDLOAD VELOCITY

Caliber .270 WIN.
Bullet 130 GR. SIERRA
Powder IMR 4631

The handload velocity graph for the .270 loads.

Data 4= Standard Vel. Deviation    Data 5= Extreme Vel. Spread    Data 6= Average Velocity

Charge Weight

Data 4, Data 5

Data 6

Page No.

gr.

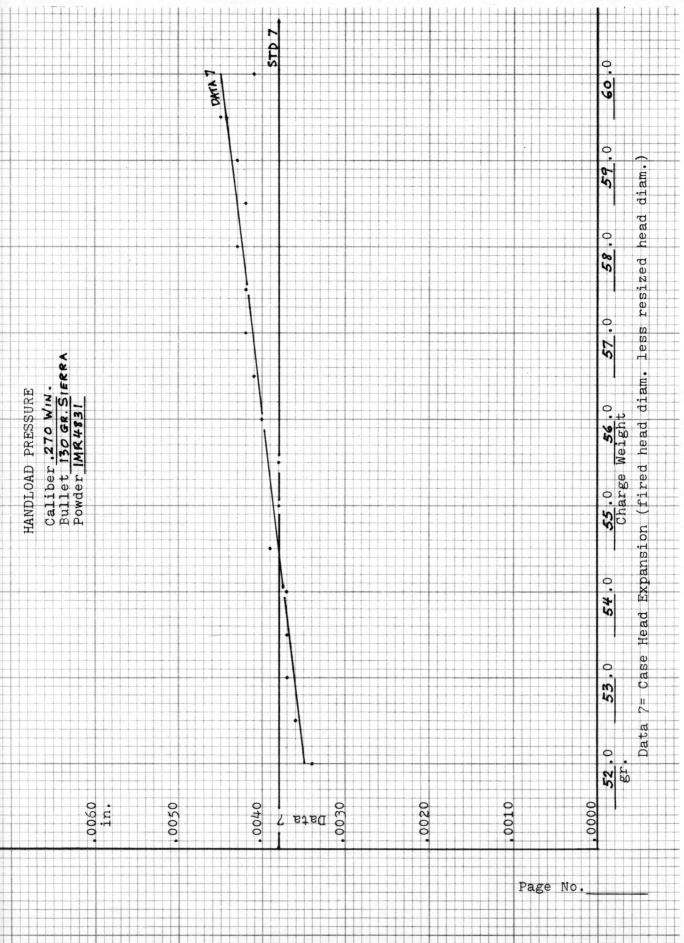

The handload pressure graph for the .270 loads.

CALIBER 7mm R. MAG BULLET WGT. 150 gr.          HANDLOAD DATA

| FIREARM: mfgr REM. | FACTY STD CARTRGE | CASE: mfgr REM (R-P) | BULLET: wgt 150 gr | POWDER: mfgr DuPONT |
|---|---|---|---|---|
| model 700 BDL | mfgr REM | avg wgt 229.5±1.5 gr | mfgr NOSLER | mfgr no. IMR4831 |
| barrel length 24 in | mfgr no. R7MM2 | trim length 2.490 in | mfgr no. 29600 | lot no. P819E28A-75 |
| twist rate 1:9¼ in | lot no. T18HD4259 | c.o.a. length 3.298 in | lot no. EF05B | PRIMER: mfgr CCI |
| TARGET: mfg/no. LEUP G-53 | bullet wgt 150 gr | *sized head 0.5117 in | type SPITZER, S.B56 | mfgr no. 250 |
| RANGE: dist. 100 yd | | * NOT USED FOR PRESS. GRAPH | clearance 1/16 in | lot no. HO7KD |

INTERNAL AND EXTERNAL FACTORS | PRECISION | VELOCITY | PRESSURE

| LOAD no. | charg wgt. gr. | date load | date fire | no. rds | wind velocity, direction, temperature, bar. pres.; precip., visibility, ch. pressure observations, other. | Dat1 Std Vert Dev. in. | Dat2 Extm Vert Sprd in. | Dat3 HtAb Aim Pt. in. | Dat4 Std Vel. Dev. fps. | Dat5 Extm Vel. Sprd. fps. | Dat6 Avg Vel. fps. | no. rds rcrd | Dat7 Case Head Exp. in. |
|---|---|---|---|---|---|---|---|---|---|---|---|---|---|
| 1 | 59.3 | 2?83 | 2?83 | 5 | Calm to 10 mph full 11:00, 68°F | 0.37 | 0.90 | 3.3 | 6 | 14 | 2,652 | 5 | 0.0057 |
| 2 | 59.9 | | | | | .44 | 0.98 | 3.5 | 8 | 23 | 2,666 | | . |
| 3 | 60.5 | | | | | .41 | 1.04 | 3.4 | 17 | 43 | 2,681 | | .0057 |
| 4 | 61.1 | | | | wind → 15 mph, gusts | .29 | 0.70 | 3.4 | 13 | 28 | 2,704 | | . |
| 5 | 61.7 | | | | | .47 | 1.21 | 3.1 | 7 | 15 | 2,738 | | . |
| 6 | 62.3 | | | | | .28 | 0.65 | 2.7 | 18 | 49 | 2,766 | | .0060 |
| 7 | 62.9 | | | | | .27 | 0.66 | 3.3 | 23 | 60 | 2,786 | | . |
| 8 | 63.5 | | | | | .33 | 0.88 | 3.2 | 20 | 55 | 2,784 | | . |
| 9 | 64.1 | | | | | .75 | 1.94 | 2.9 | 19 | 45 | 2,813 | | .0062 |
| 10 | 64.7 | | | | felt recoil similar to factory | .60 | 1.48 | 2.8 | 10 | 23 | 2,857 | 4 | . |
| 11 | 65.3 | | | | wind → 25 mph, gusts | .56 | 1.37 | 3.0 | 12 | 33 | 2,870 | 5 | . |
| 12 | 65.9 | | | | | .63 | 1.74 | 3.4 | 5 | 12 | 2,906 | | .0064 |
| 13 | 66.5 | ↘ | ↘ | → | no excessive pressure signs | .40 | 1.03 | 3.0 | 16 | 31 | 2,918 | → | . |
| 14 | . | | | | | . | . | . | | | | | . |
| 15 | . | | | | | . | . | . | | | | | . |
| 16 | . | | | | | . | . | . | | | | | . |
| 17 | . | | | | | . | . | . | | | | | . |
| 18 | . | | | | | . | . | . | | | | | . |
| 19 | . | | | | | . | . | . | | | | | . |
| 20 | . | | | | | . | . | . | | | | | . |
| 1 | facty ld | 2?83 | | 5 | | 0.54 | 1.53 | 4.1 | 38 | 69 | 2,905 | 5 | 0.0063 |
| 2 | " | " | | | one new case hard to extract | .93 | 2.29 | 3.4 | 21 | 57 | 2,855 | → | . |
| 3 | " | " | ↘ | → | | .85 | 2.30 | 3.5 | 39 | 96 | 2,872 | 4 | . |
| 4 | " | | | | | . | . | . | | | | | . |
| 5 | " | | | | | . | . | . | | | | | . |
| | facty avgs = | | | | | 0.77 | 2.04 | 3.7 | 33 | 74 | 2,877 | | |

Data 1,2,3,4,5,6 and 7 above, refer to data used in construction of the PREC., VEL. and PRESS. graphs

The handload data list for the 7mm Remington Magnum with a 150-grain bullet.

Caliber **7mm REM. MAG**   Bullet **150gr. NOSLER**   Powder **IMR 4831**

<u>NOTES</u>

Planning: Used the test objectives. Dupont guide shows 66.5/4831 for 3055 f.p.s. max. Nosler recommends 65.0/IMR4831 max. for 3255. Used range of 59.3 thru 66.5 for test. Factory cartridge: bullet = 149.4 ± 0.3 gr., powder = 68.2 ± 0.4 gr. (range 67.8 thru 68.6), tubular type; diam = .041, length = .085 (probably not IMR 4831), Case = 231.7 ± 2.1 gr. Case wgt range = 230.3 thru 233.8 = 3.5 gr or 1.5% (very good).

Loading: IMR4831 gave good loading density but some space remained between top and bottom of case shoulder area. It may load. When seated for 1/16" clearance, the Nosler Solid base bullet had its base aligned with the bottom of the case shoulder. Very little air space remained and no powder compression occurred. C.O.A.L. = 3.298 (SAMM recommends 3.290). This gave no function problems. With adjusted sizing die, a gap of 0.005 in exists between shell holder and base of die. Top of seater leaves to 0.73 in above the top of the center die body. Powder measure set at 6.00 max load + trickle to wgt. Brass was noted to 229.5 ± 1.5 gr. (228.0 → 231.0; 1.3%) and yields fairly std test charge weight. Pressure

Firing: no heavy pressure signs were noticed at any test charge weight. Pressure and charge could be increased slightly. One factory round was difficult to chamber and was hard to open bolt after firing. Velocity for this round was only 2,866, however. Probably due to extractor groove defect. Overall velocities of factory and test loads was surprisingly low.

Conclusions: Expected factory inst. velocity to be about 3,110 - 12 = 3,098 B.P.S. Disappointing. 2,877 avg. Handloads did not exceed this much, either. Best handload was #12, according to objectives. It beats factory ammo in precision and uniformity of velocity (although velocity avg. was about same (2,877 factory; 2,906 #12.) off 108 f.p.s. velocity), load #6 would be choice at loss of some velocity uniformity.

Comments on the back of the handload data sheet concerning the 7mm Mag loads.

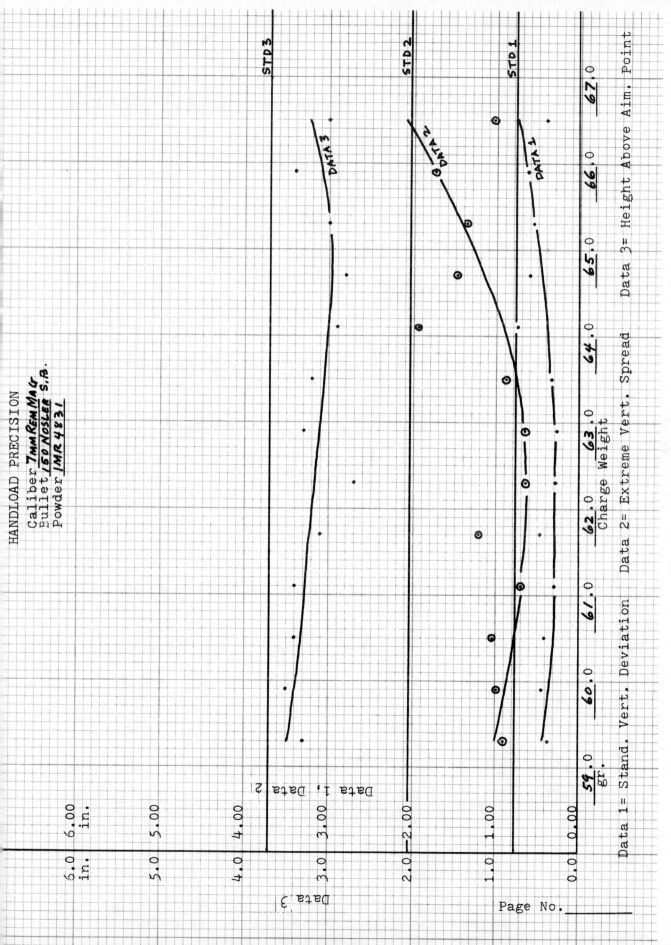

The handload precision graph for the 7mm Mag loads.

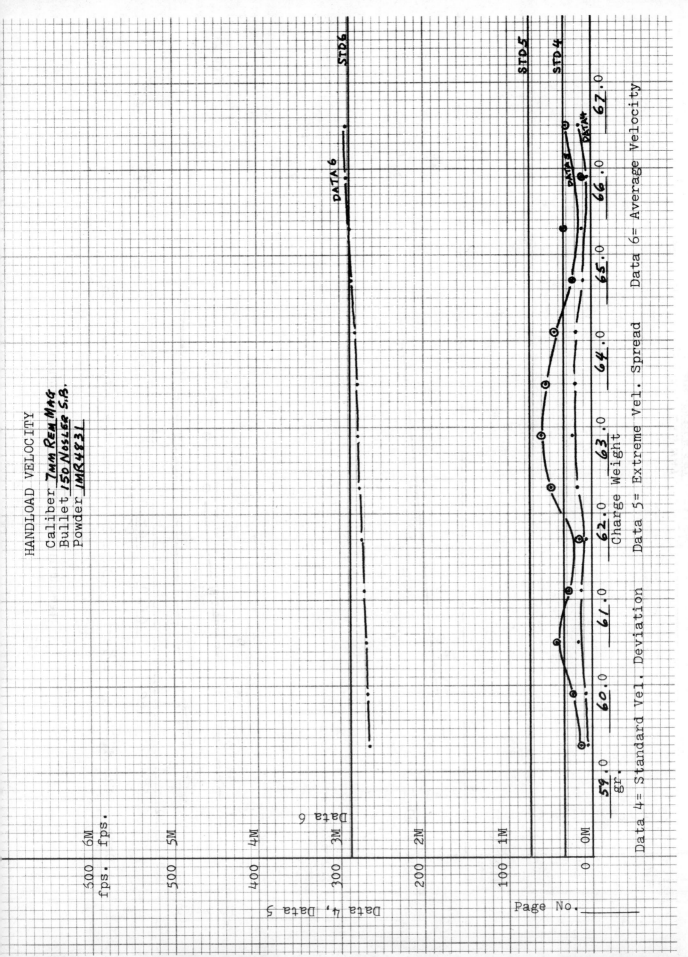

The handload velocity graph for the 7mm Mag loads.

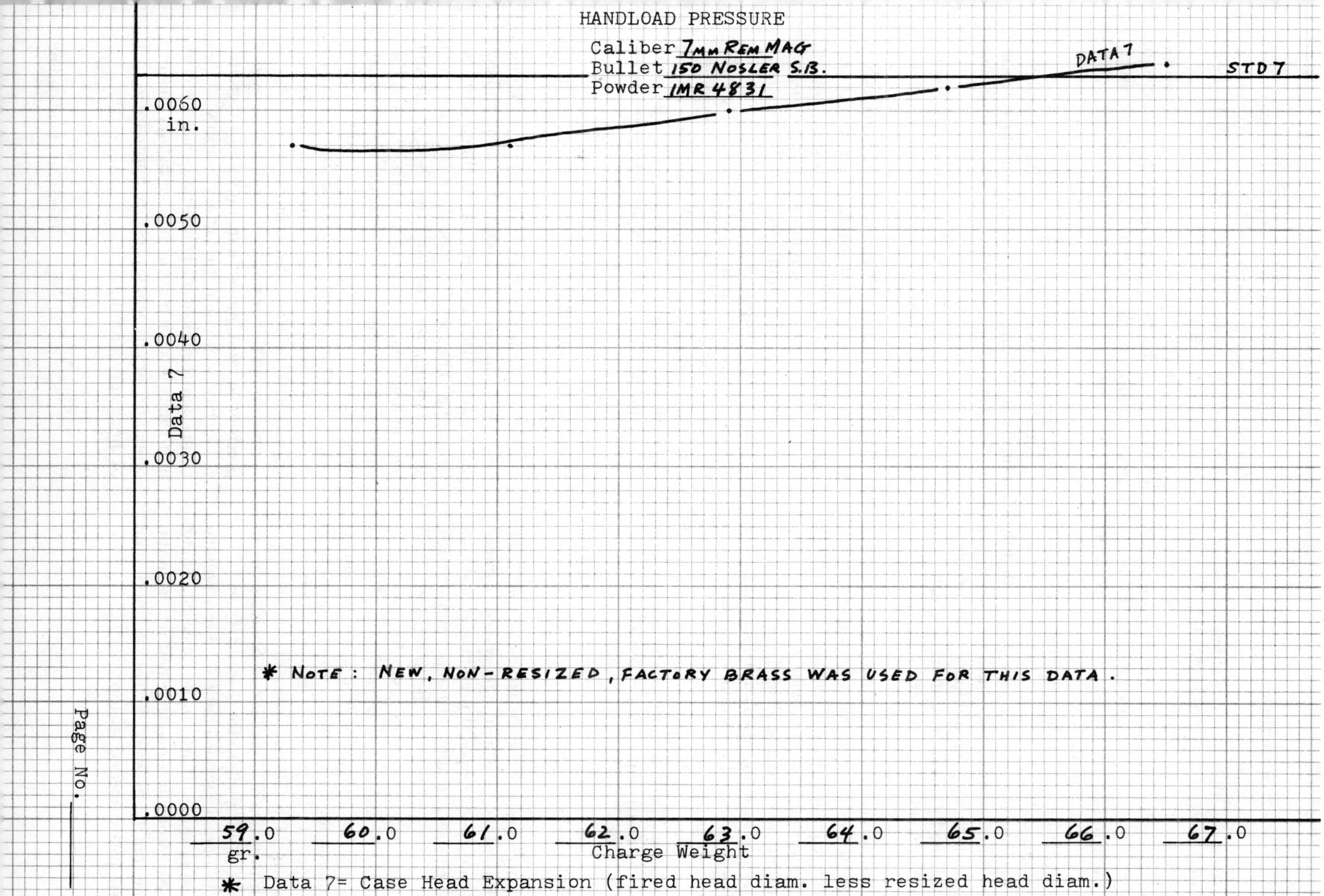

HANDLOAD PRESSURE

Caliber 7mm Rem MAG
Bullet 150 Nosler S.B.
Powder IMR 4831

STD 7

DATA 7

Data 7

.0060 in.
.0050
.0040
.0030
.0020
.0010
.0000

59.0   60.0   61.0   62.0   63.0   64.0   65.0   66.0   67.0
gr.

Charge Weight

* NOTE : NEW, NON-RESIZED, FACTORY BRASS WAS USED FOR THIS DATA.

* Data 7= Case Head Expansion (fired head diam. less resized head diam.)

The handload pressure graph for the 7mm Mag loads.

## Example 4—.30-06 Springfield

The .30-06 Springfield is the oldest of the cartridges used as examples in this chapter. But age obviously has nothing to do with popularity. Available commercially since 1908, the .30-06 remains the king of American rifle cartridges. It is fine for any big game in North America. It is as flexible as any other cartridge made for reloading, and is the standard by which all other domestic rifle cartridges are judged.

In this example, an older rifle with a slightly oversized chamber was used, which caused primer flanging with factory ammunition. This problem was eliminated by carefully adjusting the sizing die used for handloading this round.

Precision was best with around 49 to 50 grains of powder, but was better than factory performance at all points up until 51.5 grains were loaded.

Velocity equalled factory ammo speed at 49 grains and was faster at all heavier loadings. Velocity uniformity was better at all loadings.

Factory pressure was equalled at 48.5 grains, but showed very safe and consistent expansion up to about 51.5 grains.

The best load was No. 7, 50.0 grains, due to its high precision, better velocity with greater uniformity, and nearly equal factory pressure.

## Example 5—.357 Magnum

This cartridge was chosen as an example of revolver cartridges. It is a straight-walled, rimmed type. It and the .38 Special present identical concerns when sizing, seating, crimping, and so forth. Together, they represent the most frequently handloaded handgun cartridges in America.

The .357 Magnum was developed in 1935 by Smith & Wesson along with Winchester, who made the ammunition. Case dimensions are identical to the .38 Special except for the extra 0.135 inch of length of the Mag. This is to prevent chambering of the high-pressure .357 in older .38 Special guns, or any modern thirty-eights for that matter.

The 125-grain, jacketed bullets are very popular for hunting and defense loads. Slower-burning, double-based powders may give best results in this cartridge, but fresh brass, a tight case neck, and good crimps are needed for top velocity.

Handload precision only equalled or exceeded that of the factory ammo at 14.0 to 14.6 grains, a narrow range of weight. Precision is probably best around 14.4 grains.

Velocity never quite equalled that of the factory ammunition. Factory components also recorded better velocity in handloaded brass for pressure testing. The powder, primer, or bullet should be changed, starting with the powder first if equal velocity is a must.

Handloads never outperformed factory velocity uniformity results, either. Best uniformity was in the 14.4- to 14.6-grain range. These were very close to factory results, but not quite equal.

Handload pressure equalled that of the factory loads at 14.4 to 14.5 grains, and was slightly greater past that point.

The best handload with this combination was No. 16 at 14.5 grains. It nearly equalled the factory ammunition in all categories, but was never quite as good. The factory ammunition was definitely better than the handloaded ammunition in this instance.

If another attempt at loading the .357 were to be made, a powder such as WW-296, Hercules Unique, or 2400 should be tried. But, remember, that is only a guess and only for results with the components and gun in this example. Under similar circumstances, you may expect different results.

## Example 6—.45 ACP

The .45 automatic became part of the U.S. military arsenal in 1911. It was another brain child of the greatest arms inventor of all time, John M. Browning. The excellence of the design is proved by the fact that the cartridge and the gun are still held in high regard after more than 70 years. It is an excellent example of a semiautomatic pistol cartridge. The case headspaces on the mouth, so it is best to use a taper crimp die. Make sure the expander is small enough to cause a good grip on the bullet, essential for proper functioning.

Precision in this example was better than factory precision at most points, best at 6.4 and 7.0 grains.

Velocity was equal to factory velocity at 6.4 grains, and better at all points past that. Velocity uniformity was not quite as good as factory data except at 6.7 grains, when pressure approached that of the factory ammunition.

The pressure was below that of the factory cartridges at all loadings except the last.

The best loading was No. 9 (6.4 grains) for this powder. This is a more precise loading, at equal velocity and with less pressure than the factory standard. That does not mean it is the best load possible, however. Hercules Unique causes a great deal of muzzle flash with this gun. This indicates that less than ideal ignition takes place. It is a little too slow. The bullet strike is also a bit lower than that of the factory ammunition.

Using the same care in loading, a slightly faster powder may work better. Bullseye, W-W 231, or SR-7625 may be best.

Here is a Colt Government Model pistol broken down to illustrate a point. The two coil springs, for the firing pin and slide, and the combination leaf spring are designed for consistent, reliable functioning with standard ammunition (230-grain, RNMC). A change in the type of ammunition often requires changing these springs for good functioning of the mechanism.

CALIBER .30-06 BULLET 150 gr.          HANDLOAD DATA

**FIREARM:** mfgr WIN.
model 70 STD (PRE-64)
barrel length 24 in
twist rate 1:10 in
**TARGET:** mfg/no. LWS G-53
**RANGE:** dist. 100 yd

**FACTY STD CARTRGE**
mfgr FEDERAL
mfgr no. 3006A
lot no. 1B-2326
bullet wgt 150 gr

**CASE:** mfgr FED (FC)
avg wgt 186.6±1.9 gr
trim length 2.484 in
c.o.a. length 3.155 in
sized head 0.4668 in

**BULLET:** wgt 150 gr
mfgr SPEER
mfgr no. 2023
lot no. J24M
type SPT., FLAT BSE
clearance 1/16 in

**POWDER:** mfgr DuPONT
mfgr no. IMR 4064
lot no. P80MY16B-2379
**PRIMER:** mfgr CCI
mfgr no. 200
lot no. L25L

| LOAD no. | charg wgt. gr. | date load | date fire | INTERNAL AND EXTERNAL FACTORS (wind velocity, direction, temperature, bar. pres., precip., visibility, ch. pressure observations, other.) | no. rds | PRECISION Dat1 Std Vert Dev. in. | Dat2 Extm Vert Sprd in. | Dat3 HtAb Aim Pt. in. * | VELOCITY Dat4 Std Vel. Dev. fps. | Dat5 Extm Vel. Sprd fps. | Dat6 Avg Vel. fps. | no. rds rcrd | PRESSURE Dat7 Case Head Exp. in. |
|---|---|---|---|---|---|---|---|---|---|---|---|---|---|
| 1 | 47.0 | 3/6/83 | 4/6/83 | 15 from 10:00, steady, 52°F 7 gusts to 30 | 5 | 0.53 | 1.47 | 0.6+1 | 13 | 36 | 2,454 | 5 | 0.0012 |
| 2 | 47.5 | " | " | | | .18 | 0.45 | 0.3+1 | 31 | 88 | 2,511 | | .0014 |
| 3 | 48.0 | " | " | | | .31 | 0.66 | 0.9+1 | 33 | 82 | 2,524 | | .0016 |
| 4 | 48.5 | " | " | | | .66 | 1.72 | 1.1+1 | 25 | 60 | 2,545 | | .0018 |
| 5 | 49.0 | " | " | | | .37 | 1.00 | 1.2+1 | 20 | 59 | 2,568 | | .0017 |
| 6 | 49.5 | " | " | | | .30 | 0.80 | 1.6+1 | 22 | 55 | 2,620 | | .0021 |
| 7 | 50.0 | " | " | one shot hole lost in another | | .46 | 0.91 | 2.0+1 | 15 | 41 | 2,656 | | .0021 |
| 8 | 50.5 | " | " | | | .66 | 1.76 | 2.3+1 | 27 | 68 | 2,656 | | .0016 |
| 9 | 51.0 | " | " | began burning cleaner, less soot | | .49 | 1.22 | 2.7+1 | 22 | 56 | 2,700 | | .0023 |
| 10 | 51.5 | " | " | sign of minor cratering | | .93 | 2.20 | 2.8+1 | 23 | 55 | 2,752 | | .0028 |
| 11 | 52.0 | " | " | early pressure | | .37 | 0.96 | 2.5+1 | 10 | 21 | 2,770 | | .0026 |
| 12 | 52.5 | " | ↓ | powder deteriorated, end of range, did not fire this load | → | 1.13 | 3.11 | 3.1+1 | 22 | 49 | 2,795 | – | .0025 |
| 13 | 53.0 | | | did not fire this load | | – | – | – | – | – | – | | – |
| 14 | . | | | | | . | . | . | . | . | . | | . |
| 15 | . | | | | | . | . | . | . | . | . | | . |
| 16 | . | | | | | . | . | . | . | . | . | | . |
| 17 | . | | | | | . | . | . | . | . | . | | . |
| 18 | . | | | | | . | . | . | . | . | . | | . |
| 19 | . | | | | | . | . | . | . | . | . | | . |
| 20 | . | | | | | . | . | . | . | . | . | | . |
| 1 | facty ld. | 4/6/83 | | primers current during firing and flange with case expansion | 5 | 0.83 | 2.02 | 3.2+1 | 32 | 82 | 2,597 | 5 | – |
| 2 | " | ↓ | | | → | .97 | 1.99 | 2.7+1 | 48 | 104 | 2,560 | → | |
| 3 | " | | | | | .64 | 1.71 | 3.0+1 | 36 | 90 | 2,621 | | |
| 4 | " | | | | | . | | | | | | | |
| 5 | " | | | | | . | | | | | | | |
| | **facty avgs =** | | | | | 0.81 | 1.91 | 3.0+1 | 39 | 92 | 2,593 | 92 | 0.0018 |

Data 1, 2, 3, 4, 5, 6 and 7 above, refer to data used in construction of the PREC., VEL. and PRESS. graphs

* Rule 3 - see "Conclusion" notes.

The handload data list for the .30-06 Springfield with a 150-grain bullet.

Caliber .30-06 SPFLD.   Bullet _150 Gr SPEER_   Powder _IMR 4064_

<u>NOTES</u>

Planning: Test the test objectives. Factory cartridge: bullet = 149.8 ± 0.3 g., Powder = turbin grain, dimension .031 diam × .087 length. Avg wgt B charge = 47.7 ± 0.3 g., fills case to 1/8" below base of shoulder. Primer appears to std. Fed. long rifle with yellow paper cup and brass cup. avg wgt = 5.5 g. Case = FC = 186.8 ± 4.2 g.

Loading: Initial charge fills case to within 1/8 below base of shoulder. Bullet seater does not seat bullets concentric. Had to tighten clearance to 1/32 in. for compensation. Load #7 fills to base of shoulder. Had to clean, rest and adjust the seating question in order to get concentric case and good, straight bullet seating. This required unloading and reloading. 70 test rounds. This was done 3/22/03. Readjusted bullet seater for 1/16" clearance. Load #13 fills case to 1/8" of neck base. Excellent density. Powder measure set at 4.79 for reference.

Firing: Conducted on windy day. Gusts from 15 to 25 mph from 9:00 and 10:00 (crosswind). Round fore-stock of the M70 was not well fitted for lateral stability; easily moved left and right by slightest pressure on butt. The scope sight used for testing was also subject to some parallax error. Appears to be aligned and adjusted for some range other than 100 yds. Too much 3-dimension effect, difficult to use precisely. Rifle groups well, however, considering everything. Some effers analysed caused primer to unseat, initially; as one expands they be flanged by bolt face. Occurred every shot with the factory ammo. This rifle showed only to be handloads from adjusted large die. Conclusions: Best loading range was from 49.0 thru 51.0 grains. All are more precise and as fast, or faster, than factory standard. Factory premie is exceeded only slightly by these loads (#5, 6 and 7). Load #7 is best due to excellent precision, 100 f.p.s. greater velocity and very slightly greater pressure than factory. Muzzle velocity of #7 is estimated at 3.06 7 f.p.s. One (1) stick was added to add data 03 in order to keep to the height above aiming point curve from the other precision data on the precision graph.

Comments on the back of the handload data sheet concerning the .30-06 loads.

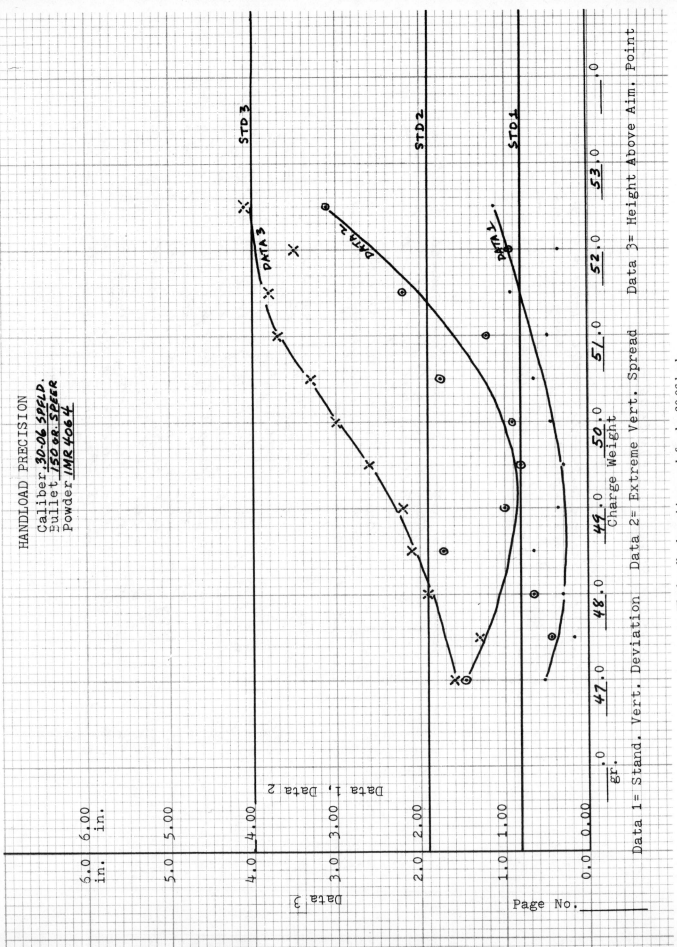

The handload precision graph for the .30-06 loads.

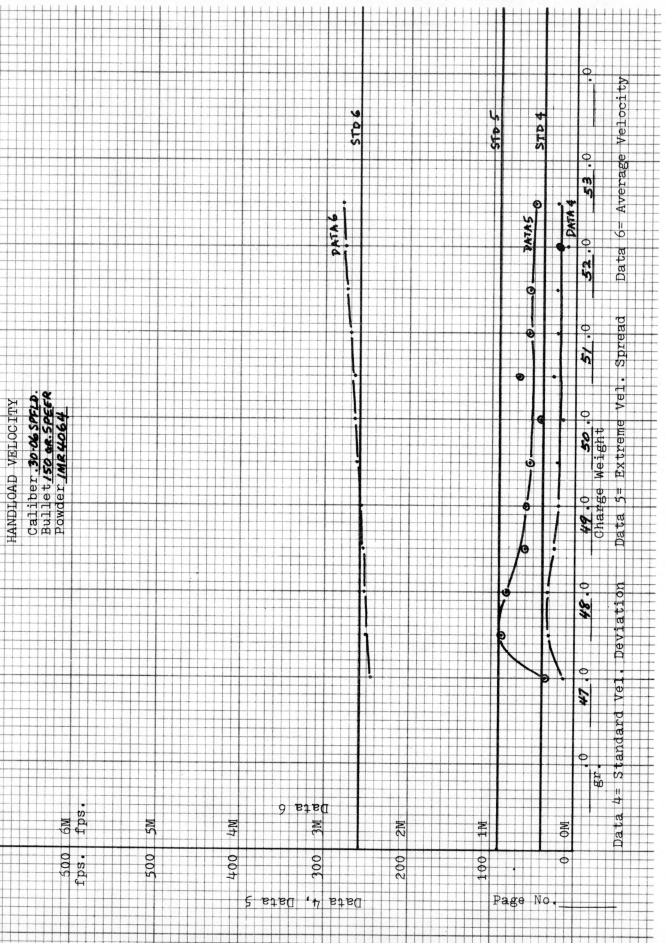

The handload velocity graph for the .30-06 loads.

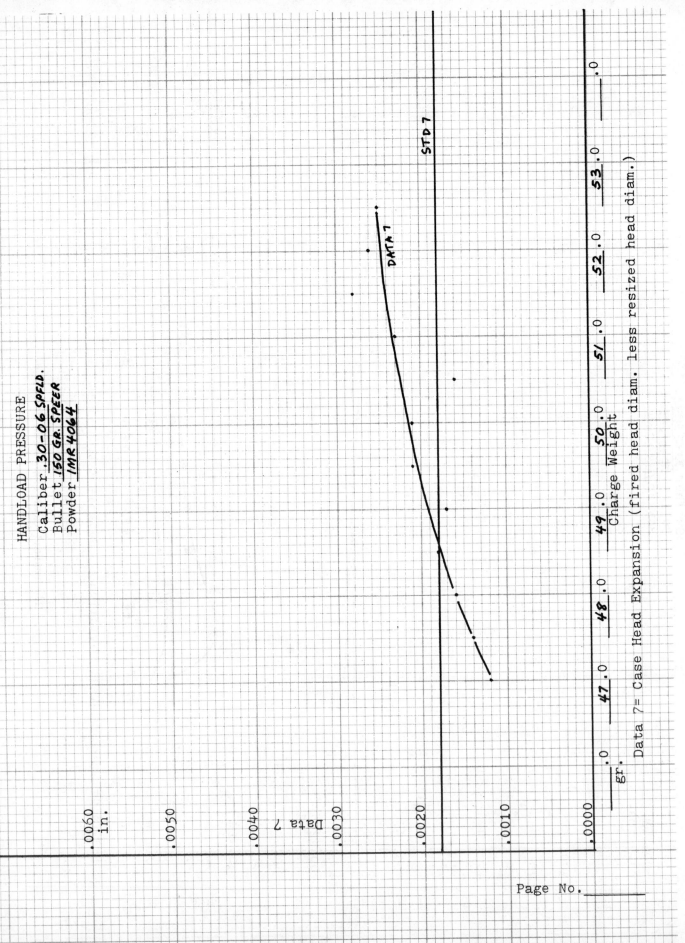

The handload pressure graph for the .30-06 loads.

CALIBER .357 MAG BULLET 125 gr.          HANDLOAD DATA

**FIREARM:** mfgr. COLT
model PYTHON
barrel length 6 in
twist rate 1:14 in
**TARGET:** mfg/no. 8" BLK.SQ.
**RANGE:** dist. 50 yd

**FACTY STD CARTRGE**
mfgr REMINGTON
mfgr no. R357M1
lot no. U16FD5968
bullet wgt 125gr

**CASE:** mfgr REM (R-P)
avg wgt 73.4±0.9 gr
trim length 1.580 in
c.o.a. length 1.565 in
sized head 0.3772 in

**BULLET:** wgt 125 gr
mfgr SIERRA
mfgr no. 8320
lot no. 300612
type JACKETED, H.PT.
clearance N.A. in

**POWDER:** mfgr HERCULES
mfgr no. BLUE DOT
lot no. B.D.048
**PRIMER:** mfgr W-W
mfgr no. 1½-108 (KWIKP)
lot no. PDL155G (S.PISTOL)

| LOAD no. | charg wgt. gr. | date load | date fire | no. rds | wind velocity, direction, temperature, bar. pres., precip., visibility, ch. pressure observations, other. 15-25 @ 9:00, 51°F | PRECISION Dat1 Std Vert Dev. in. | Dat2 Extm Vert Sprd in. | Dat3 HtAb Aim. Pt. in. * | VELOCITY Dat4 Std Vel. Dev. fps. | Dat5 Extm Vel. Sprd fps. | Dat6 Avg Vel. fps. | no. rds rcrd | PRESSURE Dat7 Case Head Exp. in. |
|---|---|---|---|---|---|---|---|---|---|---|---|---|---|
| 1 | 13.0 | 4 N 83 | 4 8 83 | 6 | light recoil every time; pulled shot #1 | .54 | 3.21 | -0.4 +2 | 79 | 236 | 1,277 | 6 | 0.0032 |
| 2 | 13.1 | | | | excellent group / do not meas. | 0.48 | 1.39 | +0.1 +2 | 114 | 333 | 1,277 | | .0031 |
| 3 | 13.2 | | | | easy extract, all primers slight flat. | 1.76 | 4.34 | +1.3 +2 | 95 | 273 | 1,292 | | .0033 |
| 4 | 13.3 | | | | | 1.70 | 4.63 | -0.7 +2 | 62 | 171 | 1,352 | | .0033 |
| 5 | 13.4 | | | | wind gusting to 35 | 2.40 | 6.27 | -0.4 +2 | 87 | 202 | 1,370 | | .0034 |
| 6 | 13.5 | | | | | 1.56 | 4.40 | -1.7 +2 | 71 | 180 | 1,381 | | .0035 |
| 7 | 13.6 | | | | | 1.31 | 3.74 | -1.5 +2 | 82 | 252 | 1,376 | | .0035 |
| 8 | 13.7 | | | | 1 round lost | 1.98 | 5.41 | -0.7 +2 | 71 | 185 | 1,394 | | .0034 |
| 9 | 13.8 | | | | | 1.43 | 4.30 | -0.8 +2 | 51 | 148 | 1,420 | | .0035 |
| 10 | 13.9 | | | | easy extract, all primers still only slightly flat. | 1.22 | 3.06 | -1.3 +2 | 33 | 88 | 1,453 | | .0037 |
| 11 | 14.0 | | | | | 1.13 | 2.74 | -1.1 +2 | 31 | 83 | 1,441 | | .0037 |
| 12 | 14.1 | | | | velocity increasing only slight | 0.98 | 3.42 | -1.2 +2 | 48 | 120 | 1,447 | | .0038 |
| 13 | 14.2 | | | | fired #13 on target #12. saved data. | 0.98 | 3.42 | -1.2 +2 | 34 | 90 | 1,432 | | .0036 |
| 14 | 14.3 | | | | | 1.17 | 2.92 | -1.0 +2 | 74 | 196 | 1,426 | | .0036 |
| 15 | 14.4 | | | | lost 3 shots; group falling to right | 1.94 | 3.77 | -1.3 +2 | 34 | 96 | 1,474 | | .0039 |
| 16 | 14.5 | | | | lost 4 shots to wind and darkness | 0.96 | 2.72 | 0.0 +2 | 21 | 57 | 1,475 | | .0038 |
| 17 | 14.6 | | | | | — | — | — | — | — | 1,518 | | .0040 |
| 18 | 14.7 | 4 N 83 | 4 8 83 | 6 | easy extraction - no excess pressure | 0.92 | 2.48 | +0.8 +2 | 33 | 91 | 1,481 | 6 | .0038 |
| 19 | 14.8 | 4 N 83 | 4 8 83 | 6 | only slight flat; cases A.O.K. | 1.52 | 4.31 | -1.4 +2 | 56 | 149 | 1,468 | 6 | .0039 |
| 20 | 14.9 | | | | similar condition but wind to 3:00 | 2.52 | 6.02 | -1.8 +2 | 31 | 91 | 1,492 | | .0041 |
| 1 | facty ld. | 4 8 83 | | | very uniform velo; cases abote | 1.12 | 2.80 | +1.9 +2 | 42 | 117 | 1,539 | 6 | . |
| 2 | " | " | | | outstanding group; amazing | 0.30 | 0.76 | +1.7 +2 | 13 | 41 | 1,520 | | . |
| 3 | " | " | | | velo uniformity | 1.83 | 5.49 | +2.4 +2 | 21 | 54 | 1,530 | | . |
| 4 | " | " | | | | | | | 25 | 71 | | | . |
| 5 | " | " | | | | | | | | | | | . |
| | | | | | facty avgs = | 1.08 | 3.02 | +2.0 +2 | 20 | 55 | 1,530 | | 0.0038 |

Data 1, 2, 3, 4, 5, 6 and 7 above, refer to data used in construction of the PREC., VEL. and PRESS. graphs
* DATA 3, see "Conclusion" notes

The handload data list for the .357 Magnum with a 125-grain bullet.

Caliber .357 S+W MAG   Bullet 125 SIERRA JHP   Powder BLUE DOT

<u>NOTES</u>

Planning: Used the test objectives. Highly conflicting and divergent guides for loading made broad range of test charge weights a requirement. Decided 2400 is too slow for this bullet. Unique would be excellent choice but decided to try the increasingly popular Blue Dot from Hercules. Used multiple sized Black Dynamite targets to chose best at 50 yard range. Factory cartridge: Bullet = 3/4 JHP. weight = 125.3 ± 0.8 gr. powder is small, flattened ball type. wgt of charges = 20.0 ± <0.1 gr. Field Case to back of bullet. Case is nickel plated. type. wgt = 73.1 ± 11.5 gr. (4.1% range). Primer had nickel-plated cup, 2 lives, brass plated anvil, small paper cover, red sealer. 33 ± 0.1 gr.

Loading: Case preparation steps: sort, deprime, anneal, ring, lube (in/out), ring, deprime (but no flare), trim to exact/equal length, lightly debur flare to min. in diam for bullet, degrease, tumble 8 hrs, detergent bath (rinse), blow dry, weight sort to 2.5% range. Prime. Charges were weighed to 0.1 gr. Bullets were seated to combine mid-jt. Roll crimp was an extra step. Critical charge weights fired to 1/8" bullet base. This eliminated double charges. Load #17 gave 100% identity. Small cylinder of powder measure set at 6.70 fps mid-charges.

Firing: Due to expected velocities, testing was done at 50 yds. The 1/8" wide front sight is more width as 8" blank square in 50 yd sight picture. Reference mark on cyl was used to insure first shot of load came from same cyl. hole. (temp). Vel. appears that best precision was in 14.2 to 14.5 gr. range (#2,13→16), but this was 50 f.p.s. slower than factory and with less uniformity. Pressure was equal to factory there, too, in Premium test rounds. This resulted in excellent velocities achieved with Blue Dot was good, safe and left cases very clean. Just is that assembled in one-fired cases with same crimp as test loads. Extreme velo spread for that = 115 f.p.s.? std. velo dev. of 46 f.p.s. = very similar to factory std. Extreme velo spread, very slightly heavier case with avg velo = 1583. Velo increase probably due to tight crimp, and different/deeper bullet seating.

Conclusions: Testing conditions were less than ideal and some retest should be made with heavier charge weight for absolute decision. Based on this available data, it appears that best precision was in 14.2 to 14.5 gr. range (#2,13→16), but this was 50 f.p.s. slower than factory and with less uniformity. Pressure was equal to factory there, too, in that velocities achieved with Blue Dot was good, safe and left cases very clean. Just is that handloads did not equal factory ammunition. Factory ammunition was best! But further testing with heavier charge (up to 15.5 gr. per Hercules), taper crimp before roll crimp, change in seating depth and possible was B Unique rz W-W 296 Overall might equal factory limits. Testing started to be done at 25 yds. Also, best handload was #6 (14.5 gr.). Two sights added to add data 3 for better graph separation on Premium graph.

Comments on the back of the handload data sheet concerning the .357 Mag loads.

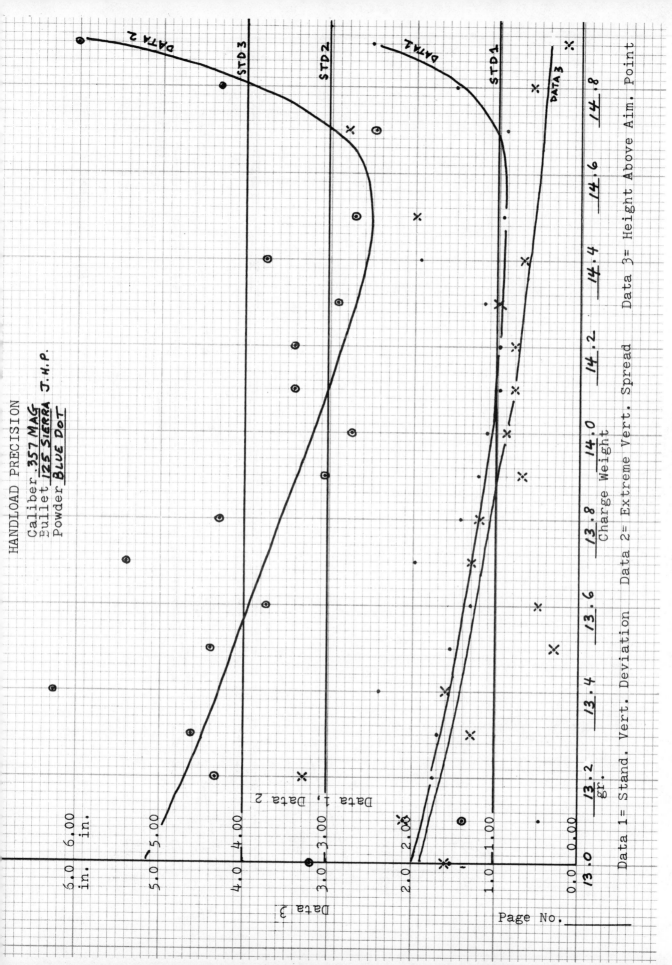

The handload precision graph for the .357 Mag loads.

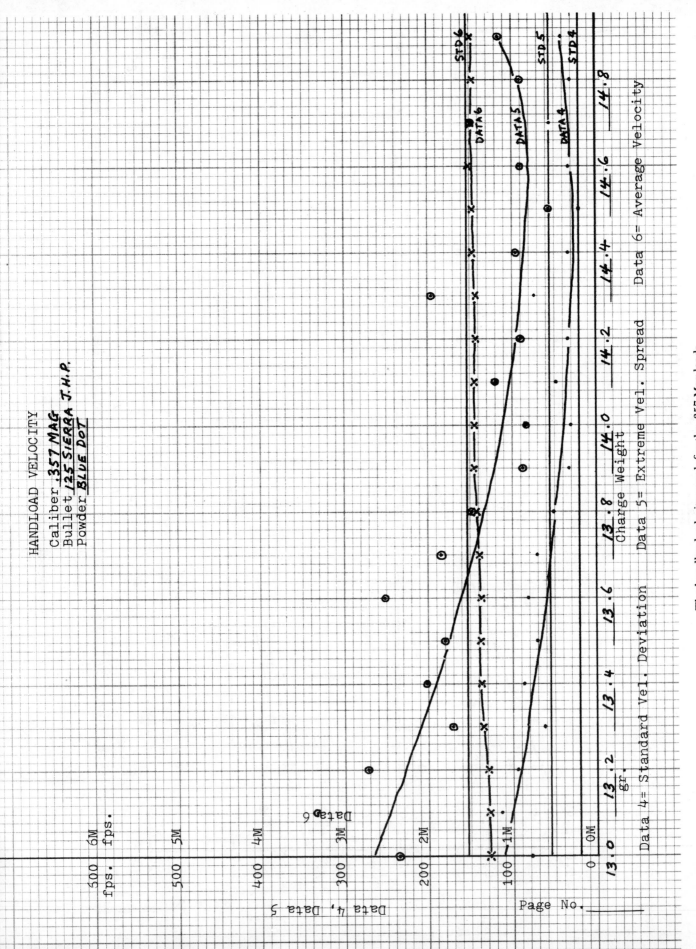

The handload velocity graph for the .357 Mag loads.

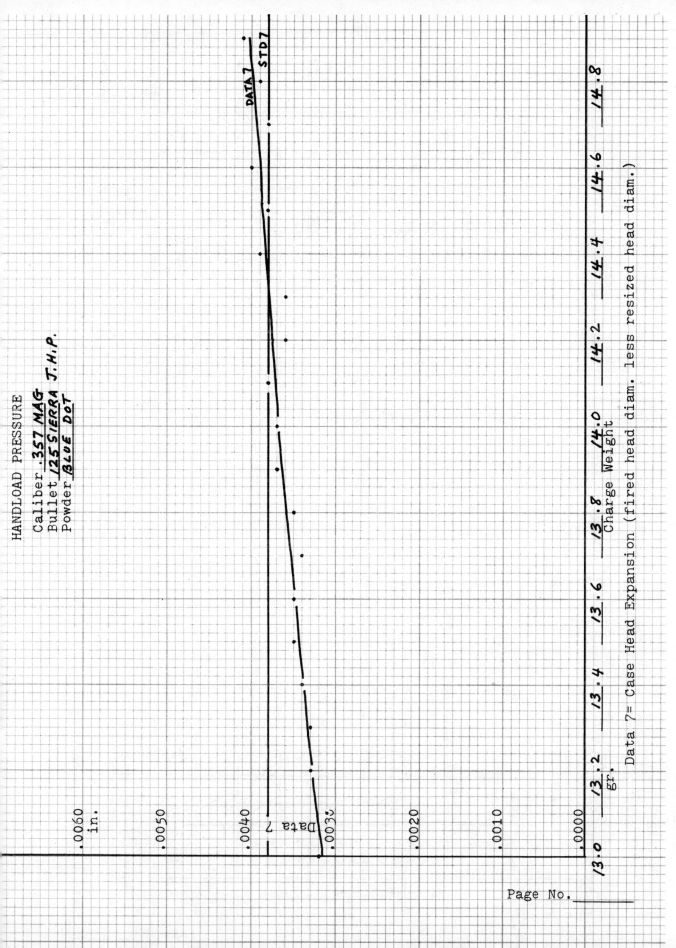

The handload pressure graph for the .357 Mag loads.

CALIBER .45ACP BULLET WGT. 230 gr.    HANDLOAD DATA

| FIREARM: mfgr. Colt | FACTY STD CARTRGE | CASE: mfgr W-W (WRA 68) | BULLET: wgt 230 gr | POWDER: mfgr HERCULES |
|---|---|---|---|---|
| model Govt., Mk IV | mfgr WESTERN-X | avg wgt 84.0 ± 1.3 gr | mfgr HORNADY | mfgr no. UNIQUE |
| barrel length 5 in | mfgr no. 45A1P | trim length 0.890 in | mfgr no. 4517 | lot no. UN.100 |
| twist rate 1:16 in | lot no. 95 INF72 | c.o.a. length 1.272 in | lot no. 8-14880-DD | PRIMER: mfgr W-W |
| TARGET: mfgr/no. 3.75" Blk Sq | bullet wgt 230 gr | sized head 0.4701 in | type ROUND NOSE, FMC | mfgr no. 7-111 (WLP) |
| RANGE: dist. 25 yd | | | clearance 0.010 in | lot no. RAL 538G (LG PIST. REG.) |

| LOAD no. | charg wgt. gr. | date load | date fire | PREC. Dat1 Std Vert Dev. in. | Dat2 Extm Vert Sprd. in. | Dat3 HtAb Aim Pt. in. | VEL. Dat4 Std Vel. Dev. fps. | Dat5 Extm Vel. Sprd. fps. | Dat6 Avg Vel. fps. | no. rds rcrd | PRES. Dat7 Case Head Exp. in. | no. rds | wind velocity, direction, temperature, bar. pres., precip., visibility, ch. pressure observations, other. |
|---|---|---|---|---|---|---|---|---|---|---|---|---|---|
| 1 | 5.6 | 4/6/83 | 4/6/83 | 1.87 | 4.12 | 2.5 | 31 | 76 | .644 | 5 | 0.0069 | 5 | 5-12 fr 3:00, 53% humid · 1 stovepipe jam – low pressure |
| 2 | 5.7 | " | " | 2.32 | 5.47 | 2.7 | 14 | 38 | .690 | | .0074 | | |
| 3 | 5.8 | " | " | 1.27 | 3.41 | 3.8 | 20 | 53 | .704 | | .0075 | | good group |
| 4 | 5.9 | " | " | 1.64 | 4.06 | 4.5 | 14 | 37 | .718 | | .0075 | | |
| 5 | 6.0 | " | " | 2.05 | 4.81 | 3.0 | 31 | 79 | .742 | | .0079 | | |
| 6 | 6.1 | " | " | 2.06 | 5.60 | 3.5 | 21 | 55 | .752 | | .0079 | | |
| 7 | 6.2 | " | " | 0.60 | 1.62 | 4.7 | 14 | 38 | .771 | | .0079 | | best vertical spread |
| 8 | 6.3 | " | " | 1.52 | 3.69 | 3.6 | 12 | 31 | .779 | | .0080 | | |
| 9 | 6.4 | " | " | 1.07 | 2.53 | 3.6 | 17 | 43 | .783 | | .0080 | | excellent group |
| 10 | 6.5 | " | " | 1.33 | 3.31 | 4.8 | 26 | 55 | .816 | | .0082 | | |
| 11 | 6.6 | " | " | 2.23 | 5.66 | 6.9 | 10 | 25 | .829 | | .0082 | | |
| 12 | 6.7 | " | " | 1.71 | 4.67 | 4.5 | 6 | 15 | .840 | | .0081 | | |
| 13 | 6.8 | " | " | 2.04 | 5.03 | 5.8 | 16 | 46 | .858 | | .0082 | | |
| 14 | 6.9 | " | ↓ | 1.93 | 4.81 | 4.5 | 31 | 77 | .876 | | .0084 | | |
| 15 | 7.0 | | | 0.97 | 2.64 | 4.5 | 19 | 47 | | ↓ | .0084 | ↓ | good group; good vel; good vel; good vel |
| 16 | | | | | | | | | | | | | |
| 17 | | | | | | | | | | | | | |
| 18 | | | | | | | | | | | | | |
| 19 | | | | | | | | | | | | | |
| 20 | | | | | | | | | | | | | |
| facty ld. 1 | | 4/6/83 | 4/6/83 | 1.75 | 4.18 | 5.7 | 17 | 36 | .803 | 5 | | 5 | |
| " 2 | | " | " | 2.52 | 6.37 | 5.8 | 6 | 15 | .804 | | | | |
| " 3 | | " | ↓ | 1.30 | 2.98 | 3.5 | 13 | 33 | .798 | | | | |
| " 4 | | | | | | | | | | | | | |
| " 5 | | | | | | | | | | | | | |
| facty avgs = | | | | 1.86 | 4.51 | 5.0 | 12 | 28 | .802 | | 0.0084 | | |

Data 1, 2, 3, 4, 5, 6 and 7 above, refer to data used in construction of the PREC., VEL. and PRESS. graphs

The handload data list for the .45 ACP with a 230-grain bullet.

Caliber .45 A.C.P.    Bullet 230gr HNDY.  Powder UNIQUE
                              RN, FMC

NOTES

Planning: Used test objectives. Much opinion exists in regard to best powder for 45 Auto. Unique chosen as a medium consensus. Others probably as good. Unique is probably as slow a propellant as usable in the 45.

Continuation of "Loading" note: Left bullet seen on bullets for pressure test rounds. Results were identical to factory. 6.3 grains Unique filled case to 1/8" of bullet base.  →

Loading: Case preparation steps: sorting, solvent bath, detergent and rinse, dry, lubricate (in and out), resizing, decapping, sort to min. case length, trim to min. case length (0.890 in.), debur with no chamfer, expansion, solvent bath, detergent bath, rinse, dry, prime. After charging by weight, bullets were seated. Taper crimp was separate and last step. Factory spec: C.O.A.L. = 1.263 ± .002 in.; bullet = 230.8 ± 0.5 gr.; case wgt = 77.5 ± 0.5 (1.3 % range); powder = 5.6 ± 0.3 gr. of flattened ball type; grey-green color and various size particles; prime = nickel plated W.W. WLP #7-111; yellow paper seal like commercial cut. Primer not crimped but had red lacquer on shell seal. Bullets seated with pitch n asphalt seal. (continued above)

Firing: Used shell catch to retrieve all spent brass for expansion measurements. Front sight is 1/10 in and subtends a 3.75 in black square at 25 yds in bench rest position. Used a dummy round loaded first into the magazine to insure equal stripping. Chambering and prevent last-round fires. Dummy loaded only 0.026 length over 105 rounds. Good fit. No malfunctions except for load no. 1. Chronograph screen did not require round/check. Loaded H.A.A.P. (Data 3) No important as this gun does not have adjustable sights.

Conclusions: Unique is probably a bit too slow to achieve identical factory ballistics. A bullet sealant might change result. It does appear to be able of higher average velocities than factory with equal pressure. This is accompanied by a good deal of muzzle flash, however. Precision trend appears best in 6.3 to 6.4 gr range, but velocity is best at 7.0 grains. If retest shows duplication of data, load #5 (7.0 gr.) is best due to high precision, near equal H.A.A.P. is factory ammo, better velocity and equal pressure. If that, loads #8 and 9 are choice due to more stable trend of precision and velo. from graphic. A second test showed also be conducted with Bullseye, WW231 or SR 7625 powder. Low muzzle velocities and 4 f.p.s. to most reading.

Comments on the back of the handload data sheet concerning the .45 ACP loads.

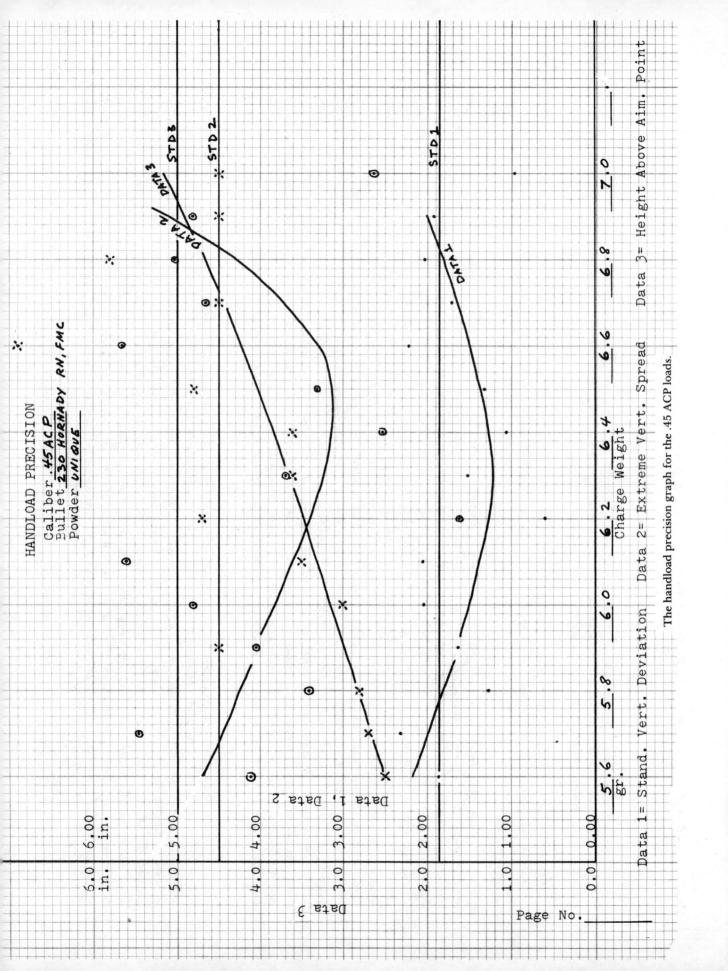

HANDLOAD PRECISION

Caliber **.45 ACP**
Bullet **230 HORNADY RN, FMC**
Powder **UNIQUE**

The handload precision graph for the .45 ACP loads.

Data 1= Stand. Vert. Deviation   Data 2= Extreme Vert. Spread   Data 3= Height Above Aim. Point

Charge Weight

Page No. _____

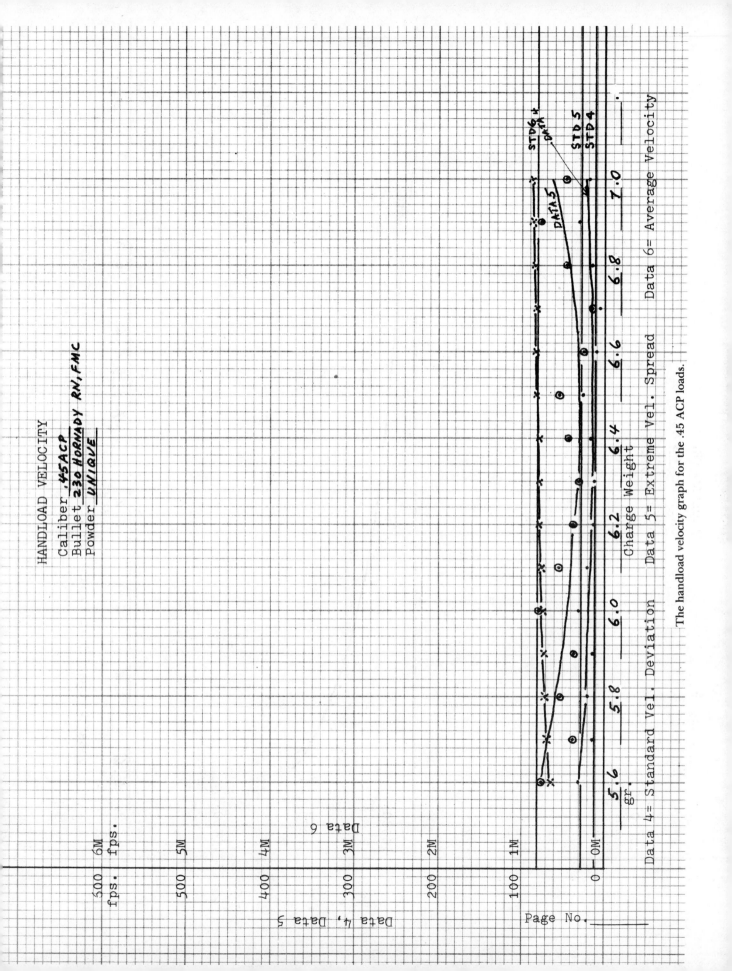

The handload velocity graph for the .45 ACP loads.

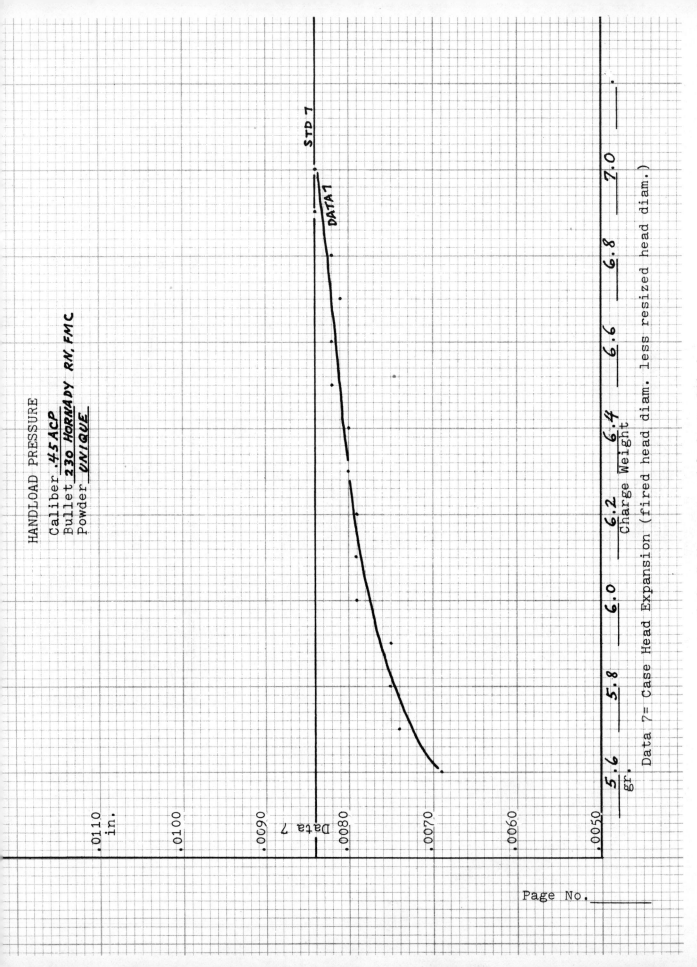

The handload pressure graph for the .45 ACP loads.

# Chapter 14

# Review of Objective Handloading

A promise was made up front stating that the methods in this book will produce positive, measurable results, while clearly identifying the best ammunition. By providing such results, the methods in this book also promise to give you the greatest confidence in your shooting. That's a lot of promising, but it's true. The reason *Precision Handloading* can make such promises is that it uses the proven method of Management by Objective.

In Chapter 1, two types of shooters were identified—reloaders and handloaders. The handloader's purpose is to develop the best ammunition possible for his needs. Unlike the reloader, the handloader is not interested in cost as much as in quality. Quality must be built into the ammunition before the ammunition can be made in quantity and cheaply. Cheap ammunition that doesn't work is of no use to anyone. After the quality is developed, the best ammunition can still be made in quantity and at low cost. The handloader can have his cake and eat it, too. With quality ammunition, the handloader can break shooting records, kill game more surely, and provide better security for home and family.

The handloader has a reason for making the best ammunition he can. His reason is to gain greater confidence in shooting. Confidence in the gun and ammunition is very important to success in any shooting sport. Handloaded ammunition gives shooters that confidence.

Without a method or plan, finding the best ammunition is difficult, if not impossible. There are so many choices of ammunition, components, and opinions, the handloader can lose confidence through confusion.

Even the excellent guides furnished by the munitions makers do not give us a method for handloading that ensures success. Their information is excellent and we can't do without it, but it doesn't tell us specifically how to get what we want—the best ammunition producing the greatest confidence. The methods we need for positive, expected results in handloading have not been available until now.

A better method for handloading does exist. The method has been around for some time, but until now has not been adapted to handloading. This book takes that method, Management by Objective, and applies it to handloading. The MBO method is used by leaders in industry and others to get what they want. We handloaders can do the same. I sometimes refer to it as handloading with a purpose, but other terminology will do as well, such as handloading by objective or handloading goals. The name is not important, only the method and the result.

The principles of goal or objective management require four steps:

I. Decide what result you want.
II. Develop plans, in enough detail, to find how the intermediate objectives will be accomplished and measured.
III. Control your activities to make sure each objective is accomplished. Don't waste time on unrelated things. The objectives are needed for the result.
IV. Set a time to get everything done.

The most important step in MBO is the first step: deciding what result you want. This is easy for handloaders. We all expect the same result—the best ammunition for our shooting needs. The hard part is getting it.

To get expected results, we have to decide what objectives are necessary. This requires careful thought for every different type of handloading project. There is a method for setting these objectives, too. It requires asking five questions of any possible objective:

1. Is the objective worth setting?
2. Is it practical?
3. Is it attainable?
4. Is it clearly stated in terms of:
   a. the task?
   b. the method of measurement?
   c. time?
5. Is the objective compatible with the result you want?

To make the MBO method more understandable, our friend, Jim, helped us set objectives for a sample handloading project. His objectives were those of a hunter. His needs fit those of many sportsmen.

After some soul searching, we decided that there were eight worthy, practical, attainable, clearly stated, measurable, and compatible objectives that would be needed for the handloading project example. Each of the objectives we decided to use can be challenged with the five objective-setting questions. Each objective provides a "yes" answer to each question. The objectives needed to create the best quality, high-velocity hunting ammunition are:

A. Precision
B. Velocity
C. Bullet preformance
D. Consistency
E. Duplication
F. Functioning
G. Pressure
H. Expense

Each of these objectives was expanded to comply properly with the objective-setting process. Each is needed to accomplish the result. Each is directly or indirectly compared to factory ammunition. Factory ammunition is the standard by which handloading efforts are best judged.

All of the above was done in Chapter 2. From that point, we started using the objectives to accomplish our result.

In Chapter 3, the decisions needed to be reached before handloading began were discussed. Safety was stressed wherever a possible danger existed. Layout of the loading area, component storage, safety concerns, safety precautions, equipment needs, materials, and supplies were all covered. Materials included the chosen factory ammunition, the components, and their selection process. Some information about the basic character of brass cases, powders, bullets, and primers was provided to help the selection process. Actual examples of the best powder and bullet selection method were given. The lubricant supplies were also discussed. Finally, the record-keeping requirements were introduced.

1. Handload data list
2. Handload precision graph

3. Handload velocity graph
4. Handload pressure graph
5. Targets

Chapter 4 took us to the loading bench and explained some basic and some finer points of handloading. These understandings are necessary to the methods of handloading by objective.

Chapters 3 and 4 briefly discussed the basics of handloading that are explained in many other books. The difference in these chapters and other books is that the special things you need to know for objective loading were stressed.

The first part of Chapter 4 took up the planning, record-keeping, and loading procedures for our methods; the second part placed Jim back into the actual loading project with a practical loading example. The loading requirements and problems were pointed out as he proceeded. In each part of Chapter 4, planning, record-keeping, and loading were described in the kind of detail needed for good, measurable results. Special emphasis was placed on setting component standards higher than the factory standards. The methods for setting these standards were explained and shown. Lastly, a checklist of equipment, materials, and supplies was furnished as a handy guide when getting started.

Chapter 5 took us to the range. How to choose a good range was discussed, and a list of the factors affecting good shooting was drawn up. These factors must be considered before firing to make best use of test time.

Actual firing involved sight adjustment, rifle preparation, bench techniques, and firing procedure. Each was explained to fit the need. The need for range safety and courtesy were pointed out. The shooter's actions before, during, and after firing were listed for complete coverage, along with the equipment, materials, and supplies needed for test firing. After completion of the handload testing, Jim discovered that he had three vital pieces of data: targets, velocity records, and fired cases. Each was to be used in the chapters following to help him decide which ammunition was best for his needs.

Precision and accuracy were defined, explained, and used in Chapter 6. We found that accuracy is not attainable until precision is first achieved.

We learned of the different ways to measure tar-

gets for precision. We also learned the best way to measure targets for our handloading needs—vertical deviation, either standard or average.

The vertical deviation of bullets from the center of the shot group was explained. The method for measuring and calculating this precision result was explained and shown. Jim used the method of target precision measurement called standard vertical deviation to measure all his targets. All the data was entered in the precision columns of the handload data list. He used this data to construct a precision graph. The graph was made up of three types of data: standard vertical deviation, extreme vertical spread, and height above the aiming point. Each data use was explained and the corresponding data from the factory standard ammunition was also placed on the graph for comparison.

The next area of data comparison was velocity, Chapter 7. As in Chapter 6, velocity was defined and explained. The methods for measuring velocity were discussed briefly. The reasons for wanting high velocity, energy, and accuracy were pointed out. Examples of old and new cartridges were shown graphically. The known velocity of any cartridge is very useful for calculating and comparing bullet energy, momentum, and downrange ballistics. The bullet trajectory can be traced to know where the bullet will strike at various distances. This is important information for long-range accuracy.

The chronograph velocity recordings gathered at the range were used to develop three pieces of data: standard velocity deviation, velocity spread, and average velocity. Each of these velocity data was explained and used to complete the handload data list and the velocity graph. The graph contained handload velocity data as well as the factory velocity data for comparison. The data was to be used for comparison of relative uniformity and objective achievement. The method of calculation for standard velocity deviation was shown.

In Chapter 8, the physical concept of pressure was introduced. Pressure, like precision and velocity, was first defined and explained. Pressure, force, and area were defined and related to each other in a formula. The differences between force and pressure were given. The reasons for knowing about pressure in handloading and the safety concerns were described.

The methods for measuring pressure in a laboratory were briefly explained for clarity, but it was pointed out that handloaders don't need to know actual pressure, only a way to compare it to factory pressure. Two methods of pressure comparison were described: observation of result and case head expansion.

The observation of result method uses felt, heard, and seen sensations to compare pressure effects to that of factory ammunition. We *feel* when the rifle recoils and the case is extracted, we *hear* the muzzle blast as the bullet leaves the barrel, and we *see* any change in the case when it is inspected.

Case head expansion involves comparing how much the handloaded ammunition expands at the base of the cartridge in relation to factory ammunition. For this test, some factory ammunition was disassembled at the bench and the components placed into brass used for the handloads for equal comparison.

Observations were noted on the data list, and head expansion was measured during and after firing. This pressure result was used to construct the handload pressure graph.

Like the precision and velocity graphs, the pressure graph compares handload test data to that obtained from the factory ammunition components. It gives a relative comparison of pressure, even though it is an indirect measure. It is adequate for our needs, even though actual pressure is not known.

How to measure for head expansion was described and shown. A micrometer that is capable of reading ±0.0001 inch is needed for these precise measurements.

After measuring and recording all expansion data, Jim constructed the pressure graph. We saw an equal gain in expansion for each equal increase in powder used.

The graphical displays of precision, velocity, and pressure were used in Chapter 9 to make a decision. That decision, based on the eight handloading objectives, was made much easier by having actual, known results of testing in front of us. Positive comparisons could be made. Guessing is not good enough for handloading. Results must be known and we must be able to compare results for sound, objective decisions.

The final decision was made through a process of elimination. In all cases, the factory results were used as the standard of comparison.

Jim first compared the data on his precision graph. We observed that the precision of his handloads got worse as the powder charges were increased. But many of the handloads were more precise than factory ammunition.

With the acceptable precision loads known, Jim compared results on the velocity graph. Here, we saw that the velocity of the handloads was slower than that of the factory ammunition at first. As propellant charges were increased, the handloaded ammunition eventually equalled and finally exceeded factory velocity. The uniformity of velocities was also compared as another objective accomplishment. This comparison narrowed the remaining choices even more.

Finally, the pressure results were compared. We saw that the best handloads were slightly below and slightly above factory pressure.

Jim made his choice of ammunition based on all these comparisons.

As a last step, we reviewed the intermediate handloading objectives to see if all had been met. This was done to ensure that our expected result was really achieved. It was found that each one of the eight loading objectives had been accomplished.

The chosen handload was the very result Jim had wanted. His purpose as a handloader was fulfilled. He had developed the best ammunition possible for his shooting. Furthermore, he could make more of this ammunition any time he needed it. It had been developed it in a no-nonsense, positive way. It was also the least expensive way.

In Chapter 10, the handloading project was completed. The remaining supplies of bullets, powder, and primers were loaded so that Jim would have a supply of the choice ammunition. This also ensured that the pertinent components would not be accidentally used in another handloading project, thereby nullifying much of his efforts and data.

Chapter 10 was also used to explain gun cleaning and lubrication. Basically, the least is the best. Different metal lubrication methods were detailed and some recommended products were named.

Storage needs were pointed out, both long term and short term.

General practice, realistic practice, and practice under stress were mentioned as ways to increase effectiveness, whether in the field or in a match. Remember, the best rifle and the best ammunition are nothing without a good marksman.

Physical conditioning for all shooting sports was emphasized.

Chapter 11 was devoted to the loading and testing of handgun cartridges. It was demonstrated that the principles of MBO can be used for handgun calibers as well as rifle loading; MBO can be used for shotshell loading, too, but there is not enough room in this book to give that subject the proper coverage it deserves. The similarities of some wildcat handgun cartridges and rifle cartridges were pointed out. This is due to the recent developments in guns and ammunition for handgun hunting and the long-range metal silhouette shooting games.

The big differences between conventional handgun and rifle cartridges were noted. Among handgun cartridges there are differences between revolver and semiauto pistol rounds. Varied loading techniques are called for.

Although the firearms are different, the basic objectives are still the same: better precision, better velocity, better uniformity, and better bullet performance. Those things don't change and are intrinsic to good shooting.

The importance of well-sorted brass of exact and equal length, tight case necks for good bullet pull, and equal, proper crimps for handgun cartridges can't be overemphasized when dealing with handgun ammunition. The selection of propellant is just as critical, perhaps more so, than for rifles.

Except for the lightest, uncrimped revolver loads, handguns in general present more difficult handloading challenges. This is true, especially if factory ammunition is honestly compared to your results. The need for a strong, clear set of objectives is absolutely necessary in order to improve on most factory handgun ammunition. It is also necessary to know if you've succeeded.

Range requirements for handguns were outlined, based on expected velocity.

Also brought up was the need for two testing periods; first, to try a variety of charge weights, and then to fine tune the handloads, often by no more than 0.1 grain of propellant.

The importance of proper target design for precision testing was noted. Round pistol targets won't do for precision measurement work. Round targets are designed to score shooting accuracy, not precision; the differentiation was explained in Chapter 6. You must make a target to suit your handgun testing needs; it doesn't have to be very elaborate.

With most patridge-, blade-, or post-type front sights and notched rear sights, a simple black square aiming point is best. The size must be correct to match the sights, sight radius, range, grip, and the shooter. Experimentation is often needed. A picture of a precision sight picture for handguns is shown in this regard.

The benchrest techniques for handgun testing were explained. Safety precautions for revolvers were also pointed out.

How partially loading a revolver cylinder or pistol magazine affects precision was detailed. Partial loading of the magazine or cylinder can have a negative effect on precision results. Positive ways to overcome these problems were offered.

Chronographing procedures for low-velocity rounds and guns with metal sights were described. Lastly, the need for extra care in testing handgun cartridges was reasserted.

Chapter 12 was a compilation of various other objectives and thoughts about handloading. The first part explained some of the objective concerns for target shooters, how to judge rimfire ammunition with the methods discussed in the text, and standards. The objectives for a shooter are a standard in themselves but there are other standards, too. Ways of upgrading standards were covered.

A simple, inexpensive method to compare bullet penetration and expansion was explained.

Improvements in the gun itself can help precision by way of various adjustments, modifications, adapters, and corrections. A proper scope mount, for one, is crucial to good precision and accuracy. It is as important as the telescopic sight itself.

Testing without a chronograph was discussed, and the plusses and minuses of doing so were given. Without a chronograph, there are still precision and pressure tools available for comparing loads. Minimal use of the chronograph was also suggested as an alternative method of testing.

Charge weight increments and the "rule of hundredths" was explained. By using one one-hundredth of the mid-weight charge and starting 10 percent below the maximum weight, about 10 or 12 test handloads will be created. This is ideal for testing. The rule can't be used precisely with very small charge weights, however.

A few comments about the relative merits of single- and double-based propellants for different types of cartridges were made; they are generalities, but basically sound.

Next, the importance of careful loading procedures for handguns was pointed out. This is especially true with case preparation and selection, bullet seating, and crimping. Handguns depend even more on these points than do rifles.

A few thoughts about targets for handload testing were brought up.

Finally, a list of conversion factors for weights and measures and some useful handloading formulas were provided.

Chapter 13 was different. Chapter 13 was a collection of handloading test results for some popular rifle and handgun cartridges. In addition to the .270 Winchester used as the text example, the .243 Winchester, 7mm Remington Magnum, .30-06 Springfield, .357 Magnum, and .45 ACP cartridges were tested. Popular weight bullets were used. The notes and comments about final decision were shown so you could get a better overall understanding of how to use handload data to meet the overall objectives.

That brings us to the concluding paragraphs in this book.

A lot of information about handloading has been presented, a bit too much, perhaps, for some readers. A lot of information, nevertheless. The fact is, handloading, like anything else, can be simple or complex. Most handloaders already know this. Some go to great lengths to improve a single facet of their shooting. Others do not. Managing handloading by objective can be simple or complex, also. As individuals, we decide how much thought and effort go into handloading. Objective management can be an involved or simple operation but its real purpose is to get results.

The most important points to remember are to decide your purpose, set your own course of objectives, and get your own results. Handload testing, using Management by Objective techniques, is the best way I know to obtain good shooting results. It takes some understanding, but only a few evenings and one afternoon at the shooting range are needed to practice it. It works for me. I sincerely hope that it will work for you.

# INDEX

instrumental velocity readings—137, 179, 214
internal ballistics—50, 136


kerosene—78
kinetic energy—139, 141


lacquer thinner—78
leade—67
Leupold and Stevens (targets)—71, 206
level (used for alignment)—110
linear velocity—135
line of probability—126


Management by Result—17
Matunas, Edward—59
methyl ethyl ketone (MEK)—78
molybdenum-based grease—182
momentum (ballistics)—141
moose—33
muzzle velocity (vs. instrumental velocity)—179


NATO—214
naphtha—78
National Rifle Association—102
National Weather Service—100
neck wall thickness—77–78, 191–92, 201
nitrocellulose—36–37, 205
nitroglycerine—36, 205
nonmercuric—46
Nonte, Major George C.—59


out-of-round cases—77
overhead baffles—100


Page, Warren—99
paint thinner—78
pet load—13–14, 68
photoelectric screens—137, 139, 195
powder lots/numbers—37–38, 62, 68, 70–71
precision (vs. accuracy)—117–18, 249
primers (standard vs. magnum)—47, 62
primer cratering—111, 155–56

primer tube—84
pressure (vs. force)—151–52
pyrocellulose—36


range courtesy—110, 249
range safety—101–02, 110, 249
reference books—14, 59–60, 99
reloaders (vs. handloaders)—11
retained weight (bullet)—198–99
rule of hundredths—204–05, 251


safety glasses—30, 65, 84, 96, 181
sample data—116–17
scope mounts/rings—106, 202, 251
sectional density (bullet)—33
Sharpe, Philip B.—59
shim—74, 91, 106
shooting muffs—86, 114
sights, adjustment of—105–07
silhouette games—117, 141, 190, 251
single-base powder—36–37, 42–43, 62, 145, 161,
    205, 251
smoke detector—28
sound baffle—195
static electricity—37
statistics, science of—115
Steindler, Bob—59
straight-walled cases—69, 159, 190, 192, 230


T-blocks—30
target mirage—104
trigger adjustment—107, 176, 201
Trzoniec, Stanley W.—59
twist rate (rifling), determining—65


unusable powder/primers, disposing of—29


varmint hunting—22, 61, 197–98, 214


wadcutter (bullet)—61
Whelen, Colonel Townsend—59
wild turkeys—198
Wooters, John—59